THE
ROYAL NAVY
AT DUNKIRK

COMMANDING OFFICERS' REPORTS OF BRITISH WARSHIPS IN ACTION DURING OPERATION DYNAMO

Dedicated to those who gave their lives
rescuing others.

THE
ROYAL NAVY
AT DUNKIRK

COMMANDING OFFICERS' REPORTS OF BRITISH WARSHIPS
IN ACTION DURING OPERATION DYNAMO

MARTIN MACE

Frontline Books

THE ROYAL NAVY AT DUNKIRK
Commanding Officers' Reports of British Warships In Action During Operation Dynamo

This edition published in 2017 by Frontline Books,
an imprint of Pen & Sword Books Ltd,
47 Church Street, Barnsley, S. Yorkshire, S70 2AS,

The individual reports and accounts are sourced from files ADM 199/792,
ADM 199/786, ADM 199/787, ADM 199/788A, ADM 199/788B and ADM
199/789 at The National Archives, Kew and licensed under the Open
Government Licence v3.0.

ISBN: 978-1-47388-672-8

For more information on our books, please visit
www.frontline-books.com
email info@frontline-books.com
or write to us at the above address.

Printed and bound by Gutenberg Press, Malta

Typeset in 10.5/12.5 Palatino

Contents

Introduction

Winston Churchill famously called the evacuation of the British Expeditionary Force from France in the spring of 1940 'a miracle of deliverance'. While it may have appeared to the world that the rescue of a third of a million men could only have been achieved by divine intervention, the reality is that it was the less miraculous but equally remarkable courage and professionalism of the armed forces and, most especially, that of the Royal Navy, that saved the United Kingdom from a disaster of unparalleled proportions.

The first hint of the possibility of an evacuation had come as early as 19 May 1940, little more than a week after Hitler had launched his attack upon France and the Low Countries. The speed and destructive effectiveness of the German attack through the Ardennes, which had broken through the weak defences on the Meuse and had penetrated deep into the heart of northern France, threatened to cut the British Expeditionary Force (BEF) off from the coast. With French resistance crumbling under the weight of the German onslaught, there seemed little hope of being able to hold back the enemy long enough for the Royal Navy to assemble sufficient shipping to transport the entire BEF back across the English Channel. Yet that is exactly what happened.

By its nature, the actions to evacuate the BEF, code-named Operation *Dynamo*, precluded the use of any of the Royal Navy's larger warships. It was an operation in which smaller vessels sailed in narrow seas and shallow shores.

As it would be from the port of Dunkirk that many of the soldiers would be embarked, the most obvious sources of transportation were the ferry and passenger ships that in peacetime had plied their trade on the waters of the Channel. Of these there were paddle steamers – such as *Royal Daffodil*, *Glen Avon*, *Duchess of Fife*, and the General Steam Navigation Company's *Crested Eagle*, the wreck of which can still be seen off the beach to the east of Dunkirk – and the faster passenger liners. The latter included those of the Isle of Man Steam Packet Company, from which ten vessels had been requisitioned by the Admiralty at the start of the war – eight of these took part in *Dynamo*, with three being sunk in and off Dunkirk.

Fortune had also favoured the Admiralty in that large numbers of self-propelled, flat-bottomed, Dutch barges, known as schuits (or 'skoots' to the monolingual British) had sailed across to Britain from Holland when the Germans invaded just days before. These were ideally suited for the task of manoeuvring close inshore, and some thirty-nine of these vessels were employed on Operation *Dynamo*, crewed by Royal Navy personnel.

It was Royal Navy personnel who also manned many of the renowned 'Little Ships', the private pleasure boats and yachts assembled from boatyards and berths along the south and east coasts. Whilst it is true that some owners not only willingly handed over their boats but also insisted in sailing them across the Channel, the majority of these boats were taken by the Admiralty, with or without the owner's consent, and, in some instances, even without their knowledge.

It was, though, the Royal Navy's own warships which would play the most important role in the drama of Dunkirk. The Royal Navy possessed numerous flotillas of destroyers, but these workhorses of the fleet were already engaged in convoy duty in the Atlantic where the U-boats were striking at the vital supply routes from North America, in battles with the Kriegsmarine in and off the coast of Norway, protecting the coastal routes of the North Sea, and facing the powerful Regia Marine (the Italian Navy) in the Mediterranean. Yet the Admiralty managed to assemble forty destroyers for *Dynamo* and it was these that not only transported more troops back to the UK than the other vessels, but their guns also helped to defend the other craft that were exposed to the persistent attacks of the Luftwaffe.

As the evacuation gathered momentum, tens of thousands of exhausted and disorganised British and Allied troops shuffled into the evacuation areas along the beaches which stretched out eastwards from Dunkirk harbour, exposed throughout to frequent aerial attack. In many instances, the men had become separated from their officers and their parent units; they were tired, hungry and leaderless. It was into this chaotic scene that Captain William Tennant stepped from the destroyer HMS *Keith* on Day 2 of Operation *Dynamo*, his task being to take over duties as Senior Naval Officer, Dunkirk. Other Royal Navy officers took up positions along the beaches, and Rear Admiral Wake-Walker sailed from Dover to organise the flow of ships into and out of Dunkirk and from the beaches.

In the early hours of 4 June, after nine days and nights, Operation *Dynamo* was concluded. Almost immediately the Admiralty issued instructions requiring ships' captains (from the largest warships to the smallest 'Little Ship') and those who served on the shore, on both sides of the Channel, to submit a report detailing their, or their ship's, actions. The most commonly stated reference for this order is No.B14/0/1101/10, which was dated 4 June 1940.

Many of these reports were duly compiled into volumes and bound – records which survive to this day in the bowels of The National Archives at Kew. It is a broad cross-section from these volumes that is presented in the following pages. Whilst the majority we have chosen to include were provided by officers and ratings who commanded a ship, of whatever size, it was felt that some of the individual accounts by shore personnel had much to offer the historian and reader, and so some of these have also been included, forming the last chapter.

As would be expected, the reports' authors all adopt differing forms and styles, from simple chronological logs through to expansive and detailed narratives. As far as possible, these accounts are reproduced in the form that they were originally written. Aside from correcting obvious spelling mistakes or typographical errors, we have strived to keep our edits and alterations to the absolute minimum. A direct consequence of this policy is that there are inconsistencies in the text – the biggest victim being the spelling of place names. In some cases there are confusing errors with times; again, these have been left as they appear. In a very few cases, particularly in the handwritten reports or where the documents have been badly damaged over time, it has not been possible to decipher the original wording – these situations are marked as 'illegible'. For consistency, we have opted to not show ship's names in capitals.

***

Without doubt, the reports that follow demonstrate the generally measured manner in which the Royal Navy evacuated the BEF under circumstances beyond anything previously experienced, or even imagined. The epic of Dunkirk has been related many times before, but these accounts provide a unique insight into the operations of the Royal Navy, from which the true magnitude of its contribution to the eventual outcome of the Second World War can be measured.

Acknowledgements

This project would not have been possible but for the help and assistance of Sara Mitchell and Leanne Mace, who tirelessly spent untold hours deciphering and transcribing many of the reports that follow, and John Grehan, for his knowledge and advice on the people and events of Operation *Dynamo*.

I would also like to acknowledge the invaluable contribution that the late Gordon Smith made to recording Britain's naval history. Gordon, who passed away in 2016, was the creator and inspiration behind the Naval-History.net website, which he allowed me to refer to whilst compiling many of Dunkirk warships' histories. His legacy lives on at www.naval-history.net.

List of Ships by Type

Armed Boarding Vessels

King Orry | Mona's Isle

Cruiser

Calcutta

Destroyers

Anthony	Esk	Grafton
Greyhound	Harvester	Havant
Icarus	Impulsive	Intrepid
Ivanhoe	Jaguar	Malcolm
Montrose	Sabre	Saladin
Scimitar	Shikari	Vanquisher
Venomous	Verity	Vimy
Vivacious	Wakeful	Whitehall
Whitshed	Winchelsea	Windsor
Wolsey	Worcester	

Gunboat

Locust

Hospital Carrier

Isle of Guernsey

Minesweepers

Albury	Gossamer	Halcyon
Hebe	Leda	Lydd
Niger	Pangbourne	Ross
Salamander	Saltash	Sutton

Motor Anti-Submarine Boat
MASB 6

Motor Torpedo Boat
MTB 67   MTB 102

MTB 107

Paddle Steamers (Auxiliary Vessels)

Crested Eagle	*Duchess of Fife*	*Glen Avon*
Glen Gower	*Golden Eagle*	*Marmion*
Medway Queen	*Oriole*	*Plinlimmon*
Princess Elizabeth	*Snaefell*	*Westward Ho*

Personnel Vessels

Biarritz	*Maid of Orleans*	*Malines*
Manxman	*Prague*	*St. Seiriol*

RAF Motor Boat
RAF Motor Boat 243

Schuits (Skoots)

Caribia	*Doggersbank*	*Fredanja*
Frisco	*Hilda*	*Pascholl*

Sloops

Guillemot	*Kingfisher*	*Sheldrake*

Submarine Tender
Dwarf

Trawlers
Arley   *Strathelliot*

Tugs
St. Clears   *Sun IV*

List of Personnel Providing Accounts

Alers-Hankey, Lieutenant Commander Conrad Byron
Allison, Commander John Hamilton
Anderson, Lieutenant Charles
Anderson, Lieutenant (Temporary) J.N.

Baker, Captain W.A.
Baker, Lieutenant G.P.
Baxter, Captain Cliff
Biddulph, Commander M.A.O.
Booth, Lieutenant Commander (Temporary) B.R.
Braithwaite, Lieutenant (Temporary) A.L.U.
Brett, Lieutenant (Temporary) Frank
Burnell-Nugent, Lieutenant Commander A.F.
Bushell, Lieutenant Commander William Charles
Buthy, Lieutenant Commander, R.H.

Cameron, Lieutenant John
Campbell, Lieutenant Commander Colin Henry
Carp, Lieutenant C.J.
Christie, Commander Arthur Edward Tolfrey
Condor, Commander Edward Reignier
Cook, Lieutenant A.T.
Corbet-Singleton, Lieutenant Commander Colin Henry
Costobadie, Lieutenant Ackroyd Norman Palliser
Cowley, Master P.B.
Crick, Lieutenant Commander T.G.P.
Cronyn, Commander St. John
Crouch, Lieutenant Commander Richard John Hullis

Darrell-Brown, Lieutenant Commander Henry Maxwell
Davies, Lieutenant (Temporary) E.L.
Dean, Commander Brian

Dechaineux, Commander Emile Frank Verlaine
Dobb, Captain R.D.
Douglas-Watson, Commander (Acting) Francis
Dover, Lieutenant Commander Laurence James
Dowding, Commander J.C.K.
Dreyer, Lieutenant C.W.S.

Elliott, Commander J.
Ellwood, Commander Michael
Ewart-Wentworth, Lieutenant Commander Michael Wentworth

Franks, Lieutenant Robert Denys
Fisher, Commander Ralph Lindsay
Fowke, Lieutenant Commander Thomas Randall

Gadd, Lieutenant Arthur
Gaffney, Lieutenant (Temporary) H.C.
Gordon, Commander Roderick Cosmo
Gray, Lieutenant A.

Hadow, Commander Philip Henry
Haig, Lieutenant Commander Rodolph Cecil Drummond
Halsey, Captain Thomas Edgar
Hare, Sub-Lieutenant D.A.
Harrison, Lieutenant Commander George Anthony Mayhew Vaughan
Hawkins, Lieutenant Commander William Alan Frank
Hill, Captain E.L.
Hine, Lieutenant Commander John Franklin William
Hinton, Commander Eric Percival
Howson, Captain John

Jones, Lieutenant E.L.

Lees, Captain Dennis Marescaux
Loynes, Lieutenant (Temporary) B.H.
Lucas, Lieutenant W.L.

Mallory, Captain G.H.
Marshall-A'Deane, Commander Walter Roger
Martin, Lieutenant J.E.L.
Maud, Lieutenant Commander Colin Douglas
McBarnet, Lieutenant D.

McBeath, Lieutenant Commander John Edwin Home
McClelland, Lieutenant Commander J.W.
McRea, Lieutenant H.C.J.
Mercer, Sub Lieutenant W.E.

Newman, Lieutenant J.C.
Northey, Lieutenant Adrian Paul

Parish, Lieutenant Commander Frank Reginald Woodbine
Parry, Commander Cecil Ramsden Langworthy
Pelly, Lieutenant Commander Peter Douglas Herbert Raymond
Penney, Master W.J.

Richardson, Commander Hector
Richardson, Lieutenant Commander Hugh Nicholas Aubyn
Robinson, Commander Cecil Edmund Charles
Robinson, Lieutenant G.W.
Ross, Commander Richard Cyril Vesey
Russell, Lieutenant Commander Archibald Boyd

Sayle, Lieutenant Commander A.R.W.
Stewart, Lieutenant Commander K.
Swift, Lieutenant Donald H.
Symons, Lieutenant George

Taylor, Rear Admiral A.H.
Temple, Commander Grenville Mathias
Temple, Commander John Bruce Goodenough
Tennant, Captain William
Thew, Lieutenant Commander Norman Vivian
Thomas, Lieutenant Commander William Scott
Thornton, Lieutenant Commander Mark
Troup, Commander H.M.

Unwin, Lieutenant Commander Harold

Vavasour, Lieutenant G.W.

Wake, Sub-Lieutenant R.
Wake-Walker, Rear Admiral William Fredric
Wells, Lieutenant J.G.
Wise, Lieutenant J.N.

Glossary and Abbreviations

AA	Anti-Aircraft
AB, A/B	Able Seaman
ABV	Armed Boarding Vessel
AC	Admiral Commanding
ADLS	Association of Dunkirk Little Ships
ADM	Admiralty
AOC-in-C	Air Officer Commanding-in-Chief
A/S	Anti-Submarine
BEF	British Expeditionary Force
Block-ship	A ship deliberately sunk to block a river or harbour entrance
Canvas Punt	A collapsible, and therefore easily transportable, long, narrow flat-bottomed boat, square at both ends
Capt.	Captain
CB	Code Books
CB	Companion of The Most Honourable Order of the Bath
CBE	Commander of the Most Excellent Order of the British Empire
C.-in-C.	Commander-in-Chief
CMB	Coastal Motor Boat; often armed with armed with torpedoes, depth charges and light machine-guns.
CPO	Chief Petty Officer
Cutter	A small boat serving a larger one by ferrying passengers or light stores between larger vessels and the shore
CVO	Commander of the Royal Victorian Order
DC	Depth Charge
DG, D/G	De-gaussing (coil)
DR	Dead Reckoning

DSC	Distinguished Service Cross
Drifter	A type of fishing boat, designed to catch herring by deploying a long net which drifts vertically below the boat into which the fish become entangled
DSO	Distinguished Service Order
ERA	Engine Room Artificer
Examination Vessel	A small ship or boat, often a civilian vessel requisitioned by the Admiralty, employed in examining and verifying the cargoes of craft entering or departing a port
GCB	Knight/Dame Grand Cross of the Most Honourable Order of the Bath
GCVO	Knight/Dame Grand Cross of the Royal Victorian Order
GMT	Greenwich Mean Time
Gunboat	A naval vessel designed for the express purpose of carrying one or more guns, often used on rivers and in shallow coastal waters
HA	High Altitude; High Angle
H/F	High Frequency
H/L	High Level
HLB	High Level Bombing
HM	His Majesty
HMHC	His Majesty's Hospital Carrier
HMHS	His Majesty's Hopsital Ship
HMS	His Majesty's Ship
HMT	His Majesty's Trawler
HMY	His Majesty's Yacht
HQ	Head Quarters
KBE	Knight Commander of the Most Excellent Order of the British Empire
KCB	Knight Commander of the Most Honourable Order of the Bath
Kedge Anchor	An anchor carried in addition to the main, or bower anchors, and usually stowed aft; often used for turning or manoeuvring a vessel
Lighter	A flat-bottomed barge used to transfer goods and passengers to and from moored ships
LS, L/S	Leading Seaman
Lt.	Lieutenant
LV	Light Vessel
MASB	Motor Anti-Submarine Boat

MB, M/B	Motor Boat
MBE	Member of the Order of the British Empire
Merchant ship	A vessel of unlimited size which carries cargoes or passengers, on a commercial basis
MG	Machine-gun
MGB	Motor Gun Boat; a fast, coastal boat armed principally with guns
M/L, ML	Motor Launch
MLC	Motor Landing Craft; a vessel specifically designed to deliver a tank to an enemy-held shore from a transport ship
MLV	Marine Loods Vaartuig; a Dutch marine pilot vessel
Motor Yacht	A power-driven, privately-owned, recreational boat
Mph	Miles per Hour
M/S	Motor Ship; Mine-Sweeping
MT	Motor Tanker
MTB	Motor Torpedo Boat; a fast, coastal boat armed principally with torpedoes
MV, M/V	Motor Vessel
MVO	Member of the Royal Victorian Order
NOIC	Naval Officer in Charge
OBE	Officer of the Order of the British Empire
OC	Officer Commanding
ON	Official Number
OS, O/S	Ordinary Seaman
Pinnace	A small boat usually carried by a warship and used to carry personnel and mail between ships
PO, P/O	Petty Officer
PV	Paravane
QMG	Quartermaster General
RAD	Rear-Admiral Dover
RAF	Royal Air Force
RA	Rear Admiral
RFR	Royal Fleet Reserve
RM	Royal Marines
RN	Royal Navy
RNLI	Royal National Lifeboat Institution
RNR	Royal Naval Reserve
RNVR	Royal Naval Volunteer Reserve
Schuit	Dutch coastal ship
Skiff	A very small boat used, often single-handed, on rivers or along coasts for fishing or leisure purposes

Skoot	*see* Schuit
Sloop	The smallest class of warship, used principally for escort and minesweeping duties
S/M	Submarine
SNO	Senior Naval Officer
SP	Signal Publications
SS, s.s.	Steam Ship
Sub.Lt, Sub/Lt	Sun-Lieutenant
T/B	Torpedo Boat
Thames Barge	More correctly a Thames sailing barge; a flat-bottomed commercial craft with a distinctively-wide upper sail-area used in the River Thames and the waters around the Thames estuary
TOO	Time Of Origin
VAD	Vice-Admiral Dover
V/S	Visual Signal
Whaler	A ship's boat with pointed bows and stern to enable it to be rowed backwards or forwards, originally used for boarding enemy vessels but also fitted with buoyancy tanks to act as a lifeboat.
WO	Warrant Officer
W/T	Wireless Telegraphy

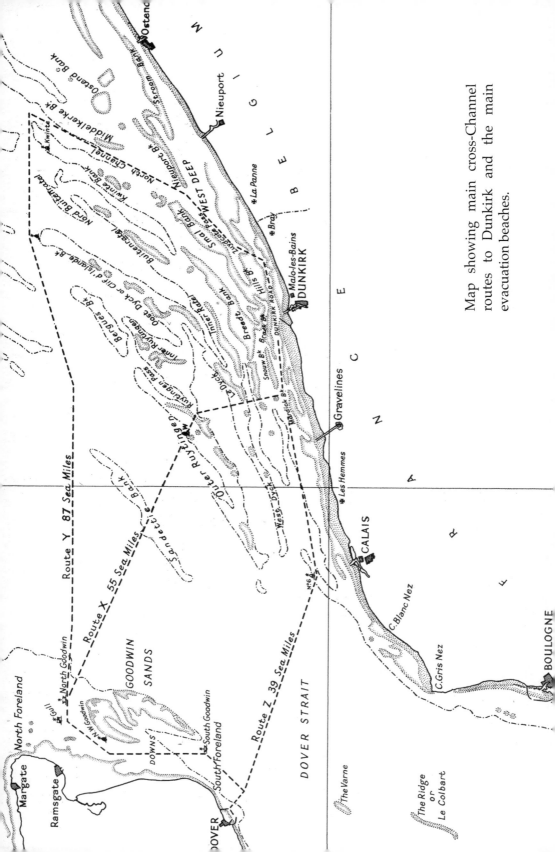

Map showing main cross-Channel routes to Dunkirk and the main evacuation beaches.

Chapter 1

Royal Navy Destroyers

ANTHONY
A-class Destroyer
Pennant Number H40
Official Rescue Total: 3,107

Built by Scotts at Greenock, having been ordered on 6 March 1928, Anthony was launched on 24 April 1929. Assigned to the 16th Destroyer Flotilla, she had been under repair prior to joining the evacuation effort. Lieutenant Commander Norman Vivian Thew's report, dated 5 June 1940, consisted of a chronological record of events:

26th May
1344   At anchor in Spithead. Received orders to escort S.S. *Kyno* to Dover and for onward routing.
1523   Passed gate with *Kyno*, proceeded to Dover.
2234   Informed Vice Admiral, Dover, that *Kyno* had no charts East of Calais.

27th May
0330   Off Dover West entrance. Landed S.P.'s, collected charts for *Kyno*, proceeded and anchored Downs. *Kyno* worried about no Pilot at Dunkirk and low water. Instructed him that we must get in.
1028   Weighed and proceeded by "Y" route for Dunkirk leading *Kyno*, two transports, two hospital ships and *Vimy*.
1220   Off "R" Buoy. Ordered return to Downs with *Kyno*. Complied.
1340   Off South Fork Buoy. Observed aircraft (? Spitfire) crash and parachutist drop in sea near Trinity Light Vessel. Proceeded all despatch to investigate via South Goodwin. French destroyer's speed boat also joined in search.

1435 No trace. Search abandoned. Proceeded Downs.
1440 Ordered return Portsmouth with *Kyno*. Proceeded.

28th May

0333 Inside Nab. Ordered *Kyno* anchor St. Helen's Roads. Ordered to return to Dover with despatch. Proceeded.
0704 Ordered proceed with all despatch via QZS 80 and 60 to meet and give support to ships evacuating B.E.F. near Dunkirk.
1005 Sighted floating French mine in channel (51° 22' N, 02° 31' E) also wreckage and oil fuel. Kept traffic clear.
1028 Mine sunk by Lewis Gun and Rifle armour piercing bullets. Proceeded.
1120 Passing through Zuydcoote Pass and reported 9 enemy aircraft passing through gap in clouds towards Dunkirk.
1125 Observed approximately 40 to 50 planes in aerial combat over Dunkirk.
1130 Aircraft crashed in sea, also parachutist, approximate position 4 miles N.W. of Dunkirk.
1220 Secured alongside *Worcester* inside Eastern Pier one berth from seaward end. Supplied *Worcester* with 12 tons oil fuel.
1250 *Montrose* slipped and proceeded, joined by *Sabre* outside.
1317 Proceeded via "Y" route with 533 troops on board.
1400 *Sabre* and *Montrose* approximately 2 miles and 3 miles ahead proceeding Dover. 15 Heinkels approached from West and commenced bombing them. Also 3 destroyers proceeding to Dunkirk in approximate position Midlekerke buoy.
1408 to 1415 Attacked consecutively by 4 aircraft from beam and stern at about 5000 feet. Avoiding action taken just before or on release of bombs. 4 salvos. In one attack from stern 2 bombs fell 10 yards port side abreast bridge but were duds. The third fell starboard side and caused one graze splinter wound to a soldier and one of pom poms crew wounded in arm. It also blew away the aerials, VC–VF Halyards, blew in the wheelhouse door and splinter holes in upper works. None penetrated the ship's side. Remainder fell wide except one on port quarter which caused no splinter casualties. In all attacks ship's company and troops were lying flat except the pom pom's crew who were in action. Barrage fire was maintained during approaches to the full low angle elevation of 30°.
1730 Arrived off Dover. *Montrose* and *Sabre* in company.
1950 Secured alongside Admiralty Pier and disembarked troops. *Worcester* secured alongside.

2100 Went with the Commanding Officer *Worcester* to report on situation at Dunkirk to the Vice Admiral, Dover.

2330 Delayed proceeding to oil owing to cloud in starboard condenser.

29h May

0344 Ferruls tightened and Canterbury test satisfactory on condenser. Proceeded to oiler.

0645 The First Lieutenant, Lieutenant Ronald de Leighton Brooke, R.N., assumed command of *Anthony*.

0714 Proceeded in company with *Worcester* and *Vimy* via "Y" route to La Panne.

1043 Anchored La Panne. Embarked troops with motor boat and whaler and one Motor Landing Craft No.15.

1525 Attacked by Heinkel high level bombing. Wide miss astern.

1635 Received W/T report of "U" Boat in vicinity, dropped one depth charge.

1645 Attacked out of sun by one Heinkel dive bombing followed by machine gunning with rear gun. Delay action bombs missed astern. No casualties.

1653 Dropped second depth charge.

1905 Secured alongside Admiralty Pier, Dover, to disembark troops. Embarked R.A.M.C. doctor and 2 orderlies.

1953 Slipped and proceeded alongside *Codrington* to fuel and ammunition at Eastern Arm.

30th May

0202 Slipped from *Codrington* to allow her to proceed.

0245 Re-berthed at Eastern Arm to embark 36 large cases containing Army maps.

0326 Slipped and proceeded via "X" channel to Dunkirk.

0400 Encountered thick fog.

0415 Anchored near Goodwin Knoll Buoy.

0455 Weighed and proceeded in low visibility.

0741 Anchored off Bray and landed one R.M. Staff Officer. Embarked 620 troops brought off by small craft of every kind. Manned several boats with crews from the ship.

0800 Sent message to Headquarters saying maps would be landed at Dunkirk.

1005 Weighed and proceeded off Dunkirk to land maps as landing them at Bray without great difficulty and damage by sea water was not possible.

3

1105 Transferred maps to Motor Yacht for landing. Proceeded via "X" route to Dover.

1330 Ship hailed in Downs by Examination Vessel and given new route from S.W. Goodwin to Dover, due to mines off entrance.

1340 Signalled and stopped two French submarine chasseurs and led them along new route.

1430 Secured alongside *Vivacious* at Admiralty Pier and disembarked troops.

1440 Lieutenant Commander Norman Vivian Thew R.N. resumed command.

1623 Slipped and proceeded Dunkirk via "X" route.

1728 Reported two suspected torpedo tracks that passed astern in position 51° 19′ N, 01° 39′E. Informed A/S trawler 2 miles ahead. These were reported by after surface lookout and 2 signalmen on Flag deck. One reliable signalman of considerable experience of Torpedo firing in *Vernon* flotilla reported that he was not certain of one that missed 1 cable astern but that the track of the miss 10 yards astern he actually saw forming.

1915 Secured alongside East Pier, Dunkirk. *Winchelsea* embarking ahead. Occasional shelling land to seaward of Quai Felix Faure from S.W.

1935 Hospital Ship left Quai Felix Faure.

1941 About 12 rounds of 4″ shell landed where hospital ship had been berthed.

1945 *Winchelsea* proceeded. Commenced embarking troops. Intermittent barrage fire was opened with *Winchelsea* at enemy aircraft to sea ward. During our loading welcome patrol of Spitfires and Blenheims were overhead.

2025 Proceeded with 1137 via "X" route.

2155 One aircraft observed over stern approximately 500 feet. He appeared to be correcting to starboard and revved up his engines. Put wheel hard a port and eased on ship answering because of top weight. Observed 5 cylindrical bombs drop in a salvo of 4 and followed by 1 single. They fell on the starboard bow or on what would have been the original course, and were delay action. The fifth felt similar to the salvo of 4 but deeper and closer. Aircraft also machine gunned ship but no casualties.

2200 Called unknown drifter or trawler to stand by as no lights, and engines had stopped. Also messengers had great difficulty in getting aft owing to crowded upper deck. One Dynamo was got working.

2205 Hull reported watertight, released trawler. Proceeded steering by engines.
2237 Gyro out of action, also magnetic compasses. W/T receivers all out of action. Sighted *Keith* who led in to Dover. Electrical steering repaired. One steering motor and dynamo with top weight made steering very sluggish. Various turbine feet cracked allowing speed up to 10 knots and only slow astern power.

31st May
0100 Secured alongside Admiralty Pier. Disembarked troops.

1st June
1800 Ready to proceed with turbines shored and one dynamo.
1835 Slipped and proceeded with *Wolsey* as escort for Portsmouth. Vibration on port turbine at speed over 14 knots or on alteration of revolutions. Only slow astern power.

2nd June
0549 Secured alongside N.W.W. (N) Portsmouth.

Lieutenant Commander Thew concluded his correspondence with a number of 'additional remarks and recommendations':

1. The very many sightings of aircraft and shipping engaged in the operation have not been recorded other than those affecting the *Anthony*.
2. Depth charge bombing at 2155, 30th May, 1940.
Five were dropped and distinctly appeared to be of cylindrical shape as described in admiralty message 1331 of 10th April, 1940. The first four went off together and produced a splash, or rather upheaval, exactly similar to depth charges. The upheaval of the fifth was not observed owing to machine gunning. The first four felt the same as a shallow depth charge asdic pattern and did not appear to affect the ship. The fifth felt deeper and closer on the starboard beam abreast the bridge. This shook the ship considerably. The signal to take cover and/or lie down had already been given, but the few ratings left standing by reason of their duty were thrown down. All the lights went out and the following major damage resulted.
(a) Turbine sliding feet fractured:
Starboard H.P. outer. Starboard H.P Inner & Outer
Port H.P. Inner and outer.

Vibration has been experienced on Port H.P. and internal examination has not yet been completed.

(b) Starboard Dynamo, turbine and gearing wrecked. All feet fractured.

(c) Gyro unbalanced and Gyro follow up system put out of action. Various leads, levels and glass broken. D.C. volt ammeter broken.

(d) All W/T receivers (including D/F) out of action. All leads in office require rewiring.

(e) "B" gun loading tray arm fractured through.

(f) 2 holding bolts of after tube mounting sheared.

(g) Starboard torpedo davit lifted and bearing distorted.

(h) Magnetic compasses shaken out of gymbals and one jumped out of binnacle.

(i) Rangefinder left window blind through shaking of prism.

(j) Various minor electrical instruments smashed on low power board.

3. The hull is intact and an interesting point is that the A/S was unaffected except for a temporary earth on the panel.

4. Bearing of Officers and Personnel. The bearing of officers and personnel throughout the operation was up to the highest traditions of the Service. No words of mine can express their fortitude, morale, cheerfulness and team spirit; also their generosity in food, clothes and comfort for the British Expeditionary Force onboard. Their regret was very genuine that the damage received prevented the ship carrying on. When the lights went out and the ship considerably shaken, it was quite understandable that the Army Officers and soldiers in messdecks and enclosed spaces below attempted to gain the upper deck as quickly as possible. A "panic" was entirely prevented by the various ratings present in the spaces who forcibly stopped and explained that the shakes were our own depth charges. On this occasion too the traditional steadfastness of the Engine Room Department was also shown, the lights being got on and the ship under weigh in the shortest possible time despite communication with the bridge being broken down.

5. Lieutenant Ronald de Leighton Brooke, R.N. Some fortnight previous to these operations I had been sick ashore and resumed duty to go to sea on completion of *Anthony*'s refit against Medical advice. This undoubtedly affected my stamina and at about 0600 on 29th May I did not consider that I was in a fit state, through lack of sleep, to continue in command without risking my ship. I was carrying an extra watch keeping officer for training and therefore signalled the Vice Admiral, Dover, that my First Lieutenant, Lieutenant R. de l. Brooke, R.N, had

assumed command. On reporting to Vice Admiral, Dover's office I was ordered to rest for 24 hours, on completion of which I again resumed command.

6. During this period *Anthony* proceeded twice to Dunkirk. Lieutenant Brooke has already been recommended in all respects for command and had previous experience in command when I was sick ashore. On this occasion, from the brief and bald facts of the attached chronological record, it will be seen these recommendations were fully justified. I would therefore submit that this officer's excellent services are favourably considered.

7. Sub-Lieutenant F. Combes, R.N.R. This officer has carried out most duties of a 2nd Lieutenant or Sub-Lieutenant in a destroyer during his period in *Anthony*. I would like to place on record his exceptional reliability and steadfastness in all respects, in particular as Navigating Officer. This duty he took over in the ship on 5th May owing to relief of the previous Navigating Officer by an Acting Sub-Lieutenant. Operating in such narrow waters, combined with the fact that he is a first class seaman, gave his Commanding Officer complete confidence and relieved him of all navigational anxieties.

ESK
E-class Destroyer
Pennant Number H15
Official Rescue Total: 3,904

The fourth ship to bear the name, HMS Esk was ordered from Swan Hunter at Wallsend on 1 November 1932 and laid down on 24 March 1933. Though she was built for use as a minelayer, her design was such that Esk could quickly be converted for use as a fleet destroyer when required. Her captain during Operation Dynamo was Lieutenant Commander Richard John Hullis Crouch, whose subsequent report is dated 9 June 1940:

2. At 1400, Tuesday 28th May, H.M.S. *Esk* slipped and sailed for Dover in company with Captain D.20 H.M.S. *Express*, subsequently proceeding to Dunkirk under the orders of Captain D.16. H.M.S. *Malcolm, Sabre* and *Scimitar* also in company. Orders were received to close the beaches and embark the B.E.F, by boat.

3. At 0015, Wednesday 29th, the force arrived, having used the North Easterly approach, boats were lowered, and the embarkation commenced. This was a slow and laborious process owing to broken water inshore and the distance out that the destroyers were forced to lie.

4. During the forenoon about 400 men were embarked from a skoot, and orders were then received from Captain D.16. to return to Dover to disembark.

5. From this time onwards I was out of touch with Captain D.16. and Captain D.20 and acted independently under the orders of the Vice Admiral, Dover.

6. At about 1700, while lying alongside the oiling jetty at the Eastern arm, I was ordered to embark the Beach Embarkation party, under the command of Rear Admiral W.F. Wake-Walker, C.B, and proceed to Dunkirk.

7. At 2100, with this party on board I slipped, and was followed to Dunkirk by *Vanquisher*, who, in due course, assisted in landing the party with his boats.

8. Embarkation of troops continued through the night and the following forenoon, using ship's boats and a variety of other small ones.

9. At 1130, with about 900 on board, I weighed and proceeded to Dover. There had been occasional shelling of the beach and sea, but no shots fell unfortunately close.

10. By 1930 I had returned to Dunkirk and then entered the harbour and embarked about 1200 men. There was shelling of the harbour as I was entering, and more after I left, but *Esk* suffered no damage.

11. This party was subsequently disembarked at Dover at 0450, Friday 31st May.

12. I then returned to Bray and embarked men from the beach. One whaler was lost inshore. During the afternoon shelling of the beaches and channel commenced, and I was forced to move to the Westward by the proximity of bursts. One soldier was killed, six seriously wounded by splinters. The ship was holed in several places and one oil fuel tank was pierced.

13. Bray, was, at this time, untenable, and Dunkirk's harbour full of ships with many more waiting outside, so I decided to return to Dover and disembark the wounded and such men as I had on board – about 100. During passage bombing attacks were carried out by the enemy. I zig-zagged up the channel at 25 knots, and *Esk* avoided any damage.

14. After disembarking troops, *Esk* fuelled and then went alongside *Sandhurst* for distilled water and temporary repairs to the ship's side and oil fuel tank, returning to Dunkirk by about 0900, Saturday 1st June.

15. On arrival off Dunkirk, a bombing raid on the harbour and shipping outside was in progress. I circled at 20 knots off the Eastern jetty and was again fortunate in avoiding any damage. When the raid ceased I entered the harbour and after embarking a few troops was ordered to proceed to the assistance of S.S. *Prague*. This ship could not be found,

but while searching, the S.S. *Scotia* was sighted on fire and in a sinking condition. I closed at full speed, and embarked about 1000 French troops including a large number of badly wounded.

16. While lying alongside the *Scotia*, enemy bombers attacked me, but did no damage. Two other bombing attacks were driven off by B and X guns who placed bursts along the line of sight to aircraft.

17. When the wreck had been cleared of men, I took on board the Captain of the *Scotia*, and returned to Dover, leaving the survivors in boats to be collected by trawlers, who had by this time arrived in adequate force.

18. At 2030, Sunday 2nd June, *Esk* proceeded to Dunkirk, and embarked about 500 French troops from the jetty. There was shelling of the harbour and jetty but not sufficiently close to embarrass us. No more troops being available, I left the harbour and returned to Dover, without further incident, and was not again required for duty in the evacuation.

19. A total of about 4500 British and French troops were conveyed to Dover.

20. The spirit and behaviour of my officers and men throughout the whole operation was beyond all praise. I cannot speak too highly of their courage, devotion to duty, and complete willingness to deal with any and every situation. The continual strain and lack of sleep appeared to leave them entirely unmoved.

21. I consider this state of affairs to be largely due to my First Lieutenant, Lieutenant C.W. Carter, R.N., who has outstanding ability as an executive officer. In addition, his personal courage on several occasions was a fine example.

23. In addition I wish to speak of the invaluable work done by the Captain of S.S. *Scotia*. With complete disregard for his own safety, his ship on fire and sinking, he was directly responsible for saving the lives of many of the wounded French troops. I regret I have no record of his name.

The Master of Scotia *was Captain William Henry Hughes, who would be decorated with the Distinguished Service Cross for his service during* Operation Dynamo. *His vessel had made two successful crossings before being attacked by Junkers Ju 87s: of at least four bombs that hit* Scotia, *one went down the funnel before exploding, with the result that the ship began to list astern and then eventually sink. In a note dated 21 June 1940, and which is appended to Lieutenant Commander Crouch's report, the following additional comment is made:*

The Master of S.S. *Scotia* has been interviewed at the Admiralty and wished to compliment Lieutenant Commander D. Couch, Captain of

H.M.S. *Esk,* and the 1st Lieutenant of that ship, on their fine work in coming full speed to his aid off Dunkirk, and bringing the ship alongside first on one side and then on the other, so as to take troops off *Scotia.*

One of Esk's crew during the evacuations was Petty Officer Herbert Vaughn. He wrote an account of his wartime service whilst a prisoner of war at the Marlag & Milag Nord PoW camp (the reason for his captivity is mentioned shortly). The following quote is reproduced from Scarborough Maritime Heritage Centre's website (www.scarboroughsmaritimeheritage.org.uk):

Then came the evacuation of the B.E.F. from Dunkirk, in this we were one of the first destroyers to take part, journey after journey from Dunkirk to Dover and back running almost without a stop for seven days and nights, being shelled and bombed incessantly but remaining to complete the final night of the evacuation, thousands of troops we must have carried, our own casualties being one killed and six wounded by shrapnel. [The] ship after running the gauntlet so much was badly damaged, but still seaworthy.

The evacuation being completed we were ordered back to Portsmouth for repairs to our ship and 48 hours' leave. For this operation our Captain, Lieut. Comdr. Crouch was awarded the D.S.O, other awards included four D.S.M.s, and several Mentioned in Despatches.

Vaughn was incorrect in stating that his captain was awarded a DSO; it was in fact a DSC. Lieutenant Commander Crouch did not live for long beyond Dynamo. On 31 August 1940, HMS Esk sailed with four other minelaying destroyers, Intrepid, Icarus, Ivanhoe and Express, to lay a minefield off the Dutch coast, north of Texel. In the darkness, Express hit a mine in a newly-laid German field and her bow was blown off. Esk closed to assist her and almost immediately struck another mine. Some fifteen minutes later, there was another explosion amidships which caused Esk to break in two and she quickly sank. A total of 135 members of the ship's company were killed, including Crouch. Such was the scale of the disaster that three ships were sunk and a fourth badly damaged.

GRAFTON
G-class Destroyer
Pennant Number H89
Official Rescue Total: 860

The G-class Fleet Destroyer HMS Grafton was ordered from John Thornycroft at Woolston, Southampton, on 5 March 1934. The ship was laid down on 30

August 1934 as Yard No.1126 and launched on 18 September 1935. She was the seventh Royal Navy ship to carry the name, first introduced in 1679. Her Captain, Commander Cecil Edmund Charles Robinson, was killed when Grafton *was sunk during Operation* Dynamo, *being torpedoed by the German U-boat U-62. The following account was therefore compiled, on 3 June 1940, by Lieutenant H.C.J. McRea:*

I much regret to inform you of the circumstances attending the loss, by enemy action, of H.M.S *Grafton*, Commander C.E.C. Robinson in command, at 0250 on 29th May, 1940, and have the honour to report the ship's proceedings as follows.

2. At about 1100 on Tuesday 28th May, H.M.S. *Grafton* arrived at Dover, from Dunkirk with about 280 troops on board. Troops were disembarked at the Admiralty Pier and at 1145 the ship slipped and prepared to secure to No.6 Buoy in the Outer Harbour. Before the ship was secured, orders were received from Vice-Admiral Dover to proceed to Dunkirk by the Northern Route. At 1310 approximately H.M.S. *Grafton* passed through the Eastern Entrance and proceeded at 30 knots.

3. No incidents developed during the passage and no enemy aircraft or surface craft were sighted and H.M.S. *Grafton* anchored close to the beach off Bray at 1445 on Tuesday 28th May. Embarkation of troops was immediately commenced, using the ship's whalers, and later power boats borrowed from H.M.S. *Calcutta*.

4. Embarkation proceeded slowly at first owing to lack of power boats. Troops were stowed as low as possible in the ship, and all Mess decks, engine and boiler rooms were filled. The more seriously wounded were placed in the E.R.A's mess and the starboard side of the fore mess deck.

5. By about 2100, 580 men had been embarked and orders were given that all ship's boats should transport troops to the schoots lying closer into the beach, and that the schoots should unload to the destroyers when they were full. During this period about 50 cases of corned beef and 50 cases of biscuits were landed for the troops on the beach.

6. At about 2310 a schoot under the command of Lieutenant McBarnet [*Doggersbank*] came alongside the starboard side and reported she had about 360 troops on board. These were embarked, but I consider that the number was probably nearer 280. The schoot then took on fresh water, and at the request of the Commanding Officer, 4 seamen from H.M.S. *Grafton* were transferred to the schoot to reinforce their small ship's company.

7. At 0015 Wednesday 29th May, *Grafton* weighed and proceeded. At this time a considerable amount of shipping was under way proceeding to and from Dunkirk. Navigation lights in all ships were switched on, which apparently attracted the attention of enemy aircraft, as several

11

bombs were heard to fall in the vicinity, and aircraft were heard to cross the line of shipping in a direction N.W. to S.E. One bomb appeared to strike a small vessel about two cables astern of *Grafton*.

8. At about 0115 I went down to the charthouse where I slept until called at 0230 through the voice pips by Lieutenant L.E. Blackmore who informed me that a ship had been torpedoed. Commander Robinson was on the bridge. He ordered the ship to be stopped and both whalers lowered. I then saw close on the starboard bow, the bows of a ship standing out of the water. There appeared to be a number of men clinging to the bows and also judging by the shouts for help, men in the water as well. I observed a buoy which I was informed was the Kwint Buoy broad on the starboard bow. While I was superintending the lowering of the whalers a signal was made to a darkened ship, which I afterwards learned was H.M.S *Lydd*, asking for information. She replied that she thought H.M.S. *Wakeful* had been torpedoed by a submarine.

9. After *Grafton*'s boats had been in the water about ten minutes, the Captain observed a small darkened vessel on the port quarter at about three cables. Believing this to be a drifter he signalled it to close and pick up survivors. I did not observe this ship closing, as my attention was concentrated on the whalers in the water. Within a few seconds, one of the lookouts on the port side of the bridge reported "Torpedo port side". This was followed almost immediately by a violent explosion. A second explosion which seemed of the same intensity followed a few seconds later. I rushed to the after end of the bridge to try and find out what damage had been done. I sent a messenger down to the Engineer Officer to make a report to the bridge as to the extent of the damage, and tried to get as many seamen as possible to keep the soldiers quiet and stationary. After about five minutes I went back to the compass platform to report to the Captain. I found that the compass platform had been wrecked. The whole of the fore screen had been blown in, and the Asdic Control and both binnacles smashed. The sides of the bridge were left standing. The bodies of Commander C.E.C. Robinson and Lieutenant H.C.C. Tanner (2nd Lieutenant) and a signalman, were buried under the wreckage and a leading signalman had been blown onto B gun deck. All four must have been killed instantaneously. The damage appeared to have originated at the port foremost corner of the bridge and been carried diagonally to the starboard after corner. It would appear to have no relation to the damage caused by the torpedo, and in my opinion would appear to have been caused by some form of grenade, or stick bomb. There was only superficial damage in the wheel house, caused by the explosion overhead.

10. Meanwhile H.M.S. *Lydd* appeared to be trying to come alongside our starboard quarter, but after hitting our starboard side she sheared off and appeared to ram a vessel on the port quarter. *Grafton* opened fire with multiple machine guns when *Lydd* was clear as we were under the impression she had rammed the M.T.B. Later the target was shifted to another vessel further away on the port quarter which was engaged by multiple machine gun and Lewis gun fire. Lieutenant Blackmore and Chief Petty Officer Chappell who manned one of the Lewis guns later reported to me that this vessel had blown up, with a bright flash. Meanwhile finding it impossible to get hold of the Engineer Officer, due to the crush of soldiers and realising the ship was not sinking rapidly, I went down to inspect the damage. It was impossible to get clear of the bridge until the soldiers had been quietened down. With the assistance of Lieutenant Blackmore, I was able to do this and pass the word for the Engineer Officer. He reported that the stern of the ship from the after magazine bulkhead, aft, had been blown off, and that the upper deck abaft the after tubes had been buckled across its entire width as though the ship's back had been broken there. The ship was still on an even keel though down by the stern. The foremost group of torpedoes were fired to lighten the ship, but the after tubes were damaged and could not be fired.

11. No ships at all were in sight, so all Carley floats, life rafts, and all wooden fittings were made ready for use. Both whalers were manned and lying off the ship awaiting orders.

12. The behaviour of the soldiers was now all that could be desired, and a tribute must be paid to their coolness and discipline. All compartments below decks had been evacuated, and auxiliary steam was being maintained. Wind and sea were freshening from the N.W., and the ship started to roll rather slowly and unsteadily.

13. About 0335 two merchant ships were observed approaching from the direction of Dunkirk. A signal was made asking them to take off the soldiers. They stopped about a mile on our port beam and lowered boats. A further signal was then made to the leading ship to come alongside. At this moment a M.T.B. was reported on the starboard bow. She was approaching at high speed from green 45 at a range of about 4,000 yards. Fire was opened with the foremost group of 4.7" guns and the starboard multiple machine gun was manned. The range was soon found and at about 1,500 yards the M.T.B. altered away quickly and was not seen again. It is not known whether she fired a torpedo.

14. At about 0400 L.N.E.R steamer *Malines* came alongside our starboard side and I gave orders for the troops to transfer to her. This was carried on mainly over the forecastle and by jumping ladders from aft. The

troops under the charge of sailors were for the most part orderly. The Master of the s.s. *Malines* handled his ship with extreme skill, and it is mainly due to him that this embarkation was carried out in an expeditious manner. It was found impossible to transfer the seriously wounded owing to the height of the *Malines* deck above our own, and to the now heavy rolling. This decided me to get the *Malines* clear as soon as possible, as *Grafton* was being badly battered and had taken up a list to starboard. I accordingly transferred such officers and men of my ship's company that I could spare.

15. Lieutenant L.E. Blackmore and Lieutenant (E) Hoskin volunteered at once to stay on board, and Surgeon Lieutenant Shields R.N.V.R refused to leave his wounded men.

16. All S.P's on the bridge were thrown overboard in a weighted bag, also all QZ charts, Fleet Charts and table of lettered positions. These were all observed to sink. It was not possible to get into the Captain's after cabin, which apart from being completely wrecked was now making water.

17. Five destroyers were seen approaching from the direction of Dover, and on a signal being made to the leading ship, *Ivanhoe* was detached and closed *Grafton*. *Grafton* was preparing to "tow for'ard" and *Ivanhoe* came alongside to take off the wounded. These were all safely transferred.

18. The ship was now listing more heavily and the sea was lapping over the after end. After consultation with Commander P.H. Hadow, R.N., the Captain of *Ivanhoe*, I decided that she would not float much longer. I therefore gave the order to abandon ship. While making a final round of the ship she began to settle more quickly. After all hands had abandoned ship, *Ivanhoe* fired three shells into *Grafton* from a range of about 500 yards and then proceeded to Dunkirk.

19. The conduct of the Officers and ship's company was exemplary. The difficult task of keeping some 850 soldiers under control was efficiently carried out, and at the same time guns and boats were manned. Lieutenant L.E. Blackmore deserves special mention. He carried out the duties of 1st Lieutenant in an efficient and cheerful manner. Lieutenant (E) Hoskin took charge of the evacuation of Engine and Boiler Rooms, and maintained steam for auxiliary purposes, and was of great assistance in assessing damage and with constructive suggestions to keep the ship afloat. Surgeon Lieutenant Shield, R.N.V.R. worked indefatigably among the many wounded and with complete disregard for his own safety visited damaged compartments in the stern, before he could possibly have known that the ship would not sink at once. He

was responsible for the rescue of at least one wounded army officer from the Ward Room Lobby.

As well as Commander Robinson, a further fifteen crew members were killed in the sinking of Grafton – *a second officer, thirteen ratings and the Canteen Manager.*

Basil Bartlett was one of the Army officers on board HMS Grafton *when she was torpedoed. The following description is quoted here from his book* My First War: An Army Officer's Journal For May 1940 Through Belgium To Dunkirk:

There was a terrific explosion as the torpedo hit the destroyer. I suppose the force of it must have knocked me unconscious. First thing I knew I was stumbling around in the dark trying to find the door of the cabin. The whole ship was trembling violently, the furniture appeared to be dancing about. There was a strong smell of petrol. I heard someone scuffling in a corner and just had the good sense to shout: 'For God's sake don't light a match.' With the greatest of difficulty I found the door and managed to get it open it.

I pushed my way out on deck. Someone said: 'Keep down. They're machine-gunning us.' I huddled against a steel door and watched the fight. Two dark shapes in the middle distance turned out to be German M.T.B.s. The destroyer and another British warship were giving them hell with shells and tracer-bullets. The M.T.B.s were answering with machine-gun fire. But one by one they were hit. We saw them leap into the air and then settle down' into the water and sink. Everyone sighed with relief ...

The deck was a mass of twisted steel and mangled bodies. The Captain had been machine-gunned and killed on the bridge. The destroyer had stopped two torpedoes. She'd been hit while hanging about to pick up survivors from another ship, which had been sunk a few minutes before. She was a very gruesome sight ...

Wounded men began to be brought up from the bowels of the ship. I learned that one of the torpedoes had gone right through the wardroom, killing all thirty-five of our officers who were sleeping there. It's pure chance that I'm alive. If I'd gone on board a little earlier I should have been put in the wardroom. I only slept in the Captain's cabin because there was no room for me anywhere else ...

There remained only one job to be done. We had to transfer our cargo. The men showed wonderful discipline. There was no ugly rush. They allowed themselves to be divided into groups and transferred from one ship to another with the same patience that they had shown on Bray-Dunes beach. It must have been a great temptation to get out of turn and take a flying leap for safety. But no one did.

GREYHOUND
G-class Fleet Destroyer
Pennant Number H05
Official Rescue Total: 1,360

A G-class fleet destroyer, HMS Greyhound was ordered from Vickers Armstrong at Newcastle on 5 March 1934. The ship was laid down as Yard No.699 on 20 September that year, being launched on 15 August 1935. This destroyer was the twenty-second British warship to carry the name which dates from 1545 when it was used for a fifteen-gun ship. Commander Walter Roger Marshall-A'Deane RN completed his narrative of Greyhound's role in Operation Dynamo on 12 June 1940:

Whilst on patrol off Calais on 25th May a German 3" H.A. battery to the east of Sangatte was located and engaged, no fire being returned. During the course of the day a number of refugees and soldiers were taken out of small boats and an R.A.F. officer, Pilot Officer Allen, rescued from the sea, he having parachuted from his damaged aircraft. These parties were disembarked at Dover during the afternoon and ship sailed again at 1750 to locate and escort the transport *Canterbury*, proceeding from Dunkirk to Dover.

On passage, when off Calais, I closed the drifter *Lord Howe*, in which an officer from the Calais garrison requested bombardment support off that town. At the same time I received your signal 1907/25/5/40 ordering me to bombard St. Pierre. To do this a course was set 067° from No.3 Buoy and fire opened.

The H.A. battery previously mentioned started firing at us from nearly right astern and very shortly, at 2000, scored a single hit through the Director, of whose crew P.O. Lush was killed, A.B. Daughtery wounded and the First Lieutenant, Lieutenant Commander H.E.F. Tweedie, was also wounded in the foot but continued the action, controlling the guns in quarters firing. The shell passed through the director and fragments killed Lieutenant Sir Marmaduke Blenner Hassett R.N.V.R. and seriously wounded Sub. Lieutenant J.P. Pigot-Moodie. Having turned to engage this battery for 15 minutes a new position for bombardment was taken up, but after a few salvoes, of which no fall of shot could be seen, it was considered that bombardment in Quarters Firing was likely to endanger friend as well as foe and target was shifted to a 6″ (?) gun to the west of Sangatte which had been firing at us. At this time *Grafton* arrived and opened fire, with whom *Greyhound* returned to Dover when darkness rendered further action nugatory.

At 1400 on 27th May *Greyhound* sailed in company with *Grafton* to establish patrol between Fairy Bank and Kwinte Buoys.

During this night orders were received to embark troops from La Panne.

Both ships arrived off this beach at 0100 and sent boats inshore, the ships being manoeuvred closer in as the tide rose.

By 0615 the beaches had been cleared and *Grafton, Greyhound, Calcutta* and three paddle steamers sailed. (Number of soldiers approximately 100).

Whilst returning to Dover *Greyhound* was detached to escort S.S. *Dorrien Rose* who had on board survivors of *Queen of the Channel;* ultimately berthing at Admiralty Pier at 1230 28th May. After discharging troops *Greyhound* proceeded to Dunkirk and went alongside the pier as soon as a billet was vacant. It was found difficult to count the troops as they came aboard and the numbers appeared to be regulated from further down the pier where detachments were assembled and detailed. *Greyhound* embarked 681 and sailed arriving alongside Admiralty pier at 0030.

At 0430 29th May *Greyhound* sailed in company with Captain D. 1st. Flotilla for La Panne – in parenthesis, this was the first time I had been at sea with my Captain D. Since 15th January.

Embarkation by whaler and motor boat was carried out steadily until 1600 when an attack was made by bombers the fourth salvo of which scored two near misses, the splinters killing 20 men and wounding 70 and causing the following damage. In the engine room one air ejector and one forced lubrication pump were put out of action. In No.3 boiler room main feed pipe was pierced resulting in complete loss of feed water, and an exhaust pipe from a feed heater punctured which caused the boiler room to fill with steam.

Greyhound, then at short stay, weighed and proceeded, her boats which returned undamaged were ordered to go to one of the two minesweepers *Sutton* and *Salamander* still at anchor, as with the number of casualties on the upper deck it was not considered possible to hoist them.

The motor boat, Leading Seaman Saunders, continued to run trips ashore until 2200 when the crew went on board H.M.S *Locust* in which they returned to Dover.

The whaler, Leading Seaman Setterfield, embarked troops continually until 2230 when she was holed and the crew taken on board *Golden Eagle* in which they returned to England.

Greyhound proceeded under her own steam, with salt water feed until 1930 when she was taken in tow by *Błyskawica*, then on patrol with H.M.S. *Vega* in vicinity of West Hindor Buoy.

Tow was slipped off Dover at 2330 and *Greyhound* was taken into harbour by tugs, berthed alongside Admiralty Pier at 0245 30th. May and landed 432 soldiers apart from casualties.

It is my opinion that the behaviour of the ship's company during these operations was excellent.

HARVESTER
H-class Destroyer
Pennant Number D19
Official Rescue Total: 3,191

A variant of the Royal Navy's H-class destroyers, this vessel was ordered by the Brazilian Government in 1938, from Vickers-Armstrong at Barrow, and laid down on 3 June 1938. She was intended to be named Jurura *but was requisitioned by the Admiralty on 5 September 1939 and when launched on 29 September given the name* Handy. *However, she was renamed as HMS* Harvester *on 27 February 1940 to prevent confusion with the destroyer HMS* Hardy *already in service. Lieutenant Commander Mark Thornton RN's record of his ship's service during the Dunkirk evacuation is dated 2 June 1940:*

At 1328/28 after 2½ days of the 3 days working up programme *Harvester* was ordered to proceed to Dover with all dispatch.
1915/28 Arrived at Dover – Oiled.
2035/28 Sailed in company with *Mackay* – route Y.
2330/28 *Mackay* grounded and *Harvester* remained near feeling the way into the deeper channel, meanwhile warning ships approaching that *Mackay* was aground.
0050/29 Sent motor boat inshore; reported that men were coming down to the beach; all boats were sent in and embarkation began. It was very slow at first, but gradually improved with the use of Carley Floats and a line from a Paddle Steamer to shore. Speed improved considerably when it was possible to get men from the Paddle Steamer aground till it fell off again as the tide left her dry.

Attempts were made to get the Army to make a pier, and Sub Lieutenant Crosswell went to arrange this.

At 1235/29 with 600 inboard I decided that the rate of embarkation would be so slow till the tide rose it was more important to remove those I had. At 1250/29 proceeded; Sub-Lieutenant Crosswell and 2 ratings not being on the beach were left behind.

Off Middlekerke buoy a medium calibre gun from Nieuport began firing. Early shots over – then short – and one very close indeed, which after, it was found had hit the transport which was being passed at that time. Inclination was altered as much as possible in the Channel and smoke made to cover the approach of a French Division of Destroyers coming down the Channel.

1540/29 Arrived Dover – disembarked troops – oiled.

2105/29 Secured to buoy.

0500/30 Sailed in company with *Javelin, Ivanhoe, Intrepid, Impulsive, Icarus, Havant,* for Sheerness – thick fog.

0836/30 Arrived at Sheerness – oiled.

1651/30 Sailed in company with *Ivanhoe, Icarus, Impulsive.*

2105/30 Detached with *Icarus* to go to La Panne but on the way not being in agreement with *Icarus* course I altered to the Southward. On closing to the land a signal was made from shore directing me to take off men there. As there was some thousands there and no ships I anchored and started embarkation. Embarkation was very slow and at 2040/30 and 2132/30 signals were made for extra boats to assist.

At 2210/30 *Icarus* reported enemy M.T.B.s. At 2306/30 torpedo passed down the Port Side missing the stern by about 5 yards. Shortly after 2316/30 second torpedo passed even less distance ahead. Leaning over the side of the bridge I could hear the hissing of the bubbles; the water was very phosphorescent.

At this time the hydrophone effect was heard on the seaward bearing. Sweeping fire to seaward with .5 machine guns and barrage fire bursting over the water were carried out. Starshell and searchlight were not used as it was thought it would disclose the other ships to the M.T.B.s. It would have been wiser to have used Starshell.

During the night at intervals there was shelling of the beach on either side and one gun which fired over *Harvester* the shots continually falling 100 to 300 yards over.

At 0426/31 orders were received to proceed to Dunkirk. 0635/31 arrived Dunkirk – secured to pier. Filled up with troops.

0638/31 At intervals fired at enemy aircraft. Some rapid fire, medium calibre passed over the ship and fell just east of the pier.

0655/31 Sailed.

0930/31 Arrived Dover.

1124/31 Sailed.

1400/31 Arrived Dunkirk. Motor boat took letters from *Icarus* for Lord Gort and took them to H.Q. Proceeded alongside transport ship and embarked troops. Air fights overhead and some rapid fire on the shore end of pier bursting close to officers and ratings hurrying up the embarkation.

1530/31 Sailed.

2010/31 Arrived Dover.

2315/15 Proceeded. At 2355/31 in position. An aeroplane approached from starboard beam with navigation lights burning; machine gunned but only hits were in beef screen. Rear gun was fired after passing over.

0218/1 Ordered to proceed to Dunkirk instead of La Panne.

0310/1 Visibility poor and it was not found possible to find No.5.W buoy being uncertain of position I remained for an hour in sight of a wreck marking buoy, unmarked on the chart; reported to S.N.O. Dover.

0540/1 Fired at enemy dive bombers.

0556/1 French Army co-operation aircraft making reconnaissance over Dunkirk was being fired at from a jetty. Information had been received that a number of these aircraft had been captured by the enemy. Not replying to the challenge, fire was opened with the barrage fire and machine guns. A few minutes later the plane went down in flames.

0610/1 Lying off Dunkirk Junkers 88 bomber let go four bombs which fell abeam 100 yards near *Winchelsea*. Barrage fire burst near, eventually plane was seen to crash.

0615/1 While firing, ship was secured alongside jetty on seaward side and embarkation commenced. 0618/1 more firing at bombers. Signal was received from V.A.D.

0715/1 Sailed. Machine gun firing from shore made funnel smoke – C.S.A smoke and smoke flat dropped to cover other ships.

Near No.5.W buoy shelled by small guns from near Gravelines. Made smoke, and turned to northward.

0743/1 Four dive bombers; one salvo fell near *Icarus*. Barrage and long range firing at these planes was so effective that they went away dropping their bombs about five miles abeam. One of these planes was hit and shortly afterwards crashed in flames.

0748/1 A plane was sighted being attacked by Spitfires flying low over the water with machine gun bullets splashing all around it. *Codrington* opened fire and [so did] the *Harvester*, and a burst of fire from .5 machine guns was seen to hit it. The plane burst into flames and gradually lost height and fell into the sea. *Codrington* then signalled that the plane had been identified as a Blenheim. Fire had been held due to the uncertainty of identification; but it seems wrong that a bomber should need to approach destroyers especially after a dive bombing attack.

0940/1 Arrived Dover.

HAVANT
H-class Destroyer
Pennant Number H32
Official Rescue Total: 2,432

A variant of the H-Class fleet destroyers, Havant *was ordered from J.S. White at Cowes by the Brazilian Government in 1937. The ship was laid down on 30 March 1938, being launched on 17 July 1939, at which point she was given the name* Javary. *On 5 September, during fitting-out, she was requisitioned by the Admiralty and renamed HMS* Havant, *a name previously used for a minesweeper sold to Siam in 1922. Lieutenant Commander A.F. Burnell-Nugent DSC's account was completed on 5 June 1940:*

I have the honour to report the proceedings of H.M.S. *Havant* under my command during the operations off the Belgian coast between 29th May and 1st June, and the circumstances which led to the loss of the ship.

2. Times throughout this narrative are from memory and are necessarily approximate.

3. After fuelling *Havant* left Dover at 1815 29th May and arrived off Bray at 2100. Motor cutter and whaler were sent in to investigate and returned with French troops, of which there were a large number on the beach. While they were making a second trip I received orders from *Hebe* to proceed further to the Eastward to La Panne, which I did. There were several warships anchored here and information was received that the British troops had gone back inland for the night.

4. I accordingly returned to Bray to continue embarking French troops.

5. I found *Bideford* here aground with her stern blown off and she asked

me for assistance. *Havant*'s stern was placed alongside *Bideford*'s port bow, the tow passed, and I then endeavoured to tow her off by going astern. But the tide was falling and she only swung round slightly. The amount of power used was gradually increased until the tow parted. I then decided that *Bideford* must be left until the tide rose, and I informed him that I would signal for a tug.

6. During operations with *Bideford* large numbers of French troops had been coming off from the shore to *Havant* in various shore boats.

7. At 0130 30th May, there being plenty of other ships waiting nearby, I proceeded to Dover, arriving at 0400 with about 500 French troops on board.

8. At 0500 *Havant* sailed for Sheerness in company with other destroyers under the orders of *Javelin*.

9. On arrival *Havant* oiled and remained at Sheerness for the rest of 30th May.

10. At 0400 31st May, *Havant* sailed with orders to embark troops from the beach to the eastward of Dunkirk, and reached Bray at 0800. German batteries in the vicinity of Mardyck fired at us rather ineffectively on the way in and their fire was returned.

11. From 0800–1300 *Havant* was at anchor off Bray embarking troops in our own boats, yachts and other small craft. At the request of an army officer, Lieut. M.G. Macleod was landed to act as pier master. The boats were in charge of Sub. Lieut. I. Hall (motor cutter) and Mid. K.N. Curryer R.N.R. (whaler), and between them these 3 officers succeeded in getting off about 400 men.

12. At 1300, I decided that, as the embarkation was proceeding so slowly, and there were plenty of other ships waiting off the beach, it would be better to enter Dunkirk and try and berth alongside.

13. This was done without difficulty. The total number of troops on board was quickly raised to 1,000, and *Havant* then proceeded to Dover, arriving at 1700. I reported by W/T that it was advisable for destroyers to berth alongside in Dunkirk harbour if possible.

14. *Havant* sailed as soon as disembarkation was complete and reached Dunkirk again at 2145. This time a berth was immediately taken up alongside, about 1,000 troops embarked in half an hour, and *Havant* then returned to Dover, arriving at 0230 on June 1st.

15. *Havant* reached Dunkirk again at 0730 and berthed alongside in the same place as before.

16. Up to this time *Havant* had not been under serious fire but at 0800 a very intense aerial bombardment began. Troops were coming very slowly down the jetty and in half an hour only about 50 had embarked.

17. At this time *Ivanhoe* was hit amidships and appeared to be on fire.

She was just outside the harbour and full of troops, and I decided to go to her assistance. I accordingly left Dunkirk and went alongside *Ivanhoe* at about 0840. There was a minesweeper alongside her other side. All troops and wounded were transferred from *Ivanhoe*. The Commanding Officer of *Ivanhoe* stated that he did not want a tow as he hoped to get under way again in a few minutes.

18. *Havant* accordingly proceeded towards Dover at full speed having onboard about 500 men many of whom were wounded.

19. On the way down the channel parallel to the beach to the west of Dunkirk we were subjected to intense dive bombing and high and low level bombing and also bombardment from shore. These were avoided by zig-zagging as much as the width of the channel permitted. *Havant* had just turned to the North Westward at the end of the channel when, at 0906, we were hit by two bombs in the Engine Room which passed through the starboard side. Almost immediately afterwards a large bomb fell in the water about 50 yards ahead. This had a delay action and exploded right underneath the ship as she passed over it, momentarily giving the impression of lifting the whole ship.

20. By this time the Engine Officer and all the E.R.As. had been killed or wounded, the after ready use ammunition lockers had blown up, and there were many casualties amongst the soldiers on the upper deck.

21. The ship was continuing to steam at moderate speed, out of control and gradually circling to starboard.

22. As we were approaching the sandbanks opposite Dunkirk it became urgently necessary to stop the ship. It was impossible to enter the Engine Room, the cut off valve on the upper deck was bent and broken and the only method of stopping appeared to be by letting the steam out of the boilers. This was done by Chief Stoker Gallor in spite of the fact that there was a fire in one of the boiler rooms, and the ship was eventually brought up in 4 fathoms by the starboard anchor.

23. Signals for assistance were then made to H.M.S. *Saltash* and a large yacht, name unknown. These came alongside one on each quarter and all the soldiers were transferred. Throughout these proceedings bombing was almost continuous.

24. *Havant* was then got in tow by *Saltash* and we proceeded at slow speed. As the ship was heeling over and settling down at a fair speed I called the (schoot)? *Aegir* (Lt. Whitworth, R.N.) alongside and transferred to her the younger members of the crew retaining onboard only the officers and about 20 men.

25. About this time we were attacked by heavy bombers, one bomb falling half way between *Saltash* and *Havant*, and another group very

close to the port quarter. I think it may have been this latter which holed the Tiller flat.

26. The situation on board had deteriorated, and after a brief conference with some of my officers, I decided that there was no hope of getting the ship back to England. I accordingly told *Saltash* of my intention to abandon ship and slipped the tow. *Aegir* was called alongside again, she had cast off during the last attack and, after transferring the wounded, and then the rest of the ship's company, I left the ship.

27. Almost all the C.Bs and S.Ps. had been transferred to the Flag Officer in Charge, Dover, before sailing. All that were onboard were thrown overboard in a weighted canvas bag in a depth of 10 fathoms before I left.

28. At the time of reaching the decision to abandon ship the damage sustained was as follows. Two large holes, about 6 and 3 feet in diameter on starboard side of Engine Room just above water line and many small holes all along the starboard side. One large hole below the water line the port side of Engine Room, the bulkhead at fore end of engine room split and water entering the boiler room from engine room, port side Engine room after bulkhead split vertically, Plummer block space flooded and water tight door buckled up, office flat flooding through this door, Port gland space flooded, Tiller flat flooded and seam on bulkhead broken. A large number of rivets were leaking. There was a fire in the after boiler room and a smaller fire in the after end of E.R. under the torpedo tubes. The ship had a heavy list to port, and water was beginning to come in through the holes the starboard side. The port side of the upper deck was almost awash. The ship being at this time in deep water I caused the magazines to be flooded to ensure that she sank before drifting onto the sandbanks.

29. I circled round the ship in *Aegir* for about 5 minutes until she rolled slowly over and sank at about 1015 in approximate position 51⁰ 0.81' N. 2⁰ 17.2'E. A few rounds were fired into her by *Saltash* just before this.

30. We were landed at Margate at about 1700 when proceeded to the Admiralty and reported the position at Dunkirk to the Assistant Chief of Naval Staff.

31. Throughout the action the behaviour of the ship's company was beyond all praise. The 0.5" guns were kept in action till the end and all the 4.7" guns until all H.A. ammunition was expended.

32. All went about their duties in a quiet and orderly manner despite grim scenes of carnage on the upper deck. During the various stages of disembarkation from *Havant* there was never any haste to leave, the soldiers and the wounded were always thought of first. About half of my seamen were ordinary seamen under 20.

33. The casualties sustained by *Havant* were 1 officer and 7 men killed and about 15 wounded, but in addition there must have been at least 25 soldiers killed or wounded onboard. The discipline of the soldiers was of the highest order.

A memorial window, installed in the north side St Faith's Church in Havant, Hampshire, commemorates all those who served on HMS Havant *at Dunkirk in 1940. A commemorative stone was also unveiled at the Royal British Legion's headquarters in Brockhampton Lane, Havant, in 1990.*

ICARUS
I-class Destroyer
Pennant Number D03
Official Rescue Total: 4,704

The fleet destroyer HMS Icarus *was ordered on 30 October 1935 from John Brown at Clydebank, being launched on 26 November 1936. She was the fifth Royal Navy ship to carry this name, which had been introduced for a Brig-Sloop in 1814 and last used by a trawler requisitioned in 1914. A busy wartime service had already been experienced prior to Operation* Dynamo. *On 10 April 1940, for example, the German merchant ship* Alster *was captured by* Icarus *in Vestfjord, north of Bodø.* Alster *was escorted to Britain were she was renamed* Empire Endurance *by the Ministry of War Transport. Lieutenant Commander Colin Douglas Maud's narrative regarding Dunkirk is dated 10 June 1940:*

Tuesday, 28th May
Icarus, in company with *Intrepid* and *Ivanhoe*, arrived at Dover from Plymouth at 2300 and proceeded to secure to No.3 Buoy while waiting orders.

Wednesday, 29th May
0145   *Icarus* sailed for Dunkirk in company with *Javelin*, *Intrepid* and *Ivanhoe*.
0545   Came to with the port anchor off Dunkirk waiting for a clear berth in the harbour.
0600   *Javelin* and *Icarus* weighed and proceeded alongside the Eastern Arm, *Icarus* inside and embarked troops.
0800   Slipped and proceeded to Dover.
1130   Secured in Dover and disembarked troops.
1215   Slipped and in the absence of other orders returned to Dunkirk, using "Y" route.

1515   Came to with the port anchor off Zuydcoote under orders of *Codrington.* I anchored as close as possible inshore to cut down the length of the boats trip but later grounded with the turn of the tide: no damage occurred and later on the Schoot *Doggers Bank* towed my stern clear without difficulty.

On anchoring I had lowered all boats, motor boat and both whalers and also four Carley floats, two large and two small. It had been my intention to try to get close enough to the shore to be able to float the Carley floats ashore on the end of a line and then haul them back to the ship, leaving the motor boat to do the towing of the whalers. It was unfortunate that the shelving beach did not allow me to get close enough to carry out this in practice. I found that actually the Carley floats were little used by the troops who were unhandy in the floats. Air raids occurred during this embarkation period, the first between 1600 and 1630, another at 1730 and again at 1830; in fact they appeared to be coming over at hourly intervals with great regularity.

It was during the first of these air raids that *Jaguar* was damaged and the S.S. *Clan Macallister* hit aft. I was proceeding to stand by *Jaguar* but *Express* was alongside her before I had got under way. *Codrington* had meanwhile proceeded to *Clan Macallister* and was playing her hoses on the stern where a fire had broken out.

After the first raid I realised that I would be at a disadvantage at anchor during a raid and therefore remained under way for the remainder of the time I was lying off the beach. This was not so satisfactory for the embarkation point of view as I could not keep as close to the beach as before but consideration of the safety of the ship outweighed this disadvantage.

At about 1730 the Schoot *Doggers Bank* came alongside to transfer her full load of some 470 troops to *Icarus.* This appeared reasonable as the Schoot could remain closer inshore and therefore embark faster, while I was able to get back to Dover and return much faster than he. This transfer was interrupted by the 1730 air raid but it was completed by about 1830 when we proceeded to Dover by "X" route.

Shortly after getting under way when approaching Dunkirk harbour, a cloud of enemy machines was sighted above us. A.A. fire was once opened as soon as suitable targets came in line. It is difficult to estimate the number of planes that were in this raid but I would say that there were at least forty. In an incredibly short time dive bombing attacks developed on all ships in sight.

A paddle minesweeper just ahead of *Icarus* and approaching on opposite courses was attacked and sunk: the harbour looked as if it was being attacked by many planes at once and then the dive bombing attack developed on *Icarus*. The channel restricted my movements considerably and it was not possible to make any alteration of course and so I did the best I could by making violent alterations of speed from "Pull Ahead Both" to "Stop Both" as the attacks developed.

The engine room department, realising what was required, worked the throttle valves as fast as humanly possible, and it is no doubt that largely due to their efforts the ship was not hit. I think that at least ten planes attacked us, some together, and some shortly after one another: there were close misses ahead which had we not stopped engines a few seconds before must have hit us, and there were close misses astern shortly after we had increased to full speed again and besides all these there were close misses due to bad aiming which fell alongside the ship.

There was one salvo of three bombs which I was certain was going to hit at "B" Gun and which actually landed in the water abreast "B" Gun three feet from the ships side and which miraculously did not explode. The ship was also machine-gunned during these attacks and it was this which caused the casualties which amounted to one killed, five seriously injured and about twenty slightly injured, all with the exception of two being soldiers.

The Germans appeared to be using a semi-armour piercing bullet inside the ordinary machine gun bullet. It was one of the small calibre bullets that penetrated the forecastle deck and killed a soldier even though he was wearing his tin helmet at the time.

The shock of the near misses damaged the starboard dynamic and also the port steering motor: no other damage was apparent at the time.

On reaching 5W buoy and altering course to 349^0 we sighted another German bomber and opened fire. This machine circled round and then lined up astern on the port quarter to make a low level bombing attack at about 1500 to 2000 feet. I made both funnel and C.S. smoke at once and as soon as the bomber was lined up to start his attack I increased to full speed. There were not so many navigational hazards and I therefore kept my alteration until the end of his attack.

The attack developed slowly, both our guns firing but apparently not deterring him much. At the moment I judged that he was about to drop his bombs I made a very large alteration of course to port and this salvo missed. The enemy plane then circled ahead and round again to the port quarter for his second attack. This time I reduced speed slightly and waited until he was about to drop his salvo. In this attack I am certain that my smoke screen caused the pilot to make a bad estimation of my course because as he was nearly in the bomb release position I saw him give quite a considerable alteration of course to port and I therefore increased to full speed again and put the rudder hard a' starboard and the second salvo fell clear to port.

The enemy then circled round ahead and to port as before. Some of our salvos seemed to be reasonably close but he was not to be deterred and approached for the third time. Once again it seemed to be the smoke that put him off and I used the same avoiding tactics as before and the third salvo missed to port: these were small bombs. So having expended all his bombs the enemy then retired to the southward. During each attack the ship was machine-gunned but there were apparently no casualties.

I returned to Dover without further incident and berthed at 2050 to disembark troops.

Thursday, 30th May

Icarus remained alongside until 0100 waiting for orders and ammunition and then proceeded alongside the Eastern Arm to complete with fuel. Both the fuelling berths were full and so I berthed at the outer end until *Anthony* had completed at 0300.

0500   Proceeded to Sheerness under orders of *Javelin* in company with *Javelin, Intrepid, Ivanhoe* and *Impulsive.*
0915   Secured to No.II Buoy Sheerness. Completed with oil fuel and ammunition.
1715   Slipped and proceeded via "X" route to Dunkirk under orders of *Ivanhoe* in company with *Ivanhoe, Impulsive* and *Harvester. Ivanhoe* and *Impulsive* were detailed off to attend on the harbour itself, *Harvester* the first beach to the eastward, and *Icarus* the second beach to the eastward.

Icarus came under fire from shore guns while passing Dunkirk: some salvoes being unpleasantly near due to the flat trajectory.

The S.S. *Clan MacAlister* made a good beacon as she was at anchor near Bray Beach and still burning. I approached as close to the beach as possible and dropped a Dan Buoy with a candle lantern on it as a mark.

Icarus, motor-boat was out of action having bent the "A" bracket and propeller shaft at Sheerness and there had been no time to either change the boat or make good these defects before sailing for Dunkirk. Consequently the embarkation had to be effected with two whalers only, and this was extremely slow work.

The beach was being shelled and Dunkirk was being bombed while *Icarus* was lying off: two officers came on board and asked if it would be possible to inform the authorities of the slow rate of embarkation. I informed them that all possible steps were being taken by the authorities but that if matters did not improve by about midnight or one a.m. I would make a signal to V.A. Dover explaining the situation at Bray Beach. This signal I made later and was informed that boats were being sent and the situation would improve in the morning.

Shortly after dawn I was able to tell the Ramsgate Life Boat *Lord Southborough* [in fact she was the Margate lifeboat] that I had not any power boats and they did magnificent work bringing loads of about seventy at a time to the ship. Unfortunately the weather began to deteriorate and the Life Boat could not get close to the shore: so the whalers ferried troops to the Life Boat and when full she brought them to *Icarus*. This was at about 0600, and shortly after both whalers were capsized ashore and the Life Boat began to get into difficulties when embarking troops ashore.

0700 Proceeded to Dover leaving crews of whalers and of *Salamander*'s motor-boat to carry on with other ships that were arriving.

1000 Arrived Dover and proceeded to disembark the troops at Admiralty Pier.

1100 Slipped and proceeded to Dunkirk by "X" route. While proceeded up the Goodwin Channel had a slight collision with *Scimitar*, but damage to both ships was slight; the worst damage to *Icarus* being the D.G. Coil which was parted aft. Temporary repairs were made by ship's staff while on passage to Dunkirk.

1400 Lay off Dunkirk harbour while waiting for berth to clear inside.

1615 Secured alongside the eastern Arm inner berth, *Windsor* and one "S" class destroyer berthing outside *Icarus*. *Icarus'* port screw was fouled by a wire in going alongside. There was an air raid on the harbour during this embarkation and A.A. fire was opened by all ships and the shore A.A. batteries. No damage was done to the ships in harbour in this raid though there were some fairly close misses. Also during this embarkation there was intermittent shelling of the harbour.

1800 Slipped and proceeded to Dover by "X" route. Between 5W buoy and F.G. buoy *Icarus* was attacked once by a dive bomber. Speed was increased to full speed at once and funnel and C.S. smoke were also made after our previous experience. Once again violent alterations of course were made and the salvo fell short. There were many ships in company and a fierce A.A. fire had been opened which, though not scoring a hit, seemed to be close enough to deter him from returning.

2045 Secured alongside Dover and disembarked troops.

2215. Proceeded to Eastern Arm to complete with fuel.

Friday, 1st June

0130 Slipped and proceeded to Dunkirk.

0415 Secured alongside the *St. Hillier* [TSS *St Helier*] in Dunkirk harbour. There was a heavy air raid during this embarkation on the harbour. It appeared that there were some fifty enemy bombers in action, but very soon our fighters appeared and scattered the bombers immediately. Some bombs were dropped but there was no doubt that these were jettisoned rather than aimed accurately as they fell all over the place. Ships replied with A.A fire when there was an opportunity and the A.A. batteries ashore were also in action. *Icarus'* D.G. Coil was shorting in two places on the fo'c'sle; damage was temporarily repaired by the ship's staff.

0730 Slipped and proceeded to Dover. As ships proceeding down this channel between Dunkirk and 5W buoy had been fired at by shore batteries, a smoke float was burnt on the forecastle and funnel smoke was also made. The wind was exactly right to afford the maximum protection from the forecastle smoke float, but whether it was due to this protection or due to the enemy guns having moved on, it is impossible to say, but fire was not opened on *Icarus* during this passage.

1015 Arrived Dover and disembarked troops.

1300 Secured to No.1 Buoy, ship's staff and dockyard fitters working on the D.G. coil.

2030 Slipped and proceeded to Dunkirk, *Windsor* in company. *Icarus* was late proceeding owing to not receiving the signal giving order of leaving harbour until 2020.

2300 Secured in Dunkirk harbour on Eastern Arm.

Saturday, 2nd June

0001 Slipped and proceeded to Dover by "X" route. Was in collision with a small trawler while proceeding westward down the channel: the visibility was extremely bad owing to the smoke from the burning oil fuel tanks at Dunkirk and in spite of my having a lookout on the forecastle, there was no time for my order of full astern to take effect before hitting. I was unable to alter away to port as I was already just outside the charted channel to port to avoid the magnetic mines, which had been laid in the channel. No major damage was sustained but the heel fitting of the P.V. boom was fractured. It is not known what damage was sustained by the trawler.

0030 Received a signal from V.A. Dover informing ships that magnetic mines had been laid indiscriminately around F.G. buoy. As my D.G. coil insulation was extremely low and had been giving continuous trouble, I decided to avoid F.G. buoy and return by another route. There appeared to be no navigational dangers between 5W buoy and the swept channel on a course of 315 degrees, but there remained the question of our own minefields. I therefore informed V.A. Dover that I intended to proceed on a course of 315⁰ from 5W buoy owing to the laying of magnetic mines at F.G. buoy and at the same time asked if there were any British minefields on this course. I judged that the minefield, if any, would be laid in the channel to the northward and therefore adjusted my speed so as to give at least half an hour in which to get an answer to my signal before entering this channel. My signal was passed by 0045 and as no answer was received by 0115 it appeared that this course was a safe one; at 0130 however, I received a signal saying that the course was useless. It was too late as by this time I was back in the normal "X" route channel.

0400 Secured at Admiralty Pier and disembarked troops.

0500 Slipped and proceeded to No.7 Buoy.

1830 *Icarus* sailing for Dunkirk cancelled owing to having only one dynamo and one steering motor in action.

Monday, 4th June

1145 Slipped and proceeded under orders of *Vivacious* to Portsmouth.

1830 Secured alongside Pitch House Jetty.

During all this period the whole ship's company behaved in a grand way. They were tireless in their energies in whatever direction they were required, either pulling the whalers to and from the beach, or landing on the jetty at Dunkirk and heartening the passage of the soldiers with cheerful words or help. I regard this magnificent spirit to be due to the example shown by my officers and heads of departments in spite of the fact that we suffered a very severe dive bombing attack on our second trip and low level bombing attacks from one plane lasting about 20 minutes this same trip, and by Saturday every man was needing rest badly.

The spirit of the ship's company was shown when, having cleared lower deck on Saturday evening and explained the final stages of the operation, there was literally a "Tooth suck" from the ship's company when the sailing cancellation was piped by the bosun's mate later.

IMPULSIVE
I-class Destroyer
Pennant Number D11
Official Rescue Total: 2,919

Built by J.S. White at Cowes, Impulsive, *the first Royal Navy warship to be so named, was launched on 1 March 1937. She was captained by Lieutenant Commander William Scott Thomas RN during Operation* Dynamo. *His report is dated 5 June 1940:*

H.M.S. *Impulsive* arrived at Dover from Immingham at 0840 on May 27th 1940, and sailed at 1140 with H.M. Ships *Skipjack* and *Halcyon* and Trinity House Vessel *Patricia* to establish and buoy searched channel from the North Goodwin Light Vessel to Dunkirk, afterwards known as Route X. This operation was completed by 1919 and *Impulsive* anchored in the Downs at 2200.

2. At 2228 on May 27th orders were received by signal to proceed with all despatch to the beaches east of Dunkirk and embark troops. *Impulsive* weighed and proceeding by route Y arrived off La Panne at 0345 on May 28th and anchored as close inshore as possible. Both power boats being broken down the two whalers were sent inshore to embark troops. These boats were employed ferrying troops from the beach to large motor boats which were lying further off the shore.

3. At 0520 *Impulsive* was ordered by *Calcutta*, anchored off La Panne, to proceed to Dunkirk and go alongside the Eastern Pier to embark troops. Ship secured alongside the outer end of the pier at 0620 and after embarking approximately 750 troops sailed for Dover. Route Y was used and after an uneventful passage ship arrived at Dover at 1110. Troops were disembarked and, when several ratings who had missed the ship at Immingham, had rejoined ship, sailed for Dunkirk at 1235 using route Y.

4. It was during this passage, off Kwinte Bank buoy, that the ship was attacked and heavily bombed by six Heinkels. By proceeding at full

speed and making frequent and violent alterations of course, the bombs, which could be seen falling, were successfully avoided and no hits were scored. Aircraft were bombing from approximately 1000 feet. On completion of the bombing three aircraft remained behind and attacked with machine guns. A northerly course was steered during these attacks in order to avoid the narrow channels, and it was during these attacks that the ship was damaged and the casualties occurred – 6 ratings being wounded, 2 seriously. B gun was put out of action by an armour piercing bullet which penetrated the gun shield, wounded the trainer and lodged in the air pipe to the run out cylinder, causing the gun to remain in the recoil position. The D/G coil was punctured by bullets and caught fire: this was quickly extinguished. On the first attack developing I cleared the bridge of lookouts and signalmen remaining up there by myself. The last lookout to leave the bridge was seriously wounded in the chest. Other ratings wounded were in the after supply party and were hit by bullets which penetrated the after screen, and on the Fore Mess Decks and in the Signal Distributing Office were hit by bullets penetrating the deck heads. All aircraft made off, presumably when they had expended their ammunition, and course was set for Dunkirk in company with *Greyhound* and *Verity*, who had by this time arrived from the eastward.

5. On arrival at Dunkirk there was no berth available alongside the pier, four destroyers being alongside already, so I anchored off and waited for a berth to be vacated. At 1730 *Grenade* sailed and I proceeded alongside in her place. Smoke floats and a whaler for placing them were then handed over to the Naval Officer in charge of embarkation. About 1000 troops were embarked and I sailed, with *Jaguar* in company, by route Y, arriving at Dover after an uneventful passage at 0100 on May 29th.

6. At 0400 after disembarking troops I moved out to No.11. buoy to repair damage which had been caused during the machine gun attacks. The pipe from B gun and two copper pipes in the engine room which had been fractured by the detonation of near bomb misses, were sent to *Sandhurst* for repair and efforts were made by the ship's staff to repair the D/G coil. By 1300 the ship was once again ready for sea except for the D/G coil, which was temporarily repaired later in the day.

7. At 0500 on May 30th *Impulsive* sailed for Sheerness in company with *Javelin*, *Intrepid*, *Ivanhoe*, *Icarus*, *Havant*, and *Harvester*, arriving and securing to No.10 buoy at 0900. At 1600 orders were received to proceed with all despatch to Dunkirk, and *Ivanhoe*, *Icarus*, *Impulsive* and *Harvester* sailed in company by route X. On arrival *Impulsive* proceeded alongside the East Pier, the inshore berth, and embarked 1300 troops. This was the largest number embarked and I did not consider there was room for

any more. The passage back to Dover by route X was uneventful and at 2400 the ship secured alongside Admiralty Pier, after a long wait in the outer harbour for a berth to become vacant.

8. At 0400 on May 31st, the ship sailed for Dunkirk by route X, with orders to embark troops from Dunkirk beach, and arrived off the beach at 0700. Although there were thousands of soldiers on the beach there were very few boats to bring them off. *Impulsive* had no power boats and only one whaler. The only power boat in the neighbourhood, a large War Department motor boat with Colonel Hutchings in charge, came alongside. This boat, towing a cutter and *Impulsive's* whaler, did magnificent work under difficult conditions and between 0800 and 1315 had transferred approximately 450 troops from the beach to the ship.

9. It was whilst the ship was lying off waiting for boats to come alongside that *Impulsive* grounded aft on an uncharted wreck. The details of this incident have already been reported.

10. At 1420 *Impulsive* returned to Dover by route X at twelve knots on one engine. Heavy bombing attacks on Dunkirk had just started, and the shore battery abreast No.7W Buoy was shelling ships using the West Channel. Passage to Dover was uneventful, and at 2000 the ship secured alongside Admiralty Pier and disembarked approximately 450 troops.

11. This was the last trip *Impulsive* made to Dunkirk, and at 1715 on June 1st the ship sailed for Sheerness to de-ammunition before proceeding to Blackwall Dock for repair.

INTREPID
I-class Destroyer
Pennant Number D10
Official Rescue Total: 661

Launched on 17 December 1936, Intrepid *was the seventh British warship to carry the name which was introduced in 1747 for a French Prize. It was previously used for a blockship sunk at Zeebrugge in 1918. Commander Roderick Cosmo Gordon completed his report on 5 June 1940:*

27th May 1940
2100 H.M. Ships *Intrepid*, *Ivanhoe* and *Icarus* off Folkestone Gate detached to proceed to Western Approaches. Set course via Searched Channels in force. Speed 23 knots.

28th May 1940
0700 Ships arrived Plymouth – Oiled and secured to buoys.

0930   Commanding Officers waited on Commander in Chief and received their orders.
1230   All orders cancelled. Received orders to raise steam and prepare to sail forthwith.
1320   Slipped and proceeded out of harbour. Set course for Dover via Searched Channels. Speed 28 knots.
2300   Arrived Dover and secured to buoys awaiting orders.

29th May 1940
0130   Slipped from buoys. Joined H.M.S. *Javelin* outside breakwater. H.M.S. *Vimy* also joined. Proceeded in company to Dunkirk by route 'Y'.
0500   Arrived off Dunkirk. Anchored off the harbour.
0530   (approx) S.S. *Mona's Isle* who was anchored astern of us blew up on a magnetic mine. Lowered motor boat to assist in rescuing survivors. H.M.S. *Vimy* also lowered boats. *Ivanhoe* had been detached to assist *Grafton* off Kwinte buoy. *Javelin* and *Icarus* had proceeded into Dunkirk harbour.
0730   Entered Dunkirk Harbour and proceeded alongside Eastern arm. S.N.O. Dunkirk and staff came onboard and were given a meal. Embarked 675 troops (6 Officers included)
0840   Slipped and proceeded independently to Dover via route 'Y'.
1200   Arrived Dover. Disembarked troops at Admiralty Pier.
1400   Proceeded to Dunkirk by route 'Y'.
1700   Attacked by enemy aircraft between Middelkerke and La Panne. Engaged aircraft with 0.5 M.Gs, Lewis Guns and 'B' and 'X' 4.7 guns. ('A' and 'Y' guns were not on board).
       Owing to the sun and a thin mist at about 3000 feet it was difficult to see aircraft before they attacked. One bomb exploded on impact with the water close alongside the Port side just for'ard of the bridge and did considerable damage.
       One piece of shrapnel pierced the side abreast No.1 boiler room and subsequently the main steam pipe in this boiler room. In this connection the Stoker P.O in the boiler room (Acting Sto. P.O. A.F. Taylor O.N. C/KX 79114) is deserving of special mention for quick action in shutting down the boiler room which was rapidly filling with steam, thus preventing a boiler explosion. The side was pierced in a number of places (about 70 in all) especially the after end of the seamans and stokers mess decks. Fires were started on both these decks due probably to hot pieces of shrapnel landing near hammocks etc. And also electric leads being damaged also by shrapnel the fires on both these messdecks took

some time to extinguish owing to the difficulty of locating their origin. This in turn was due to the exhaust steam pipe to the capstan being severed and filling the upper messdeck with steam. This could not be shut off as the valve is in No.1 boiler room which had to be evacuated.

On the stokers messdeck electric leads had been shot away by splinters putting this compartment and the magazine and shell room below in darkness. Both these fires were eventually got under control about an hour later but in the mean time I had given orders for the forward magazine and shell room to be flooded.

Two ratings were killed and seventeen wounded nearly all of whom were supply or repair parties stationed in the galley flat or messdecks. 'B' gun's crew received two casualties and a flying fragment bent the mantlet plate putting the gun out of action as it could not be elevated.

Several further attacks occurred subsequently but no hits or near misses were received. Course was continued towards Dunkirk until the Engineer Officer reported that he was unable so far to extinguish the fires in the messdecks, when taking into account the other damage which had been received and having given orders for the fore magazine and shell room to be flooded I decided that the ship must be considered out of action until repairs had been effected.

Course was then set for Dover which was reached at 2000 and ship proceeded alongside Admiralty Pier to disembark wounded. A signal was then made asking for dockyard assistance to make good defects incurred in action and ship, after oiling, secured to a buoy in Dover Harbour.

30th May 1940

0500 Sailed from Dover in company with *Javelin, Ivanhoe, Icarus, Impulsive, Havant* and *Harvester*.

0845 Arrived Sheerness, oiled and secured to buoy. Representative of Commodore in Charge came onboard at once and inspected defects and reported the situation to the Commander in Chief, The Nore.

Subsequently *Intrepid* was ordered to leave Sheerness for Middlesbrough at 0400 on Saturday 1st June. Ship sailed accordingly and arrived Middlesbrough at 1730 on that day where she was taken in hand at once.

IVANHOE
I-class Destroyer
Pennant Number D16
Official Rescue Total: 1,904

HMS Ivanhoe *was ordered from Yarrow's at Scotstoun on 30 October 1935, being launched on 11 February 1937. She was the second Royal Navy warship to carry the name.* Ivanhoe *had been undertaking mine-laying duties when she was redeployed for* Dynamo, *her part in which is recounted here by Commander Philip Henry Hadow, his report being dated 3 June 1940:*

Wednesday, 29th May
0148 Sailed from Dover in company with *Javelin, Intrepid* and *Icarus.*
0430 Detached off Kwinte buoy to stand by *Grafton.* Proceeded alongside and embarked survivors. Grafton was sinking slowly and this was accordingly accelerated by gunfire.
0615 Proceeded to Dunkirk.
0856 Secured alongside mole and embarked troops.
1115 Sailed for Dover.
1610 Secured alongside Admiralty Pier Dover and disembarked troops. (Approximately 600.)
1745 Sailed for Dunkirk.
1820 Picked up four of crew of aircraft K.8773, crashed in vicinity of S.W. Goodwin buoy. Crew transferred to a nearby drifter.
2100 Off Dunkirk.
2240 Recalled to Dover.

Thursday, 30th May
0250 Arrived Dover.
0500 Sailed for Sheerness in company with *Javelin, Intrepid, Icarus* and *Impulsive.*
0930 Arrived Sheerness and completed with oil fuel.
1715 Sailed for Dunkirk in company with *Impulsive, Icarus* and *Harvester.*
2115 Started embarking troops from beach 1 mile East of Dunkirk pier.

Friday, 31st May
0315 Proceeded alongside Dunkirk pier and embarked further troops.
0415 Sailed for Dover.
0800 Arrived Dover and disembarked troops (Approximately 1,300).
0955 Sailed for Dunkirk.

37

1300 Off beaches. Ordered by R.A. Dover to act as organising centre for embarkation at beach 1 mile East of Dunkirk and as V/S link between Dunkirk and the Admiral.

Started embarking troops, as far as above duties permitted.

During the afternoon this area was subjected to heavy bombing attacks.

2145 Arrived off La Panne and started further embarkation which proceeded throughout the night.

Saturday, 1st June

At about 0230 the situation ashore was obscure owing to a heavy and incessant artillery bombardment, and I received reports that either there were no more troops left to embark or that what troops remained had taken cover or moved along the beach to the Westward. The motor boat was sent inshore to find out the exact situation and it was discovered that a large body of British troops had just arrived on the beach. Their embarkation was accordingly immediately proceeded with.

From dawn for a period of about one hour the ship and beach were subjected to a continuous machine-gun fire from low flying aircraft. One and possibly two, of these were shot down.

At 0715, having embarked approximately 1,000 troops I received orders from R.A. Dover to proceed. When abreast Bray, in company with other destroyers and light craft the ships were subjected to heavy level bombing attacks by a large number of enemy aircraft. These attacks were all avoided.

When abreast Dunkirk dive bombing attacks developed and at about 0800 *Ivanhoe* received damage from a salvo of 3 bombs. Two were near misses on either side whilst the third after presumably hitting the port whaler's after davit exploded a few feet above the upper deck near the base of the foremost funnel. The bombs appeared to be dropped from about 1,000 feet.

The resulting damage was as follows:

a) The deck above No.2 Boiler room was pierced in many places, and bomb splinters entered the boiler room damaging the boiler and the steam leads from No.1 Boiler Room.

b) Fires developed in the uptake to No.1 Boiler Room, the drying room, and at the base of the foremost funnel.

c) All deck fittings in the vicinity were destroyed as far as, and including, the 0.5" gun platform and the 0.5" guns were completely put out of action.

d) The ships side above and below the waterline, and nearby superstructure, was pierced in many places.

e) No.1 and No.2. Boiler Rooms subsequently became flooded.

f) There were in all 26 killed and 30 wounded.

In view of the fires the foremost magazine was flooded. As soon as it was clear that the ship was not in immediate danger of sinking I remained in the channel and requested *Havant* and *Speedwell* to come alongside and remove the soldiers. This was done and some twenty wounded were also transferred to *Havant*. By this time all fires were under control and the engineer Officer, had been able to master the situation below, and the ship was able to proceed at approximately 7 knots partly under our own power, from steam in No.3. Boiler, and with the valuable assistance of the tug *Persia*.

During the subsequent hour the ship was attacked by a large number of level bombers on two occasions. During each of these attacks, after the first salvo of bombs had fallen a smoke float was ignited in the bows to simulate that the ship had been struck. This ruse had the desired effect and undoubtedly saved the ship from further damage.

The remainder of the passage to Sheerness was without incident and Admiralty tugs took over the ship when inside the Edinburgh Channel.

The conduct and bearing of all the officers and men both during the operation and after the ship had been struck was highly praiseworthy.

Silvester MacDonald was a Royal Navy medical orderly sent on board soon after Ivanhoe docked at Sheerness. His account is quoted here from War's Long Shadow: 69 Months of the Second World War:

The *Ivanhoe* just about made the crossing without sinking and was immediately placed in a dry dock so that she would not sink overnight. The soldiers and ship's crew who had survived were disembarked and the wounded were removed and taken to hospital. Such were the conditions when our little party arrived at dockside. It was a beautiful summer morning, but there was an unnatural quietness hanging all around. Even the view from dockside brought a hushed feeling to all who looked.

It was a macabre scene that the devil himself could not have imagined to see bodies hanging over the bridge rails, lying around gun turrets, sprawled on the decks both fore and aft and the bodies in navy blue and in khaki that were entangled in death in a grotesque heap on the after deck.

It took little imagination to hear the ghostly echoes of far off bugles calling for their spirits to assemble again and be counted. We just went back to the barracks and did not even discuss it before we tried to sleep.

I believe that it was a very rude awakening for me. The fun and games were definitely finished.

JAGUAR
J-class Destroyer
Pennant Number F34
Official Rescue Total: 700

Ordered from William Denny at Dunbarton on 25 March 1937, Jaguar *was launched on 22 November 1938 as the first Royal Navy ship to carry the name. Lieutenant Commander John Franklin William Hine's report is dated 1 June 1940:*

2. At 0214, 28th May, slipped and proceeded from Harwich in company with *Codrington*, *Javelin*, and *Grenade* to patrol between North Goodwin Light Vessel and Kwinte Bank in accordance with Commander-in-Chief, Nore's 0253/28.

3. At 0600, wreckage, boats and rafts were sighted. Proceeded to pick up survivors in accordance with Captain (D) 1's 0605. Embarked one woman, six men, and a dog, of whom one man subsequently died. Patrol was resumed at 0648 and at 1012 survivors of S.S. *Aboukir* were transferred to *Grenade*. Master reported that ship had been torpedoed by submarine.

4. Having proceeded to Dunkirk in company with *Javelin* and *Codrington*, in accordance with Vice Admiral, Dover's 1007, on arrival off harbour *Javelin* and *Jaguar* were sent to embark troops from Braye beach. Remained underway, five cables from shore, lowering motor cutter and whaler. These boats were inadequate for the large number of troops waiting, and it was decided to pick up a derelict whaler and skiff a mile to the eastward. Returned and embarked one boat load. Aircraft were engaged on several occasions but no bombs were dropped.

5. Being ordered to proceed to Dunkirk by *Javelin*, left at 1550 and entered Dunkirk, finding great difficulty in securing to Eastern Arm during strong flood tide. Boats were left in charge of *Javelin*. Seven hundred troops were embarked between 1730 and 1900.

6. Slipped and proceeded to Dover in company with *Impulsive*, remaining there until 0830/29 to complete with ammunition and fuel.

7. Sailed at that time in company with *Grenade* and *Gallant* in accordance with Vice Admiral, Dover's 0550, proceeding by route "X" with all despatch.

8. At 1155, when to the westward of the Snouw Bank a force of dive bombers was sighted and was engaged as it closed to attack. Aircraft dispersed and attacked all three ships, *Gallant* in particular.

As attack on *Jaguar* developed, director jammed on port after stop but close range weapons were engaged continuously.

Approximately six aircraft attacked ship, dropping one bomb each, which all missed, though the nearest was less than a hundred yards off the starboard bow.

Gallant was seen to be damaged and retiring. One aircraft was seen to be hit by pom-pom and whilst losing height was despatched by a fighter. An aerial combat developed and it is thought that others were destroyed.

Freedom of manoeuvre was impossible owing to narrow waters and changes in speed were the only method of avoiding.

9. Secured alongside *Grenade* at Eastern Arm, Dunkirk, at 1250, embarkation of approximately a thousand troops commencing at 1400 and continuing until 1525. Though enemy level bombers were being held off by fighters and ship and shore A.A. fire during this period, two patterns of heavy bombs were dropped close to Eastern arm without damage to ships.

10. Following verbal orders were received from the Commander on the staff of S.N.O, Dunkirk whilst alongside: i. "Embark all possible troops, at least a thousand"; ii. "Do not impair fighting efficiency by overcrowding"; iii. When this latter order was received, some eight hundred troops had been embarked; iv. "Provide A.A. cover as far as possible for transport *Loch Garry*. It was ascertained that this vessel had a speed of 12 knots.

11. *Loch Garry* was seen off entrance to be steaming for "Y" route and she was closed and hailed. Original intention of returning by "X" route was abandoned, owing to a submarine report.

12. Whilst taking station ahead of transport, a dive bombing attack developed, and attacks were continuous from all angles from 1550 to 1605. Owing to the narrow waters in the vicinity of 8E buoy, there was little freedom of manoeuvre with a transport astern and several wrecks. Aircraft attacks were concentrated on *Jaguar* who received about fourteen, the transport one, aircraft dropping salvoe of four bombs.

13. There were many near misses, and towards the close of the attack a bomb exploded close on the port side abreast the break of the forecastle. This did considerable damage to ship and personnel, and engines and steering were put out of action. Steering was carried out from tiller flat, and from a position close to 8E buoy a course was shaped up the channel, but headway was soon lost and ship stopped close to a wreck whose upperworks were visible.

A transport, ahead and inshore, was hit by level bombers, and *Codrington* was seen closing her.

Messengers had to be sent to engine room to ascertain damage, owing to break-down of telephone, and the report seemed serious, holes above and below the water line, leaking oil fuel tanks, and pierced steam, oil and water pipes indicating that ship was likely to be out of action for some time.

Water was flowing into number one and two boiler rooms, and low power room, an increasing list to port developed, and it was feared that ship would sink slowly until those holes above the water line were also submerged, and thus increase the likelihood of foundering, unless steam could be raised. An additional handicap was the extra load of seventy tons of troops, who hampered all movement above and below decks. Under these circumstances it was decided to jettison torpedoes and depth charges.

Preparations to be taken in tow were in progress, and torpedoes were fired after removal of pistols from warheads. Unfortunately the stop valves of at least four had not been closed and they ran onto the beach at Braye, where it is hoped they burnt themselves out. Twenty three depth charges and pistols were also jettisoned.

14. Meanwhile *Express* closed and offered assistance at a moment when *Jaguar* was slowly drifting on to the wreck less than 50 yards off. *Express* was asked to tow alongside in order to get clear quickly, which she did at 1710.

Express continued towing alongside at a speed of about four knots until more open water was reached, during which time the majority of troops transferred.

A level bombing attack was experienced during this operation though it might have been aimed at other ships passing.

Recent engine room reports suggested the possibility of having steam soon, though there was still doubt, owing to many minor punctures in piping and the uncertainty of obtaining fuel free from water.

15. Scoot *Rika* closed *Express* and removed more troops and a more pessimistic report was received from engine room that steam would be delayed at least an hour.

It was then decided to tow by hawser, and at 1800 *Express* slipped, sustaining damage to torpedo davit and "X" gun deck, as *Jaguar's* overhanging bow passed down her starboard side.

It was intended to tow with at least three shackles of cable on the 4½ inch wire, but it was feared that veering so much cable in shallow water might result in anchoring both ships. Accordingly, only a shackle and a quarter were veered. The port anchor had to be slipped to avoid fouling the tow as it tautened. A speed of nine knots was attained, when the tow parted near the outboard end at 1850.

16. *Express* then signalled "Anchor instantly. I will come alongside to collect your wounded" and ship was anchored and tow recovered. *Express* came alongside at 1905, embarked wounded and slipped at 1940, having requested Vice Admiral, Dover, to send a tug or other vessel to tow.

17. *Jaguar* remained at anchor, and another tow was being prepared when engine room reported likelihood of having steam. At 1945 engines were tried and found to be working.

18. At 1950, weighed and proceeded, gradually working up to a speed of twenty knots.

19. At 2014 a level bomber attacked, and was engaged. Course was altered but the stick of heavy bombs straddled very close astern though no apparent damage was done.

20. At 2026 another level bomber attacked and was engaged. Bombs were avoided by a bold alteration of course.

21. A zig-zag course was steered until reaching "R" buoy. An aircraft believed hostile, was glimpsed in the Downs and *Bliskawica* [*Błyskawica*] reported having sighted aircraft dropping parachute mines.

22. Entered Dover harbour at 2350, where temporary repairs were carried out by *Sandhurst*, sailing at 1600/31 for Immingham, for repairs, arriving 1000/1.

REMARKS

Great appreciation was felt of the timely and efficient aid of H.M.S. *Express*, by which the ship was saved from drifting on to wreck and towed clear of the narrow channel. It was essential too, to get rid of the troops in order to lighten the ship and have room to repair damage.

2. It is considered that enemy aircraft made a mistake in concentrating attacks on *Jaguar* when a large and fully loaded transport was astern. Their misjudgement alone justifies the use of an overloaded destroyer as an A.A. escort to a slow ship. Fortunately casualties were light, which would not have been the case, had the transport been attacked and it was an extremely lucky case of two "wrongs" making a "right".

3. Ship had no boats. They were still in use at Braye beach.

4. The morale of Officers and men was excellent and there were many instances of high initiative and bravery. The troops, already weary, showed an excellent spirit, though there was a move to hurry off the mess decks during attack. They also lost no time in transferring to *Express*. There was one instance of failure in action but this man is an epileptic, frequent attempts having been made beforehand to relieve him.

5. The fact that some torpedoes ran on to the beach is disappointing. The Gunner (T) had very definite orders about closing stop valves before jettisoning, but he was wounded when it was done. The L.T.O of the forward tubes was away in charge of a boat and most of the torpedomen were either jettisoning depth charges or on electrical repair work. It was impossible to fire to seaward, owing to *Express*.

6. The gunnery problem of a sustained dive bombing attack is the subject of a separate report. With aircraft attacking in steep dives from an elevation above that of the 4.7" guns, close range weapons are the only protection and they have great difficulty in shifting target with effect.

7. H.M.S. *Jaguar* was fitted experimentally to tow a kite balloon in November, 1939, and these trials were successful. It is suggested that a kite balloon might be a deterrent to dive bombers and should be fitted in waters where enemy aircraft have supremacy.

8. It is considered that, when the tow parted, *Express* was undoubtedly right in returning to Dover. From the level bombing attacks which were experienced afterward, it is possible that both ships might have been damaged when towing at low speed, and many of the wounded probably owe their lives to *Express* collecting them after anchoring.

REPORT IN ACCORDANCE WITH H.G.O. 032.

Ship was attacked by Dive Bombers when approaching Dunkirk in company with *Grenade* and *Gallant*, the latter receiving damage. All bombs of at least six attacks missed and one aircraft was brought down by A.A. fire and others by Fighters.

One high bombing attack on jetty was experienced while embarking a thousand troops alongside.

On leaving A.A. cover was provided by *Jaguar* for a transport and whilst still in narrow waters, a dive bombing attack developed, about twelve attacks on *Jaguar* and one on transport. There were several near misses and one bomb exploded close to the Port side, killing twelve and wounding thirty. Steam and fuel pipes were pierced by splinters and ship was unable to steam for three and three quarter hours.

After a quarter of an hour *Express* came alongside and towed ship away from a wreck towards which she was drifting. As ship was holed near water-line torpedoes and depth charges were jettisoned, and troops transferred to *Express* and Scoot, *Rika*.

As ships were again bombed, and progress was slow, *Express* proceeded to tow *Jaguar* from aft. But tow parted and ship was anchored whilst *Express* came alongside and embarked wounded.

After remaining at anchor for an hour, steam was raised and a speed of twenty knots was eventually reached. High level bombing attacks were being carried out on neighbouring ships and *Jaguar* was twice attacked, one stick of four straddling very close astern.

Ship then proceeded to Dover.

MALCOLM
Scott-class Flotilla Leader
Pennant Number D19
Official Rescue Total: 5,851

HMS Malcolm *was laid down on 27 March 1918, being launched on 29 May 1919 as the first Royal Navy warship to carry the name. Her build was completed in December 1919. Captain Thomas Edgar Halsey RN's report of his ship's participation in Operation* Dynamo *was completed at the Royal Naval Barracks Chatham on 10 June 1940 (of interest is the fact that fifteen days later Halsey was replaced as* Malcolm's *commander by Captain Augustus Willington Shelton Agar VC, DSO, RN):*

I have the honour to submit a brief report of events mainly compiled from H.M.S. *Malcolm*'s deck and signal log.

The days went by so quickly and one was so intent on one's own small section of the job in hand that I find it difficult to remember a great deal of what occurred, or to do justice to the good work of other ships working nearby.

After the period from 0200 on 29th May during which *Malcolm* was largely concerned with trying to distribute destroyers and boats to the best advantage between various beaches and Dunkirk Pier, the ship ran almost solely as a ferry between Dunkirk Eastern Pier and Dover.

In this connection I feel it should be pointed out how much harder it must have been for the Commanding Officer of private destroyers than for a ship with a Captain (D)'s staff. Commanding Officers of these ships had to rely almost entirely on themselves, without the assistance of the additional officers borne in a leader.

I was very little concerned with the work on the beaches after Wednesday 29th, which was before the very large number of auxiliary boats arrived, but I must comment on the admirable work of the transports at Dunkirk Pier. These ships were handled with skill and coolness under shell fire and bombing which would be expected from His Majesty's Ships but which is an enormous credit to their masters and crews.

The following is a brief diary of events:

Tuesday, 28th
1422 Slipped from North Western Wall Ports.
2010 Spoke Dover. Ordered to proceed to beaches East of Dunkirk by route Y with H.M.S. *Esk*, H.M.S. *Shikari* and H.M.S. *Scimitar* in company.

Wednesday, 29th
0215 Anchored off No.8 E. Zuydcotte buoy. Sent in one whaler in tow of *Express*'s motor boat, Sub-Lieutenant Brooke-Alder R.N.R. in charge, with orders to investigate and commence embarking soldiers if a concentration had been found.
0245 Sent in second whaler in tow of another's ship's motor boat. Put Lieutenant Nelson, R.N.V.R. in charge with similar orders.
0630 Closed abandoned shore motor boat, which we repaired. Sent First Lieutenant in shore to beach a schuyt for use as a pier for boats embarking soldiers on shore.
0945 *Shikari* came alongside bringing First Lieutenant and E.R.A. from shore motor boat which broke down completely and had to be abandoned. From 1500 onwards heavy bombing took place on beaches, Dunkirk and ships during which *Malcolm* was straddled and machine gunned.
1630 Proceeded alongside *Clan Macalister* (she had brought a number of A.L.C.s which were then in use embarking soldiers from shore. I had previously ordered her to remain off the beach and fill up with troops) who had been hit by a bomb and was on fire aft. Embarked the soldiers and wounded members of the crew from *Clan Macalister* and instructed her that she might return as soon as she could get under way. By this time I had approximately 600 soldiers and a number of wounded on board.
1800 Proceeded to Dover via route Y.

1940 Spitfire aircraft crashed near ship in position VXWY 1902. Aircraft broke into small fragments with no trace of survivors.
2200 Secured alongside *Icarus* at Admiralty Pier, disembarked soldiers and wounded.

Friday, 30th
0128 Secured at Eastern Arm, embarked 140 tons of oil fuel and ammunition.
0518 Proceeded by route X.

0810 Arrived Dunkirk.

0833 Secured at E. Pier. Embarked approximately 1000 soldiers.

0852 Slipped and proceeded to Dover via route X.

1205 Berthed alongside transport at Admiralty Pier. Disembarked soldiers. *Shikari* alongside me also disembarking.

1308 Slipped and proceeded.

1610 Alongside Eastern Pier Dunkirk. Embarked approximately 1000 soldiers.

1700 Slipped

1850 Secured alongside *Whitehall* at Admiralty Pier and disembarked soldiers including two German prisoners who were put in the forecastle cable locker.

2123 Proceeded.

2350 Delayed trying to pick up light on No.6 W. Buoy, ship's estimated position being just North of Snouw Bank. Finally, hearing No.7 W. Whistle buoy and assisted by use of asdics, cleared Snouw Bank.

0112 Spoke *Ivanhoe* off Dunkirk.

0120 Spoke S.N.O. Dunkirk, entered.

0130 Owing to my misjudgement of distances in the dark was in heavy collision with Dunkirk Pier with considerable damage to ship's forefoot, but making no water abaft the forepeak bulkhead.

0215 Finally secured alongside. Embarked 1000 troops and proceeded.

0600 Secured at Admiralty Pier. Disembarked soldiers.

0643 Slipped and, after considerable search for oil berth secured alongside Eastern Arm and embarked oil fuel.

1135 Slipped.

1430 Arrived Dunkirk and secured Eastern Pier. Embarked approximately 1000 soldiers. Soldiers were coming down slowly at this time and demolition stores were put on shore at request of Commander Clouston, acting as Piermaster, in order that breach might be blown in Pier if necessary to enable last beach party to embark in motor boats.

1747 Slipped and proceeded Dover via route X.

1941 Picked up crew (2) of crashed British Defiant fighter.

2125 Secured alongside Admiralty Pier and disembarked soldiers. Some delay was caused in landing by the difficulty of disembarking the wounded airmen and their disposal.

2346 Proceeded.

Saturday, 1st June

Weather was thick and ship was in collision with French trawler which altered to port when sighted right ahead on opposite course. Ship was holed abreast the bridge port side above the water line, D.G. circuit being severed. Visibility at this time and place was about 50 yards.

0309 Arrived off Dunkirk Pier. Spoke *Worcester* who was outside lying off. Entrance was obscured by clouds of black smoke. At this time the Engineer Officer informed me that he had used up the water in reserve feed tank and had run down one boiler and anticipated being able to steam for another 2 hours approximately.

0315 Entered. Secured alongside Eastern Pier which was crowded with soldiers and no other ships alongside. Embarked approximately 1000 soldiers. Soon after this other destroyers and transports entered.

0442 Slipped and proceeded to Dover via route X.

0758 Secured alongside *Anthony* at Admiralty Pier. Disembarked approximately 1000 soldiers.

0850 Secured alongside *Sandhurst* for distilled water and repairs.

1318 Slipped from *Sandhurst* (no tugs were available) and proceeded although unable to obtain permission from Vice-Admiral, Dover. At the eastern entrance was ordered by Vice-Admiral, Dover to return. Secured to No.9 buoy and subsequently reverted to one hour and then 2½ hours' notice to steam. Whilst alongside *Sandhurst* ship's company were very exhausted and, but for the fine example of Officers and Petty Officers, might have given way. It was perhaps fortunate that Vice Admiral, Dover shortly after this put the ship at longer notice and gave them a nights rest. The spirit of the ship's company the next day was immensely improved.

1930 Fuelled from *War Sepoy*.

2215 Secured to No.11 buoy.

Sunday, 2nd June
In harbour. During forenoon diving party examined propellers, ship's company cleaned up ship and mess decks and piped down at 1050.

2000 Embarked scaling ladders.

2206 Slipped and proceeded to be off Dunkirk at 0200 in accordance with Vice-Admiral, Dover's 1715 and 1740/2/6.

Mon, 3rd June
0145 Arrived off Dunkirk. Several destroyers and small vessels were lying off awaiting their turn to proceed alongside.

0212 Ordered by R.A.D. via D.1 that all destroyers were to return to Dover except two detailed by me. *Malcolm* and *Whitshed* were detailed, the remainder sailed.

0248 R.A.D. ordered all destroyers return to Dover which we did empty, to our sorrow.

0530 Secured alongside *Codrington* at Eastern Arm.

1600 Embarked new A.S. dome.

1730 Embarked victuals for French troops and 2 French Naval ratings to assist in their embarkation.

2108 Slipped so as to be off Dunkirk in accordance with Vice-Admiral, Dover's 1224/3/6.

0023 Arrived off Dunkirk. Found several destroyers and other vessels waiting their turn to go in also *Locust* lying off, embarking men from small craft coming out from the inner harbour. Ships proceeded in and berthed in accordance with R.A.D's orders.

0210 Secured alongside Eastern Pier. Embarked approximately 800 French troops. This disappointing number was due to difficulty of stowing French troops with the enormous packs they carried. The ship seemed fuller than it had ever been. While *Malcolm* was alongside embarking troops, *Locust* had completed embarkation of troops from small boats and signalled she had room for about another 100 or so and proceeded alongside pier ahead of *Malcolm* at about 0225 and filled up. This was not part of the duties for which she had been detailed. Light was not then far off and I consider this showed initiative and courage on the part of the Commanding Officer of *Locust* whose name is unknown to me.

About this time R.A.D. told me verbally by loud speaker from a M.T.B that the last two ships were to use their discretion about remaining later than 0230 and *Express* was told by me to leave not later than 0300. It is understood that she remained until 0318 before shoving off full of French troops and the Naval Beach Party, which I consider most creditable to the Commanding Officer, Captain J. Bickford.

0245 Slipped. Outside Dunkirk met *Shikari* and signalled her to return to Dover. Found she was escorting a block ship. At this time a magnetic mine exploded alongside the block ship just after *Malcolm* passed her at about a half cable's distance. It is understood from subsequent signals that *Shikari* went alongside to take off further French troops who were still on the pier. In the circumstances I consider this showed courage and initiative on the part of the Commanding Officer, Lieutenant Commander H.N.A. Richardson, R.N. Beach party had already been embarked in *Express* and destroyers had been ordered to return to Dover. On my way back during thick weather near North Goodwin heard cries of distress in the water and picked up survivors, mainly soldiers, from "Schuyt" which had been sunk by collision with one of our minesweepers. A French motor boat who was picking up survivors and whose propeller had been disabled by wreckage, asked me for a tow. I took her in tow and found that Admiral Abrial, French Commander-in-Chief, Dunkirk, was on board her.

0600 (approx.) Secured alongside Admiralty Pier and disembarked French troops and French Commander-in-Chief who was received by Vice-Admiral, Dover.

The behaviour of officers and ship's company of *Malcolm* was all that I had hoped for. The ship's company had had a very hard 24 hours stowing ammunition, etc., and hurrying the ship forward at Portsmouth. *Malcolm* slipped with a good deal of the ammunition still on the Upper Deck which was stowed below during the passage to Dover.

The First Lieutenant and Engineer Officer, who replaced previous casualties, only joined shortly before sailing, and the ship was still short of a Gunner (T) and about 15 ratings, previous casualties who had not been replaced.

MONTROSE
Scott-class Flotilla Leader
Pennant Number I01
Official Rescue Total: 925

Ordered from Hawthorn Leslie at Newcastle in April 1917, HMS Montrose *was launched on 10 June 1917 as the first Royal Navy ship to carry this name. She was completed on 14 December 1918. Commander Cecil Ramsden Langworthy Parry wrote his account whilst* Montrose *was berthed in Millwall Dock, London, on 2 June 1940:*

2. At 1535 on Monday 27th May, *Montrose* slipped from *War Kindoo* at Milford Haven and set course for Dover at a speed of 20 knots. This maintained until 0500 the following day when speed was reduced to pass through traffic making for Dover. When off this port a signal was received ordering *Montrose* to proceed at once to Dunkirk to assist in evacuating soldiers. When clear of the Downs speed was increased to 28 knots and a course laid for Dunkirk via the Northern Channel, Zuydcoote Pass.

3. The weather was fine and calm on the way across with fairly high

clouds. At one period a tremendous air battle was heard going on above the clouds but none of the actual fighting was seen. The Pass was reached at 0945 and soundings were taken as the ship went through. It was nearly low water at the time and minimum depth obtained was 3½ fathoms. While making for Dunkirk Pier much shouting was heard from a mined Merchantman where a number of British Soldiers were seen on board. *Sabre* who was astern of *Montrose* was ordered to pick up these men.

4. *Montrose* berthed alongside the seaward end of the pier at 1015 with *Sabre* outside, having had to wait for a short while until *Mackay* had got clear. At 1120 *Worcester* and *Antony* [*Anthony*] secured ahead. The embarkation of troops was carried out as expeditiously as possible and all stretcher cases were taken aboard *Montrose* as *Sabre* had not got a Doctor on board.

5. At 1134 several enemy aircraft attempted to bomb and machine gun the pier and ships were driven by gun fire from *Montrose* and shore batteries. Vast columns of smoke were drifting westwards from the burning oil tanks ashore and houses on the sea front burst into flames from time to time. The crash of exploding bombs and the thudding noise of anti-aircraft weapons was continuous and frequent air combats were seen during the forenoon. The long pier jammed with troops made a particularly selectable target for enemy aircraft and it was very fortunate that they were prevented from machine gunning the soldiers as the latter awaited embarkation.

6. By 1240 there was no further accommodation left on board and *Montrose* and *Sabre* slipped and proceeded for Dover via the Northern channel. When clear of the pass, speed was increased to 26 knots, several other Destroyers were passed on their way in to collect troops. At 1430 *Montrose*, *Sabre* and *Antony* and a "G" class Destroyer were attacked with bombs and machine guns by successive waves of enemy aircraft. The attacks lasted for about an hour and it is estimated that at least 45 hostile planes took part.

7. Early in the battle one aircraft attacked *Montrose* from about five thousand feet and when his bombs were seen to be released, the wheel was put hard over and emergency full speed ordered. Five bombs fell close together abreast X gun, the nearest being 20 feet away (for damage done see Appendix I), avoiding action was rather cramped owing to proximity of sand banks to starboard and other Destroyers to port. Persistent machine gun attacks were made on the ship but by frequent alteration of course no hits were obtained. Steady and constant fire from the Ship's two Pom-Poms and 3 inch H.A. gun kept the attackers from coming low, the average height being about eight thousand feet. 250

rounds of pom-pom and 45 rounds of 3" H.A. ammunition were expended. All guns functioned perfectly and in the last attack one hit was scored on an enemy bomber which was subsequently seen to crash and burst into flames on the shore.

8. The Ship's company and Soldiers behaved admirably during the attacks and the military gave great assistance in maintaining the supply of ammunition from the magazine. It is considered that unless a ship has an adequate and up to date high angle armament, the only sure way of minimising the effect of air attack is by intelligent handling of the ship.

9. The weather now started to deteriorate and it rained steadily until Dover was reached 1630. Some doubt was felt as regards the position of the ship during the afternoon, as the gyro had failed. Visibility was not too good and the complicated manoeuvres of the ship made it difficult to keep an accurate D.R. The ship secured alongside the Admiralty Pier at 1817 and disembarked the soldiers. The latter were feeling much better after a rest, plenty of hot tea and food in the ship and went ashore in excellent heart. It was remarkable how good was their morale and behaviour from the time they arrived on the pier at Dunkirk until they left at Dover. It was computed by Military sources that *Montrose* had transported some 1200 men and 28 stretcher cases, several of the latter being seriously wounded.

10. Having completed the disembarkation *Montrose* proceeded towards [*War*] *Sepoy* to fuel. Due to minor delays this was not completed until 2230. The ship then slipped and proceeded again for Dunkirk. It was at 0013 Wednesday 29th May that the ship suddenly ran into a patch of fog and collided with the Tug *Sun V*. The details of this mishap were reported in my letter 29th May. *Montrose* was towed back stern first to Dover by the tug *Lady Brassy* where she arrived at 1550. Late in the forenoon the ship was moved to the inner basin alongside *Sandhurst* to make temporary repairs to the stem, so that *Montrose* with *Mackay* in company was able to proceed to Sheerness at 0600 the following day.

11. The passage to Sheerness was uneventful, many tows of barges and ships' lifeboats steaming towards Dover being met on the way. At 1415 the ship secured to No.20 Buoy at Sheerness and de-ammunitioned. At 0400 on Friday 31st May *Montrose* slipped and proceeded up the Thames to the Royal Albert Dock where she was berthed at 1035. Owing to the neighbouring dry dock not being available she left the basin at 0930 the next day and secured in Millwall Dry Dock at 1200.

12. It is desired to express once more the excellent conduct of the ship's company and the military, while under constant attack from enemy aircraft and the general disappointment of all concerned at the most

unfortunate and regrettable collision which prevented the ship continuing to assist in the re-embarkation of the B.E.F..

APPENDIX I

Five bombs burst close together on the port side abreast X gun, the nearest being about 20 feet away. The wheel was hard over at the time, speed 29 knots.

2. No casualties to personnel or material were cased either by splinters or machine gun bullets. The effect of detonation of the bombs aft were very violent. Officers on their bunks in cabins were hurled to the deck, cabin and Wardroom furniture and fittings were thrown about and nearly all the Wardroom crockery smashed. No splinter or bullet holes were found.

3. When the ship docked a few days later, it was observed that the plating on the port side of the rudder had been opened up and several rivets were missing. It is considered that further steaming at high speed would have undoubtedly caused the plating to have opened out still further and finally become detached.

4. The shock of the explosion caused the rocker arm of the Port Dynamo to jump forward, foul the risers and short circuit part of the dynamo armature. This caused the latter to catch fire, but the machine was stopped before the latter became serious. As the ring main was split no great inconvenience resulted from the sudden stopping of one machine.

SABRE
S-class Destroyer
Pennant Number H18
Official Rescue Total: 5,765

Laid down on in September 1917, and launched on 23 September the following year, Sabre was as the first Royal Navy ship to carry this name. Her build was completed during 1919 and the ship commissioned for Fleet service. By 1938 she had been de-militarised for use as a target ship but brought forward for a return to service in 1939 despite her age and unsuitability. Commander Brian Dean's account is dated 8 June 1940:

On arrival off Dover at 2300 on 27th May, was ordered by signal to proceed to beaches east of Dunkirk, embark troops in our own boats and leave not later than 0330. Proceeded at 27knots, stopped at 0120 two miles east of Dunkirk harbour entrance and brought off six boatloads (two trips for three boats) about 100 troops. While waiting *Sabre* was machine gunned by an aircraft and sustained one slight casualty. Fire was opened on the aircraft. Two drifters came alongside and transferred their troops.

It was found that Chart No.1872 was not held. The return passage was therefore made direct via "Z" route. Secured alongside Admiralty Pier at 0520 and proceeded again at 0618. At 0830 took station astern *Montrose* and followed her through the Zuidcoote Pass. At 1030 went alongside a wreck one mile east of Dunkirk and took off about 20 troops. While waiting off the harbour entrance observed a "forced landed" Hurricane aircraft on the beach west of Dunkirk. The motor boat was sent in to take off the crew. In so doing she grounded on a falling tide and got sand in the engine.

At 1100 *Montrose* berthed at the east pier and *Sabre* berthed on her. About 800 troops were embarked (the propeller draught being 20 feet) and at 1230 both ships shoved off and returned via the "Zuidcoote Pass". At 1410 the ships were attacked by a squadron of high level Bombers. By zig-zagging at high speed all bombs were avoided though some fell near enough to shake and splash the ship. No damage was sustained. A continuous fire from 12 pdr and 0.5" M.G.'s was kept up as long as the bombers were in range. Arrived at Dover at 1820.

Having completed with oil fuel, sailed at 2130/28 and proceeded by "Z" route so as to arrive before daylight. On arrival off the E beach the whaler was sent in (the only remaining boat), but no troops were found. When searching further to the eastward a number were observed in a wreck. Went alongside and took off a small number of British troops. The remainder were all French and were taken off by a French Gunboat.

More British destroyers were found off La Panne and *Sabre*'s whaler was utilised for bringing off troops from there. At 0515/29 *Sabre* was ordered to proceed alongside East Pier leaving whaler and 1st Lieutenant behind. Shoved off at 0550 having embarked about 500 troops and returned via route "Y". A number of dive bombing raids occurred during the morning, but *Sabre* was not hit. Arrived at Dover at 1030.

All the ammunition (H.A.) being expended, proceeded alongside Eastern Arm where ammunition and oil fuel were taken in. 100 depth charges were landed. At 1600, having embarked the naval Officers for Dunkirk, proceeded via route "X". On arrival it was found that the pier had been cleared owing to air raids, but the ship was placed alongside without wires and the naval party disembarked. A few troops were seen coming down the pier and were embarked. The pier was bombed by dive bombers but *Sabre* was apparently not noticed. Prodigious quantities of ammunition were however expended and one bomber was seen to crash, another appeared to be damaged. Both were Junkers 87s.

After the first raid *Sabre* left the pier and on arrival outside found some men struggling in the water. Having no boats left it was necessary to place the ship alongside each man and hoist him in with a bowline. The survivors included the Second Engineer of the *Crested Eagle* and a stoker from *Grenade*, both badly burned; also some Frenchmen from a raft. During this time *Sabre* was repeatedly attacked by dive bombers but sustained no damage.

Then proceeded off Bray to land portable wireless set, loudspeakers, etc, with the telegraphists in charge of them. Some time was spent in searching for a boat (*Sabre* having none), and a small motor launch was eventually headed off and pressed into service. The dive bombing attacks were continuous and a number of ships were seen to be hit including *Bideford* and *Saladin*, three transports and a trawler.

Sabre kept zig-zagging at high speed and thus escaped, though she was severely shaken by near misses, and every man on deck was blackened with oil fuel splashes. At 2010 (by which time all ammunition was expended) destroyers were ordered to withdraw. Returned in company with *Verity* and *Saladin* who could only do 15 knots.

At 0515/30 secured alongside at Dover and landed troops. Then proceeded to eastern arm, embarked ammunition and borrowed a whaler from *Sandhurst*. Proceeded at 0830 and returned to Dunkirk. Secured to East Pier at 1145 and embarked troop. On shoving off it was found that the ship was aground, but by moving troops forward she was got off without delay. Some damage was sustained by the propellers and asdic dome.

At 1530 secured at Dover. At 1615 proceeded again taking route "Z" on account of low visibility. A drifting mine was sighted and was sunk by M.G. fire. The fog gradually dispersed; *Sabre* was shadowed by a reconnaissance aircraft, and just before reaching No.6 Calais buoy, came under fire from shore batteries. Speed was increased to "Full" and the wheel put over at each gun flash, keeping them between 20 and 70 degrees abaft the beam. The range was quickly found, however, and several hits sustained on the bridge and upper works.

Course was therefore altered to the northward, smoke was made, and the ship continued to zig-zag as much as possible without showing herself clear of the smoke. Just before turning away, however, a shell passed through the Petty Officer's mess deck. It did not explode, but it passed through the Master Gyro compass, and a splinter from it penetrated the deck and so admitted water to No.2 Oil Fuel tank. With this tank out of action there was insufficient oil fuel remaining for the round trip to be completed. The D.G. cable had been pierced in four places and the magnetic compass was therefore practically useless.

The ship was therefore steered by the sun (fortunately visible) until traffic on route "X" was discerned. Thereafter it was possible to go from buoy to buoy. *Sandhurst's* whaler was severely riddled with shell splinters but the damage to the ship (except for the gyro compass and oil fuel tank) was only superficial and not a man was touched. Arrived at Dover at 2030.

Defects were taken in hand forthwith, and at noon on the 31st *Sabre* proceeded alongside eastern arm to facilitate the work. Nothing could be done about the gyro compass in the time available, but the D.G. cable was repaired and a great deal of other repair work was done by *Sandhurst*, of whose services I should like to express my appreciation. A 16ft motor skiff was borrowed in lieu of the damaged whaler, and *Sabre's* own motor boat was recovered having been repaired.

All hands had been utterly exhausted and the day and night in harbour gave them a new lease of life.

At 2120/31, having completed with oil, *Sabre* again sailed for Dunkirk, and at 0115/1 both boats were again sent in to the eastern beach. No troops were found there, so proceeded to search further east.

Hearing "S.O.S" being sounded on a siren, steamed towards it and found a drifter stranded on a submerged wreck. Went alongside and took off the crew and troops. Just before dawn some more destroyers were found off Bray, and *Sabre's* boats were sent in to bring off troops which could now be seen in large numbers. On *Shikari* filling up a cutter was taken over from her. The towage of this, full of troops, proved too much for the motor boat and the troops had to pull off to the ship. Two trips were made in this way.

Meanwhile on orders from R.A. Dover (in *Keith*) *Sabre* went alongside a tug, took off her troops and sent her to tow *Speedwell* off. During this time a single aircraft (apparently a Messerschmitt 109) approached and made some rather half-hearted machine gun attacks. Intense A.A. fire prevented these from being pressed home. There was also an unsuccessful dive bombing attack by a Junkers 87. Numerous British fighters were seen, and our freedom from serious interference was presumably due to them. At 0700 having about 500 troops aboard, *Sabre* returned to Dover, arriving at 1000.

At 2030/1 proceeded to Dunkirk in company with *Codrington* at 28 knots. At 2315 secured to the east pier and filled up with troops. Shoved off at midnight and returned, fortunately coming up with *Icarus* who was followed as far as the Downs (*Sabre's* compass still being unreliable). Arrived at 0400/2 and landed troops.

At 1845/2 proceeded to Dunkirk in company with *Shikari* who was sent ahead at the North Goodwin L.V. until arrival in Dunkirk Channel. When passing near Ruytingen bank buoy H.M.H.S. *Paris* was seen to be sinking and to have boats away. A cross channel steamer which had just been overtaken was sent to her assistance, and a report sent by W/T. It is not known whether *Paris* was bombed, torpedoed, or mined; but a drifting mine was sighted not far away.

Shortly afterwards, the ship came under fire (which was returned) in the vicinity of No.5W buoy: smoke was made and no damage was suffered.

At 2110 secured inside the wrecked trawler at East Pier and embarked troops. These were all part of the rearguard of the B.E.F. and included men of the Green Howards. Only 15 came on board in stretchers, but a further 50 odd were carried by their comrades and the seamen: most of these collapsed on arrival and over 50 had to be hoisted out on stretchers at Dover. Their courage was magnificent and I never heard a complaint and hardly ever a groan.

On leaving the harbour, flashing signals were observed from the wreck of the *Mosquito*: the bow was placed alongside her, and three men taken off. They turned out to be Royal Artillery officers who had evaded capture by paddling off in a small boat. The boat had evidently been made fast with a "Soldier's hitch" and had drifted away leaving them stranded: they were fortunate in finding a signal lantern and so being able to attract attention. Proceeded with *Shikari* at 2200 and arrived at Dover at 0120/3.

Left Dover at 2020/3 for the final trip. *Venomous*, who was in company, had been delayed, but caught up with *Sabre* near Ruytingen bank buoy. Entered Dunkirk harbour at 2250 and lay off while the transports berthed: *Sabre* then berthed between two transports where there would not have been room for a larger destroyer. *Whitshed* had arrived earlier but had not yet berthed: her stern was placed alongside *Sabre* bow and troops were passed over to her until there was room for her to berth at the pier.

By this time *Sabre* was full up, having embarked nearly 600 French troops and Admiral Abrial's Flag Lieutenant. Shoved off at 0025/4, getting out with some difficulty owing to the mass of ships trying to berth or to get away. A number of imminent collisions were narrowly averted and *Sabre* eventually got clear and headed approximately westward. A minesweeper was soon caught up and followed until a faster ship came up (a transport), when allegiance was transferred to her. She in turn was lost when fog was encountered near U buoy. The

Goodwin L.V was, however, found by sound, after which it was possible to go from buoy to buoy until Dover was reached at 0500. The French troops were in excellent spirits and keenly appreciated being addressed in their own language, however imperfectly. Jokes about the comparative comfort of *Sabre* and *Normandie* were well received ...

It is pointed out that *Sabre*'s engines are 22 years old and have been submerged and full of salt water for 48 hours after a collision last October. To avoid bombs and shell fire it was necessary to make most exacting demands on the engines such as might well have taxed those of a new ship. In every case the response was immediate, all that could be desired, and far greater than could be reasonably expected. It is submitted that this reflects great credit on the engine-room department, to whom is unquestionably due the fact that we are all still alive and unhurt and our ship safely in dock, and the far more important fact that upwards of 5,000 troops were safely transported ...

Where the whole ship's company worked so well – often till they dropped from sheer exhaustion – it is difficult to differentiate ... Whatever awards may be made, it will be made clear that (as in the case of my own decoration) it is the ship which is being decorated rather than the individual.

As regards other ships, it is again difficult to differentiate; but I was struck by the rapidity and accuracy of *Shikari*'s shooting which appeared to silence the guns west of Dunkirk. *Verity* also did well in landing her medical unit under continuous dive-bombing attacks.

SALADIN
S-class Destroyer
Pennant Number H54
Official Rescue Total: -

Ordered from Alex Stephen at Govan in April 1917, Saladin was launched on 17 February 1918 as the first Royal Navy ship to carry the name. In 1939 she was manned by Fleet Reserve personnel when she attended the Review of the Reserve Fleet by HM King George V during August 1939. The following report, penned by Lieutenant Commander Laurence James Dover RN on 1 June 1940, was 'submitted with reference to the Air Raid at Dunkirk on 29th May 1940':

H.M.S. *Saladin* was approaching Dunkirk at about 1845 to comply with Vice Admiral Dover's signal 1625/29, it was seen that an air raid was taking place over the town, but as the orders were to proceed to *Hebe* with all despatch the ship continued. Soon after entering the channel one bomber attacked the ship, this was the first of approximately 10 (Ten) attacks.

2. As H.M.S. *Hebe* was not anchored at the entrance to the harbour ship proceeded up the coast where other H.M. Ships could be seen. In view of the very inadequate Anti Aircraft guns (one 2lb. Pom Pom and 2 Lewis guns) carried in this ship, it was considered that some protection would be obtained from the guns of the other ships.

3. H.M.S. *Saladin* appeared to be selected by the enemy for attacks possibly because less fire could be brought to bear, than by other ships in the vicinity. Avoiding action was taken by swinging the ship and increasing speed as the bombers dived to attack, and all bombs were avoided. The bombs from all attacks fell near the ship the nearest being about 5 (Five) feet away.

4. In one of the early attacks, splinters which penetrated the Engine Room fractured the Starboard dynamo exhaust pipe and the throttle to the Port dynamo, thereby putting both dynamos out of action, and filling the Engine Room with steam. Owing to loss of vacuum, speed was reduced until temporary repairs had been made. E.F. Reddell, Chief E.R.A. P/MX57144., carried out extremely good work in temporarily stopping the leaks in the damaged pipes by securing rubber insertion round the fractures. W. Adams, Ldg. Sto. P/KX79401., showed resourcefulness in restarting the Starboard dynamo under the instructions of Lieutenant (E) A.J. Lee whose good organisation soon had the ship capable of steaming again.

5. After one attack a fire was reported Aft, Lieutenant J.H. Edwards (Rtd) by my instructions went aft to deal with it. He found the ready use cordite in the after gun position burning; after having to lie down twice when attacks were made he, with two Able Seaman, threw the burning charges from one box and the other box which was alight over the side; I consider this was the saving of a very large fire aft and carried out under great personal danger.

6. One slight casualty only occurred in the ship (W. Noyes A.B. P/J28942. being landed at Dover), I consider this due to the fact that the ship's company had been instructed to lie down in the event of an air attack. This is not possible in the Engine and Boiler Rooms but on this occasion no casualties occurred there although splinters penetrated the Engine Room. It was possible to steer the ship when ratings were lying down with the Coxswain and one rating either side of the wheel. The Commanding Officer had to take occasional glances over the bridge rails as the attacks were carried out in confined waters and other ships were in the vicinity.

7. The reports given by Lieutenant J.W.G. Payne R.N. and the Anti Aircraft look outs were most valuable to the Commanding Officer as he only actually saw, owing to the bridge being covered, about one attack which came from the bow. The manoeuvring of the ship on other occasions was carried out on reports received. During one attack three bombers in formation were approaching the ship when one fired the correct Allied recognition signal, the order cease fire was given, until it was seen from the markings that they were enemy.

8. The behaviour of the officers and ship's company during those series of attacks was most creditable; as it was a case of knowing the attack was being delivered and waiting to see if a hit would be registered.

9. When the attacks finished the ship proceeded towards the harbour to find H.M.S. *Hebe*, on arriving off the entrance a signal was received from the harbour to keep clear and return after dark. On clearing the channel the damage to the ship was reviewed and as the pipes in the Engine Room had been fractured and the boilers starting to show a density, it was evident that high speed could not be used and very possibly the ship might be brought to a stop; in which case one would probably be hindering the operation; so in view of the above, ship returned to Dover.

10. The main damage received was leaking condensers, due probably to concussion; butt straps on water drums on all boilers leaking, and brick work in all boilers loosened. Two steam and exhaust pipes in Engine Room fractured. Rifling of after gun indented by splinters. Numerous holes in ship's side (Leaks in Engine Room and Provision Room). Funnels and upper deck casings from bomb splinters and machine gun bullets.

SCIMITAR
S-class Destroyer
Pennant Number H21
Official Rescue Total: 2,711

Ordered from John Brown at Clydebank in April 1917, HMS Scimitar *was laid down on 30 May the same year and launched on 27 February 1918 as the first Royal Navy ship to bear this name. Her build was completed on 29 April 1918 and the ship served briefly with the Grand Fleet before the Armistice in November 1918. In 1938 she was deployed with the Portsmouth Local Flotilla and used for training purposes. Lieutenant Robert Denys Franks OBE's account is dated 8 June 1940:*

I have the honour to report on the proceedings of H.M. ship under my command between 26th May and 4th June as follows.

2. I received orders to sail for Dover at noon/28th and I arrived at Dover at about 2000 28th May. At about 2100 I was ordered to leave under the orders of Captain (D) 16 in *Malcolm*. On arrival at Bray at about 0130 I was ordered to proceed a mile to the eastward and send in boats. My motor boat with whaler in tow proceeded inshore under Lieutenant J.R.G. Trenchman and embarked troops. After about two hours my whaler was swamped inshore due to being rushed by troops. My motor boat continued to assist in towing and I embarked troops from various other boats. Later I secured another whaler and embarkation proceeded more rapidly.

3. At about 1230/29 I considered the ship was full (about 350 troops) and I was ordered to return to Dover. I sailed by route Y in company with *Shikari*. I arrived at Dover at about 1630/29 and disembarked troops and then proceeded to oil.

4. I sailed for Dunkirk again at about 2000/29, starting via route Y, joining *Worcester* and then proceeding via route X to the beaches East of Bray. Good progress was made during the night embarking troops using our own motor boat and captured whaler and various other boats. In the morning I had 350 troops on board and proceeded via route X leaving my motor boat and whaler inshore under the command of Midshipman Ball R.N.R. Fog patches were encountered on the way back and I arrived at Dover at about 1000/30.

5. After disembarking troops I sailed again at about 1130 and was ordered to go to Dunkirk harbour via route Z. I arrived and went alongside at about 1330/30 and embarked about 500 troops very quickly. I returned via route Z being shelled and bombed off Calais. The shelling was of small calibre but fairly accurate; no damage was sustained. I arrived at Dover at about 1630/30 and disembarked troops.

6. I sailed again about 1830/30 for La Panne via route X. Near Dunkirk I sighted my motor boat and recalled it. After waiting sometime at La Panne, where there were several other ships, I was ordered by *Worcester* to go to Bray. I collected a string of derelict boats and sent them in with my motor boat under Sub-Lieutenant J.N. Coldwell. Good progress was made in embarking troops and at about 0600/31 I had 500 on board and sailed after transferring my motor boat and string of other boats to the trawler *Olivina*. I proceeded via route X to Dover in company with *Harvester*.

7. I arrived at Dover at about 0930/31 and after disembarking troops sailed again about 1030. Whilst proceeding through the Downs at 25 knots, I was navigating as close as possible to the starboard hand buoys and had just reached the N.W. Goodwin buoy when I was overtaken by H.M.S. *Icarus*, who cut across very close, and although I altered to

starboard as soon as the buoy would allow, I was drawn in towards him. I stopped both and went hard a starboard when he was about abreast me but I was sucked over and hit his stern with my stem. I found that my bows were crumpled in on the water line with a definite rent allowing water pressure on to the collision bulkhead. However, after securing a collision mat, in view of the extreme urgency of the operation, I thought I could go on at slow speed and proceed at 8 knots, later at 10. The reasons for this collision and a report on the damage sustained have been more fully reported to Captain (D) 16.

8. I arrived at Dunkirk at about 1300/31 and was ordered to go to Bray beaches. I spent this afternoon and evening in company with *Vivacious* and *Shikari* off Bray under intermittent bombardment and bombing during which no damage was sustained. During one bombing attack at about 1700(?) an aircraft was shot down; it is thought that this was from *Scimitar*'s A gun. I myself was watching A[A] gun bursts, which appeared close to the target and at the moment the aircraft caught fire a burst from A gun appeared nearly in line. The aircraft fell in the sea and was obviously a total loss. During this period no troops were embarked as I had no boats and no other boats came near. There seemed to be trouble in embarking due to choppy water.

9. At nightfall/31 the weather improved and troops were very quickly embarked, principally from the "skoot" *Hilda* which was doing excellent work. I sailed at about 2300 with 500 troops, proceeding at 8 knots. During the passage numerous aircraft were heard but no attacks were made. A slight collision occurred with an unknown trawler, in which my port propeller guard was damaged. I arrived at Dover at about 0600/1 and after disembarking troops proceeded to oil. A further examination of the damage was made.

10. At 1000/1 I was ready and was ordered to proceed to Dunkirk again, but when near the North Goodwin L.V. I was ordered to return. At this time I had just sighted S.S. *Prague* in difficulties so I went to his assistance. He asked me to take some of his troops so I went alongside while under way and embarked 500. I then stood by while he proceeded through the Downs and at about 1530/1 I arrived at Dover and disembarked troops subsequently proceeding to a buoy.

11. At 0600/2 I proceeded to Sheerness to disembark ammunition, thence to London for repairs by Messrs Harland and Wolff. Repairs are expected to take 14 days.

12. *Scimitar* being short-handed compared to other destroyers, all ratings had to work very hard and it was noteworthy that Engine room ratings not only steamed the ship with full efficiency and took their place at ammunition supply parties, but also assisted on deck in

embarkation etc. Nearly all seaman took part as boat's crews at one time or another, using skill and determination in trying conditions. The following are considered particularly worthy of mention or award.

SHIKARI
S-class Destroyer
Pennant Number D85
Official Rescue Total: 3,589

Though she had been ordered in 1917, HMS Shikari's build was delayed due to the restrictions on naval expenditure after the First World War. Finally launched on 14 July 1919 she was taken in tow to Chatham for completion by HM Dockyard. This name had previously used by a trawler hired during 1915. Lieutenant Commander Hugh Nicholas Aubyn Richardson's account is dated 8 June 1940:

Tuesday, 28th May
Returned from night Convoy to Cherbourg at 1400. Landed S.P.'s and fuelled.
1430 Sailed independently for Dover at 28 knots.
1930 Arrived off Dover. Instructed to join *Malcolm*.
2000 Sailed under Captain D.16's Orders to carry out evacuation.

Wednesday, 29th May
0100 Arrived off Beach at La Panne. Commenced work, using Motorboat and Whaler. Heavy surf running. Whaler capsized owing to military rushing boat in the surf. With daylight evacuation speeded up and this was greatly assisted by Naval Landing Craft. As in subsequent work, drifting boats were being towed in by the motorboat with boatkeepers from *Shikari*. Kedge anchors were used when surf was heavy and boats veered to the shore. During all operations, hands not required at the Guns were in boats or assisting to embark the military. Supply Parties only closing up when the Guns fired.
1215 Ship full. Returned to Dover. Disembarked troops, fuelled.
1745 Left Dover for La Panne. Many bombing attacks on ships in vicinity, when near Oost Dyck buoy. Closed paddle steamer *Gracie Fields* who had been hit, but as sufficient craft were available to take off her troops, proceeded. Zig-zagging at high speeds was employed whenever bombing attacks took place or were threatened.

Thursday, 30th May

Ran aground on approaching the Coast but got off on the rising tide, three hours later, at Dawn. Continued embarking troops.

0800 Full. Returned to Dover. On passing Nieuport Buoy came under fire from a battery behind Nieuport for seven minutes. It is thought that the fire was controlled by an observation balloon over Nieuport. This fact was reported by signal but the balloon was up for the next few days. No hits were registered. Smoke screen and zig-zagging was commenced after the first salvo.

1300 Arrived Dover. Disembarked. Many of these troops from the beaches had only Half Kits and were wet through. The Ship's Company did all they could for the soldiers and now in consequence have depleted kits. The Coxswain, his Staff and the Cooks and Stewards did great work in supplying the soldiers with food and drink, under most trying circumstances; especially as in *Shikari* it is impossible to keep the Galley fire going when steaming at high speeds. A burst steam pipe to one of the oil fuel pumps necessitated proceeding to a buoy while *Sandhurst* made repairs. This was rapidly done.

1930 Ready for sea again. Sailed for La Panne. Gyro Compass failed when approaching Dunkirk by "X" Route for the first time.

2230 Darkness slowed down evacuation considerably, and our boats took soldiers to light draught ships close inshore when uncertain of *Shikari's* position. This added considerably to the time spent off the beaches.

Friday, 31st May

0400 R.A. ordered *Shikari* to Dunkirk. Proceeded alongside East Jetty and very soon had the ship full. During this operation there was a bombing attack, which was most inaccurate due to heavy A.A. fire.

0520 Sailed for Dover disembarked.

0930 Sailed for La Panne. Near No.6. W. buoy of the Dunkirk Channel, came under fire from shore battery to the West of Dunkirk. Fire was returned. During the whole time embarkation was taking place, the Nieuport batteries were firing at the ships. When straddled moved West towards Bray, the motorboat and tow filling up small craft in their vicinity, before rejoining *Shikari* at Bray. Beaches shelled.

1800 Bombers attacked. A.A. fire was opened. This continued until dark and rather disorganised embarkation. Our boats were asked for to bring off Lord Gort's luggage. The embarkation speeded up under cover of darkness.

Saturday, 1st June
At dawn shelling was resumed with greater intensity.

0600 Though reported nearly full, *Shikari* was ordered to complete to full capacity at Dunkirk. This was done.

0620 Sailed with other ships for Dover. Used smoke screen and only a few shots were fired at us off No.6.W. buoy. On the voyage, had several attacks from the air. Enemy aircraft being engaged by our fighters.

1000 Arrived Dover, disembarked troops. Each batch had several stretcher cases which lengthened the disembarkation. From today, Saturday 1st June, no more day evacuation was attempted, owing to shelling and bombing. The troops today were part of General Piroux's army. Oiled and ammunitioned ship.

2130 Sailed for Dunkirk, arriving at 0225.

Sunday, 2nd June

0200 Ship full. Returned to Dover. Most of the voyage was under cover of darkness, and there was no trouble.

0540 Arrived Dover. Disembarked troops. Scaling ladders were supplied.

1845 Sailed under orders of *Sabre* for Dunkirk. The shore batteries opened fire as we rounded No.6. W. Buoy. Under cover of a smoke screen no hits were obtained. Fire was returned at the flashes seen.

2200 Ship full. Sailed for Dover. Though unable to see aircraft, they were heard and flares were seen. Probably mine laying.

Monday, 3rd June

0130 Secured and disembarked troops.

1800 Captain Dangerfield and his Staff arrived onboard. Sailed for the Downs and anchored for two hours near the three blockships. A conference of C.O.s was held in *Shikari*.

2030 Sailed for Dunkirk. Speed 7 knots. Acted as guide for the blockships. Route "Z" was used. Arrived off Calais at dusk. No fire from the shore.

0130 Anchored near Dunkirk harbour entrance.

0230 Ordered to weigh by Captain Dangerfield who had transferred to an M.T.B. *Shikari* led the blockships to the entrance. On weighing, a mine blew up on our port bow and soon after the leading blockship following in our wake, blew up, presumably mined. M.T.B. picked up survivors. The remaining two blockships carried on with their job. *Shikari*, in waiting, proceeded alongside and embarked 400 troops, French who had been left after the last ship evacuating had sailed. Among these troops was General Bathelemy [Barthélemy], commanding the Flanders Garrison, who stated that 12000 still remained in Dunkirk. This was reported. By this time it was light and firing at the jetty had commenced, one shell hitting the jetty, causing many casualties.

0340　Ordered to withdraw by Captain Dangerfield. An uneventful passage.
0645　Arrived Dover. Disembarked troops.
0950　Received signal to return to Home Ports.
1130　Proceeded to Plymouth under orders of Captain D. *Codrington*.
2100　Arrived Devonport.

VANQUISHER
V-class Destroyer
Pennant Number D54
Official Rescue Total: 3,941

Laid down on 27 September 1916 end launched on 18 August 1917, Vanquisher was the first Royal Navy warship to carry the name. Between the wars she served in the Atlantic and Mediterranean Fleets and in 1938 was attached to the 1st Anti-Submarine Flotilla at Portland. Lieutenant Commander Conrad Byron Alers-Hankey's report is dated 10 June 1940. It begins with a very concise diary of movements, in which, he states, the 'times are approximate':

Monday, 27th May
1400　Sailed from Devonport.
2400　Arrived off Dover.

Tuesday, 28th May
0200　Proceeded to Dunkirk via route "Y" in company with *Icarus* and *Ivanhoe* under orders of *Javelin*.
0430　Passed Kwinte Buoy.
0545　Anchored about 1 mile east of entrance to Dunkirk Harbour.
0945　Entered Dunkirk Harbour. Went alongside East Pier and embarked troops.
1030　Left Pier and proceeded to Dover.
1430　Entered Dover and secured alongside Admiralty Pier. Disembarked troops.
1615　Secured alongside oiling berth at East Arm.

2100 Proceeded with *Esk* to Dunkirk following route "X".
2330 Stopped off Malo Beach.

Wednesday, 29th May
0100 Closed Malo Beach and anchored in three fathoms.
0400 Weighed and entered Dunkirk going alongside Eastern Pier. Embarked troops.
0630 Sailed for Dover.
0900 Entered Dover and secured alongside Eastern Pier. Embarked troops.
1600 Sailed for Dover.
1900 Arrived Dover and secured alongside Admiralty Pier. Disembarked troops.
2300 Proceeded to *War Sepoy* for fuel.

Thursday, 30th May
0430 Moved from oiler to enable *Windsor* to sail. Resecured alongside oiler.
1300 Secured to buoy.

Friday, 31st May
1700 Sailed for Dunkirk.
2030 Entered Dunkirk. Embarked troops.
2100 Sailed for Dover.

Saturday, 1st June
0030 Entered Dover and secured to Admiralty Pier. Disembarked troops.
0200 Sailed for Dunkirk.
0530 Entered Dunkirk. Secured alongside *Icarus*. Embarked troops.
0630 Sailed for Dover.
0930 Entered Dover. Secured alongside Admiralty Pier. Disembarked troops.
1430 Secured to No.10 buoy.

Sunday, 2nd June
1325 Sailed to investigate reported attacks on trawlers off "R" buoy.
1730 Returned to Dover and secured to No.10 buoy.
2130 Sailed for Dunkirk.

Monday, 3rd June
0030 Arrived off entrance to Dunkirk Harbour.

0230 Ordered to return to Dover.
0445 Entered Dover and secured alongside Admiralty Pier.
       Disembarked troops.
0700 Secured alongside East Arm and oiled.
2045 Sailed for Dunkirk.
2400 Arrived off Dunkirk.

Tuesday, 4th June
0200 Entered Dunkirk. Secured alongside Eastern pier. Embarked
       troops.
0240 Sailed for Dover.
0430 Anchored off North Goodwin Lightship in thick fog.
0615 Entered Dover. Secured alongside Admiralty Pier. Disembarked
       troops.
1030 Went alongside *Malcolm* at East Arm.
1500 Sailed for Chatham in company with *Malcolm* and *Sabre*.

Troops carried (Numbers approximate.)

28th May	One trip only	250 troops.
29th May	First trip	700 troops.
	Second trip	700 troops.
31st May	One trip only	700 troops.
1st June	One trip only	1200 troops.
3rd June	One trip only	35 troops. (French)
4th June	One trip only	400 troops. (French)
	Total	4000 troops (approximately.)

EVENTS

28th May
While at anchor awaiting entry into Dunkirk on 28th May, S.S. *Mona's Queen* was blown up and sunk at about 0630 a short distance from the ship. As it was thought that this might have been due to an M.T.B. attack cable was slipped and the ship manoeuvred to reduce the size of target presented. The starboard anchor and four shackles of cable were thus lost. The whaler was sent away to pick up survivors. 32 were recovered, including the Master. One of the survivors died on the return trip to Dover and was buried at sea. It became apparent later that S.S. *Mona's Queen* was sunk by a mine. She sank within two minutes.

29th May
Esk, carrying Rear Admiral Wake Walker and beach parties, and

Vanquisher arrived off Malo beach at about 2300/28. *Esk* proceeded towards Bray and La Panne Beaches. In the absence of orders, I remained off Malo beach where there were many thousands of troops waiting to be embarked. Having anchored as close in as I could, I sent away the motorboat, whaler, and skiff to embark the troops.

At this time *Vanquisher* was the only ship at this beach. Signals were accordingly made to ships and boats passing towards Eastern Beaches (which appeared to have an adequate number) to remain at Malo Beach. When two or three ships arrived, I proceeded to Dunkirk to carry out V.A. Dover's instruction (received by signal) that the practicability of entry into Dunkirk should be investigated by the ship best placed to do so. The boats and crews were left behind. The latter only were recovered later that day.

The entrance to Dunkirk was found to be practicable and a signal to that effect was sent to V.A. Dover.

Enemy bombers attacked the ship while manoeuvring in the entrance to the harbour but the bombs missed.

After reaching Dover I requested a berth for oiling but was ordered not to take more than was necessary for a round trip in view of the pressing nature of the situation at Dunkirk.

As I had sufficient fuel to undertake another round trip, I proceeded to Dunkirk without oiling.

The ship was noticeably unsteady on the return journey. General Watson took passage in the ship on this trip. During the return trip I found that my sight and judgement had become impaired to such a degree that, observing the importance of the operations, it was no longer safe for me to retain command of H.M.S. *Vanquisher*.

Consequently I reported to the Chief of Staff V.A. Dover who arranged for a temporary relief so that I could have a rest.

The remaining officers and ship's company were also in great need of rest.

Enemy aircraft manoeuvring for attack were fired on while the ship was at Dunkirk on this occasion.

30th May
At about 1200 Lieutenant Commander Buchell [Bushell] R.N. and Mr. Rathbone Gunner joined to relieve myself and Mr. F. Edwards. I landed at 1300 with Mr. Edwards (Gunner) and Lieutenant (E) Tribbeck (Engineer Officer) who had been sent sick by the Medical officer.

Mr. Edwards and myself were accommodated at the Grand Shaft Barracks where we were very hospitably received by the Colonel and Officers of the Green Howards.

31st May
Lieutenant (E) Blair joined as Engineer Officer vice Tribback landed sick the previous day.

1st June
A bombing attack was made on the ship while alongside the pier at Dunkirk.

2nd June
I resumed command at about 1100. Mr. Edwards rejoined with me and Lieutenant Commander Buchell [Bushell] and Mr. Rathbone, Gunner, left the ship.

3rd June
Owing to surplus of ships waiting off Dunkirk to embark troops I was not required to enter the harbour. About 35 French troops were embarked from a small boat while lying off. When about three miles off Dunkirk I observed a transport collide with a vessel I understand to have been a block-ship. Lieutenant R.N. Hankey R.N. (1st Lieutenant) was landed for rest.

4th June
Owing to strong offset from the pier and delay in securing the stern wires, considerable difficulty was experienced in berthing the ship alongside the pier at Dunkirk. This delayed the embarkation of troops by about five minutes but I was able to remain alongside ten minutes after the time I had been told to leave by the Pier Master (probably Commander Buchanan). The French soldiers were very slow embarking and were much hampered by their equipment.

The ship's company behaved magnificently throughout this operation. While it is not known how their degree of exhaustion compared with that of other ships, a contributory factor to their condition was undoubtedly the employment of the ship prior to reaching Dover.

This was as follows:
Wednesday, 22nd May	2200. Left Liverpool.
Thursday, 23rd May	0530. Rendezvous with *Montrose* off the Smalls.
23rd, 24th, and 25th.	Patrolling off S.W. Ireland.
Sunday, 26th May	0300. Arrived Milford Haven.
	1800. Sailed from Milford Haven.

| Monday, 27th May | 0600. Arrived Plymouth. |
| | 1400. Sailed for Dover. |

Thus from 23rd May till 26th May inclusive the ship's company were without proper rest and so were not fresh when the operations began on the night of the 27th May. The number of officers and ratings landed for rest or sick were as follows:

| Officers: | Sick – 1. | Rest – 4. |
| Ratings: | Sick – 2. | Rest – 9. |

I was very grateful for the assistance of Lieutenant Symons R.A.M.C and two R.A.M.C orderlies who were lent to the ship by the Military Authorities for the period of the operations. This officer took over the duties of Medical Officer of the ship in the absence of Surgeon Lt. E. Penn R.N. who was landed for 24 hours rest on 2nd June and proved himself extremely competent in a field that must have been strange to him.

Owing to the concentration that was essential in handling the ship on passage to and from and at Dunkirk, I am unable to comment specifically on the work performed by other ships or remember in any detail events as they affected this ship.

I cannot, however, refrain from mentioning my admiration for the skill and coolness with which the transports were handled.

The skill, control and coolness exercised by Commander J.C. Clouston R.N. (Piermaster) on Dunkirk East Pier was of the utmost value and was responsible at least for the expeditious embarkation of troops by this ship.

The ratings acting as berthing party also behaved extremely well under Commander Clouston.

As detailed by Lieutenant Commander Alers-Hankey, in his absence HMS Vanquisher *was commanded by Lieutenant Commander William Charles Bushell. Bushell's normal command, HMS* Wivern, *was being repaired and refitted and therefore unable to participate in Operation* Dynamo – *the damage occurred on 14 May during Operation* Ordnance, *the evacuation of Allied personnel from Hook of Holland. Bushell's account of his time with* Vanquisher *is dated 19 June 1940:*

H.M.S. *Wivern* was undergoing refit and damage repairs consequent upon enemy action, and had been taken over by a Care and Maintenance Party supplied by R.N. Barracks while the Ship's Company were on leave.

On Thursday 30th May with the Executive Officer, Lieutenant J.W. Harbottle, I had been attending to various matters connected with the refit prior to proceeding on leave when instructions were received from the Commander-in-Chief, Portsmouth, addressed to Lieutenant Harbottle and myself by name to report to the Vice Admiral Dover immediately. It was discovered that the next train left in half an hour and with some difficulty it was caught by a narrow margin, and Dover reached in the early hours of the next morning, Friday 31st May.

I was detailed to relieve the Commanding Officer, H.M.S. *Vanquisher* and Lieutenant Harbottle was instructed to accompany me in case a relief Executive Officer should also be required. On joining *Vanquisher* at 1100 this was not found to be the case but Lieutenant Harbottle was most anxious to come and it seemed desirable to retain him as the exhaustion to which the Commanding Officer of *Vanquisher* had succumbed might well overtake his Executive Officer if operations became further protracted. His assistance was of greatest value throughout. He took over the armament completely, and shared other duties with the Executive Officer, providing the latter with opportunities for rest which could not otherwise have occurred.

I had been instructed by the Chief Staff Officer to the Vice Admiral Dover that there was a possibility of *Vanquisher*'s screws and rudder having been damaged, and that having regard to this I was to sail for Dunkirk as soon as possible. Soon after I arrived on board, divers came off and carried out underwater examination. Screws and rudder were undamaged but Asdic dome had been removed and oscillator tube bent straight aft, being cracked at the bend and leaking slightly. The compartment was therefore kept battened down in case the tube should snap off and the crack become enlarged. Meanwhile the Engineer officer had also gone sick and had to be landed. A relief was requested as the C.E.R.A. though professionally competent to steam the ship was physically exhausted.

As soon as the relief Engineer Officer joined, the ship was sailed for Dunkirk, i.e. at 1700 Friday, 31st May. No interference from enemy action was experienced on passage though between F.G. Buoy and W. Buoys some bombing was observed about a mile ahead, apparently ineffective. R.A.F. fighters soon appeared and no further enemy air action was observed.

On arrival at Dunkirk *Vanquisher* was berthed at the eastern pier about two ships lengths ahead of the wrecked drifter. The inner end of the pier was being shelled. Troops were embarked and were taken to Dover and disembarked at Admiralty Pier, and *Vanquisher* was again sailed for Dunkirk about 0230. After passing F.G. Buoy, 9 fighters were observed and at first thought to be friendly. They were later seen to be Messerschmitt's and soon after this had been established, they attacked a ship about 3 cables on the port quarter with tracer ammunition.

Fire was opened and was effective in preventing further attacks. Other fighters approached later and were identified as Spitfires. On arrival at Dunkirk it was low water and only the outer berths at the east pier could be used. That nearest the shore was already occupied by *Icarus*, and *Vanquisher* was berthed alongside her. Shortly afterwards *Windsor* berthed outside *Vanquisher*. Mess tables were rigged across "B" Gundecks of inside ships and troops were hurried across to outside ships with all despatch. *Vanquisher's* electrical hailing equipment was of great value here, as all the troops were French and various exhortations in that language backed by ample power produced a marked effect. The pier was crowded and every effort was made to embark the greatest possible number which is believed to have been not less than 1200.

During the proceedings enemy aircraft were much in evidence. Bombs were dropped to the eastward of the pier, apparently aimed at one of the numerous wrecks. Both barrage and close range fire were frequently opened, and one bomber, despite heavy fire, pressed home his attack and dropped a salvo of 4 bombs which fell near *Vivacious'* port bow.

The sky was cloudy and bombers were several times seen dimly through the cloud directly overhead at 1500 to 2000 feet. Fortunately they dropped no bombs. *Vanquisher's* aerials were shot away by *Icarus'* 0.5" machine guns. Troops were disembarked on return to Dover and ammunition to complete was requested.

Meanwhile it was clear that *Vanquisher's* Ship's Company had reached a state of exhaustion which made it most undesirable to take them to sea again without rest. This was reported to the Vice Admiral's Office and the ship accordingly reverted to 2½ hours' notice.

The following day, Sunday 2nd June, orders were received at 0437 to raise steam for full speed with all despatch, but later reverted to ½ hour's notice. I had now decided that there was no longer any reason to retain Lieutenant Harbottle in *Vanquisher*. He was anxious not to leave while operations were still not complete, but he was in need of leave and I also felt it desirable that he should be available to handle *Wivern's* refit in case my absence became protracted. I therefore discharged him a.m. Sunday 2nd June and requested the Vice Admiral's Staff that if not urgently required elsewhere he might be sent on leave.

A few hours later the Commanding Officer of *Vanquisher* re-joined and took over command. I reported to Vice Admiral Dover and was instructed to proceed to Folkestone with 1 Leading hand and 8 A.B's

73

and go on board the transport *Tynwald*. It was emphasised that I was not to consider myself in command of the ship but to employ all possible means to get her to sail for Dunkirk as a number of the officers and crew were apparently unwilling to do so. Owing to the efforts of the company which owns the ship, and their agent in Folkestone, this presented no difficulty whatsoever.

The Chief Officer – Mr Whiteaway – had been recalled from leave and relieved the Master; the Second Officer became the Chief Officer with a new Second, the Chief Engineer and several Engineers were relieved, and all men unwilling to sail had been replaced by others sent down from London by bus. These were not only willing but eager to sail.

Naval and military Lewis and Bren guns crews were carried, and were in charge of the Military Liaison Officer, Captain Nicholson, who was one of the greatest assistance throughout. The ship left Folkestone at 2115/2nd June and berthed at the outer end of Dunkirk east pier at about 0100/3rd June. This presented some difficulty as the Master was clearly new to ship handling and there was no one on the pier to take lines. This was done by Captain Nicholson and a rating who jumped for it. Another transport was struck once and the pier twice before berthing was completed.

No troops could be seen on the pier and Captain Nicholson proceeded along it towards the inshore and to pass the word that the ship was waiting and capable of taking thousands. All this time the pier was being shelled and fire was frequently opened on aircraft that could be heard overhead.

French troops began to arrive in small numbers about 0215. I was ordered to leave about 0245 but as troops were then coming better, an endeavour was made to embark more. Definite orders to leave were however repeated and the ship cast off at 0305 and proceeded to Folkestone. Troops were disembarked on arrival and I was instructed to return to Dover with my party.

I reached Dover about 1045 and was there instructed to rest until 1300 and then return to the *Tynwald* at Folkestone with the same party and sail so as to reach Dunkirk at 0045/4th June. This was done and this time after waiting off the entrance for about ½ hour *Tynwald* was berthed at a shorter jetty to the west of the east pier. This jetty was crowded with French troops.

Every possible means of embarkation was used, the Naval ratings took up previously arranged stations in gangways and at ladders to ensure that the ship was filled from the bottom upwards, and in about ½ hour all space was occupied. From observation and from conversation with French Officers who knew what units were onboard the number is estimated to have been about 4000. No enemy interference was experienced. The return trip was eventless except that a very heavy explosion was felt shortly after leaving Dunkirk harbour. This was thought to be a mine that exploded about 2 cables astern. Troops were disembarked at Dover which was reached about 0700 on 4th June.

I was instructed to report at Admiralty whence I returned to H.M.S. *Wivern*.

I feel it right to remark that most of the officers and ratings of *Tynwald* who declined to sail for Dunkirk were elderly men who had already been there and were possibly shaken by the sight of their sister ship *Fenella*, sunk at the end of the east pier. It was also known that two other transports had been sunk and hospital ships attacked. At the same time I feel that very high praise is due to those who did sail, and who all remained completely calm and efficient throughout this trying experience. In this respect I would particularly mention the acting Master, Mr Whiteaway, and the acting Chief Officer, Mr. Watson.

VENOMOUS
W-class Destroyer
Pennant Number D75
Official Rescue Total: 4,410

A modified W-Class destroyer ordered in January 1918 from John Brown at Clydebank, this ship was laid down on 31 May 1918, being launched on 21 December that year. She was originally to have been named HMS Venom *but this was changed in order to avoid confusion with the Torpedo School, HMS* Venom. *Lieutenant Commander John Edwin Home McBeath RN wrote his account on 6 June 1940:*

2. H.M.S. *Whitehall* and H.M.S. *Venomous* left Dover Harbour at 0035/31, and arrived off Bray at 0350. During the passage, searchlights were observed burning from the shore seawards near Calais. H.M.S. *Venomous*, after waiting off the beach for one hour proceeded, on the receipt of orders from R.A.D., to berth alongside Dunkirk Eastern breakwater. Having remained alongside for thirty minutes, H.M.S. *Venomous* left harbour with 1200 troops on board, entering Dover Harbour at 0800.

3. At 0940 31st May 1940 H.M.S. *Venomous* left harbour with orders to proceed to Bray or La Panne beaches to embark troops. The ship arrived

off Bray at 1530, and finding no small craft available, I lowered my motor boat and whaler to embark troops. The motor boat broke down and was towed back to the ship. H.M. Motor Boat *Balquhain* (a Sub-Lieutenant was in command) used the whaler and ferried some 200 troops from the shore to the ship. During this period, repeated high level bombing attacks were carried out on the beach and ships lying off. Barrage fire was opened as opportunity presented. At 1700 H.M.S. *Venomous* was ordered by R.A.D. to proceed alongside to embark troops. While waiting for a berth, aircraft appeared and dropped bombs. Since the H.A. ammunition in H.M.S. *Venomous* was nearly exhausted, H.M.S. *Venomous* requested permission to return to harbour to replenish ammunition. At 1900 the ship was ordered to proceed alongside by S.N.O. Dunkirk. The ship proceeded alongside but no troops arrived. 60 German aircraft were observed approaching from the S.E. Fire was opened with all guns. The gun recoil parted all my wires and as no berthing party was available on the jetty, I proceeded out of harbour so as to retain mobility of the ship during the air attack. All H.A. ammunition was now expended and on receipt of orders from V.A.D. H.M.S. *Venomous* returned to Dover to replenish ammunition, arriving at 2220.

4. The ensuing twelve hours were spent in refuelling, repairing damage to the D.G. equipment and ammunitioning ship.

5. At 1245 1st June 1940 H.M.S. *Venomous* left harbour with orders to proceed to Dunkirk. At 1430 all Destroyers were recalled by V.A.D. and accordingly I returned to Dover at 1545.

6. At 2050 1st June 1940 H.M.S. *Venomous* embarked a beach party, consisting of ten Officers and ninety men, with orders to proceed to a position off St. Malo-les-Bains and embark troops. At 0030 2nd June 1940 the ship arrived but no boats appeared from the shore. Number One landing section (Lt. Cdr. Craig R.N.) pulled ashore inship's whaler to investigate. Nothing further was seen of this party. At 0200 R.A.D. ordered the ship to berth alongside and embark troops. He stated that he would order one of the M.S. to take over the whaler and berthing party. After half an hour alongside 1100 troops had been embarked and H.M.S. *Venomous* returned to Dover at 28 knots, arriving at 0515.

7. H.M.S. *Venomous* was ordered to arrive alongside Dunkirk Breakwater at 2150 2nd June 1940 to embark troops. The ship left Dover at 1910 and arrived alongside at the ordered time. During the passage an enemy seaplane was sighted and reported in position 090°2 miles North Goodwin Light Vessel. Owing to the prevailing wind and tide, great difficulty was experienced in getting alongside. Eventually, with the assistance of an M.A/S.B., the ship was berthed. After half an hour,

having embarked 1500 troops, the ship returned to Dover, arriving at 0125. During the return passage, an enemy seaplane, evidently returning from a minelaying expedition, machine gunned the ship but was driven off by barrage and close range fire.

8. H.M.S. *Venomous* left harbour at 2030 3rd June 1940 with instructions to arrive at Dunkirk for the embarkation of troops at 2245. On arrival, I entered harbour but owing to the very congested state inside, I was ordered to wait off the harbour mouth. At 0130, on receipt of orders from R.A.D., I entered harbour and proceeded alongside. Having embarked 1100 French troops, H.M.S. *Venomous* returned to Dover. Thick fog was encountered and the ship anchored off the North Goodwin Light Vessel at 0430. After half an hour the fog lifted and I weighed and arrived at Dover at 0610.

9. During these operations it was impossible to observe whether the gunfire of the ship inflicted any casualties on enemy aircraft, but it is considered probable that one aircraft that crashed on the beach, to the west of Dunkirk on the 31st May 1940 was brought down by the guns of the ship.

VERITY
V-class Destroyer
Pennant Number D63
Official Rescue Total: 504

HMS Verity *was laid down on 17 May 1918 and launched on 19 March the following year. She was the first Royal Navy warship to carry the name. Between the wars she served in the Atlantic and Mediterranean fleets. She served under two captains during Operation* Dynamo. *The first was Lieutenant Commander Arthur Ronald Mawson Black; after he was seriously wounded, Lieutenant E.L. Jones took over. It is the latter who provided this narrative:*

I have the honour to forward the following Report of Proceedings of H.M.S. *Verity*, for Monday 27th May, 1940.

Verity at No.10 buoy with steam at half an hour's notice.

0322   Signal received from Vice Admiral, Dover ordering *Verity* to escort *Biarritz* and *Arkangel* to Dunkirk.

0342   Slipped and proceeded.

0348   Cleared Eastern entrance. Set course for Dunkirk, via Calais Channel, at 16 knots.

0520   Shore batteries around Oye Church opened fire on *Verity* and

Convoy. Convoy proceeded on course with *Verity* zig-zagging, and laying smoke on the engaged side. The batteries were straddling *Verity* continuously with High Explosive and S.A.P. Fire was returned at about 7000 yards.

0523 Lieutenant Commander A.R.M. Black was seriously wounded, Sub-Lieutenant C.F. Alington slightly, and also A.B. M. Gibson, R.N.V.R., seriously wounded; compass platform personnel.

0530 Lieutenant E.L. Jones R.N. assumed command.

0528 Convoy ordered to return to Dover as the fire was getting stronger as Gravelines was approached.

0554 Shore batteries ceased fire.

0555 Informed V.A. Dover that *Verity* was returning to Dover with Convoy.

0558 *Verity* ceased fire and lead convoy into the channel.

0600 *Biarritz* reported that she was damaged in the Engine Room, and had difficulty in keeping steam; this was reported to V.A. Dover, who ordered her to return to Dover. *Arkangel* reported 'all well'. *Verity* sustained two direct hits with 4 inch S.A.P. shell, which penetrated the after boiler room, causing minor damage. Little damage was caused by H.E. Shell.

0608 Ordered by V.A. Dover to return to Dunkirk.

0623 *Biarritz* was then detached to Dover and *Arkangel* ordered to follow *Verity* at 15 knots.

0655 Man overboard; lowered Whaler.

0700 Man recovered, Whaler hoisted and proceeded.

0748 Observed Hospital ship and small vessels being shelled from French coast lines. Considered that owing to the heavy fire, slow speed (15 knots) of the convoy, and exhausted ammunition, it was advisable to use the Northern route to Dunkirk.

0749 V.A. Dover informed of this intention.

0838 Rounded South Goodwin Light Vessel and proceeded through 8Q.Z.F.

0845 *Arkangel* reported she would not have sufficient fuel to make the round voyage.

0856 Informed V.A. Dover that *Verity* and *Arkangel* were returning to Dover, and proceeded back along the channel.

0943 Entered harbour and secured to No.10 buoy.

Damage to After Boiler Room: Fan intake casings port and starboard, and escape hatch torn and holed. Deck between casings holed, allowing air pressure to escape from Boiler Room. The deck abreast starboard air casings damaged but not holed. Voice pipes to after Guns and Torpedo tubes damaged. The conduct of the Ships' Company was highly commendable. All guns and instruments functioned correctly.

Some records state that Lieutenant Commander Robert Henry Mills assumed command of HMS Verity *on 29 May 1940, though examination of the ship's Dunkirk account suggests that the remainder of the text was also written by Lieutenant E.L. Jones:*

Report of proceedings of H.M.S. *Verity*, from 1345, 27th May to 0130, 30th May, 1940.
The morale of the Ship's Company had been undermined by the shelling from shore batteries and aerial bombing during the last few days; it is considered that this was aggravated by long hours and lack of sleep. This situation came to a climax during the first Dog, when one rating attempted to commit suicide. This incident caused a marked increase to the men's uneasiness. Shortly afterwards a report was made by the Leading Seamen that the ship's company were considering breaking out of the ship.

I reported this state of affairs to V.A. Dover. V. Admiral Summerville [Somerville] returning to the ship with me and addressed the ship's company.

I was then informed that *Verity* would not be required until A.M., Tuesday 29th, endeavouring to allow the men a night's rest; this news when broadcast greatly relieved the men.

During the embarkation of the B.E.F. troops off Bray the Ship's Company greatly assisted and worked hard in comforting the wounded and feeding the troops. Again on the 29th May, the men showed determination in repelling the dive-bomb aircraft, and seemed in good fettle on the return journey.

On Thursday 30th May, when *Verity* had secured alongside in the Submarine Basin, members of the ship's company broke out of the ship, of these three were detained at the Dockyard gate and three returned A.M., Friday 31st May. Six men are still absent. The men who had returned, on being interrogated, stated that their nerves had given way and they could not 'stand it'. *Verity* was then ordered to stay in Harbour.

It is considered that this situation was caused by lack of rest, and the fact that our 'Chummy ships' of the Dover Patrol had been damaged by enemy action causing casualties, and then steadily growing belief that *Verity*'s turn was certain to come. The final effect being the attempt of suicide in the Mess Deck, and later this was increased by one rating developing shell shock.

I wish to emphasise the devotion to duty of Ch.E.R.A. Hill and S.B. Whitter, during these operations off Dunkirk.

CHRONOLOGICAL SUMMARY
Tuesday 28th May, 1940
Verity at No.11 buoy, with steam at 15 minutes notice, and alongside *War Sepoy* fuelling.

1330 Slipped from Oiler, and proceeded to Dunkirk, via Northern route. Speed 28 knots. Off Dyke buoy joined company with *Greyhound* and *Impulsive*. Occasional enemy aircraft were fired at during the voyage.

1705 Came to anchor off Bray, and lowered boats to embark B.E.F. During the night occasional bombing raids on the ships at anchor.

29th May

0148 Weighed with about 400 troops on board including 30 stretcher and wounded men, and proceeded to Dover.

0602 Entered Dover Harbour and proceeded alongside Admiralty Pier.

0645 Disembarked troops.

1145 Slipped from Admiralty Pier and proceeded to Oiler *War Sepoy*.

1415 Slipped from Oiler and proceeded to Dunkirk via route 'Y' at 28 knots.

1700 (approx). Passed Dunkirk Harbour, and received orders from S.N.O. Dunkirk, to proceed into Dunkirk.

1720 Proceed alongside East Mole Pier ahead of *Grenade* and trawlers.

1735 (do) Heavy dive bombing by aircraft on pier and ships.

1745 (do) One trawler hit, *Grenade* hit forward and commenced sinking. *Verity* was continuously straddled for thirty five minutes.

1800 (do) Slipped and turned ship in channel. On clearing the Trawlers and *Grenade* it was considered *Verity* touched forward.

1805 Cleared entrance, and proceeded to Bray.

1820 Off Bray, in company with *Sabre* and *Saladin*, being bombed, *Saladin* ahead being hit.

1840 A Paddle Trooper was observed on fire endeavouring to beach. Instructed Trooper to stop and let *Verity* get alongside and embark her troops. This was not possible as she could not stop.

1845 Embarked 20 B.E.F., and remained under way in the channel.

1850. Dunkirk and Bray under heavy bombing, during which time *Verity* especially was under constant bombing and machine gun fire.

1910 Embarked 20 more B.E.F.

2010 Bombing ceased, and as ammunition was expended, and no embarkation boats were available and ships whaler holed. *Verity* proceeded towards Dunkirk. As Dunkirk was again heavily bombed I followed *Sabre* out of Dunkirk Roads to Dover.

30th May
0130 Secured alongside *Express* at Admiralty Pier, disembarked troops.

VIMY
V-class Destroyer
Pennant Number D33
Official Rescue Total: 2,976

Ordered from Beardmore at Dalmuir, Glasgow, Vimy *was laid down on 30 June 1916. Launched on 28 December 1917, she was originally named HMS* Vancouver, *the first Royal Navy to carry this name which was used to commemorate the name of Captain George Vancouver (1757-1798) who gave his name to the island and town in British Columbia, Canada. Completed in March 1918, after service in the Grand Fleet* Vancouver *was deployed in the Baltic and took part in actions against Russian forces during support of the defence of countries under threat from the Red Army. In April 1928, whilst placed in Reserve, the ship was renamed HMS* Vimy *to enable her former name to be used by the Royal Canadian Navy for its destroyer HMS* Toreador.

HMS Vimy *was unusual in that she had three captains during the period of Operation* Dynamo. *These were Lieutenant Commander Richard George Kirby Knowling (missing), Lieutenant Adrian Paul Northey (temporary), and Lieutenant Commander Michael Wentworth Ewart-Wentworth. As a result, there are two reports detailing* Vimy's *part in the evacuations. The first, dated 3 June 1940, was written by Lieutenant Adrian Paul Northey:*

Monday, 27th May 1940
2. Slipped in company with S.S. *St. Helier* and *Royal Daffodil* at 0630 and proceeded for Dunkirk via French Coast. Searched Channels (Route Z).
3. Orders to return to Dover were received at 0710 on account of reported enemy batteries at Gravelines. Anchored in Dover at 0810.
4. At 1054, having received verbal orders to proceed weighed in company with H.M.S. *Anthony*, S.S. *Kyno* (10 knts), *St. Helier* and *Royal Daffodil* and proceeded northward through Downs.
5. At 1140 Hospital Ships *St. Andrew* and *St. Julian* joined company as they had no charts for Route 'Y'.

6. At 1230 H.M.S. *Anthony* and S.S. *Kyno* parted company to return to the Downs.

7. Convoy then increased speed to 20 knots and proceeded to Dunkirk via Route 'Y'.

8. At 1445 when between West Hinder and Kwinte Bank buoys two bombing attacks were made on the Hospital ships by two twin engine aircraft. Both salvoes missed.

9. Joined *Wolsey* who was laying off Dunkirk Breakwater at 1622.

10. Both transports then proceeded inside the harbour, the hospital ships remained outside.

11. By 1740 both transports had left the harbour and were lying off outside. *Royal Daffodil* was then ordered to remain off the harbour and we proceeded in company with *St. Helier* and the two hospital ships for Dover by Route 'Y' at 1750.

12. During the period the ship was off Dunkirk the town was continuously bombed by twin engine high level bombers. The ship was not attacked but several bombers passed nearby, and the A.A. armaments were frequently in action.

13. On arrival in Downs at 2200 the convoy anchored and *Vimy* remained off the P.W.S.S. at South Foreland for orders.

14. At 2308 V.A. Dover's signal timed 2238 was received and *Vimy* proceeded in accordance with this at 20 knots.

15. At about 2355 the Captain (Lieut. Cmdr. R.G.K. Knowling. R.N.) left the bridge. He had not returned by 0015/28 and I had the ship searched without result.

Tuesday, 28th May 1940

16. At 0030 I took command and increased speed to 26 knots.

17. The circumstances of the loss of Lieut. Comdr. R.G.K.K. Knowling R.N. were reported in my signal timed 0115 and confirmed in my No.154/5/1 dated 29th May 1940.

18. Arrived off beach 3 miles E of Dunkirk at 0320 finding S.S. *Brighton Bell* [sic] already embarking Troops from a French canal boat, and a small pulling boat. Boats were lowered and sent to the beach to assist filling up the *Brighton Belle*.

19. At 0445 received information that conditions were better at East Pier. Left boats with *Brighton Belle* and proceeded alongside.

20. Having embarked about 600 Troops from East Pier slipped and proceeded for Dover via Route 'Y' at 0545.

21. Embarkation was assisted by a heavy pall of smoke from burning buildings ashore which obscured the harbour from the air. Although

several different aircraft were seen flying high which were reported, no attacks were made.

22. While on passage to Dover various hostile aircraft were seen flying high, which were reported. No attacks were made.

23. Arrived Dover and proceeded alongside Admiralty Pier at 1015. Troops were disembarked as soon as possible.

24. At 1105 slipped and proceeded for Dunkirk via Route "Y".

25. Between Kwinte Bank and Nieuport Bank at 1415 about 20 Heinkel bombers attacked, in groups of two and three, *Vimy* and four other Destroyers in the vicinity.

26. Avoiding action as far as possible was taken and anti-aircraft fire opened. All attacks were high level with salvoes of five heavy bombs from each aircraft. Aircraft endeavoured to attack from astern. No hits were received but two salvoes burst within 20 yards of the ship one off the bow and one off the quarter, no damage resulted.

27. Several more bombers flew over the ship while off the Bray; anti aircraft fire was opened and attacks were made on the ships lying closer inshore.

28. Entered Dunkirk harbour and secured alongside *Grenade* at East Pier at 1532.

29. Having embarked about 650 Troops, slipped and proceeded for Dover via Route 'Y' at 1807.

30. While lying alongside flying conditions were poor owing to low cloud and rain, but several bombers and reconnaissance aircraft were seen and engaged. No attacks were made on the ships alongside.

31. Arrived in Dover and secured alongside Admiralty Pier at 2250. Disembarked Troops.

Wednesday, 29th May 1940

32. Slipped from Admiralty Pier at 0305 and proceeded alongside *Worcester* alongside *War Sepoy*.

33. Delay was experienced owing to congestion at the oiler and *Vimy* sailed in company with *Worcester* and *Anthony* at 0705 for Dunkirk via Route 'Y' only 86 tons of fuel had been embarked owing to the delay in oiling.

34. V.A. Dover's signal timed 0941 was received at 1018 while off Bray. Proceeded into Dunkirk at 1040 passed important letter for S.N.O. Dunkirk to *Ivanhoe* and sailed immediately for Sheerness.

35. Arrived Sheerness at 1545 and secured to No.6 Buoy.

36. On arrival Lieut Comdr. M.W. Ewart Wentworth R.N. joined the ship and took over command.

The second report on HMS Vimy *is dated 11 June 1940. It was written by Lieutenant Commander Ewart-Wentworth:*

29th May 1940
2. Sailed from Sheerness at 1905 to rendezvous with remainder of Force 'D' for operation D.F.
3. Admiralty's signal timed 1938 was received at 2102 and ship proceeded to Dover.
4. Arrived off Dover at 2230 and waited off the Eastern entrance for orders.

30th May 1940
5. Sailed in accordance with V.A. Dover's signal timed 0353 at 0425 and proceeded by Route X to Dunkirk.
6. H.M.S. *Vanquisher* reported Dunkirk harbour practicable at 0645. Proceeded alongside East side of East Pier at 0712.
7. Embarked troops and proceeded for Dover at 0731.
8. Arrived Dover at 1100 and disembarked approximately 600 troops at Admiralty Pier.
9. Proceeded in accordance with V.A. Dover's signal timed 1111 via Route X to Dunkirk at 1248.
10. Arrived off Dunkirk at 1615 and lay off outside to await opportunity to go alongside East Pier.
11. An attempt was made to secure 'Bows out' at 1717 but owing to the shelling of the pier by shore artillery this was not possible.
12. A further attempt was made at 1802 I secured and embarked troops, proceeding for Dover at 1825.
13. Arrived at Dover and secured alongside Admiralty Pier to disembark troops at 2132.

31st May 1940
14. Proceeded to No.2 buoy and secured with slip rope at 0048.
15. Proceeded in accordance with V.A. Dover's signal timed 2153/30 at 0445.
16. Clearly sighted periscope and conning tower of submarine on the starboard beam in position between North Goodwin buoy and N.W. Goodwin buoy, apparently steering West. Own speed was 20 knots. One depth charge was dropped and A/S hunt started between latitudes of Goodwin Knoll buoy and S.W. Goodwin buoy.
17. H.M.S. *Sheldrake* joined the hunt in accordance with C in C Nore's signal timed 0708.
18. Proceeded for Dunkirk at 1030 leaving hunt to H.M.S. *Sheldrake* and Trawlers in accordance with C in C Nore's signal timed 1001.

19. Arrived off Dunkirk at 1230 and secured alongside East Pier, bows out, at 1300.

20. The falling tide made it necessary to shift berth further to seaward on two occasions between 1300 and 1335 and at 1400 I left to secure alongside the end of the pier bows in.

21. While troops were being embarked intermittent shelling by shore batteries was observed at the landward end of the pier.

22. Proceeded for Dover at 1538.

23. Arrived Dover to disembark troops securing to Admiralty Pier at 1856.

1st June 1940

24. Completed with oil fuel and proceeded for Dunkirk at 0100.

25. In collision with H.M.Y. *Amulree* in position 270° N.W. Goodwin buoy 1 cable at 0156.

26. A single white light was sighted ahead. The engines were put to Full Astern and the wheel Hard-a-Starboard. *Amulree* apparently altered to Port as *Vimy*'s stem entered her starboard bow. As soon as the ship gathered stern-way *Amulree* went clear and sank immediately. Own speed before collision 15 ½ knots.

27. The Skiff, being the only remaining boat, was lowered to pick up survivors, and at 0233 I proceeded for Dover having recovered all members of *Amulree*'s crew.

28. Arrived Dover and secured to No.2 Buoy at 0349.

2nd June 1940

29. Proceeded in accordance with V.A. Dover's signal timed 1942/1 for Cardiff at 0605.

30. Proceeded in accordance with Admiralty's signal timed 1514 for Portsmouth at 1540.

31. Arrived at Portsmouth and secured at North Corner Jetty alongside *Verity* at 1620 to be taken in hand for repairs.

Further information on the fate of Lieutenant Commander Richard George Kirby Knowling is provided in a letter dated 21 June 1940 – this was sent to Mrs D.K. Knowling (a copy, quoted here, is held in file reference ADM 358/110 at The National Archives):

I am commanded by My Lords Commissioners of the Admiralty to inform you, with reference to their letter of 30th May, that further information is now available concerning the death of Lieutenant-Commander R.G.K. Knowling, R.N., who was presumed to have been lost overboard from his ship, H.M.S. *Vimy*, on the night of 27th-28th May last.

It appears that, just before midnight on 27th May, he left the bridge with the intention of going below; when he did not reappear shortly afterwards, a search of the ship was made, but no trace of him was discovered. The rails and life-lines were all properly secured and in order, and the only conceivable explanation appeared to be that while the ship was turning at speed, Lieutenant-Commander Knowling might have been thrown off his balance and gone overboard. He was known to be suffering from a sprained ankle at the time, and this, coupled with the fact that the ship had in fact changed course shortly after he was last seen, lent some colour to this suggestion.

VIVACIOUS
V-class Destroyer
Pennant Number D36
Official Rescue Total: 1,999

HMS Vivacious *was laid down in July 1916 and launched on 3 November that year as the first Royal Navy warship to carry this name. She was completed in December 1917 and was fitted for use as a minelayer. During 1919-1920* Vivacious *was deployed in the Baltic and was in action against Russian warships. Later she served in the Atlantic and Mediterranean fleets until the mid-1930s when placed in Maintenance Reserve at Rosyth. She was brought forward in August 1939 for the Review of the Reserve Fleet by HM King George VI at Weymouth. The ship remained in commission and began her war service in the Western Approaches. Lieutenant Commander Frank Reginald Woodbine Parish RN completed his account on 12 June 1940:*

I have the honour to forward the following report of proceedings for H.M.S. *Vivacious* for the period 26th May until 4th June 1940 inclusive.
2. *Vivacious* left Immingham at 2200 on 26th May 1940 and proceeded to rendezvous with Admiral Commanding 2nd Cruiser Squadron in H.M.S *Galatea* in position 'X' at 1215. C.S.2. Parted company at 1800 and orders were received to patrol in company with *Gallant* and the Polish Destroyer *Blyskawica* [Błyskawica] between North Goodwin Light and 'T' buoy.
3. At 2200 ships were ordered to a position one mile East of Dunkirk to evacuate the B.E.F. and arrived at 0030. The town was undergoing continual bombardment and flames from ammunition dumps and oil fuel depots reached two to three thousand feet. During these raids

'whistling' bombs were heard, their noise being similar to that of a siren.

4. Two enemy aircraft came through the thick smoke cloud and attacked the ships with machine guns. The *Blyskawca* shot down one of these in the harbour.

5. *Vivacious'* section of the beach was cleared at 0330 with the aid of drifters and the whaler, and a report having been received from a personnel boat that the East Jetty had been cleared, the ship returned to Dover with 353 military personnel.

6. The ship sailed again for Dunkirk at 1030 on 27th proceeding by the Eastern Route.

7. Intense aircraft attack by about twenty-five enemy machines was encountered off the Eastern Entrance with about 100 bombs being dropped on the ships and three enemy machines were shot down (two Junkers 88 and one Heinkel 111). One burst into flames and crashed on the beach, and another with the port engine on fire crashed into the sea. The third was not seen to crash but the pilot was seen to leave the plane by parachute.

8. Arrival at point three miles East of Dunkirk was made at 1230 and after five and three quarter hours some 553 military were taken by ships boats, M.T.B. 16 and a Dutch Scoot. The return journey was made in company with *Codrington* and *Javelin* as all A.A. ammunition had been expended.

9. Orders were received to proceed to Sheerness with Woolsey and Vimy to arrive at 1300 for special service. Operation 'D' was commenced at 1800. This was cancelled at 2100 and the ships were ordered to return to Dover.

10. While at Sheerness Surgeon Lieutenant S. Grice R.N.V.R. collapsed owing to injuries and strain and was relieved by Surgeon Lieutenant P.A. Smyth R.N.V.R.

11. Before reaching Dover *Vivacious* was ordered to return to Dunkirk arriving at 0300, using the Western Route, the orders being to evacuate troops one mile east of the town.

12. On arrival a broken down M.T.B., which had been picking up the survivors of the *King Orry*, was taken in tow until repaired.

13. It was most distressing to hear the cries of a few men in the water, but these had to be left in order to carry on with the operation. A drifter, however, was sent to rescue as many as possible and it is believed that most of these men were picked up.

14. During the day low misty weather made aircraft conditions difficult and 650 men were taken off the beach with hardly any embarrassment from the air.

15. On arrival at Dover I was relieved by Commander E.F.V. Dechaineux R.A.N. by order of V.A. Dover.

16. The report of proceedings of Commander Dechaineux for the remaining part of the operation is attached herewith.

REPORT OF PROCEEDINGS OF COMMANDER E.F.V. DECHAINEUX.

1. Commander E.F.V. Dechaineux R.A.N. was ordered by V.A. Dover to assume command of H.M.S. *Vivacious* in place of Lieutenant Commander F.R. Parish R.N. who, due to overstrain, was granted sick leave.

2. *Vivacious* remained in Dover Harbour until 0530 on 30th May, when she sailed for Bray on the Belgian Coast, arriving at about 0700.

3. My object was to embark as many troops as possible and to provide supporting fire to the army ashore.

4. Throughout the day a fresh breeze was blowing from the East North East causing in the shallow shore a line of breakers extending about fifty yards off shore. These conditions made embarkation difficult and together with the small number of suitable boats caused the evacuation to be very slow.

5. By 1700, 175 British troops had been evacuated.

6. Intermittently throughout the day the ship and those in company were bombed. At 1500 a very thrilling dog-fight between nine spitfires and a larger number of Messerschmitts and various types of German bombers was witnessed. Two spitfires were shot down and two enemy bombers. A fifth unaccounted plane was also shot down. Most of the enemy aircraft attacks were high level bombing from over 10,000 feet.

7. It was particularly distressing to see an increasing number of troops assembling on the beach, which in the circumstances prevailing gave me a feeling of impotence. Towards late afternoon a general movement Westward to Dunkirk was apparent.

8. Throughout the afternoon a shore battery believed to be two, and later four 4" guns situated on the coast to the Eastwards had carried out desultory and inaccurate fire on the anchorage, the principal target appearing to be an abandoned merchant ship at anchor in the roadstead.

9. At 1800 this battery commenced a controlled and accurate fire on *Vivacious* who was under way and pointed along the line of fire. When it was obvious that the target was the assembled ships (*Shikari*, *Esk*, and *Mosquito*), I ordered a retirement to the Westward. *Vivacious* was hit on the Foxle by what is believed to be a 4" graze fuze shell, causing three deaths and twelve casualties to the troops on the upper mess deck. Two near misses caused about forty small shrapnel holes on the waterline

abreast the engine room and the after torpedo tubes. These near misses punctured two fuel tanks rendering them unfit for use. The central store was flooded partially, the lubricating pipe to the stern was punctured and the De-Gaussing circuits were cut in eight places. The batteries were out ranged by a two mile movement to the Westward.

10. Throughout the night *Vivacious* patrolled between La Panne and Bray but no noteworthy incident occurred.

11. At about 1900 on 30th May *Codrington* had returned to Bray and took over the senior officers duties.

12. At about 0530 on 31st May rear Admiral Wake Walker in H.M.S *Keith* ordered *Vivacious* to proceed to Dunkirk to embark troops.

13. At about 0610 on 31st whilst waiting to enter Dunkirk the ship was attacked by a Junkers 88 in a dive attack. Five 250 or 500lb bombs were released from 1000 feet but fortunately missed the ship by about 20 feet. No damage was caused.

14. A difficult alongside was made successfully at 0630 during an air attack. 650 troops were embarked by 0645 and the ship sailed arriving at Dover without incident, except for slight and inaccurate enemy gunfire at No.6 buoy.

15. *Vivacious* arrived at Dover at 0915 on 31st May, remaining there until 1800 on 2nd June.

16. At 1800 on 2nd June *Vivacious* sailed after embarking Captain Dangerfield R.N., to escort three block ships whose object was to block Dunkirk Harbour. A conference of Captains of the Blockships (S.S. *Westgrove* [*West Cove*], S.S. *Edward Nissen* and S.S. *Holland*) and of the M.T.Bs of the blocking force was held in the Downs. At 2030 *Vivacious* leading the blockships, with M.T.B. 107 in tow, and M.A.S. 07 in company moved off from the Downs at 7 knots through 'Z' route arriving off Dunkirk at 0220. Captain Dangerfield in M.T.B. 107 at 0230 and proceeded to Dunkirk.

17. On arrival off Dunkirk the Block ships were anchored and at 0245 ordered to weigh and proceed to block the channel. It subsequently transpired that S.S. *Holland*, the last in the line, had been rammed about five miles west of Dunkirk.

18. The blockships *West Cove* and *Edward Nissen* entered Dunkirk at 0300 and 0310 respectively.

19. It is unfortunate that the block was not completed and navigation in the approach channel to the docks is still possible. M.A.S. 07 and M.T.B. 107 brought off the crews of the blockships to *Vivacious*, who had by this time moved three miles to the Westward. It is indeed fortunate that this movement was made as at 0350 shore batteries to the Eastward opened a well-aimed fire on the ship. Embarkation of the crews

however was almost complete and *Vivacious* retired to the Westward without damage.

20. *Vivacious* arrived at Dover at 0630 on 3rd June. Two serious casualties from among the *Holland's* crew were landed with the remainder of the Blockships crews.

21. At 1145 on the 4th *Vivacious* sailed with *Icarus* in company for Portsmouth. *Esk* had been ordered to join but owing to fog had failed to join. *Vivacious* and *Icarus* arrived Portsmouth at 1830.

WAKEFUL
W-class Destroyer
Pennant Number H88
Official Rescue Total: 639

The W-Class destroyer HMS Wakeful *was ordered from Beardmore at Dalmuir in December 1916. Laid down on 17 January 1917 and launched on 6 October that year, she was the first Royal Navy warship to carry the name. Her build was completed on 16 December 1917 and she served in the Grand Fleet during the First World War. Before going into Reserve,* Wakeful *attended the surrender of the German High Seas Fleet. Commander Ralph Lindsay Fisher's report, written at the Royal Naval Barracks Chatham, is dated 30 May 1940:*

I much regret to inform you of the loss, by enemy action, of H.M.S *Wakeful* while under my command at 0045 on 29th May 1940 and have the honour to report my proceedings as follows.

2. At 1430 on Monday, 28th April, while at Plymouth at short notice, orders were received to proceed to Dover with all dispatch and the ship sailed half an hour later.

3. On passage all Confidential Books and all except a few essential Signal Publications were put in sealed bags.

4. Dover was reached at 0100 on Tuesday, 28th May and the ship proceeded alongside the oiler but, before she had secured, orders were received to proceed to the beach east of Dunkirk with utmost dispatch to embark troops.

5. Six bags of Confidential Books and Signal Publications were handed to the Master of *War Sepoy* and H.M.S. *Wakeful* sailed immediately.

6. The Southern route was taken and as ship passed Dunkirk Harbour a signal from Senior Naval Officer, Dunkirk was read ordering her to proceed alongside East Pier. Six hundred and thirty-nine troops were

embarked in about 25 minutes. These were landed at Dover at 0930 on Tuesday, 28th May.

7. H.M.S. *Wakeful* sailed for Dunkirk again unaccompanied at 1130 with orders to proceed by the Northern route and embark troops from the beach at Le Braye.

8. At about 1300, near the Kwinte Whistle Buoy, a level bombing attack by nine four-engined German aircraft developed. They attacked nine times in groups of three. The ten rounds per gun of barrage ammunition carried was quickly expended and I regret to report that no damage was inflicted on the enemy, but the bombs were avoided by waiting for their release and then putting the wheel hard over. Out of about forty or fifty bombs one fell about thirty yards from the ship's side and made a hole in the engine room above the water line, wounding one man seriously and two slightly. The coolness and efficiency of Sub-Lieutenant Percival-Jones during this attack were highly commendable. He identified the aircraft in the first place and informed me of each bomb release.

9. H.M.S. *Wakeful* anchored of the Braye Sanatorium at 1500 on Tuesday, 28th May and, during the next eight hours, embarked about 640 troops by ship's boats. Sub-Lieutenant Percival-Jones volunteered to go in the boats and did splendid work on the beach marshalling troops, at one time at the point of the revolver.

10. All mess-tables and stools and other available timber was placed on the upper deck for life-saving purposes and the troops were stowed as low in the ship as possible to preserve sufficient stability for rapid manoeuvring in case of air attack. Engine-room, boiler rooms and store rooms were all utilised.

11. At 2300 on Tuesday, 28th May H.M.S. *Wakeful* weighed and sailed for Dover by Zuydcoote Pass and North Channel. The night was dark, but phosphorescence was very pronounced.

12. Twelve knots was maintained while in the narrow channels and every time the sound of aircraft engines was heard speed was reduced to slow to reduce wake.

13. I felt that it was very probable that some form of attack would be made near the Kwinte Whistle Buoy and five miles before reaching it speed was increased to 20 knots and a zig-zag of 40 degrees every four minutes was started. All guns crews and bridge personnel were warned and were keyed up and were keeping a specially good lookout.

14. At 0045 (Wednesday, 29th May) when the ship was two cables west of the Kwinte Whistle Buoy, two parallel torpedo tracks about 30 yards apart one slightly ahead of the other were seen approaching 150 yards away on the starboard bow. They appeared to be running practically on

the surface and the tracks were very bright with phosphorescence. No survivor can say what fired them, but it is evident from subsequent events that they were fired by a motor torpedo boat which was probably lying stopped close to the buoy.

15. The wheel was put hard a port and the ship swung sufficiently to cause one to miss ahead. The other hit in the forward boiler room. The ship broke in half and the two portions sank within about 15 seconds, each remaining standing with its mid-ship end on the bottom and the bow and stern standing about 60 feet above the water.

16. All Signal Publications were in the W/T Office and must have gone down with the ship. The following secret documents were on the chart table and may possibly have floated to the surface: Chart in use on which Dover Strait minefields were lightly marked; Current table of lettered positions.

17. Most of the guns' crews floated clear and thirty men and an officer remained on the stern portion. All the troops were asleep below and went down with the ship except one, and all H.M.S. *Wakeful*'s engine room department except one or two were lost. I floated clear of the bridge.

18. After about half an hour the motor drifters *Nautilus* and *Comfort* came on the scene and started to pick up those still swimming. *Nautilus* picked up six and *Comfort* 16 including myself. H.M.S. *Gossamer* arrived soon after and lowered boats which picked up about fifteen.

19. The swimmers and rescue ships had drifted some distance away with the tide and, after cruising for about half an hour shouting, I directed *Comfort* to go back to the wreck to take off the men clinging to the stern while *Nautilus* carried on to Dunkirk. When we got there the stern had fallen over and many men were shouting in the water. H.M. Ships *Grafton* and *Lydd* were close to the wreck and I went alongside the former's starboard quarter to warn her that she was in danger of being torpedoed. At that moment (0250) a torpedo hit her in the wardroom and the *Comfort* was lifted in the air, then momentarily swamped and as she bobbed to the surface again I was washed overboard. I was able to grab a rope's end, but as the *Comfort* was going full speed ahead with no-one on deck I soon had to let go.

20. The *Comfort* then came round in a wide circle and suddenly both H.M.S *Lydd* and H.M.S. *Grafton* opened a heavy fire on her with Lewis guns and, I think, four inch. I realised that they very naturally thought she was enemy and kept under water as much as possible when the bullets were coming near me.

21. I understand that all the *Comfort*'s crew except one and all H.M.S. *Wakeful*'s survivors onboard her except four were killed during this

affray. Of these four, two were later found wounded in the *Comfort*'s skiff and picked up. Sub-Lieutenant Percival-Jones is known to have been amongst those killed.

22. The firing ceased and I swam to the *Comfort* which had stopped engines and was drifting towards me slowly. As I reached her bow and was feeling for a rope's end, H.M.S. *Lydd* bore down on her at full speed and rammed her amidships on the opposite side, cutting her in half.

23. I was submerged but came to the surface after an interval and swam about till about 0515 when I was picked up by a boat from the Norwegian ship *Hird* carrying 3000 troops from Dunkirk.

24. I very much hope that some expression of Their Lordships' appreciation can be sent to the widow of Mr Tucker, Warrant Engineer, on whose high zeal, efficiency and sense of duty I have previously reported to the Commander-in-Chief, Western Approaches, and who dealt personally with a burst auxiliary steam pipe at the time of the bomb damage on May 29th. He was unhappily killed with practically the whole of his staff when the ship was torpedoed.

WHITEHALL
W-class Destroyer
Pennant Number H94
Official Rescue Total: 3,453

HMS Whitehall *was laid down in June 1918 and was launched as the first British warship to carry the name. After launch, work was suspended and she was towed to HM Dockyard, Chatham. The build was finally completed in July 1924 when* Whitehall *entered service. Due to economic reasons this ship had limited operational use until the outbreak of war. During the Dunkirk evacuation she was captained by Lieutenant Commander Archibald Boyd Russell, whose narrative is dated 4 June 1940:*

Whitehall proceeded from Plymouth at 0700/29 and arrived at Dover at 1900/29. At 0130/30 proceeded to Dunkerque Roads by X route, arriving at 0510. Between 0530 and 0550, 600 troops and survivors from *King Orry* were embarked from two trawlers. During this time a few enemy aircraft were bombing. At 0550 proceeded to Dover by X route arriving at 0950.

At 1120 proceeded from Dover to Dunkerque via Z route arriving at 1350. During passage *Princess Maud* about 2 miles astern was heavily engaged by either shore batteries or bombers. 1415 entered Dunkerque

Harbour, embarked 800 troops and proceeded to Dover by X route, arriving at 1900.

2. After disembarking troops, Ship completed with fuel and at 0025/31 proceeded to Dunkerque, *Venomous* in company, by Z route, arriving at 0300. During passage through Dunkerque Roads Ship fouled sunken wreckage between Nos. 13 and 14 Buoys. Senior Naval Officer, Dunkerque, ordered *Whitehall* into harbour at 0330, but, due to Starboard engine being practically out of action, this order was not obeyed for fear of Ship becoming uncontrollable and obstructing the entrance to the harbour. At 0415 Starboard screw had cleared itself and ship entered the harbour, embarked 1300 troops and returned to Dover via X route, arriving at 0815. During this trip little bombing was seen but Dunkerque was under artillery fire.

At 0950 proceeded to Dunkerque via X route arriving at 1250. At 1315 stood by *Impulsive* who was aground on sunken wreck off N 10 E buoy. At 1400 *Impulsive* had cleared and ship proceeded to Bray. As there were an ample number of destroyers at Bray and La Panne, ship returned to Dunkerque at 1530 and was ordered by Senior Naval Officer, Dunkerque, to await orders to enter Dunkerque. Whilst waiting, 12 French troops were embarked in ship's whaler. Bombing had been intermittent throughout the afternoon. At 1710 about 40 or 50 Dive bombers were overhead and at 1717 almost simultaneous attacks were made on *Ivanhoe* and *Whitehall* who were to Eastward off harbour waiting to enter. Attack was a "near-miss" by delay action bombs, and landed about 30 yards from Starboard bow, bursting under water on Starboard beam. A/S set and rangefinder put out of action.

At 1830 entered harbour and secured alongside *Winchelsea*. Armed Yacht *Grive* (the Hon. G.I. Lambton), secured outside. At this time two minesweepers, *Venomous* and drifters were secured to wall to seaward of *Whitehall*. At 1910, during embarkation of troops, a large force of dive bombers and fighters was sighted approaching from the N.E. *Whitehall* ordered *Grive* to slip and leave harbour and *Winchelsea* to follow *Whitehall* out. At 1912 *Grive* proceeded followed by *Venomous*, *Whitehall* and *Winchelsea*. *Grive* stopped close outside the entrance and *Venomous* just avoided her. As *Whitehall* passed through the entrance going astern at 15 knots, Grive went ahead. *Whitehall* stopped but was unable to check way of ship due to *Winchelsea* following her out. At 1920 *Whitehall* was in collision with *Grive*. *Grive*'s stem hit *Whitehall*'s port quarter, damaging after superstructure and holing ship's side at 155 station. The Ward Room and Provision Room were holed and No.155 Bulkhead was torn and buckled just below the upper deck. During this period enemy bombers were being engaged with all guns and *Whitehall's* after group shot down one.

Venomous and *Grive* left roads at full speed and at 2000 *Whitehall* re-entered harbour. Enemy were active over Dunkerque Town, but were not bombing the harbour. At 2055 completed embarkation of 700 troops, and proceeded to Dover by X Route arriving at 0045/1.

Whitehall completed with fuel and H.A. ammunition and sailed for Dunkerque at 0830/1. During passage through Downs spoke *Windsor* who advised use of Y Route. Ship proceeded accordingly.

At 1223 ship was at Middlekerke Buoy, and sighted *Basilisk* out of action and aground off Bray. *Basilisk's* ship's company had abandoned ship and were embarked from boats and Carley Floats. A French drifter and one whaler proceeded to Westward across the banks and due to it being low water, *Whitehall* was unable to pick up these survivors. *Whitehall* shelled *Basilisk* at 1310 and set her on fire below the bridge. At 1325 four torpedoes were fired at *Basilisk* at a range of 2000 yards. As *Basilisk* was aground on a shallow bank and t was low water *Whitehall* could not get closer to her. One torpedo is thought to have hit abreast the foremost funnel. During this period *Whitehall* was shelled intermittently by a small calibre shore gun.

3. At 1340, after consultation with *Basilisk's* Commanding Officer, it was decided to return to Dover. Shortly after, destroyers were recalled to Dover. *Whitehall* arrived at Dover at 1740 and left for Plymouth at 2300 taking survivors from *Basilisk* with her.

Whitehall arrived at Plymouth at 1115/2.

WHITSHED
W-class Destroyer
Pennant Number D77
Official Rescue Total: 1,038

A Modified W-Class destroyer, HMS Whitshed *was built by Swan Hunter at Wallsend on Tyne, Newcastle, in April 1918. Launched on 31 January 1919, she was the first Royal Navy warship to carry the name. The month of May 1940 was a hectic period for this ship and her crew. The beginning of the month saw* Whitshed *involved in the following: Demolition and evacuation duties at Ijmuiden and Amsterdam; transporting supplies and men of the Irish Guards to Dunkirk on the 13th; participating in Operation* Ordnance *(the evacuation at Hook of Holland); assisting in the evacuation from Ostend between the 16th and 18th; and providing escort to ships taking Guards battalions to Boulogne on the 22nd. Having remained on station off Boulogne on the 23rd, Whitshed was hit by shore fire and sustained casualties. It is from this point on that her captain, Commander Edward Reignier Condor, takes up the story:*

I have the honour to report that in accordance with your instructions H.M. Ship under my command was expeditiously repaired, guns being lifted and roller paths cleaned and adjusted. The Commander-in-Chief, Portsmouth also authorised the removal of the after set of triple torpedo tubes and the fitting of a twelve pounder H.A. gun in this place and the conversion of the warhead magazine for H.A. ammunition stowage. Ship also received a lot of plating as splinter protection. Boilers were cleaned and repairs made to engines and hull.

New officers and ratings joined and ship proceeded at 2000 Friday, 31st May to Spithead. Ship's company were drilled that evening and the following forenoon until the magnetic mines in the entrance had been exploded and the port re-opened to traffic when ship at once sailed for Dover, arriving there at 1730.

Ship sailed at 2240, 1st June for Dunkirk arriving there at 0130 and berthing at the other berth on the western side of the Eastern arm. On passage an aircraft which dropped a large object ahead of the ship was fired at. French destroyers off Dunkirk were frequently firing at heard aircraft and a signal was sent asking whether these were friendly or not as if so it was most desirable that firing should cease. No reply was received.

The jetty was empty and no troops could be found. However by using the loud hailer army landing craft from the beach on the other side of the pier started to bring troops to the ship, while I landed and finding a bicycle proceeded up the pier until I had collected enough troops, English and French to fill the ship. The bicycle also provided useful transport for two wounded men, and I was able to help in berthing two other destroyers and directing troops to board them.

I slipped at 0300 as dawn was breaking and proceeded without incident to Dover arriving at 0530.

Ship left Dover at 2135 and proceeded to Dunkirk arriving there at 0030. Just past W. buoy whistling was heard and eventually I found one aircraftsman survivor from Commander Clouston's R.A.F. launch. A Messerschmitt had got them about 1830 and Commander Clouston had refused to be rescued by their consort and had ordered it away into Dunkirk. They were machine gunned in the water. The congestion in the harbour made berthing impossible and together with many other craft ship lay to outside.

The Rear Admiral (D) gave me orders to use my loud hailer and stop other ships entering and this was done. Some 80 troops and 10 civilians and others were embarked from small craft. Orders were received to return to Dover as no more troops were available and ship proceeded at 0245. When at No.5 W. Buoy H.M.S. *Holland* was observed apparently splitting in half and sinking. I stood by her but survivors were taken off by M.T.B. 102 so I proceeded, arriving Dover at 0530.

A Dutch scoot flying the white ensign had rammed me in Dover harbour the previous afternoon piercing No.3 oil tank. While off Dunkirk with H.M.S *Malcolm* lying across my bows an unknown paddle minesweeper rammed my stern and carried away part of the depth charge racks. Ship accordingly proceeded alongside *Sandhurst* where the damaged stern was made watertight.

My ship's company were in very good heart and although lying at one time alongside H.M.S. *Hebe* were unaffected by their hysteria.

Embarking Commander Buchanan, R.A.N. and the pier party, ship sailed at 1900 for Dunkirk with the harmonica band playing.

Ship arrived Dunkirk at 2215, 3rd June. A Transport jammed me in the entrance and the wind and tide were setting ships off the Eastern arm. I got my bows alongside in No.5 berth and a wire out but this parted. I put part of the pier party into the M.T.B. that had Rear Admiral (D) aboard and again went alongside, but the French troops would not take my wires. The harbour was now full of ships of all sorts and sizes backing and filling.

Eventually I got my bows alongside a transport's stern and my stern alongside H.M.S. *Sabre* who had slipped in inside me. I gave a special brow to the transport to assist them in embarking troops as they only had some three or four hundred on board and one very small narrow brow. She, however, decided that as the tide was falling she must leave and H.M.S *Sabre* went about the same time. By now I had almost 200 troops on board. Perforce I backed down the harbour with the others and then went alongside again and embarked a further four or five hundred. With this number on board and my plating I can only use 10° of wheel at high speed and so with no more troops in sight I sailed at 0245 having been warned that enemy M.T.B's were in the vicinity. One salvo of shells fell uncomfortably close to the ship while manoeuvring in the harbour. Ship arrived Dover at 0530 the passage from U buoy to within a mile of the breakwater being made in dense fog.

After making arrangements about the administration of the 19th Flotilla of which H.M.S *Whitshed* was the only one left at Dover, ship sailed for Portsmouth with H.M.S *Winchelsea* in company at 1315 arriving Portsmouth at 1730.

WINCHELSEA
W-class Destroyer
Pennant Number D46
Official Rescue Total: 4,957

Launched on 15 December 1917, Winchelsea *was the seventh Royal Navy ship to carry the name, which was introduced in 1694 – probably after the 6th Earl of Winchelsea (1647-1730) who was a Lord of the Admiralty in 1679 and a supporter of William II.* Winchelsea's *captain during the evacuations was Lieutenant Commander William Alan Frank Hawkins, whose report is dated 5 June 1940:*

In accordance with Flag Officer in Charge, Liverpool signal 1500/28 *Winchelsea* slipped and proceeded to Plymouth at 1600/28. The ship arrived at Plymouth at 0630/29th.

2. At 1230 *Winchelsea* slipped from No.5 buoy and proceeded to over with all despatch, as ordered by Commander-in-Chief, Western Approaches. At 2200/29 *Winchelsea* was off Dover Breakwater and at 2300 proceeded to Dunkirk.

3. The whaler was sent away at 0211/30 and four survivors of H.M.S *King Orry* were picked up. A trawler was detailed to pick up the remainder; *King Orry* had been bombed and hit by six bombs at 1700/29. Boats were lowered and the embarkation of troops from Braye Beach was commenced at 0315. At 0515/30 one enemy aircraft was attacked by gunfire and driven off. By 0630/30 *Winchelsea* had embarked 480 British French, Belgian and Belgian Colonial troops and proceeded to Dover: Visibility was bad and a thick fog made it necessary to anchor. This cleared considerably at 1040/30 and *Winchelsea* proceeded into Dover.

4. *Winchelsea* returned to Dunkirk at 1415 in company with *Codrington* and secured alongside Dunkirk Pier at 1800/30 to embark troops, returning to Dover at 1940. Troops were disembarked at 0015/31, and finally secured to East Wall Dover.

5. At 0730/31 *Winchelsea* slipped from East Wall and proceeded to Braye Beach. Due to bad weather conditions and lack of suitable boats to embark troops the progress was very slow. At 1645 an attack was carried out on the fleet by 40 enemy dive bombers *Winchelsea* was attacked at this time and all bombs fell ahead on either bow. During this raid it is believed that one enemy aircraft was shot down by the ship. In view of the very slow rate of embarkation, Colonel Hutchings, the Admiralty Liaison Officer who was on board at the time, suggested to Senior Naval Officer, Dunkirk that ships should go alongside the pier and troops be

marched down to the mole. The ship proceeded alongside at 1832. At 1930 50 enemy bombers were observed and bombing was carried from about 5,000 feet. No hits were obtained on ships. *Winchelsea* left the jetty directly on the commencement of the raid and secured alongside on its completion. Some 1200 French and British troops were embarked; *Winchelsea* berthed alongside Admiralty Pier, Dover at 2345/31.

6. Ship returned to Dunkirk at 0130/1, securing alongside the Pier at 0630. Ships alongside were heavily bombed at 0745, the *Ivanhoe* was observed to be hit between the foremost funnel and the bridge; but proceeded under her own steam matter. *Winchelsea* was again bombed at 0830/1 while proceeding through the channel but all bombs fell to port about 30 yards away. No casualties or damage were sustained beyond broken glass. The number of troops carried was again about 1300. The ship returned to Dover at about 1100.

7. In accordance with Vice Admiral Dover's orders, *Winchelsea* again proceeded to Dunkirk in company with *Whitshed* at 2240 and secured to the Pier at 0230/2. As ordered the ship slipped and proceeded at 0300 with about 1100 Allied troops on board and returned to Dover. The complete evacuation of troops was not finished as expected. The signal from *Lydd* referring to arrival of the Rearguard on the beach at 0230 was not received by *Winchelsea* until 0411, when approaching Dover, *Winchelsea* was thus unable to comply with this signal.

8. Vice Admiral over's signal 0710/2 was received at 0730 and defects to Forced Lubrication coolers were made good. *Winchelsea* proceeded so as to arrive at Dunkirk Pier at 2300/2. The pier was shelled by shore batteries during embarkation and the ship was machine-gunned by land forces on leaving harbour at 2341. After leaving the pier several parachute flares were seen to drop over the end of the mole, but no bombing attacks were observed. *Winchelsea* was machine-gunned by an enemy plane on leaving the channel, but no casualties were sustained.

9. *Winchelsea* remained in harbour during the night of 2/3rd June.

10. While manoeuvring to avoid enemy aircraft dropping bombs *Winchelsea* grounded on a shoal patch on the morning of the 30th May and the A/S Dome was damaged.

11. No casualties or serious damage were sustained by *Winchelsea* at any time. The spirit and morale of the ship's company were magnificent throughout the whole operation in spite of hard steaming, long action stations, discomfort and lack of sleep. Mention of initiative and courage of individual ratings is being forwarded by separate letter where differentiation is possible; but special mention is deserved by all Stokers, P.O.s and younger ratings particularly R.N.R. and R.N.V.R ratings borne.

12. In accordance with orders received from Vice Admiral Dover, *Winchelsea* proceeded to Portsmouth at 1330, arriving at 1800/4.

WINDSOR
W-class Destroyer
Pennant Number D42
Official Rescue Total: 3,991

HMS Windsor *was ordered from Scotts at Greenock in December 1916 and launched on 21 June 1918. She was the third ship to carry this name, which had been introduced in 1695 for a 4th Rate and was used for a trawler in the First World War. Having been involved in the rescue of the Dutch Government earlier in May,* Windsor*'s captain during Operation* Dynamo *was Lieutenant Commander Peter Douglas Herbert Raymond Pelly. His report is dated 14 June 1940:*

I have the honour to report that at 2300, 25th May, I left Dover in company with *Verity* with orders to cover the withdrawal of small vessels which were waiting off Calais to carry out the evacuation if it was ordered.

2. After passing the Eastern entrance, a magnetic mine was dropped close to the ship. This was reported at once.

3. While patrolling off Calais at 0140/26 three soldiers were picked up from a raft.

4. The decision was made not to evacuate Calais and at 0300/26 the small craft started to withdraw and I assisted *Verity* to escort them back towards Dover. At 0645 dive bombing attacks were made on the two destroyers but no hits were obtained.

5. I anchored in the Downs at 0745/26, disembarked the three soldiers in a hospital boat belonging to H.M.S. *Fervent* and at 1700 returned to Dover.

6. At 0635 May 27th I left Dover with orders to carry out patrol OC.1. and OC.2.

7. At 0904/27 I closed *Mona's Isle* who was full of soldiers and had been heavily machine gunned. Going alongside her I transferred Surgeon Lieutenant Shutte and escorted the ship to Dover, waiting off the breakwater until Surgeon Lieutenant Shutte rejoined. He informed me that he was able to give first aid to nearly all of the wounded and undoubtedly saved many lives.

8. Patrol OC. 1. And OC.2. was resumed at 1515 and continued without incident save the occasional sinking of mines until 1145 28th May. At

this moment the ship was close to No.1. Buoy near the South Goodwin Light Vessel, and was attacked by 15 dive bombers who were supported by 10 fighters.

9. No direct bomb hits were obtained but extensive damage was done to the ship by bomb splinters and machine gun bullets. Wireless was put out of action; D.G. gear shot through in several places; electric leads shot through all over the ship; asdic gear put out of action; the starboard side riddled like a pepper box and 30 casualties.

10. I returned to Dover, landed the casualties and secured alongside *Sandhurst* at 1400.

11. From then until 0930 May 30th, the ship was patched up by the *Sandhurst* and made seaworthy. This was a very trying period as the nerves of my ship's company had been badly affected by the bombing. My Officers and many of the senior ratings worked splendidly to restore our reduced morale, but even so when I sailed at 0930/30 to assist in the evacuation of the B.E.F. from Dunkirk, still with 30 ratings short, I was nervous as to what would be the reactions of my ship's company to further enemy action.

12. The first trip to Dunkirk however completely restored the confidence of the ship's company. By 1330/30 the ship was close inshore off the beaches near La Panne and the soldiers started to embark from small boats. At 1530 Rear Admiral Wake-Walker transferred with his staff from *Hebe* to *Windsor*, but shortly after this the ship was loaded to capacity and so at 1700 the Rear Admiral transferred to the *Worcester*, and the *Windsor* returned to Dover.

13. Thereafter five more trips were made to Dunkirk and in each case the soldiers embarked from the East Pier.

14. I do not intend to describe each trip, because on no occasion did the ship sustain damage or casualties. Each operation although fraught with endless unpleasant possibilities, proved to be simple and entirely free from incident worthy of mention.

15. During the sixth and final trip carried out between 1900 June 2nd and 0100 June 3rd, I found difficulty in getting the ship alongside the east pier as there was a strong set off the pier. However the ship was clear of the harbour one minute before the next destroyer was due to enter.

16. It was impossible to keep an accurate tally of the soldiers embarked but I am confident that an average of 750 was kept to in all six trips.

17. At noon June 4th *Windsor* was ordered to Portsmouth where the ship was docked to repair the damage sustained when we were bombed on 28th May.

WOLSEY
W-class Destroyer
Pennant Number D98
Official Rescue Total: 3,337

The first Royal Navy ship of the name, HMS Wolsey *was ordered on 9 December 1916. Lieutenant Commander Colin Henry Campbell RN was one of the last to complete his* Dynamo *report, on 12 June 1940, the reasons for this he gave thus: 'The delay in forwarding this report is regretted but, firstly, I did not think that reports from individual ships would be required for such a large operation and further, your letter ... was not seen by me until my return from leave on 11th June.' His account continues in this manner:*

2. H.M.S. *Wolsey* was ordered to proceed to Dunkirk at 1913 22nd May. Ship berthed at the Felix Faure jetty and about 200 wounded soldiers (all walking cases). Ship sailed for Dover at 2105, secured to Admiralty Pier at 0140/23 and disembarked wounded, finally securing to buoy at 0230.

3. At 0915/23 *Wolsey* slipped and proceeded to the Downs to instruct Hospital Ships *Isle of Thanet* and *Worthing* to proceed to Dunkirk. Hospital Ships were instructed to stop at Dover for route but as they had not the necessary charts, *Wolsey* had to lead. Ships berthed alongside at Dunkirk at 1430. *Wolsey* embarked approximately 180 Officers and other ranks of the Army G.P.O. and other non-combatants. Ships sailed in company 2045. Hospital Ships were ordered to Newhaven, *Wolsey* secured to Admiralty Pier 2330 and disembarked troops, finally securing to buoy at 0415/24.

4. Friday 24th May *Wolsey* in company with *Windsor* proceeded to Le Havre with demolition parties. On return *Wolsey* was ordered to embark ammunition for Calais. This was cancelled AM Saturday and *Wolsey* proceeded to buoy. On passage to buoy, *Wolsey* fouled mooring cable of fixed buoy of Western Entrance boom and destroyed dome (already reported).

5. At 1445/26 *Wolsey* in company with *Wolfhound* proceeded to Calais and carried out bombardment of the road to Seaward of the Scouring Basin, returning to Dover 1850. At 1930 *Wolsey* was ordered to proceed to Dunkirk to act as W/T link ship. Fog was encountered on passage but *Wolsey* finally secured to Felix Faure jetty 2350. *Wolsey* shifted berth at 0530/27 to allow troop transports to come alongside. Ship remained under way in anchorage but finding communication with Shore signal Station difficult I berthed alongside East Pier 0700. I calculated I could remain there until one hour before Low Water but at 0915 I found water getting shallow, and as Air-Raid began at 0930 I decided to move to

anchorage immediately. In endeavouring to move ship, propellers grounded (reported by signal) and ship was eventually hauled off by French Tug at 1030. Ship proceeded to anchorage and remained there for the rest of the day, maintained V/S touch with the Shore Signal Station with great difficulty due to the dense clouds of smoke and almost continuous Air-Raid. Ship was at Action Stations all day, over 70 rounds per gun being fired. *Wolsey* claims to have brought down one plane, but this is not confirmed. Anchorage was bombed on six occasions but no bombs fell dangerously near *Wolsey*. At about 1800 *Wolfhound* arrived and proceeded alongside. *Wolfhound* and *Wolsey* subsequently anchored as close inshore as possible and embarked troops. Both ships anchored as close inshore as possible and embarked troops. Both ships sailed for Dover at 0100/28 *Wolsey* bringing back approximately 150 troops.

6. During the morning of 28th May *Wolsey* oiled and ammunitioned ship. At 1850 *Wolsey* proceeded to Bray beach by route 'Y' arriving there at 2300. Boats were immediately lowered and embarkation of troops began. *Wolsey* sailed at 0400 for Dover with 500 troops on board. At 1100/29 *Wolsey* was ordered in company with *Vivacious* and *Vimy* to proceed to Sheerness. Ship sailed from Sheerness at 1830 for Operation F.D. This operation was cancelled by Admiralty and *Wolsey* returned to Dover. Ship remained alongside while one rating injured by berthing wire was discharged to Hospital and proceeded to Dunkirk at 0615/30. *Wolsey* secured alongside East Pier Dunkirk at 0915 and embarked approximately 800 troops. *Wolsey* returned to Dover disembarked troops, and again proceeded to Dunkirk at 1525. *Wolsey* again secured to East Pier and embarked 1060 troops returning to Dover at 2235. Troops disembarked *Wolsey* oiled and proceeded to Bray beach at 0600. Colonel Blake R.A.M.C and Medical Stores were embarked before proceeding. At 0703 *Wolsey* was in collision with S.S. *Roebuck* (Already reported). *Wolsey* proceeded alongside East Pier Dunkirk, disembarked Colonel Blake and stores then proceeded to Bray Beach. After being there two hours and embarking 40 troops I was ordered by *Codrington* to proceed alongside. Secured alongside, embarked 500 troops, returned to Dover at 18 knots, disembarked troops, and at 1830 slipped from Admiralty Pier and returned to Dunkirk. Whilst inside Dunkirk Harbour and proceeding alongside East Pier *Wolsey* D.G. Coil fused and caught fire. This may have been caused by a shell splinter as Dunkirk was being shelled at the time. While 600 troops were being embarked the electric light party endeavoured to repair the D.G. coil. At 2330 the E.A. reported to me that he had done all he could and that the coil was 30 per cent efficient. I considered the risk justifiable and having announced repairs completed, sailed for Dover. Either the coil in the condition was efficient

against Magnetic Mines or *Wolsey* was lucky and the passage was made safely. The Phosphorescence was extremely noticeable and several aircraft were heard, so *Wolsey* proceeded at 12 knots for the first hour and a half. *Wolsey* secured alongside Admiralty Wharf 0425 and disembarked troops, subsequently securing to buoy to effect repairs to D.G. coil. At 1300 *Wolsey* reported ready for sea and at 1600 *Wolsey* was ordered to proceed to Portsmouth for repairs.

Lieutenant Commander Campbell appended the 'following report of circumstances in which H.M. Ship under my Command was in collision with S.S. Roebuck *at about 0705 on Friday, 31st May 1940':*

H.M.S. *Wolsey* was proceeding to Dunkirk via route "X" and shortly before entering Dunkirk approach channel, S.S. *Roebuck* was observed by me about 1 mile on port bow steering a roughly parallel course.

Wolsey altered round No. 5.W.Buoy and at 0701½ steadied on the new course, 090° about 100 yards to East of No.6.W.Buoy and close to it. S.S. *Roebuck* was then sighted on the port bow about 6-7 cables distant, entering the approach channel between Nos. 5 and 7 W. buoys and steering a course nearly at right angles to the channel.

I held my course and speed and S.S. *Roebuck* came right across the channel across my bows. When it was seen that collision was imminent, I ordered Full Speed Astern both, and then Hard a Starboard, sounding 3 blasts. This appeared to cause S.S. *Roebuck* to sight me for the first time and she altered to port. Collision was nearly avoided, the large iron-bound rubbing strake of S.S. *Roebuck* causing most of the damage to *Wolsey*.

WORCESTER
W-class Destroyer
Pennant Number D96
Official Rescue Total: 4,545

A modified W-Class destroyer, HMS Worcester *was ordered from J.S. White at Cowes on the Isle of Wight in April 1918. Launched on 24 October 1919, she was the eighth Royal Navy warship to carry the name that had been introduced in 1651 for a forty-eight-gun ship which was, ironically, later renamed* Dunkirk. *Commander John Hamilton Allison RN's 'report of operations off Dunkirk' was completed at Tilbury on 7 June 1940:*

Having proceeded at maximum speed (26½ knots) with fuel available from a position about 120 miles north of Lands End, *Worcester* arrived off Dover at 0715 on the 28th May. Then on account of reduced fuel I was forced to make the passage to Dunkirk by "Y" Channel at a speed of 18 knots ...

On journey 1 attempts were made to refuel from *Anthony* but only 10 tons was taken on board. The return journey was made at 15 knots leaving less than 5 tons on board on arrival at Dover. Numerous enemy aircraft made towards the ship during the afternoon but all were driven off by gunfire. Destroyers astern were seen to be bombed. Attacked possible S/M off West Hinden Light Buoy. 1 pattern of depth charges. Result – wreckage but no oil.

Fuel was taken in before journey 2 (Route X both ways) which took place without incident except for a heavy bombing attack on East Pier while embarking troops. The continuation of this attack subsequently sunk the *Grenade* 10 minutes after leaving the pier.

Journey 3. (Route X both ways). Troops were embarked from boats off Bray. All ships boats were left behind. Very few enemy aircraft approached the ship on this trip and any that looked dangerous were driven off by gunfire.

Journey 4. Sailed on route Z but altered back to route X on receiving information of enemy shelling on Z. It was expected to embark troops from the beaches again but was ordered to carry R.A. Dover and Staff until dawn. A full load was taken from boats at La Panne and Bray after his departure. On return X channel was taken at dead low water and owing to rounding No.5 Buoy Dunkirk roads too close, grounded on a shoal 337° 2.5 cables from that buoy. When the ship was refloated it was discovered that 18-20knots was the maximum safe speed.

Occasional firing was carried out on enemy aircraft in the vicinity during the evening of 30th May.

Journey 5. As soon as ship had refuelled and had the propellers examined by divers, a passage was made at 18 knots to the beaches which were reached at dusk on 31st May.

East Pier was full at this time and it was evident that difficulty was being experienced in getting men to the minesweepers already at the beaches. I visited all the beaches in turn and finally anchoring at La Panne. The minesweepers further inshore were getting small loads but none came the greater distance to *Worcester*. At dawn *Worcester* came under shell fire from shore batteries and I decided to slip the cable and proceed to East Pier where a full load of troops was embarked.

Journey 6. June 1st. On approaching C channel about 1500 in the vicinity of No.5 buoy, two recent wrecks of transports were sighted; small craft and destroyers were picking up survivors. A few survivors were picked up. At this time a signal was received from V.A. Dover to return to harbour forthwith. It seemed, however, not worthwhile to return so close from Dunkirk and so I continued my course through the roads where some French soldiers were picked up from an open boat and the crew of a small service motor launch which had broken down.

On arrival at Dunkirk I was ordered to go to West Pier. I deemed this inadvisable and said no. Also it was suggested that I should pick up French soldiers from the beach inside the harbour. Without boats this was impracticable.

Alongside East Pier a full load was taken, but not before I had cast off and returned owing to a misunderstanding. While alongside, a hulk two cables east from the pier was heavily bombed by two waves of dive bombers. The second attack was in progress as I left the pier and aircraft were engaged by the entire armament. Dive bomber attacks on leaving Dunkirk.

During the next half hour the ship was attacked by successive waves of dive bombers consisting of three or four squadrons of about nine each.

The first attack took place in Dunkirk roads where avoiding action was not possible. The maximum available speed was 19 knots. In this attack about half the bombs dropped were time delay and the nearest appeared to be about 50 yards away. Although the ship was lifted in the water a number of times no structural damage was done.

Succeeding attacks took place in the channel leading northward from No.5 buoy. In these attacks the majority of the bombs burst on impact with the water and caused great damage to personnel. Some of these dropped as near as 10 yards.

In all it is estimated that over 100 bombs were dropped near the ship.

Attacks were pressed well home even down to 200 or 300 feet and it can be said that the bombing was accurate, only a miracle preventing the ship being struck. After releasing bombs the aircraft fired their guns, but it seemed without great accuracy.

Throughout these attacks the behaviour of the gun crews was magnificent. A heavy volume of fire was kept up all the time except at short intervals when death or wounds prevented a crew from functioning.

Two aircraft were certainly shot down and probably three.

Six Bren guns were found to be a useful addition to the armament.

By my order men were told to lie down whenever possible and on the bridge this was done whenever bombs were seen to be released until after they had exploded. The only man killed on the bridge was Sub. Lieut. Humphreys who was standing up firing a Bren gun.

A number of casualties occurred when an H.E. shell in the rack was detonated by a splinter outside the sickbay.

As a result of this action there were 46 dead and 180 injured on board and numbers of splinter holes all over the ship. Those in oil fuel tanks subsequently stopped the ship about five miles from the North Goodwin light vessel. Others wrecked electrical circuits including the D.C. gear, and the gyro compass. Only three holes were found below the water line.

Five miles from the North Goodwin, water in the fuel tanks caused stoppage of main engines and the Tug *St. Olaive* [*St. Olaves*] was signalled to take us in tow. However after three quarters of an hour engines were reported ready and course was shaped for Dover.

Entering the inner harbour about 2030 Worcester collided with S.S. *Maid of Orleans* on the way out. I attribute this largely to the loss of manoeuvring power both of screws and rudder from damage sustained in recent operations.

In an appendix attached to his report, Commander Allison noted the following 'expenditure of ammunition off Dunkirk': a) 266 rounds of 4.7" H.E. (fuzed); b) 360 rounds Pom Pom H.E. (graze fuze); c) 6 depth charges; and d) 10,000 rounds of .303 ammunition. He added that about 35% of a), 75% of b) and 50% of d) had been expended during Journey 6.

Chapter 2

Royal Navy Warships

ALBURY
Hunt-class Minesweeper
Pennant Number J41
Official Rescue Total: 1,536

Launched in the First World War, but not commissioned in time to see active service, HMS Albury was commanded by Lieutenant Commander Colin Henry Corbet-Singleton during Operation Dynamo. Corbet-Singleton, who would be awarded the Distinguished Service Cross and the Croix de Guerre for his part in the evacuation, completed his narrative on 9 June 1940:

I left Harwich at noon on May 28th in company with the Fifth Minesweeping Flotilla, arrived off Zudecotte Beach at 2130 and, anchoring as close as possible, sent boats inshore to embark troops. The rate of embarkation was then slow as the tide was low and a small surf was troublesome on the beach. The troops were in good spirits though short of rations; I landed a quantity of dry provisions in the skiff.

About 2330 a bomb was seen to drop about one mile to seaward of the ship, but no interference was caused to the work in hand.

At 0230 on May 29th I got under way and proceeded without incident to Margate, where the troops were disembarked.

I then returned to Zudecotte, arriving there at 1930 on May 29th; a considerable amount of bombing was in progress. On arrival the roads were fairly empty, as we had passed, on the way, a number of loaded ships returning.

I made towards a burning Paddle-steamer, which had grounded and, being full of troops and survivors, appeared to be in a bad way. All boats and Carley floats were sent away and many survivors were picked up. Bombs were being dropped continually around the ship and the

Paddle-steamer during this operation, and two Machine-gun attacks were carried out. I have nothing but the utmost praise for all concerned, the majority of whom are very young and had certainly never been in action before. Continual anti-aircraft fire was kept up by the Twelve Pounder. I sent a signal for Fighter assistance, which arrived later in the evening.

Fifty seven cot-cases alone were brought off, mostly suffering from severe burns; the Commanding Officer and other survivors from His Majesty's Destroyer *Grenade* were amongst those embarked. After having cleared the steamer out as far as was known, I proceeded down the coast towards Bray, and picked up troops from several boats, which they had found on the beach. A Captain Churchill, from the Headquarters Staff, came off and told me that he had to get over to England to see his uncle, the Prime Minister, by 0600.

I proceeded to Margate, arriving at 0530 on May 30th, disembarked troops, survivors and Captain Churchill, then sailed for Sheerness for coal and ammunition.

I left Sheerness at 0300 on May 31st and arrived without incident off the beach just to the East of Dunkirk, at 0930. The rate of embarkation was slow owing to considerable surf on the beach, but valuable assistance was given by a large power boat. It was necessary for me to leave at 1230 in order to unload and be at my rendezvous by 2200 on May 31st for the evening operations.

I sailed from Margate to comply with previous instructions and proceeded, under the orders of the Senior Officer of the Fifth Minesweeping Flotilla, to my appointed station off the beach; navigation at this period was difficult, as the absence of wind allowed the smoke from Dunkirk to settle over the channel, so that visibility was poor. On anchoring at 2345 a shell from a shore battery landed about a cable to seaward; this was repeated spasmodically. Reports were then received of magnetic mines being dropped in the channel.

About 0230 the Flotilla was ordered to carry on embarkation, using ships' boats. Shortly after dawn a bombing attack took place, and from then on these attacks were practically continuous. Several Heinkel 111 type aircraft were observed, but the majority of the attackers were identified as Junkers 87 dive-bombers. Embarkation was carried out, though the rate was slow.

His Majesty's Ship *Speedwell* was seen to be aground; a wire was passed and I towed her off. During this operation the ship came under machine-gun fire from the air, and great credit is due to my First Lieutenant for the speed and coolness with which he carried out the evolution.

I then received orders from the Flag Officer afloat to proceed alongside in Dunkirk harbour, and to complete landing with troops there. As troops were being embarked, bombs were dropped in the harbour and a machine-gun attack was delivered, but no casualties were incurred.

Just before I slipped, with a full load of troops on board, His Majesty's Destroyer *Ivanhoe* was hit by a bomb outside the harbour. Two ships went to her assistance, so I proceeded at full speed.

While leaving the channel and coming up to the Breedt bank, the most intense bombing attacks were experienced. Repeated near misses were registered on His Majesty's Ship *Gossamer*, ahead of me. His Majesty's Destroyer *Havant*, who had just overtaken me, was hit in the vicinity of number Three gun; continuing at high speed, she described a large circle to starboard, and when last seen was steaming in a Southerly direction. Near misses were also registered on His Majesty's Ship *Albury*; Fighter assistance was requested.

These bombers came in relays and pursued the ship well out to sea. The Twelve pounder was kept in action the whole time, and it was very noticeable that if fire was withheld until aircraft approaching from astern were close, they were forced to sheer off and go round again. Effective use was made of Lewis and Bren guns, the latter obtained from and manned by the troops.

I proceeded to Sheerness, landed the troops, replenished supplies of coal and ammunition, and sailed for Dunkirk at 1600, on June 2nd.

On arrival in Dunkirk harbour at 0015 on June 3rd, I went alongside the Eastern arm. French troops were embarked, though there did not appear to be many waiting, and it was necessary to send along the jetty towards the town to collect them. During the time that His Majesty's Ship *Albury* was alongside, intermittent shelling was taking place, apparently directed at the harbour and ships alongside. I sailed eventually about 0215 with two hundred troops on board.

While returning I encountered a floating mine off "U" buoy, which I reported to you. It was slightly conical in shape, and from its appearance might have been a Dutch mine. I sank it and proceeded to Sheerness to land the troops and to coal.

I sailed again for Dunkirk at 1630 on June 3rd in company with His Majesty's Ships *Gossamer* and *Leda*, and was detached off "W" buoy to act independently, in order to arrive at the harbour at 0020 on June 4th. I was ordered alongside the West pier, filled up with French soldiers, and left the harbour at 0130.

Fog was encountered between "U" buoy and the North Goodwin Light-vessel, and I overtook His Majesty's Ship *Leda*, who had been in collision; I stood by her until relieved by His Majesty's Ship *Kellett*.

In the vicinity of the Elbow buoy, the French Auxiliary Naval Vessel *Emile Deschamps*, crowded with troops and refugees, was passed. I was about five cables ahead of her, and signalling her the course to the North Goodwin Light-vessel, which she had missed, when she blew up and sank within half a minute. I turned to pick up survivors, and reported to you that she had been sunk by a mine.

The London Fire Brigade Fire-float *Massey Shaw* was on the spot and assisted with the rescue work. During the operation the Master of this vessel informed me quite confidently that he had seen a periscope shortly before the explosion, so I sent out an Enemy Submarine report. I proceeded to Margate with the survivors, forty of whom, men and women, were severely wounded, and landed them with the troops.

The morale, courage, and endurance shewn by all on board during this period, was exceptional, an encouraging fact as the average age is very low. Sub-Lieutenant F.R.A. Turnball R.N. did excellent work on the beach with the boats, and Sub-Lieutenant B.P. Cahill R.N.V.R. spent long hours on the bridge with unremitting attention to duty.

SPECIAL MENTIONS

Lieutenant J.R. Gower R.N. – the First Lieutenant, by his coolness and courage was an inspiration to the Ship's Company. This Officer's services were invaluable, and by his cheerfulness and boundless energy he set a very high example to all ratings working on the Upper deck.

Commissioned Engineer L.J. Brading R.N. – the Engineer Officer, kept his engines working at full speed for hours at a stretch, when it was necessary, and also kept his department working and happy. He was of invaluable assistance on the upper deck, organizing the disposal of the wounded, and traffic in general, and by his cheerful manner and good power of command was of the greatest help to the First Lieutenant.

Chief Petty Officer F.R. Wills, D/J96305 – was untiring in his efforts throughout the six days, as Chief Boatswain's Mate, Coxswain of a boat, Officer of the quarters at the Twelve pounder during intensive dive-bombing attacks, and was of great assistance to the First Lieutenant, when refloating His Majesty's Ship *Speedwell*. His example was reacted in the seamen throughout the ship.

Chief Engine Room Artificer L.H. Earley, P/MX53797 – is recommended for unremitting devotion to duty, below, during the whole period, during which time both thrust bearings required constant attention, and, but for his efforts the Main Engines could not have been worked.

Leading Cook G.M. Bowman, D/MX50163 – did excellent work as one of the ship's First Aid staff. With little experience he was always ready to dress wounds, make tea, supply comforts to all onboard and when not thus employed, was always ready to lend a hand on deck.

Leading Stoker C. Davies, C/KX8017 – was outstanding in the ship's Whaler and untiring in his efforts to help with the wounded on the upper deck and in hoisting boats.

Acting Leading Stoker F. Putt, D/KX84370 – for untiring and excellent service in the ship's Cutter Gig. He was of great assistance when his boat became overturned and swamped, and was directly responsible for saving the lives of several soldiers, by jumping in and cutting their equipment off them.

Both these men carried out these duties in addition to their normal Engine Room duties, over a period of six days.

Canteen Manager A. Harris – this man who had only been at sea for a month, did magnificent work throughout the six days, was continually supplying comforts, food and necessities to the troops and wounded, and was invaluable in the First Aid Station, though the work obviously revolted him and made him very sick.

Chief Petty Officer C. Carr, D/J95908 – as Coxswain of His Majesty's Ship *Albury* was most useful in attending the wounded and assisting in the First Aid Stations. In addition he was at the wheel for long periods and carried out his duties in a most efficient manner.

CALCUTTA
C-class Light Cruiser
Pennant Number D82
Official Rescue Total: 1,856

Ordered from by Armstrong's at Newcastle in June 1917, the C-class light cruiser HMS Calcutta *was laid down on 18 October 1917. Launched on 9 July 1918, her build was completed on 21 August 1919. After 1927 HMS* Calcutta, *the fifth Royal Navy warship to carry the name, was placed in Reserve and used for the training of Boy Seamen.*

In August 1938 work began at Chatham Dockyard to convert HMS Calcutta *into an anti-aircraft cruiser. This conversion involved the removal of all guns and torpedo tubes, followed by the fitting of eight QF 4-inch Mk.XVI naval guns in four twin mounts, a close-in armament of a quadruple 2-pounder pom-pom and two quadruple Vickers .50 machine-guns mounts. The refit was completed in July 1939.*

Having only taken over command of HMS Calcutta *on 18 March 1940, Captain Dennis Marescaux Lees's report is dated 6 June 1940. In his opening comments, Lees described his ships involvement in the evacuation as a 'minor part', adding that 'in view of the vast number of reports which you will receive, it has been made as brief as possible in the form of a chronological time table of events with covering remarks at the end':*

Monday, 27th May
2310 Sailed from Trinity Bay, The Downs for La Panne.

Tuesday, 28th May
0115 Loud explosion about 5 cables on starboard beam probably from torpedo fired by enemy submarine or M.T.B.
0125 Torpedo track crossing from port to starboard missed ship about 100 yards astern.
0135 M.T.B. heard and vaguely sighted bearing Green 60°. Ship manoeuvred under large helm. No subsequent torpedo tracks or explosions seen or heard.
0248 Anchored in position 005° La Panne, air light, 3'10 Motor Cutter and both whalers sent in to beach to commence evacuation into paddle mine sweepers *Sandown* and *Gracie Fields* who were much closer inshore. *Grafton*, *Greyhound* and *Impulsive* also evacuating from this beach.
0500 Opened fire on one Heinkel.
0523 Opened fire on one Ju 88.
0615 *Impulsive* ordered to proceed to Dunkirk and go alongside East pier.
0621 Opened fire on 3 Heinkels.
0625 Evacuation of beach completed. *Grafton* and *Greyhound* proceeded. Paddle Minesweepers *Sandown* and *Gracie Fields* ordered alongside to disembark their 700 troops into *Calcutta*.
0641 Opened fire on 1 Heinkel.
0715 Weighed and proceeded to Sheerness.
1215 Arrived Sheerness, disembarked 700 troops and completed with oil fuel and provisions.
1710 Slipped from buoy and proceeded to La Panne.
2157 Anchored in position 014½° La Panne Air Light, 2'.6 Boats sent in to the same beach as had been used previously. Heavy surf running and conditions for embarking troops extremely difficult. Only one Schoot to assist in embarkation of about 70 wounded.

Wednesday, 29th May
0300 All wounded that could be moved evacuated into Schoot or ship's boats all of which returned to *Calcutta*.
        Schoot with a certain number of wounded, sent back to

England as she was nearly unmanageable with her steering gear in a precarious state.

0345 Boats sent in again to collect more troops as they arrived and if possible to connect with Lord Gort in view of your message 0127/29th May.

Officer in charge of *Calcutta*'s boats, Mr. F.J. March, Gunner, made personal contact with Lord Gort about 8 miles inland, and placed *Calcutta* at his disposal for his or his staff's evacuation. Lord Gort courteously refused to be evacuated at this stage.

0430 One of *Calcutta*'s whalers lost.

0520 Opened fire on one Dornier.

0710 *Calcutta*'s boats returned with more troops and sent in again to La Panne with relief crews.

0735 *Sutton* alongside to disembark her troops into *Calcutta* and return close inshore opposite La Panne.

0810 *Salamander* alongside and as for *Sutton* above.

1210 Party of tugs and drifters towing own boats sighted, proceeding homewards full of troops. All ordered alongside *Calcutta* to disembark their troops and return to La Panne for more.

1227 *Java* towing launch alongside.

1228 *Golden Sunbeam* towing launch alongside.

1230 *Lord Rodney* alongside.

1237 *Lord Keith* towing launch alongside.

1247 *Lord St. Vincent* alongside.

1250 *Lord Collingwood* alongside.

1335 Captain (D) 1st D/F, who was senior officer at La Panne at this time, informed that tugs and drifters were being sent in to load up again.

1350 *Calcutta*'s boats returned to ship.

1357 Weighed.

1900 Arrived Sheerness. Disembarked 1000 troops and completed with oil fuel and ammunition.

Friday, 31st May

1940 Slipped from buoy at Sheerness.

2130 Anchored off East Margate buoy with *Mallard* and *Shearwater* in company.

Saturday, 1st June

0315 Weighed and proceeded with *Mallard* and *Shearwater*.

0500 Commenced patrolling on X route between W and Y buoys.

0938 Ordered to return to Sheerness.

1015 Opened fire on one Heinkel who had attacked and damaged *Mosquito*. Heinkel shot down.
1018 Opened fire on two more Heinkels diving from broken clouds.
1024 Detached *Shearwater* to stand by *Mosquito*.
1312 Anchored off Nore Light Vessel.
2015 Weighed.
2140 Anchored off East Margate Buoy, *Mallard* and *Shearwater* in company.

Sunday, 2nd June 1940
0245 Weighed and proceeded with *Mallard* and *Shearwater*.
0430 Commenced patrolling in vicinity of W buoy.
     French destroyers *Epervier* [*Épervier*] and *Leopard* at U and V buoys respectively.
0710 Last homeward bound ship passed W buoy.
1035 Attacked by 3 Ju 88 diving from out of the sun.
     4 bombs very close on port beam.
     4 bombs very close on port bow.
     4 bombs missed well ahead.
     French destroyers left patrol.
1050 Attacked by 1 Heinkel dive bombing. 4 bombs missed well out on starboard beam.
1140 Attacked by 1 Heinkel with machine gun from 4,000 ft.
1155 Attacked by 1 Ju 88 who would not come through *Calcutta*'s barrage and dropped 4 bombs well astern.
1350 Orders received to return to Sheerness.
1459 *Mallard* detached to stand by Hospital Ship *Worthing* who had been bombed and damaged.
1644 Anchored off Nore Light Vessel to make good condenser trouble and slight damage from near misses.

Monday, 3rd June
0510 Weighed.
0550 Secured to buoy at Sheerness. Discovered further condenser trouble and serious cloud in all reserve feed tanks. All defects made good by 1400 on Tuesday, 4th June.

During the period at la Panne, *Calcutta* had to lie too far from the beach to be of any use for direct embarkation of troops so the principle adopted was to order any small ships alongside when they were full, disembark their troops into *Calcutta* and return close inshore for another load.

In the two salvoes each of 4 bombs which fell very close to *Calcutta* on Sunday 2nd June it appeared that one bomb in each salvo had a delay action and burst some way under the water whereas the other three burst on impact.

The conduct and behaviour of my ship's company and of the military forces evacuated has been exemplary throughout.

DWARF
Submarine Tender
Pennant Number T92
Official Rescue Total: -

Commanded by Sub-Lieutenant D.A. Hare, the submarine tender HMS Dwarf *was normally based at Gosport as part of the 5th Submarine Flotilla. Hare's account is dated 6 June 1940:*

I have the honour to report the following proceedings of H.M.S. *Dwarf* in connection with evacuation of the B.E.F. from Dunkirk.

H.M.S. *Dwarf* sailed from Portsmouth 2100 on Wednesday 29th May 1940 for Ramsgate. During the passage there was nothing of interest to note, and *Dwarf* arrived at 1700 on Thursday 30th May.

After provisioning, coaling and embarking two Lewis guns, *Dwarf* sailed for Dunkirk at 2000 using route "X".

At about 0030 on Friday *Dwarf* was some 6 miles North West of Dunkirk, so waited till daylight, before attempting to enter the buoyed channel to Dunkirk. During the passage up the channel a formation of German reconnaissance aeroplanes appeared overhead. Every ship in the vicinity, as well as the soldiers on the beach, opened fire. *Dwarf's* starboard Lewis gunner registered several tracer bullets in one of the machines which turned away to the South.

On reaching Dunkirk *Dwarf* was ordered by a destroyer to proceed to La Panne. However, after steaming for about ¾ mile the motor barge *Viking* hailed for assistance. She had 150 soldiers on board, and in attempting to get off the beach, burnt out her clutches. She could now only go in the astern direction. At the time there was a fresh North West wind and rising tide, as well as several wrecks and ships at anchor, which made operations in order to get her in tow very difficult.

Dwarf got alongside *Viking* and took off 34 soldiers to relieve the congestion. *Dwarf* then towed *Viking* closer to the beach with a view to lying alongside her while at anchor and embark more soldiers. The tow rope parted before this object could be achieved. She drifted towards the beach so I told her to anchor. The water under her was too shallow for *Dwarf* to go alongside.

Due to the danger both vessels were facing I decided to take *Viking* in tow and make for Ramsgate. During the proceedings of taking her in tow, the tow rope fouled my rudder and could not be cleared.

About half way back on the return journey I signalled the A/S Trawler *Olvina* [*Olivina*] to take her in tow as I was only making good about 2½ knots. *Dwarf* then proceeded alone towards Ramsgate.

No other boats were entering Ramsgate at the time due to the state of the tide, so I followed the rest of the shipping to Dover, arriving at 2000. *Dwarf* anchored off the harbour until 2130, then proceeded to the North end of the Military Jetty to disembark the soldiers.

I now had to wait until dawn to clear my rudder and take on more provisions and ammunition. *Dwarf* sailed again for Dunkirk at 0800 on Saturday 1st June.

At 1500, when 2 miles North West of the buoyed channel to Dunkirk, shore batteries at Gravelines opened fire. I turned round to wait until dark before attempting to go in. However, only about ½ hour later a formation of Heinkel bombers appeared. They split up and dived on a small armada.

Two bombers dived towards *Dwarf* on the starboard side and dropped six bombs, all of which missed by feet. They turned round, machine-gunned the ship and bombed a second time.

During this machine gun attack my Coxswain P.O. [*illegible*] was shot in both legs by a bullet which ricocheted off the temporary protection rigged over the bridge before sailing from Portsmouth. This second bomb attack damaged the steering engine. I now took over the wheel and zig-zagged towards a group of small boats which had been sunk to pick up survivors.

Before I could reach them one Heinkel bomber dived down and dropped a large bomb, or possibly several smaller ones, which exploded very close to the starboard quarter. This explosion "lifted the ship right out of the water". The force of impact on returning to the water cracked the main circulator, damaged both engines, and the starboard boiler which was due to the escape of steam in the Engine Room. The Stoker on watch lashed the circulator up with a piece of rope and got out of the Engine Room on account of the steam.

The engines were now only just moving and making a deafening noise. They would only move for a few more minutes, so I hailed a Drifter to take me in tow. The Main Stop was shut and the fires drawn.

While being towed we were once again attacked and the bombs, as on previous occasions, just missed.

117

Just before dusk the bombers disappeared the Chief Mechanician went round the ship to see if there were any leaks. There were two minor leaks – one in the Engine room, the other in the Capstan Flat.

The Drifter anchored with *Dwarf* astern, about 4½ miles E.N.E. of Ramsgate at 2300 to wait for the tide. The drifter wirelessed for medical assistance but could not get in touch with the shore station. At about 0030 on Sunday 2nd June a small motor boat passed close to *Dwarf* on her way into Ramsgate with a full load of soldiers. I hailed her to send for medical assistance on reaching harbour. At about 0400 a Doctor arrived and took my Coxswain with him.

The Drifter proceeded towards the harbour at 0500 with *Dwarf* in tow. The tow was cast off and *Dwarf* laid alongside a French Trawler until a tug was sent out to take the ship into Ramsgate inner harbour.

On Monday forenoon I handed H.M.S. *Dwarf* over to the Naval Officer-in-Charge at Ramsgate, and proceeded with the crew to Portsmouth.

There is a separate short report attached to Hare's account. Dated 9 June 1940, and having the title 'Gallantry in Action – Dunkirk Evacuation', it was written by Lieutenant Commander A.R.W. Sayle RNR:

I have the honour to inform you that it was reported to me by the Sub-Lieutenant R.N. (name unknown) in command of H.M.S. *Dwarf* tender to the Submarine Depot, Portsmouth, that the coxswain of the *Dwarf*, although shot through both knees when under heavy machine gun fire, remained at his post of duty refusing to be relieved and later refusing "morphine" although in considerable pain. I understand this coxswain is now in Ramsgate Hospital; the Sub-Lieutenant has now returned to Fort Blockhouse.

GOSSAMER
Halcyon-class Minesweeper
Pennant Number J63
Official Rescue Total: 3,169

Authorised as part of the 1936 naval programme, the Halcyon-class minesweeper HMS Gossamer was laid down on 2 November 1936. Built by William Hamilton & Co. Ltd, she was launched on 5 October the following year. From 21 February 1940, Gossamer's captain was Commander Richard Cyril Vesey Ross RN, who, in a long naval career, had witnessed the scuttling of the German High Seas Fleet at Scapa Flow in 1919. The following account was written by Ross, who was subsequently awarded the Distinguished Service Order for his part in the evacuation from Dunkirk as the CO of the 5th Minesweeping Flotilla:

I have the honour to submit the following despatch on the operations of H.M. Ship *Gossamer* under my command during the evacuation of Dunkirk, for the information of Their Lordships.

We made six trips in all, and transported, as accurately as can be ascertained, 3214 British and French troops to this country. A list of recommendation for awards is appended. At the same time the entire ship's company did as much to deserve a medal as those few I was able to single out.

When this operation is compared with the glorious feat at Zeebrugge in 1918, I am inclined to believe that it imposed greater strain on the officers and men. This was particularly so due to the constant repetition in the belief that each trip was the last. Again there were the long hours off the beaches in momentary expectation of the arrival of enemy aircraft (an expectation which was seldom disappointed). Then the six hour passage home with constant reports of the presence of enemy M.T.B.'s on the route, and in the knowledge that we had six or seven hundred souls on board and no boats whatsoever.

Gossamer sailed from Harwich at 1230 on 28th May, 1940, in company with H.M. Ships *Kellett, Albury, Ross, Lydd, Pangbourne* and *Leda*. H.M.S. *Saltash* was left in the Tyne boiler cleaning. The flotilla arrived at Zuidcote Pass at 2030 and stopped off Bray at 2115. There appeared to be a large wood close to the shore but on approaching nearer this was seen to be a mass of troops on the sand. Two ships were left there and the remainder proceeded to the East Pier at Dunkirk which at that time was intact.

As it was low water it took half an hour to embark troops down improvised ladders, but *Gossamer* sailed at 2215 with 420 on board. From now on it was impossible to exercise control over the flotilla as a unit, and this narrative is concerned with *Gossamer* alone.

Just outside the Zuidcote Pass, we came upon the *Manxman* aground, and S.S. *Prague* stopped, without charts. *Manxman* was given directions, and a boat was sent to *Prague* with a chart of Dunkirk. As will be seen this delay saved our lives.

Proceeding towards Kwint Buoy we soon came into a patch of water filled with men crying "Help!", and heads could be seen all around in the sea. I stopped and lowered boats (three whalers and a skiff). I was then hailed by Commander R.L. Fisher of H.M.S. *Wakeful* who said he had been torpedoed and that the Submarine was still nearby. In actual fact I believe he was attacked by an M.T.B. But my boats and almost all my officers were now lost in the night, and it took some time to recover them with such few men as they had been able to pick up. The skiff was left alongside a drifter. No doubt we were wrong to stop, but at the time I thought otherwise. We then steered so as to avoid Kwint Buoy, and proceeded without further incident to Dover, arriving there at 0655 on Wednesday 29th May.

Ship sailed from Dover at 0850 on 29th May, did a day's minesweeping and arrived off Dunkirk, lit by the red flames of the burning oil tanks, at 0040 on 30th May. On this occasion troops were embarked off Bray Dune in our own boats and canvas punts. There were no incidents of note, and we sailed at 0515, arriving Dover at 1015 on Thursday morning. All boats were left on the beach by order of the Rear Admiral, Dover.

Third trip. Sailing from Dover at 1330 with a party of signalmen for La Panne, we arrived off Bray at 1830. Admiral Wake Walker came on board for passage to La Panne, where we transferred him to H.M.S. *Worcester* and anchored at 1930. I can recall no features of this trip, which was eclipsed by the incidents of the following one. We proceeded at 0118 and arrived Dover at 0600.

Fourth trip. In order to comply with Vice Admiral Dover's 0400/31 12 hours were spent at Dover. A small motor-boat, the *Handy Billy* [*Handy Billie*], was requisitioned. We left at 1800 and anchored as ordered, one mile west of La Panne and four cables from the shore, at 1207.

Sub-Lieutenant M. Phipps proceeded to search the shore in *Handy Billy* and reported no answer to his hails. Inside an hour, however, the situation had changed, and thousands were massing abreast the ship. I called for more boats by searchlight up and down the coast, and was eventually much assisted by H.M.S. *Ivanhoe* who lent me a motor-boat. The vital need now was for more boats. About this time Lieutenant-Commander McLelland swam off from shore with a message for V.A. Dover which he was just able to gasp out before collapsing. The troops had been forced out of La Panne and were marching West. We also embarked a Major, 2nd in Command 2nd Coldstream Guards, and on his advice ordered the bulk of the troops to move West of Dunkirk in small groups.

I decided to remain where I was and to embark the wounded and such troops as refused to move on. *Ivanhoe* remained with me.

At this time a paddle minesweeper most gallantly grounded herself close inshore to save as many as possible. I do not know her name.

At 0500 as I had expected a flight of Messerschmitt 109's appeared from Eastward, flew over the beaches and sprayed ships and men with machine-gun fire. The silvery tracer bullets were clearly visible in the morning light. Our fire did something to disperse these machines and casualties did not appear to be heavy.

At 0600 Captain (D) in H.M.S. *Codrington* asked me my intentions and as I had 675 troops on board I replied I was proceeding. He ordered me to Dunkirk to "fill up".

On our way there we went alongside H.M.S. *Skipjack* who required 8 oz. chloroform. We then berthed East Arm just beyond the break and very quickly embarked some 170 French troops. The enemy was now bombing the town and massing off the harbour entrance. As I went astern *Ivanhoe* was hit whilst steaming full speed past the pier head. We set course west, and were about to turn north at 5 W Buoy when we were attacked by some five Junkers 87 dive bombers. These were followed by nine or ten others a few minutes later. It was at this time that H.M.S. *Havant* was hit. During these attacks I attribute our escape to the coolness and precision with which Lieutenant P.F. Manisty and Yeoman of Signals J. Young (C/JX 131436) observed each aircraft as it turned to the attack, and assisted me in handling the ship. The salvoes of four small bombs and one large one fell very close; on two occasions it was only our swing during the flight of the bombs that saved us.

The 0.5" machine-gun fired until all the force springs fell off. The 4" guns were hampered by the swing of the ship.

This was a most trying time for the troops between decks who could not tell whether or not we were hit. A great deal was done to calm them by P.O. Steward A. Hockney (L 14824) who actually sat on the ladder to the messdeck and sang to the soldiers.

This was between 0840 and 0850 on Saturday June 1st. There were no further incidents. Our own fighters passed us about 0915 and we arrived at Sheerness at 1345.

It was now necessary to replenish ammunition. Signs of exhaustion were beginning to show. I may say as evidence of our fatigue that I myself burst into tears in the staff office on shore. It was too late to send us back that night and sleep did much to restore us.

There were two more trips after this, on the nights of Sunday 2nd and Monday 3rd June, both to the harbour. There was some shrapnel on the first occasion, but on the Monday all went smoothly. On both nights M.T.B.'s were reported on our return journey. As the whole route was full of motor-boats it was hard to know how to identify these, and the strain was considerable.

In all *Gossamer* transported almost exactly one hundredth of the total number of troops evacuated. Two men were slightly wounded by shrapnel. One was landed with shock.

S.P.O. H.W.R. Hook (KX 75635) who was left behind in the skiff on the first night was subsequently reported missing believed killed. Two soldiers who died of wounds were buried at sea. An Army Chaplain took their particulars. There is one small shrapnel hole above the water line. We are ready for service.

Petty Officer Stoker Harry William Robert Hook is recorded as having been killed, aged 33, on 29 May 1940. The husband of Alice Ellen Mary Ann Hook, of Lowestoft, Suffolk, Hook is commemorated on the Chatham Naval Memorial.

Commander Ross supplied two appendices with his report. The first detailed the numbers evacuated on each trip:

1.	420	All British
2.	487	All British
3.	502	All British
4.	845	675 British and 170 French
5.	470	All French
6.	490	All French

Ross' second appendix listed those 'officers and men specially recommended for awards':

Lieutenant P.F. Manisty
Yeo. Sigs. J. Young (C/JX 131436)
For cool and accurate observations of enemy during dive bombing attacks.

Sub-Lieutenant M. Phipps
For constantly returning to the beaches to organise the embarkation of the troops.

P.O. Ed. Wm. Higgs (C/JX 133416)
For his services at the 0.5" machine-gun during dive bombing attacks, and his courage and activity throughout the operation, including several rescues from the sea.

P.O. Steward A. Hockney (L 14824)
For his coolness and resource in calming the French troops between decks during dive bombing attacks by singing to them.

Asst. Cook (O) T.H. Ward (MX 59579)
For constant activity and gallantry including five rescues of exhausted men from the sea.

GUILLEMOT
Kingfisher-class Patrol Sloop
Pennant Number L89
Official Rescue Total: 460

Launched in July 1939, HMS Guillemot was one of nine Kingfisher-class patrol sloops. Later classed as Corvettes, these vessels were designed for duties in UK coastal waters, and as such had a limited range and supply of depth charges. Captained by Lieutenant Commander Henry Maxwell Darrell-Brown, Guillemot was based at Harwich for escort duties in the North Sea and English Channel which she was called upon to participate in the Dunkirk evacuation. Darrell-Brown penned his report on 11 June 1940, whilst HMS Guillemot was at Harwich:

On Wednesday 29th. May *Guillemot* received orders to proceed to Sheerness, and arrived there at 0700. On arrival she was ordered to embark fuel and stores and proceed to Margate and act as base ship. She arrived at Margate at 2030, and at 2200 H.M. Schoot *Horst* came alongside for stores and lubricating oil. She cast off at 2300.

On 30th. May H.M.S. *Golden Eagle* came alongside for fuel and water at 0625. At 0950 *Guillemot* cast off from *Golden Eagle*, weighed anchor and proceeded alongside *Royal Eagle* to supply stores, water and oil fuel to her. At 1100 we cast off from *Royal Eagle* and anchored. At 1840 *Medway Queen* came alongside for oil fuel and water, and at 1950 H.M. Schoot *Delta* came alongside for diesel oil. *Medway Queen* cast off at 2000 and *Delta* at 2115.

At 2345 *Golden Eagle* came alongside for oil fuel and water and cast off at 0425 the following morning. During the day a supply of victualling stores was landed on Margate Pier for supply to ships' companies of ships going alongside pending the arrival of stores from Ramsgate. Signalman Allen was landed to assist the Signal staff ashore, which duty he performed until the ship sailed for Dunkirk.

At 1110 on 31st. May oil lighter *Brendor* came alongside for orders as it had been arranged with N.O.I.C. Margate that *Guillemot* would take charge of all fuelling. *Brendor* carried about 30 tons of diesel oil and was extremely useful fuelling Schoots and other Diesel engine craft. *Hopper W24* came alongside for oil and stores during the forenoon.

At 1135 H.M. Schoot *Horst* secured alongside and Lieutenant Sargent R.N.R., 1st Lieutenant of *Guillemot*, took over command of her from Lieutenant Commander Fardell R.N. Her crew was relieved by a volunteer crew from *Guillemot* as her Officers and men had been three days and nights without sleep. *Horst* sailed at 1315. Lieutenant Sargent's narrative is attached [missing].

123

During the afternoon of the 1st. June four coal barges were brought down the river by a tug and secured alongside. They were later towed to Ramsgate by H.M. Tug *Sprite*.

On 1st. June *Queen of Thanet* came alongside for fuel and water at 0820 and *Westward Ho* at 0845. Lieutenant Sargent and temporary crew of *Horst* returned to the ship at 0900 and the original crew of *Horst* were discharged to shore. *Westward Ho* cast off at 1040 and *Queen of Thanet* at 1100. As *Guillemot's* oil fuel was running low an oil fuel lighter was asked for from Sheerness. *Golden Eagle* came alongside for oil fuel and water at 1145 and cast off at 1420. During the afternoon 40 rounds of 4inch H.E. ammunition were supplied to H.M.S. *Kingfisher*.

On 2nd. June oil lighter *Phero* secured at 0805 and *Guillemot* oiled from her. She remained alongside all day and supplied oil fuel to various ships. H.M.S. *Kingfisher* oiled from *Phero* at 1215 and cast off at 1530, when *Queen of Thanet* came alongside for fuel and water.

At 1600 H.M.S. *Oriole*, a coal burning paddle steamer, came alongside for water and requested the loan of some stokers to assist in trimming her bunkers. Six stokers from *Guillemot* volunteered but it was decided that only two could be spared, and lots were drawn and stokers S. Hiorns and C. Sawyer were sent. At 1700 *Duchess of Fife*, secured alongside *Queen of Thanet* and at 2020 *Oriole*, *Duchess of Fife*, and *Queen of Thanet* cast off and proceeded. At 2135 oiler *Phero* cast off and anchored astern.

On 3rd. June orders were received to proceed to Dunkirk in company with *Kingfisher* escorting *Lady of Man* and *Auto Carrier* across, then to embark troops from Dunkirk Pier and return to Margate. At 1630 beef and bread for 250 men were embarked. Lieutenant R.C. Norwood R.N. and Sub Lieutenant W.G.H.T. Bonham R.N. came on board at 1800. These officers had obtained permission of N.O.I.C. Margate to accompany us as they had both had previous experience of Dunkirk and its approaches. They both proved of great assistance, Sub Lieutenant Bonham's accurate navigation being particularly valuable.

Guillemot and *Kingfisher* weighed and proceeded at 1910 and met *Auto Carrier* with *Lady of Man* some distance astern at the North Goodwin Light Vessel at 2200. Two floating mines were sighted while on passage, and a third was sunk off Gravelines by *Guillemot* by orders of *Kingfisher*, at 2215.

Ship arrived off Dunkirk at 2300 and went to the Western Mole at 2355. It was high water and owing to the shape of the Mole the ship could not lie close enough for the brow to reach. This difficulty was solved by heaving the bow in and utilising the flare of the bow. The ship secured past H.M.S. *Speedwell* which was lying at the outboard end of the Mole.

There were about six hundred French troops ashore, and after thirty one minutes of embarkation the ship was full, and cast off from the Mole, leaving about two hundred troops behind. Boats were seen approaching the Mole and it was thought that the remaining troops would be collected by them. *Guillemot* cast off at 0225. There was considerable congestion at the entrance and collision was with difficulty avoided. Aircraft flares were seen on the return journey but no attacks were made on the ship. Thick fog came down at daylight, and the ship anchored near the Foreland Buoy at 0428 for one hour, arriving at Margate at 0700 and disembarked 387 Officers and men.

Commander Henry Maxwell Darrell-Brown RN was killed on 10 November 1942 when the sloop HMS Ibis was sunk by a torpedo dropped by an Italian aircraft in the Western Mediterranean off Algiers. HMS Guillemot survived the war, being sold on 6 June 1950.

HALCYON
Halcyon-class Minesweeper
Pennant Number J42
Official Rescue Total: 2,271

HMS Halcyon was the first of the twenty-one ships of the class that bore her name to be constructed. She was laid down on 27 March 1933 at the J. Brown yard on the Clyde, being commissioned on 18 March 1934. Though Halcyon was initially commanded by Lieutenant Commander John Mark Symonds Cox DSC during Operation Dynamo, from 28 May 1940 the minesweeper's captain was Commander Eric Percival Hinton MVO. For his involvement in the evacuations, Cox was awarded a Bar to his DSC on 7 June 1940, whilst Hinton, for his part, was awarded the DSO on 16 August 1940. It was Hinton who responded to the Admiralty's instructions, providing his report in diary form. It is worth noting that each entry was numbered by Hinton; for the sake of clarity these have been deleted from the following:

Sunday, 26th. May.
Arrived Dover 2015 in company with H.M.S. *Skipjack*.

Monday, 27th. May.
Slipped and proceeded to the Downs, anchoring there at 1244.

1530. Weighed and proceeded with *Impulsive, Skipjack* and *Patricia* to sweep new channel and lay U, V and W buoys, anchoring off Goodwin Knoll at 2225.

Tuesday, 28th. May.
0600. Weighed and returned to Dover, securing to 20 buoy at 0750. Commander E.P. Hinton took over command of the ship from Lieutenant Commander J.M.S. Cox. Royal Navy.
1447. Slipped and proceeded to a position 7 miles East of Dunkirk, H.M. Ships *Sutton, Skipjack, Fitzroy* and *Salamander* joining company in the Downs.
2115. Anchored and sent Sub. Lieutenant Worthington in charge of motor boat and two whalers to embark troops.

Wednesday, 29th. May.
A swell made boatwork difficult. 192 troops were embarked 0525. Weighed and proceeded, shortly after which a large and unaccountable explosion occurred just off the bow. It is considered that this may have been a delay action bomb or a torpedo.
1240. Arrived Admiralty Pier and disembarked troops.
1600. Sailed for Dunkirk. Enemy aircraft were engaged in the vicinity of Dunkirk and a deliberate attack on a Hospital Ship was observed. One wounded man from this ship was picked up out of the water. On arrival at Dunkirk destroyers leaving the harbour informed me that we were to keep clear until dark. Later H.M.S. *Sharpshooter* joined company and we anchored just to the Eastward of the burning wreck of H.M.S. *Crested Eagle.*

Thursday 30th. May.
0330. Weighed and proceeded with 232 troops, leaving motor boat for destroyers remaining. On passage back to Dover another unexplained explosion occurred in the water off Dunkirk.
0820. Disembarked troops at Dover. Having completed with fuel and stores, sailed for Dunkirk at 1556 in company with *Skipjack* and *Salamander.*
2100. Anchored off Bray and embarked 422 troops, with the assistance of a large private motor boat, the exhausted Naval crew of which were relieved by Sub. Lieutenants Vann and Worthington and ratings. After this boat had broken down *Skipjack*'s motor boat was borrowed and used for towing whalers and then handed over to the destroyers.

Friday 31st. May.

0325. Weighed and returned to Dover, disembarking troops at 0830.

1820. Sailed for Dunkirk. The passage up Dunkirk roads was more difficult than usual owing to the number of new wrecks in the channel, which fortunately were avoided, the complete darkness and the large amount of traffic. A Magnetic Mine was seen dropping off 12E buoy, about half a cable from the ship.

Saturday, 1st. June.

An intense bombardment was in progress and shells were falling into the sea when we anchored off La Panne at 0050. A motor yacht was hailed alongside and reported that there were plenty of boats ashore and that embarkation had been proceeding steadily up to 2200, but that it had ceased temporarily owing to the bombardment.

When dawn came a number of troops were seen on the beach, but with no power boats. Whalers under oars and under command of Sub. Lieutenant Jellicoe and Worthington were sent in and troops paddled themselves off in rubber boats or swam off.

During this operation two close range machine gun attacks by thirty enemy fighters were made on the ship, her boats and the beach.

Lieutenant Nigel Thurston, Royal Navy, was seriously wounded and has since died in hospital. The two whalers were riddled with bullets when on their way inshore and one rating was seriously injured. Three other ratings aboard were slightly injured. One of our fighters crashed into the sea near the ship, and the pilot, although he had been machine gunned in the water, was rescued unscathed.

The troops on the beach were by this time moving along towards Bray, so anchor was weighed with the intent to embark them further down. Orders were received, however, to go alongside in Dunkirk harbour. This was done during a heavy dive bombing attack. While embarking French troops another dive bombing attack by about forty enemy planes took place and bombs straddled the mole and ship without causing damage.

0840. Sailed for Dover. Shells from shore batteries West of Dunkirk missed astern. Off W buoy and while near the trooper *Prague* a dive bombing attack was carried out and four heavy bombs fell between the two ships. *Prague* later reported that she was making water aft and while *Halcyon* was closing her about thirty darts were dropped falling close on either side of *Halcyon*. Having escorted *Prague* for a few miles, *Halcyon* went on ahead as she had seventeen seriously wounded onboard and there were other H.M. ships in the vicinity.

1340. Arrived Dover and disembarked 508 troops. Having expended the full outfit of H.A. Ammunition, arrangements were made to draw a new outfit at Admiralty pier as soon as possible. As her berth was urgently required however *Halcyon* was ordered to a buoy and the ammunition was sent off by lighter. As it did not arrive until 2000 there was not time to embark and fuze a percentage of it and get to Dunkirk before daylight and accordingly the ship was ordered to revert to two and a half hours' notice.

During the night enemy aircraft were engaged by close range weapons.

Sunday, 2nd June.
2025. Sailed for Dunkirk.

Monday 3rd June.
0125. Secured alongside Eastern arm, Dunkirk. Embarked 416 French troops, during which mole and ship were straddled by Artillery fire from La Panne, and a few troops on the pier were wounded.
0150. Sailed for Folkestone, securing alongside pier at 0650.
0900. Proceeded, arriving Dover at 0955. Boiler brickwork was found to be bad and there was distinct danger of fire. Consideration was given to doing the trip on one boiler but it was eventually decided to do the trip on both boilers in view of the congestion in Dunkirk harbour.
1800. Sailed for Dunkirk securing alongside Porte Avante at 2358, delay in arriving being caused by dealing with a floating mine off F.G. buoy.

Tuesday 4th June.
0020. Sailed with 501 French troops. Dense fog was encountered off North Goodwin Light Vessel and ship anchored for about half an hour until the fog lifted somewhat.
0650. Secured alongside and disembarked.

It was not possible to keep an exact record of all air attacks, but these were, of course, very frequent. Flares were observed in the Dunkirk area over land and sea every night. A particularly sinister type of machine gun bullet was found onboard after machine gun attacks, which was hard but would give a dum dum effect. A specimen was given to the Inspector of Ordinance, Dover.

To sum up, during six trips to Dunkirk, 2371 (by careful count) British and French Troops were evacuated.

After sixteen years' service with the Royal Navy, HMS Halcyon *was sold for scrapping at Milford Haven on 19 April 1950. Lieutenant Commander Cox was killed, aged 32, when the Halcyon-class minesweeper he commanded, HMS* Britomart, *was bombed whilst at anchor in Rye Bay on 15 March 1941. Having attained the rank of Captain, Hinton retired from the Service on 7 July 1956.*

Whilst it is not a Commanding Officer's report, the following account provides an interesting insight as to what it was like to be rescued by the Royal Navy during Operation Dynamo. *Private 3654379 S.V. Jones was serving in 'A' Company, 1st Battalion The South Lancashire Regiment (Prince of Wales' Volunteers) when he found himself at Dunkirk. His memoir is in the care of the Imperial War Museum Document Archive (reference 11629 03/28/1), the section below being quoted on www.halcyon-class.co.uk):*

I wandered around the beach for a while and then much later decided to have another go at wading out as far as possible, perhaps a passing small boat would pick me up. By this time my shoulders were aching madly, and I realised it was the weight of all the Bren gun magazines I was carrying, all fully loaded, plus the others tucked in behind my gas mask.

Later in the day I saw three chaps pulling a canvas collapsible boat across the sand towards the water, so I went across to them in the hope of being able to join them. Inside the boat they had a wounded companion. Another chap reached them at the same time as I and we were told, 'Only room for one'. The other chap must have taken pity on me seeing the state of me, and said, 'You go then mate!'

We managed to reach the water's edge pushed the boat into the sea, and then clambered in to it. The two chaps took a paddle each and began to paddle, but not in rhythm. The first wave flowed over us into the boat, almost causing us to sink. I took my steel helmet off and began to bale out the water, and shouting 'In-Out!' So we finally got the boat heading smoothly to a naval ship immediately in front. It turned out to be a minesweeper, HMS *Halcyon*.

Tied up alongside, I bent down to retrieve my equipment which I had taken off in case the boat had capsized and thrown me into the sea. 'Leave that' called out an officer of the ship: 'It's you we want'. With hindsight I should have picked the equipment up and brought it aboard as about an hour later, whilst we still lay off the beach, I was asked to go round the ship and collect all the ammunition people were carrying.

On boarding the ship I had been pushed into the foc'sle under the forward gun, and given a large bowl of soup and a quarter portion of a loaf. It was like Manna from heaven. As I sat there relishing the hot soup, immediately above my head came an enormous explosion, and a rat tat tat, as empty cartridge cases fell upon the deck. I jumped out of my skin thinking we had been bombed and were being machine gunned.

As I rushed out on deck a sailor told me it was the forward gun firing on hostile planes, Stuka dive bombers which were attacking all and sundry beneath them. Soldiers picked up from the beach were ringing the deck of the ship and letting fly at the planes with any weapon they had. I could have done with all those Bren gun magazines I had carried for miles only to leave them in the canvas boat.

Now that I was aboard the ship I thought that it was high time that we pulled up anchor and made our way back to England. We continued however for several hours picking up troops, and even going down to Dunkirk to lay off shore as small craft came out to us. The scene and the entire area was a sight of pure living hell. The ship eventually slipped away during the late afternoon and we disembarked at Dover Harbour.

HEBE
Halycon-class Minesweeper
Pennant Number J24
Official Rescue Total: 1,140

Ordered from HM Dockyard Devonport on 2 March 1936, HMS Hebe *was laid down on 27 April 1936. The eighth Royal Navy warship to carry the name, which had been introduced for a forty-gun ship taken as Prize in 1794,* Hebe *was completed on 23 October 1937. Lieutenant Commander John Bruce Goodenough Temple's account is dated 7 June 1940:*

Orders were received at approximately 2145 for *Hebe* and *Sharpshooter* to sail for Dover. The passage, which was started at 2250, was made without incident except for thick fog from Kinnaird Head to Bell Rock. Both ships arrived at Dover at 1723 on May 28th and secured to buoys. 2. At 1830/28 I was ordered to raise steam and proceed with all dispatch to La Panne, taking passage by Route Y to embark troops from the beach. Difficulty was experienced in finding the Whistle Buoy marking the channel off Braye. This was eventually found and *Hebe* anchored off La Panne at 0110. On passing the Whistle Buoy a heavy explosion occurred about ¼ mile to Westward which was believed to be due to a magnetic mine. No information was forthcoming as to whether any British ships were damaged.

3. Embarkation of troops continued till dawn, using ship's boats about 100 troops were embarked, including a number of stretcher cases.

4. *Hebe* weighed and proceeded at 0350 and arrived alongside at Dover at 1010. After disembarking troops, ship secured to No.19 buoy and took on board water and fresh provisions.

5. *Hebe* proceeded for La Panne via Y channel at 1410 and arrived off Whistle Buoy at 1840. A very intense air raid by dive bombers was in progress at this time and it was decided to postpone entry into the Roads until this was over. Various enemy aircraft were engaged, and *Hebe* was attacked by three Heinkel Bombers, two of which had already dropped their bombs, and opened fire with machine guns; the third attacked with what was believed to be incendiary bombs. No hits were scored by the enemy.

6. After these attacks, a voice was heard crying for help and a floating figure was observed. With the help of a loudspeaker I rescued this man (who turned out to be a wounded R.A.F. Officer) and came to his assistance. He was picked up in very shallow water.

7. In accordance with instructions I then proceeded to Dunquerque and embarked Capt. E.W. Bush, D.S.C., R.N. At 2115, I embarked survivors from a troop ship which had been sunk in the air raid at 1900. There was several severe casualties suffering from burns.

8. I arrived at La Panne at 2230 taking my orders from Capt. Bush. At 0045/30 a signal was received from *Esk* to send boat for R.A. and staff, who arrived on board 0100.

9. Troops were embarked from boats at various places from La Panne to Braye, up till 1000, when *Hebe* proceeded alongside at Dunquerque and filled to capacity.

10. On leaving Dunquerque proceeded under orders of R.A. until 1515, when he and his staff transferred to *Keith*. *Hebe* then sailed via Route X for Dover where she arrived at 2000. Disembarkation was completed at 2345 and ship secured to No.20 buoy, and replenished ammunition. Left Dover again at 0618 with Capt. Bush on board and arrived at La Panne at 1035. Troops were embarked during forenoon and afternoon from ships and other boats. During these operations ship's motor boat broke down, capsized and was lost, and one whaler was sunk in collision. No casualties were sustained. During this period H.M. ships at anchor at La Panne and Braye were subjected to bombardment from shore guns in the neighbourhood of Nieuport and inland. Constant manoeuvring was necessary to avoid this shell fire.

11. At 1700 approximately an intense air raid started and *Hebe* was attacked by four dive bombers, and twelve heavy bombs were dropped by three of them, all of which fell very close to the ship. The fourth plane

machine-gunned the ship. Apart from all lights being temporarily extinguished, the seizing of one boiler-room fan engine and the collapse of boiler brick work, only superficial damage was caused, such as the breaking of crockery & trivials. It is remarkable that greater damage was not sustained as the ship was very badly shaken. One Heinkel bomber was shot down in flames by the .5 machine gun.

12. At 1800 a signal was received from shore saying that G.H.Q. would embark from La Panne. I proceeded there, and then received further instructions that G.H.Q. would embark from a point two miles to the Westward instead. Arrangements were made for boats to go to this place and Lord Gort and his A.D.C. arrived on board at 18.30. The remainder of G.H.Q. are all believed to have embarked in *Keith*. While Lord Gort was embarking, another air raid and considerable shelling started. It was noticed that the shelling was directed at the beach, where G.H.Q. would have originally embarked. Approximately forty air craft took part in the raid and many bombs were dropped on shore and ships. During these attacks I proceeded at high speed, altering course frequently and kept as far away from *Keith* as possible, believing that the enemy had information that Lord Gort and G.H.Q. were on board her. At 2000 I returned to La Panne to continue embarkation of troops. This continued till 0300.

13. Lord Gort transferred to *Keith* at 0015.

14. From 2300 onwards the beach and town at La Panne were subjected to a very heavy bombardment, and by 0300 much of the town was on fire. Due to this bombardment Capt. Bush gave order for troops at La Panne to move to the Westward or Dunquerque to embark in ships where possible. At 0350 I proceeded towards Braye to assist in embarkation there and it was found that all small boats were fully occupied in transport to ships already there, and I therefore proceeded to Dunquerque where I filled up to 420 troops. A larger number was not taken on board as the ship was short of ammunition and fuel, and was consequently very 'tender'. During all embarkation operations, fire was frequently opened on enemy aircraft of all types. Proceeded at 0420 to Dover via X channel, arriving there at 0830.

15. Having taken in oil and ammunition *Hebe* remained alongside to make good defects to boiler brickwork and fan engine. During the following 24 hours one officer and 28 members of the crew collapsed due to shock and were sent to *Sandhurst* for treatment. I reported this fact to Vice Admiral Dover who ordered me to sail for Portsmouth at 0900 on June 3rd and give leave.

16. Although they had very little sleep and were continually at action stations, the conduct of the officers and ship's company has been beyond praise. Further report will be made on individual cases.

KINGFISHER
Kingfisher-class Patrol Sloop
Pennant Number L06
Official Rescue Total: 640

HMS Kingfisher *was ordered by the Admiralty on 15 December 1933, as the lead ship of a new class of coastal sloops. The class was intended to be used as coastal escorts, suitable for replacing the old ships used for fishery protection and anti-submarine warfare training in peacetime, while being suitable for mass production. On 5 June 1940,* Kingfisher's *CO, Lieutenant Commander George Anthony Mayhew Vaughan Harrison RN, completed the following 'report of proceedings' in relation to Operation* Dynamo:

Wednesday 29th May.
P.M. Received orders to land Experimental gear and remove Experimental Dome, and be ready to sail for Dover by 0600 Thursday 30th. This operation took less time than was anticipated due to the good work of the Scientific Staff and my Ship's Company. Reported ready to proceed at Midnight.

Thursday 30th May.
0001 Proceeded.
0900 Arrived at Dover and secured to No. 19 Buoy.
1317 Slipped and proceeded to Dunkirk by Route "X" with large Motor Boat *Sambra* in tow. Speed 12 Knots. Magnetic Mine exploded by Sweeper 1 mile ahead of *Kingfisher* in swept channel 3 miles E. of Dover.
1930 Arrived at Malo Beach, Dunkirk and embarked troops using Motor Boat and Whaler and *Sambra*.
2300 Proceeded with 180 British troops on board.

Friday 31st May.
0510 Alongside Ramsgate Pier. Troops disembarked. Had to wait for the tide before going alongside.
0533 Proceeded back to Dunkirk.
0800 Arrived Malo Beach and embarked troops with Motor boat and Whaler. No other boats were available.
1100 Had 80 troops on board, one seriously wounded, and 20 French. It was nearing low water and a small ship which had been beached and which the boats had been using as a jetty was of no further use. There was sufficient surf on the beach to make embarkation extremely difficult and produce considerable risk of

133

losing my only means of transport, also there were no more British troops ready to come off probably due to the fact that the Germans had started to shell the beach and the troops had taken cover. I decided to proceed with what I had and return as soon as possible, by which time the state of the tide would be more favourable.

1440 Alongside Margate Pier, disembarked troops.

1518 Proceeded back to Dunkirk.

1835 Arrived Malo Beach. Where there appeared to be very few troops and a large number of Tugs and small boats waiting off. Decided to try the Harbour but had to wait for a berth.

1900 High bombing raid commenced, engaged enemy Aircraft and considered *Kingfisher* shot one down, possibly, already damaged by our fighters.

2010 Alongside Eastern Pier embarking troops.

2105 Proceeded with 180 British troops.

Saturday 1st June.

0005 Anchored off Margate.

0133 Alongside Margate Pier, disembarked troops.

0240 Ordered to anchor off Margate and await orders.

0700 Ordered to proceed to Dunkirk.

1000 Alongside Eastern Pier, Dunkirk Harbour, embarking troops. More or less continuous High level Bombing in progress engaged enemy Bombers.

1130 Proceeded with 210 British troops, and 5 stretcher cases.

1235 In position 342° No.5 Buoy 1 Mile, steering 342° with two transports ahead. One being a large two funneller and the other a Paddle steamer (names nor known), both carrying French troops. We were all attacked by 16 Enemy Dive Bombers which were hotly engaged. Both transports were hit, and *Kingfisher* "near missed". The smaller ship appeared to be sinking and the larger on fire, but still under way, and under control. A number of small Drifters proceeding to Dunkirk, were close at hand and proceeded to pick up survivors. I commenced to turn, with the same intention but sighted two destroyers two miles to the Northward, one British and one French, both without troops. I informed them by light and they closed at full speed. I then decided that the help *Kingfisher*, who was already full, could add, did not justify my risking the loss of my troops by remaining in the vicinity, so proceeded.

1442 Anchored off Margate Pier.

1555 Alongside Margate Pier disembarking troops.

1635 Proceeded and anchored in Margate Roads, ordered to remain at 1 hour's notice in case required.

Not included in Saturday Night's operations.

Sunday 2nd June.

No fresh orders received, took the opportunity to replenish ammunition, 113 4" H.E. H.A., return empties, and to oil. During the dark hours several Parachute flares were seen to drop, off North Foreland.

Monday 3rd June.

1910 Weighed and proceeded, *Guillemot* in company, to rendezvous with, and escort, *Lady of Man* and *Auto Carrier*.

1955 Formed escort on *Auto Carrier*, who informed me that *Lady of Man* was still in Dover.

2130 Off 'W' Buoy. *Salamander* firing at floating mine.

2149 Sighted two floating Mines about 12 feet apart with a line between them. Ordered *Guillemot* to sink them.

2255 Went alongside West Pier, Dunkirk Harbour and embarked 210 French troops, who were very well organised for embarkation, and appeared much fresher than any of our own. They also still possessed practically all their equipment.

2319 Slipped and proceeded. There was considerable congestion in the harbour.

2331 Just cleared Harbour entrance when *Kingfisher* was rammed by French Trawler *Edmond Rene* [some accounts give the name as *Edmund Rene*], and her Port Bow, 20 feet from the stem opened up to the water-line "M" and "F" Degaussing circuits were cut. The two ships swung alongside one another after the collision and troops transhipped to the trawler who was undamaged.

Tuesday 4th June.

0005 Received orders to return to Margate. *Kingfisher* was making a little water in the Asdic Compartment.

0010 Proceeded. Speed 7 Knots. Ordered to proceed to Sheerness.

0505 In company with H.M.S. *Lida* [*Leda*] who had been in collision and requested *Kingfisher* to stand by.

0540 Sighted French Destroyer with damaged bows, at anchor near N. Goodwin Lt. Vessel, who had been in collision.

0545 French Destroyer got under way and proceeded to the South.

0615 Observed heavy explosion in position 51° 23' N, 1° 31' E., and unknown ship sink. Several of the H.M. Ships including H.M.S. *Aulbury* and H.M.S. *Kellet* near the position picked up survivors.

0714 H.M.S. *Lida* and *Kingfisher* arrived off Margate. Decided to anchor attempt repairs to D.G. Circuits before proceeding.

0745 Thick fog. Requisitioned steamer *King George V* hit *Kingfisher* on the Starboard Bow when entering Margate Road but caused practically no damage.

1200 D.G. Circuits temporarily repaired. Received orders to proceed to Lowestoft at daylight on Wednesday. During the evening M.A.S.B. No.1 came alongside and reported one engine out of action and requested a tow up the swept channel to abreast Harwich.

Wednesday 5th June.

0400 Proceeded with M.A.S.B. No.1. in tow.

0926 North Knock Deep Buoy. Slipped M.A.S.B. No.1. who proceeded to Harwich.

1620 Berthed in Lowestoft Harbour.

In a covering letter, Lieutenant Commander Harrison wrote that 'throughout the operations the conduct of all ranks and ratings in Kingfisher *was excellent. Everybody put all they had into the job displaying the greatest keenness and cheerfulness at all times. It is difficult to single out anybody for special mention … The Engine Room Department deserve special mention. No Ventilation Fan is fitted in the Engine Room and under Action conditions it is almost impossible to remain on the platform for more than half an hour, the temperature being 125°F., yet no complaint was made until completion of the operations and then only with a view to improving conditions for the next trip.'*

Kingfisher was under repair until July 1940. She was damaged again during the Battle of Britain, this time during a Luftwaffe raid on Portland Harbour on 14 August 1940. Kingfisher was sold for scrap on 21 April 1947.

LEDA
Halcyon-class Minesweeper
Pennant Number J93
Official Rescue Total: 2,848

Ordered from HM Dockyard Devonport on 1 July 1936, HMS Leda was launched on 8 June 1937. She was the sixth Royal Navy warship to carry this name which, derived from classic Greek legend, had been introduced for a fifth-

rate built at Rotherhithe in 1783. It was whilst Leda *was deployed in the North Sea with the rest of her flotilla that she was detached to take part in the evacuation. Lieutenant Commander Harold Unwin described his ship's involvement in a report dated 14 June 1940:*

At 1200 28th May 1940 H.M.S. *Leda* under my command proceeded in company with the 5th. M/S. Flotilla to Dunkirk Beaches. On receiving the order to act independently I came to a single anchor in a position Braye Dunes Hotel bearing 123° distant 7 cables at 2120.

Four whalers, a skiff and motor boat were at once lowered, Sub. Lieutenant Jamieson R.N. being in command of the landing party. The embarkation of troops proceeded until 0320 when all boats were hoisted and the anchor weighed.

Following the route by Dyck Buoy I arrived off Margate Pier at 0917 29th May and disembarked 365 soldiers.

Disembarkation was completed by 1015 and a fresh supply of provisions had been taken on board, I then slipped and proceeded towards the French coast by the same route.

At 1445 I came to a single anchor in a position Braye Dunes Hotel bearing 093° distant 1.4 miles. All boats were again lowered and proceeded to embark troops. This time the embarkation was exceptionally rapid owing to there being a large number of Army self propelled boats already under way.

Enemy bombers became active at 1545 and were engaged, it is considered probable that one bomber was damaged. There were now 525 troops on board and in view of the danger from enemy action I weighed and proceeded to Margate at maximum speed.

Three whalers and the motor boat were left inshore under the command of Sub. Lieutenant Jamieson with orders to assist other ships.

After passing Middlekerke Buoy enemy bombers were observed attacking a Hospital ships [*sic*] and H.M.S. *Kellett* and *Pangbourne*, who were bound for the beaches.

At 2044 I secured alongside Margate Pier and disembarked troops. This was completed by 2155 when I slipped and proceeded towards the French coast by the Dyck Buoy.

No ships were sighted during this passage, and at 0130 when off the Dyck Buoy, my suspicions about this route were aroused. Reports of enemy submarines in the vicinity were received and I decided to return to the North Goodwin L.V. and proceed by "X" route.

I came to a single anchor in a position Braye Dunes Hotel bearing 170° distant 1 mile and proceeded to embark troops.

A search was made for *Leda*'s landing party but without success.

By 1220, 30th May 650 troops had been embarked so I weighed and proceeded towards Margate arriving at 1815.

Whilst alongside Margate Pier Sub. Lieutenant Jamieson returned on board and made the following report: "After H.M.S. *Leda* left I used the motor boat and whalers for embarking troops in the *Gracie Fields*, *Locust* and other ships lying off La Panne Beach. This continued until 0200/30 when only the motor boat was left, the whalers having been sunk during the air raid the previous afternoon. The motor boat was abandoned through engine trouble and lack of fuel."

All troops had been disembarked by 1955 and so slipped and proceeded towards Dunkirk.

Whilst approaching Dunkirk it was observed that the enemy were now shelling Dunkirk harbour. I signalled my arrival to the signal station on the East Pier and received a general message to the effect that boats were urgently required for embarking troops from the beaches. All my boats having been lost, I decided that it would be a waste of time to go to the Beach and consequently I entered Dunkirk harbour and secured alongside the East Pier at 0015 31st May.

About fifty stretcher cases were then embarked and 350 troops. At the time it was considered that there were more troops on board than this, but it was very difficult to check them as they came on board.

At 0135 I slipped and proceeded out of harbour. After rounding "FG" buoy a collision occurred with an unknown scoot which attempted to cross my bow from port to starboard. Slight damage was done to the port side above the water line. After the collision mat had been placed in position and a careful examination made I continued on my way.

On arrival at Margate all troops were disembarked and I then proceeded to Sheerness to have a temporary patch put on the port side. This was completed by 1700 and I was able to rendezvous with M.S.5 at 2200 off "W" buoy. I would like to mention at this point the expeditious and efficient manner in which repairs were carried out by the Sheerness Dockyard.

Leda anchored in a position La Panne Church bearing 100° distant 1.6 miles at 2359. Whilst awaiting troops shells were observed to be falling close to the waiting ships and these appeared to come from German guns to the East of La Panne.

At 0230 1st June it was apparent that few boats were available for the embarkation, and M.S.5 approved my request to proceed towards Dunkirk in search of boats. I then weighed and proceeded, and at 0300 a motor boat and three launches were acquired and manned by seamen from *Leda*.

630 troops were then embarked from the beach and I remained in a position Zuydecoote Sanatorium bearing 150° distant 8 cables. During this period enemy fighter planes attacked with machine guns and were engaged. At 0715 I proceeded towards Sheerness.

During the passage through Dunkirk Roads a heavy concentration of enemy bombers attacked the ship H.M.S. *Keith* when about 4 cables ahead of me was seen to be seriously damaged, and steamed round at high speed out of control. A collision was narrowly averted.

Whilst passing Dunkirk breakwater H.M.S. *Ivanhoe* was seen to be damaged and disembarking troops to *Skipjack* who was alongside her. Enemy bombers proceeded to attack the ships ahead of *Leda* including H.M.S. *Havant*, and finally attacked us but without success. At 0815 bombing attacks ceased and I proceeded without further hindrance.

Throughout this intensive bombing the gun's crews behaved magnificently, in particular P.O. Collins who by his cool and steady manner inspired the remainder and gave them that necessary confidence during the early part of the attack. Altogether 118 rounds of 4", 3200 rounds 0.5" and 2700 rounds of .303 were expended.

At 1410 I arrived at Sheerness and secured to No.26 buoy and disembarked troops. On arrival a number of ratings had to be treated by the Medical Officer for complete exhaustion and most ratings fell asleep where they stood.

Leda did not proceed to Dunkirk on the night of Saturday 1st June as she was unable to arrive there during dark hours.

During the forenoon of Sunday 2nd June ammunition was embarked to complete establishment. At 1645 I slipped and proceeded towards Dunkirk and arrived off entrance to the harbour 2300. After securing alongside the East Pier no troops were to be seen.

At 2350 orders were received from the officer in charge of berthing to slip and proceed. I left harbour at 0010 3rd June with no troops on board. During the period alongside the enemy were bombarding the entrance with shrapnel, but no damage was done to *Leda* except for a hole in the funnel.

On arrival at Margate orders were received to proceed to Sheerness and at 0928 I secured No.26 buoy.

Orders for the final evacuation were received during the afternoon and at 1600 *Leda* slipped in company with *Gossamer* and proceeded towards Dunkirk.

In accordance with the berthing arrangements I secured alongside the West Pier at 2310 and commenced embarking French troops. By 0022, 4th June 484 French soldiers had been embarked and I slipped and proceeded out of harbour. At this point I would like to pay tribute to the excellent arrangements at West pier for the embarkation, and also the high standard of discipline of the French troops, they were magnificent.

At 0300 fog was encountered, speed reduced and fog signals made. During this fog a collision occurred with the Belgian scoot *Marechal Foch* which sank. *Leda* sustained damage to her bows, but the forward bulkhead held. It is not known how many survivors were taken off. A detailed report of the accident has been forwarded through the usual Service channels H.M.S. *Kellett* remained in company whilst I proceeded at a moderate speed to Margate. Owing to dense fog off Margate it was not possible to disembark troops until 1020.

On completion of the disembarkation I went to an anchorage off Margate, the signal that Operation *Dynamo* had been completed was received at 1100.

In a further report dated 15 June 1940, Lieutenant Commander Unwin listed three members of his ship's crew who he felt deserving of further recognition:

Lieutenant William McKee, Royal Naval Reserve:
Throughout the evacuation this officer worked unceasingly with great vigour and cheerfulness, he was an inspiration to his men by his steady manner. I consider his work to be worthy of a "mention in despatches".

George Bertram Head, Chief E.R.A. Portsmouth. M.34498:
C.E.R.A. Head by his unflinching determination and attention to duty during long hours in the Engine Room at "Action Stations" under very trying conditions was instrumental in making possible the evacuation by H.M.S. *Leda* of 3,055 troops. I consider that his conduct is worthy of the Distinguished Service Medal.

John Collins, Petty Officer, Portsmouth. O.N. J90457:
Petty Officer Collins was mentioned by name in my letter of proceedings of the 14th June for his action during enemy air attacks on the morning of 1st June 1940. His coolness and steady manner as Captain of "A" Gun deserves the highest praise and I consider that he is worthy of the Distinguished Service Medal.

In time, the above men received the awards requested by Unwin. He himself would be awarded the Distinguished Service Cross.

One of the men brought home from Dunkirk by HMS Leda *was Corporal 2067466 M.E. Booth. Serving at the time in No.2 Section, 248 Field Company*

Royal Engineers, his account, Let Battle Commence, *can be seen on the BBC People's War website (www.bbc.co.uk/history/ww2peopleswar):*

On the beach in front of Bray Dunes we actually found an officer and he was looking for R.E.s. Some of the lads were getting lorries from the other side of town, driving them onto the beach and making a pier with them. My little group joined a party who had found some bridging lorries with folding pontoons, our job was to unload the pontoons, take them to the sea, erect them and then ferry parties of soldiers out to larger craft off shore, unload and then return for another party. If we came too far into the beach we found that the pontoon filled up very rapidly and we were aground, nobody wanted to get off to enable us to refloat and things got a bit hairy at times. Eventually common-sense prevailed and several of the lads got of and we were refloated, they pushed us out into deeper water and then climbed on again.

After that we always stopped out to sea and they had to wade out to us. On one trip we had a young officer with us, he was waving his revolver and behaving like Captain Bligh of the *Bounty*. I shouted at him and told him if he used his energy rowing instead of blowing we would get along a lot better. To my surprise he put his revolver away and started rowing!

Later in the afternoon an RSM came on my pontoon. When we got to the ship he said, 'Right lads, you've done your bit for today, go on board, somebody else can take her back'. My lads and I made our way to the side of the pontoon, grabbed the net hanging down the ship's side and were up and over in a flash. When I landed on the deck one of the ship's officer[s] saw my revolver and said, 'Just what I want, a revolver'. Just to keep him happy I passed it over to him, telling him to clean it before he used it as it was full of French soil!

We were then told to go below decks out of the way. I found myself sitting on a seat with my back to the side of the ship up forrad underneath the ack-ack gun. The sailors were grand, they gave us hot tea and sandwiches out of their own lockers and we settled down for a rest whilst the ship loaded up. Eventually we were full up and off we started for England. I fell asleep when suddenly there was a series of loud bangs and the door of the locker above me fell on my head. Eventually the banging stopped and a sailor came down and told us that we had been attacked by a Stuka but they had shot it down and we would soon be in England.

Once the excitement was over I soon fell fast asleep; eventually a sailor came along shouting 'wakey wakey, get yourselves ashore, unless you want to go back again'.

Everybody declined his offer and we all made our way ashore to find that we were in Margate. We marched to the railway station, at the station there were lots of Red Cross people handing out sandwiches, cigarettes, chocolate and filling our mugs with hot sweet tea. Strange how most of the lads managed to hang onto their mug! They also produced postcards and pencils which they gave us so we could inform our families that we were safe and sound, there were people from lots of other organisations doing all they could to help us. It was a wonderful reception as we had all been wondering what the people in England would think about the poor show that we had made.

LOCUST
Dragonfly-class River Gunboat
Pennant Number T28
Official Rescue Total: 2,329

Launched on 28 September 1939 and commissioned on 17 May 1940, HMS Locust *was one of four Dragonfly-class river gunboats constructed for the Royal Navy. Having survived the Dunkirk evacuations,* Locust *went on to play a key role in the Dieppe Raid and participate in the Normandy landings, during which she was hit by a shell. In the introduction to his subsequent report,* Locust's *captain, Lieutenant Ackroyd Norman Palliser Costobadie RN, made the following comments: 'I beg to state that the behaviour of both officers and men under my command was exemplary, especially in view of the fact that the ship has only been in commission since 13th May, and that nineteen of the Ship's Company are Hostilities Only, or, Short Service, Ordinary Seamen. The fine example of leadership and untiring zeal set by Lieutenant John Arundel Holdsworth, Royal Navy, the First Lieutenant, was particularly worthy of note.' Costobadie went on to write:*

29th May.
H.M.S. *Locust* and H.M.S. *Mosquito* were ordered to sail for La Panne and Bray Dunes respectively, and proceeded at 1348.

At 1730 *Mosquito* parted company and at 1845 *Locust* arrived in position off La Panne Beach.

Large numbers of both British and French Troops were seen to be waiting on the beach, and it was decided that a first attempt at embarkation should be made by grounding the fore part of *Locust* and trying to get the soldiers to wade out and climb on board over the bow. Ladders were accordingly rigged forward and the ship steamed in to the beach. The kedge anchor was let go over the stern and at 1900 the ship took the ground forward. After hailing the beach a few soldiers started to wade off, but gave up the attempt, and as the tide was falling the ship was got off and anchored, and embarkation started by means of the Ship's two whalers.

At 1950 engaged enemy aircraft and continued to do so intermittently until 2130. Enemy aircraft were carrying out bombing attacks on the beaches.

At 2200 *Locust* signalled Commander Cordeaux in *Royal Eagle* for information, as embarkation was proceeding very slowly, and there appeared to be no Power boats available. Reply from *Royal Eagle* that Commander Cordeaux was incapacitated and that *Locust* was S.N.O. La Panne.

As there were no powerboats in sight, and a number of pulling boats could be seen stranded on the beach by the receding tide I decided to land in order to organize the troops into pulling themselves off from the beach.

At 2220 S.N.O. "A" in *Hebe* approached and approved my landing. I accordingly landed at 2230 and found six R.N. cutters and three Merchant Service (pulling) Life boats stranded on the beach about 300 yards from the water's edge. There were about 1000 British Troops who appeared to be in charge of Non-commissioned Officers. The boats had swung across the beach and were jambed [*sic*] together, half full of water and in many cases imbedded in the sand. The soldiers took some little time to understand what was required of them, but eventually all the boats were emptied and got down to the water's edge. They were then pulled out to *Locust* and other ships present by the Soldiers.

30th May.

At midnight, 29th/30th the ships and the beach were again bombed by enemy aircraft which caused some slight delay in the embarkation, but by 0300 all the available boats were off the beach and I returned on board.

During the time that I was ashore I was accompanied by Signalman E.E. Roden, Offl No. C/D 360, who behaved with great courage and resource, and was personally instrumental in getting two boats down to the water, organising the Military party in handling the boats and detailing the men to go off in them. His initiative and encouragement set a very fine example to the Soldiers, who would certainly not have succeeded in launching the two boats without his leadership.

At 0310 having 620 British and French Troops on board, *Locust* proceeded to the assistance of H.M.S. *Bideford* at Bray Dunes. *Bideford* was found to be unable to steam or steer due to having been bombed aft, and was aground.

At 0330 tow was passed to *Bideford* and at 0425 *Bideford* came off and ships proceeded. At 0445 and 0540 tows parted, and at 0605 *Locust* secured *Bideford* alongside and towed her clear of shoal water, passing tow astern again at 0930. After one stop, due to *Bideford* having a man overboard, (at 2235), tow parted at 0340/31st and *Locust* again secured alongside and both ships entered Dover Harbour at 1200 on 31st May.

31st May.
Troops were disembarked at 1300 and ships secured alongside. P.M. *Locust* was ordered to proceed to Dunkirk and embark British Troops and return. At 1840 sailed, and entered Dunkirk Harbour at 2240. On arrival the Harbour was completely deserted and no sign of any Troops could be seen. No signals were made to *Locust* and after ship had been laid close alongside shore end of Pier and still no signs of any troops were apparent I turned and proceeded to Malo Centre Beach. As ship left Dunkirk Harbour a dive bombing attack was carried out by two enemy aircraft. These were engaged and both retired, one with both engines on fire and losing height.

1st June.
At 2400 31st/1st anchored off Malo Centre Beach. The First Lieutenant, Lieutenant J.A. Holdsworth, and Signalman H.O. Carter, C/SSX. 17317, were sent ashore to reconnoitre and try to start embarkation. At 0045 embarkation commenced in Ship's whalers and by 0400 about 150 troops had been embarked. During this time the beach and roadway were heavily bombed on several occasions, and this accounted for the slowness of the embarkation. Again the lack of power boats was seriously felt, and Lieutenant Holdsworth did very well in hunting for small parties of troops in the cover of the sand dunes, and conducting them to the boats. At 0415 weighed and proceeded inside Dunkirk Harbour, and went alongside Eastern Mole, where 500 troops were embarked.

The Mole and Ships alongside were heavily bombed by Dive bombers and Mole was shelled from the Eastward. The enemy aircraft were repulsed by fire from the Destroyers alongside.

At 0610 proceeded, and arrived at Dover at 1015, and disembarked 650 Troops.

At 2000 received orders (F.O.C. Dover Most Secret Memorandum No. A.14/0/40.) to proceed to vicinity of Bray to lend support and covering fire. Owing to low visibility and necessity for oiling before starting *Locust* was one hour late in position. Took ship close inshore but coast was very misty and no targets could be seen. Heavy small arm firing was heard in Bray, which was also being shelled from apparently the village of Furnes. After some waiting *Locust* was fired at by machine guns from a position approximately half way between the foreshore and Adinkerke. This was replied to by 0.5 machine gun fire from *Locust*. Further fire was directed at the ship from the direction of La Panne, and this was answered with 4" H.E. I then attempted to silence shore batteries which were shelling Bray from Furnes, and 30 rounds of 4" H.E. were fired. This apparently achieved some result as the firing died down, and several explosions causing fires were observed.

2nd June.
0300. Ceased firing and proceeded.
0350. Tug *Fossa* signalled she was ashore and required assistance. In attempting to close, *Locust* took the ground but came off again, and I decided it was impracticable to close *Fossa*. A Motor Landing craft was therefore hailed and brought alongside and her troops, 51 in number were transferred to *Locust*, and the M.L.C. was sent to rescue the crew of the Tug, and any troops she had on board.
0450. Proceeded, and at 0545 overtook a small armed yacht in the charge of a Major R.A., who had 28 men with him. Party was transferred to *Locust*, and Major gave information that covering fire of *Locust* had been effective.
1005. Arrived Dover, and disembarked 79 troops.
1820. Slipped and proceeded to Dunkirk Harbour.
2223. Went alongside East Mole, Dunkirk and commenced embarkation of British troops.
2302. Sailed with 650 British and 70 French Troops.

3rd June.
0408. Arrived Dover.
1845. Slipped and proceeded.
2300. Anchored off Dunkirk Mole and commenced embarking troops from Motor boats.

4th June.
0015. Demolition party consisting of Lieutenant Holdsworth and 6 men left by Motor boat for wreck of *Mosquito*. On arrival it was found that the wreck was submerged to the level of the battery deck, and despite repeated efforts of Lieut. Holdsworth who attempted to enter the Captain's Quarters, the forward charge had to be placed in the wheelhouse. The after charge was placed in the after magazine. The demolition party were working under great difficulties due to the movement of the wreck in the swell and to

the darkness, and great initiative was displayed by Lieut. Holdsworth in placing the charges which were heavy and difficult to handle, and were somewhat dangerous. The demolition party returned on board at 0205 having fired the charges. The explosion blew off the fore part and after part of the wreck and should have prevented anything of value falling into enemy hands.

0235. Proceeded with 200 French Troops and arrived at Dover at 0635. During the above operations no casualties were suffered by *Locust*, and the majority of the damage sustained was caused during the towing of H.M.S. *Bideford*.

LYDD
Hunt-class Minesweeper
Pennant Number J44
Official Rescue Total: 1,502

Ordered in 1918 from Fairfield's at Govan, HMS Lydd *was launched in December 1918 and completed during 1919. After service in the Mediterranean she was put in Reserve at Alexandria. Before the outbreak of war this ship was brought forward for service off Palestine, intercepting ships carrying illegal immigrants. She was diverted from minesweeping duties off the East Coast to participate in Operation* Dynamo, *its involvement in which represented, as is clear in Lieutenant Commander Rodolph Cecil Drummond Haig's following report, a somewhat hectic period, including, for example, the ramming and sinking of the drifter* Comfort *(60 GRT) off Dover, the latter having been mistaken her for an enemy vessel. Haig's account was dated 7 June 1940:*

At noon on Tuesday the 28th May 1940, H.M.S. *Lydd* under my command left Harwich in company with the 5th M/S Flotilla arriving off Bray at about 2115. I was there ordered to proceed into Dunkirk harbour to embark troops. I secured alongside the Eastern jetty and embarked about four hundred, leaving again at 2250.

At 2318 about two miles to the eastward of the entrance a drifter was sighted ahead crossing from port to starboard about twenty five yards away, fine on the port bow. The engines were put full steam astern, but it was too late to avoid a collision. The crew of the drifter were taken aboard another drifter, which was close by. It is understood that the drifter in collision with *Lydd* was the *Girl Pamela* which subsequently sank. No damage was sustained by *Lydd*.

At 0200 29th May when passing the Kwinke buoy, flares were sighted and shouting heard close at hand. The light from the Aldis lamp revealed the bow and stern portions of H.M.S. *Wakeful* appearing above water with men clinging to them. I immediately lowered a whaler and two carley floats. Shortly after this H.M.S. *Gossamer*, which was close by, ordered me to put my light out and drop a depth charge. I could not at once comply with the latter order as I was too close to the wreck and would have killed the men in the water; I therefor asked what the situation was, to which I received no reply; nor did I see *Gossamer* again. I kept the ship moving while the whaler and carley floats were picking up survivors and had just got twenty alongside when H.M.S. *Grafton* appeared. I asked her if she would pick up the rest, and she asked me to circle round her in case of enemy submarines. It was the discovered from one of the survivors that *Wakeful* had been torpedoed by an M.T.B. I at once passed this to *Grafton* and continued circling round.

I had just completed one circle and was heading west with my stern to *Grafton*, when at about 0307 an explosion occurred at her stern. I continued my circle to port and sighted an M.T.B. about fifty yards away on the starboard beam, steering about south-west and nearly stern on to *Lydd*. Sub-Lieut. E.M. Britton R.N. who was on the bridge, opened fire with the starboard pair of Lewis guns and raked her up the stern; bullets being seen to hit her wheelhouse and superstructure in a cloud of sparks. It was thought that she was disabled. I then closed *Grafton* with the idea of taking off survivors should she be sinking; but as she appeared to be alright I circled round to starboard to finish off the M.T.B. if she were still afloat.

A dark object was sighted ahead in the direction in which the M.T.B. was last seen and fire was opened with Lewis guns and 4inch; *Grafton* also opened fire. The supposed M.T.B. was then rammed, as she was hit figures sprang at the ship and it was thought that an attempt was being made to board; fire was therefore opened with rifles. During this firing A.B. S.P. Sinclair, O.N. C/JX 152005 who was on the Forecastle attempting to repel the boarders was accidentally shot. It is very much regretted that he died about an hour later from his wound. After investigation I have come to the conclusion that the bullet which struck him must have glanced off some portion of the vessel rammed. Two men were taken off her. I then set course for home, *Grafton* being apparently well able to look after herself.

It was then discovered that the vessel rammed was the drifter *Comfort* and not the M.T.B. V.A. Dover was informed of the circumstances as far as I knew them; I also informed *Jason* and *Javelin*, met with shortly afterwards, of *Grafton's* plight. On further questioning the two survivors of the *Comfort*, it was ascertained that she had been picking up survivors from the *Wakefield* [*Wakeful*], when an explosion threw all on board into the water and disabled the vessel. Three men managed to scramble back again, of whom two got on board *Lydd* and the other who was apparently badly wounded, went down with the vessel when she was rammed.

I landed the troops at Ramsgate and returned to Dunkirk by Y route.

When off Nieuport Bank buoy at 1700 a large number of enemy aircraft started dive-bombing ships arriving and leaving, paying particular attention to the hospital ship *St Julien* which had repeated attacks made on her.

I arrived off Bray at 1730 and sent boats inshore to embark troops. I did not anchor but lay to off the beach. At about 1745 an urgent call for assistance was received from SS *Clan MacAllister* which was on fire aft. I passed this to *Pangbourne* who was just arriving, as I had already started embarking troops. *Pangbourne* then went alongside the burning ship.

Embarkation was not much hampered as far as *Lydd* was concerned by the almost incessant bombing attacks; but it was noticed that ships at anchor had heavy bombs directed at them, whereas *Lydd* who was under weigh was only treated to light stuff. During the embarkation H.M.S. *Crested Eagle*, which had [been] bombed aft and caught fire, beached herself close by and the troops on board began to jump into the water. *Lydd*'s boats immediately went to their assistance, picking up a large number, including twenty five very badly burnt and injured men. H.M.S. *Albury* arrived shortly after this and her assistance was called for, which was at once rendered.

As there was no doctor on board it was deemed essential to get the wounded home as quickly as possible, and I left the scene at 2100, with three hundred troops onboard.

When off the Middelkirke Buoy at 2200 it was reported to me that the D.G. cables had caught fire and had had to be switched off. It was discovered that they had been pierced by bomb splinters, the steering compass was now so sluggish that the ship had to be steered by a star when visible. Temporary repairs to D.G. cables were carried out next day.

At 2205 an S.O.S. was received from the Trawler *Tor Bay 2*. On closing her it was discovered that all she had wrong was a foul propeller. I explained about the necessity of getting my wounded home quickly, told her that there were other ships following, continued on my way, and reported the matter on arrival at Margate.

I arrived at Margate at 0515 30th May, but could not get alongside to disembark until 0855, owing to the large number of ships already there.

I then proceeded to Sheerness to coal and ammunition, sailing again in company with *Sutton* and *Ross* at 0230, May 31st arriving off Bray by X route at 0915.

As there were no enemy aircraft in the vicinity, I anchored. Troops were embarked and at 1130 *Sutton* and *Ross* transferred their troops to me and all proceeded to Margate where I disembarked five hundred.

At 1915 I proceeded towards the rendezvous off W buoy, being ordered at 2145 to assist Tug *St. Abbs*, one of whose tow of three Thames barges had broken adrift. I picked up this barge and towed her to Dunkirk, arriving at 0330, 1st June. At about this time a vessel which was unidentified was seen to blow up, presumably on a magnetic mine, in the neighbourhood of the whistle buoy off Bray.

About two hundred and fifty troops had been embarked when a message was brought off from the Brigadier to say that he had stopped embarkation from the beaches, which were being shelled, and was retiring to Dunkirk. I passed this message to *Keith*.

During the embarkation low flying aircraft machine-gunned boats and ships. Several hits were registered on one machine, which was afterwards seen to crash on the sand dunes, by a Bren gun in *Lydd* fired by one of the troops embarked. Another machine was also thought to have been hit by the starboard pair of Lewis guns fired by Ord. Sea. W.F.R. Duxbury. O.N. G/JX 173054.

At 0625 I proceeded by route X to Dover arriving at 1120. On the way enemy bombers appeared but after a few salvos were driven off by our fighters who were seen to bring down two.

At 1920 I again proceeded by route X to Dunkirk, anchoring in the roads about half a mile east of the harbour entrance at 2350. The beach and roads were being shelled, and there did not appear to be much boat traffic. I sent the motor boat inshore and it brought off the Brigadier of the Brigade then embarking, who asked that a message from the acting C-in-C might be sent to V.A. Dover asking that the embarkation should be diverted to the beach, as French soldiers were causing congestion on the piers. It was also stated that the rearguard would arrive about 0230. I informed V.A. Dover and all the forces at Dunkirk of this by W/T. The difficulty at the beach appeared to be lack of boats. With *Lydd*'s boats about two hundred were embarked by 0245, 2nd June.

Having received no reply to my signal, I again read V.A. Dover's signal ordering withdrawal before 0300, and saw that it referred only to Minesweepers. I therefore assumed that the destroyers were carrying on till a later hour, and withdrew, passing the harbour entrance at 0300. Owing to smoke haze it was impossible to see how many other craft were still off the beach.

At 0320 V.A. Dover's signal was received ordering the Minesweepers to remain if necessary after 0300, by which time I had nearly reached W buoy and therefore continued on my course arriving at Margate shortly after 0600.

The D.G. coil was again found to be defective, which prevented the ship taking part in any further operations. This has since been temporarily repaired at Sheerness.

The only other damage received apart from a few minor splinter holes and dents, was a hole torn in the bow plating and the port hawse pipe fractured when the *Comfort* was rammed.

NIGER
Halcyon-class Minesweeper
Pennant Number J73
Official Rescue Total: 1,245

Commissioned at Devonport on 4 June 1936, the Halcyon-class minesweeper HMS Niger *was the sixth Royal Navy vessel to carry the name. By the time she was called upon for* Dynamo, Niger *had become accustomed to being under fire. On 7 October 1939, for example, she had been minesweeping off the Swarte Bank in the North Sea when she was attached by enemy aircraft, being slightly damaged. The next attack took place off Invergordon on 30 January 1940. On this occasion German bombers dropped twenty bombs; despite only suffering slight damage, three of* Niger's *crew were wounded. Then, in the days leading up to the evacuation of the BEF,* Niger *was operating off the French coast near Gravelines when she was dive-bombed and set on fire on 20 May.* Niger's *captain since 8 April 1940, Commander St. John Cronyn RN gave this account of his ship's role at Dunkirk:*

30th May, 2145
Whilst on passage to North Goodwin Light in company with *Dundalk*, signal was received instructing *Niger* to carry out ferry service between Sheerness and La Panne. The route to be used was given.

31st May
0400   Arrived North Goodwin. Informed V.A.D. and R.A.D.
0700   Arrived La Panne. Lowered both whalers and motor-boat and sent them inshore. Anchored 5 cables off beach. A considerable surf was running. There was no one in charge ashore and as soon as the boats arrived in they were seized by soldiers. One was swamped, the other overloaded and capsized.

0825 V.A.D.'s signal regarding the final evacuation was received giving the groups of ships, the rendezvous and time. As *Niger* had then scarcely any troops on board I made signal No.1 to R.A.D. in *Keith* with the idea of saving time. This was not approved (2) but R.A.D. instructed yachts to fill up *Niger* first. The result being that at 1045 *Niger* had over 200 troops on board when it was necessary to sail.

1045 Sailed for Dover not Sheerness in order to save sea-time. Before sailing Signal No.3 was made to R.A.D. In consequence Lieutenant R.P. Hichens R.N.V.R. was left behind. He moored two yachts as pontoons, secured grass lines to the pier of lorries and organised the boats pulley-hauly on these lines. I was later informed that his work made the most tremendous difference to the rate of embarkation of troops apart from making it comparatively safe and avoiding the risk of drowning soldiers which was extremely high in the early morning, when boats were capsizing frequently.

1445 Arrived Dover. Secured at Admiralty Pier.

1715 Intercepted Signal No. 4. Sailed immediately.

2240 Anchored off Bray Dunes in 3½ fathoms. *Niger* and group 3 were to westward. At first no boats were lowered as the evacuation was timed for 0300 and it was also understood that fast shore motor boats would be used.

2315 A boat under oars came off with some 30 soldiers under the command of Sub.-Lieut. Byggott, R.N. This boat had been towed by tug *Tanya*. Sub.Lieut. Byggott who had severely damaged his thumb reported that there were 150 soldiers abreast the ship but that all others had moved to the westward to Bray. Two whalers and the motor boat were at once lowered and sent in. A fairly heavy surf was still running.

2350 A Sub-Lieutenant R.N.V.R. (Name unknown) from the tug *Sun VIII* reported that his motor-boat and a ship's boat were aground with some 60 soldiers: that he had got off 30 in another boat and that there were about 50 more waiting. *Niger*'s boats returned empty about this time and reported that they could find no troops. They were at once sent in with orders to tow the other boats off and also fill up. The Cox'n reported later that the boats had got off before he reached the beach and that there were no soldiers left.

1st June

0100 A large shore boat under the orders of Lieut.-Comdr. Craig came alongside with 40 soldiers including Brigadiers Robb and Towel.

He asked me to move further to the Eastward as all the troops were off Bray. I pointed out that all the other minesweepers were to eastward of me. Shortly afterwards our boats returned with troops. Flashing was also seen from the shore and from this time onwards troops were brought off regularly but slowly.

0330　As dawn came very large numbers of troops were seen to be on the beach and endeavouring to hasten transport, *Niger* lowered her Carly floats. These took a large number of soldiers but towed very slowly. Lifebelts were also sent in and some soldiers out these on and swam off. At this time which was nearly low water, *Niger* was about three cables from the beach in 2½ fathoms. Bray was shelled continuously from Nieuport throughout the night.

0500　Enemy aircraft carried out machine-gun attacks on the ships and beaches. Several attacks were made.

0610　With approximately 330 troops on board *Niger* weighed and proceeded, *Sutton* in company. Not many troops remained and a message was received from Major General Montgomery through *Salamander* that the troops had been ordered to proceed to Dunkirk.

1800　Slipped and proceeded *Sutton* in company, in accordance with signal No.5.

2215　Let go port anchor 1 mile east of Dunkirk, 3.5 cables from shore. In accordance with verbal instructions from Admiral's motor boat, *Sutton* proceeded into Dunkirk to embark troops.

2225　No boats being worked from the beach, the motor boat was lowered together with one whaler and a ship's boat borrowed from S.S. *Vrere* in Dover, the other whaler having been lost in the morning.

2230　Boats proceeded ashore Lieutenant Hichens, R.P., R.N.V.R. in charge. Lieutenant Hichens could see no troops on the beach waiting and no other boats being worked. He landed and proceeded along the beach towards Dunkirk. About 5 cables westward he found large detachments of French troops drawn up on the beach. He endeavoured to get these troops to start embarkation but had considerable difficulty. Finally he found an officer who spoke a little English who took him to the Commanding Officer in Malo-les-Bains who gave orders for the evacuation and embarkation to commence. The boats were called up and some 50 French troops taken off.

2nd June

0000　On return to the ship Lieutenant Hichens was instructed that there were British troops some 6 cables further Eastward. He landed considerably further to the East and found some more

French troops and 3 British sentries who informed him that the remaining British troops had not yet come but were expected shortly. As he had 3 boats waiting himself and two other large boats were also waiting from a paddle minesweeper, believed to be the *Marmion* anchored near *Niger*, he asked to be taken to the Commanding Officer in order to ascertain how quickly the men could be brought on. Lieut. Hichens found the Colonel in charge who had a considerable number of British troops waiting in the streets near the shore. These were at once sent forward to the beach and embarkation proceeded.

0246 Boats hoisted in accordance with signal No.6. Approximately 300 soldiers on board.

0255 Weighed and proceeded.

2055 Proceeded to Dunkirk.

3rd June

0015 Entered Dunkirk and secured Port side to alongside East Arm. Embarked approximately 700 French soldiers.

0120 Slipped. Whilst turning an unknown French craft passing from Starboard to port crossed *Niger*'s bows and was rammed. She appeared to be all right and a few minutes later came back and rammed *Niger*. The Skipper came on board after the first collision and was landed at Folkestone being turned over to the Military Authorities.

2100 Weighed and proceeded.

2233 Dense fog. Visibility 1½ cables, reduced to eight knots.

4th June, 0030

Visibility had not improved. It was not possible to reach Dunkirk in time to effect any reasonable embarkation and leave by 0230 in accordance with instructions. Furthermore *Niger* was the last ship and would be the only one proceeding East against a large stream of traffic going West. It was felt that the risk of collision outweighed the doubtful possibility of a small embarkation and the passage was therefore abandoned.

0135 *Niger* anchored approximately 3 miles from North Goodwin Light.

The signals referred to by Commander St. John Cronyn were listed at the end of his narrative:

R.A.D. [Rear Admiral Dover] from *Niger*. V.A.D.'s 0357 intend to fill up with troops now and if unable to make rendezvous in time tonight will ask him to supply spare ship.

Niger from R.A.D. You should leave in time to make rendezvous tonight full or not.

R.A.D. from *Niger*. I have one officer who has volunteered to stay ashore and assist on the beach. He is confident that with a grass line and a yacht anchored in close he will get all soldiers off quickly. I have great confidence in him and intend to leave him behind.

Most immediate. F.O. Dover. S.N.O. Dunkirk from V.A.D. Army wishes to commence evacuation 2030. Instruct [illegible] beaches at this time.

N.O.i/c Ramsgate 1st, 4th, 5th, 6th M.S.F. C. in C. Nore, Speedy N.O.i/c Sheerness from V.A.D. All available ships operating under V.A. Dover and M.S.F.s' addressed are required to evacuate tonight Saturday. Ships to sail to arrive off beaches between Dunkirk and a point 1½ miles East at 2200/1st June. Ships which have not D.G. equipment are not to sail. Ships report forth with whether they can comply. A dimmed light is to be shown shoreward when in position. 1510/1/6.

Evacuation tonight Saturday from west end of beach and from harbour only to cease at 0300. Can embark about 9000 from beach if weather remains calm. Drifters and destroyers will enter harbour. 2045/1/6.

In a further report dated 12 June 1940, Commander St. John Cronyn listed those officers and other ranks he felt deserving of further recognition. The following two officers were, he noted, worthy of a decoration:

Lieut. Robert Peverell Hichens, R.N.V.R.:
This Officer landed on Friday 31st May as a volunteer to organise the beach at La Panne. He succeeded in getting Yachts moored and grass-lines secured from them to the beach, thus hastening considerably and making vastly safer the transport of troops to the waiting ships. He remained ashore and rejoined *Niger* next day. The beaches were under shell-fire and air attack for a great part of the time. At 2230 on Saturday 1st June he landed again at Malo-les-Bains to supervise the embarkation of troops. He had twice to go into the town in order to find Senior Military Officers and get the troops down to the beaches and boats. By his initiative and leadership he performed extremely valuable work and saved a tremendous amount of time.

Lieut-Comdr. Lionel James Spencer Ede, R.N. :
I wish to submit to your notice for a decoration Lieut-Comdr. Ede, Commanding Officer of H.M.S. *Salamander* whose report you will already have had. I was not in company when *Salamander* was damaged

but she is one of my Flotilla and I feel that his conduct is worthy of mention. I must also add that the Torpedo Coxswain of H.M.S. *Salamander* requested to see me on behalf of the Ship's Company with a view to bringing forward Lieut-Commander Ede's name as in their opinion he gave them a great lead and was a source of inspiration when things were unpleasant.

The following men were identified by Commander St. John Cronyn to receive a Mention in Despatches:

Lieut. Colin Benson Cathie, R.N.:
The Flotilla Navigating Officer who twice anchored the Ship at night within four cables of the beach and also guided in other ships of the group.

C.P.O. John Horace Brown, C/J.30520. Torp. Cox'n:
For good spirit, care and attention to the soldiers as they arrived on board, especially with regard to organising rations and comforts for them.

Ch. Stoker Ernest James Day, C/K.61574:
Was of great assistance in helping the Soldiers on board and generally guiding them to suitable parts of the Ship and seeing to their comfort. He showed a fine spirit.

Ldg.Sea. Clive Frederick Mane Cooper, C/JX.137062:
Coxwain [*sic*] of the *Niger*'s motor boat who showed excellent leadership and seamanship in towing the boats to and from the beaches. He ran every trip that the motor boat made on *Niger*'s three evacuations from the beaches, and was quite tireless. He also rescued many soldiers in danger of drowning. If *Niger* had been more often under fire I should have no hesitation in recommending this Rating for a decoration.

Ldg.Sea. George Frederick Crick, C/J.45439:
Coxwain [*sic*] of the whaler, performed excellent work in assisting the embarkation of the troops from the shore and showed considerable leadership.

L.S.B.A. Arthur Vernon Lionel McIllroy, C/MX.50059:
Was most able in the work which he had to do helping the wounded. He showed untiring willingness in aiding the exhausted soldiers and was of great assistance to the Medical Officer.

Whilst Commander (later Captain) St. John Cronyn DSO, RN, survived the war, retiring in January 1953, HMS Niger did not. During the return to Britain of Convoy QP 13 on 5 July 1942, Niger (then captained by Commander Arthur Jelfs Cubison, DSC and Bar, RN) led a column of merchantmen in bad weather with visibility reduced to one mile. Niger's crew had been unable to take bearings due to the weather but made a sighting of land, which was in fact an iceberg. Unfortunately the convoy had strayed into a British minefield off Iceland. She was mined at 22.40 hours, as were six of the merchants she was escorting. All but one also sank.

PANGBOURNE
Hunt-class Minesweeper
Pennant Number J37
Official Rescue Total: 1,026

The evening of Saturday, 25 May 1940, found HMS Pangbourne berthed alongside the quay at North Shields. A Hunt-class minesweeper launched in 1918, Pangbourne was a half-leader of the 5th Flotilla – the Fighting Fifth. It was shortly before midnight when her captain, Commander (Acting) Francis Douglas-Watson, received orders to sail for Harwich. Those officers and men ashore were immediately recalled. The duty officer recalled that it was 'a pretty tall order to recover sixty men in a town the size of North Shields', though within hours the task had been completed and the minesweeper underway. By 11.00 hours the next morning Pangbourne had docked at Harwich and work immediately began to prepare the small warship for whatever lay ahead. Commander Douglas-Watson's account of his ship's part in Operation Dynamo was written on 5 June 1940 whilst HMS Pangbourne was underway at sea:

At approximately midnight on Sunday 26th. May, H.M.S. *Pangbourne* in company with the remainder of the 5th M.S. Flotilla less H.M.S. *Saltash* slipped from Union Wharf, North Shields, and proceeded to Harwich, arriving at about 2300 Monday 27th. May. The ship coaled and provisioned a.m. Tuesday 28th. May, and proceeded to the beach east of Dunkirk at 1200. On arrival off the beach *Pangbourne* was ordered into Dunkirk harbour, and secured alongside the East mole at 2145. Some difficulty was experienced in getting alongside properly as a wire cable was discovered across the stem which prevented the ship going ahead far enough to clear the *Gossamer*, who was secured alongside in the next berth to seaward. *Pangbourne's* stern was thus outside

Gossamer's stem which meant that embarkation of troops could only take place over the lower bridge and a ladder on the forecastle.

When about a hundred to a hundred and fifty troops had embarked Commander J.C. Clouston R.N. who was N.O.I.C. on the jetty informed me that an unknown number of badly wounded were isolated on a jetty the other side of the entrance about one and a half miles further up, and asked me if I could go and collect them. I pointed out the presence of the wire across my bow, but he assured me that the centre of the channel was clear, as he had just seen some French destroyers go up. I backed out clear and proceeded as directed, turning before going alongside. In this I was assisted by the light of blazing buildings although the wharf itself was in deep shadow. On securing alongside I found about one thousand troops including a large number of stretcher cases and several hundred walking cases.

Owing to the tide being low and still ebbing it was necessary to rig wooden gangways from the boatdeck to the wharf, and the stretcher cases and walking cases were embarked by this method. It soon became apparent that we could not accommodate all the stretcher cases; the quarterdeck, passages, Wardroom etc., were soon full so non-wounded were embarked over the bridge forward until the ship was full. The troops on the mole behaved well and carried out instructions, but as there appeared to be very few officers or N.C.Os. ashore to take charge there was, when it became apparent that the entire party could not be taken off, a certain amount of crowding round the gangways.

At 0030 on Wednesday 29th. May I slipped and proceeded down harbour. After rounding No. 6E whistle and bell buoy I found myself in among two or three French destroyers, stopped in the channel, and as a result missed No. 1E bouy [sic] and went aground on sandbank north of Zuydcoote Pass. Engines were put to full astern and the ship slid off into about ten fathoms. In order to ascertain my exact position and wait until unlit bouys [sic] could be seen I anchored and very shortly picked up the Nieuport buoy. While waiting the ship was roughly fixed and found to be in position 51 degrees 7 minutes 30 seconds North, 2 degrees 28 minutes 48 seconds East, and clear of the channel. I proceeded without further incident to Margate. Just before dawn gunfire was observed ahead and shortly afterwards several destroyers passed me proceeding towards the French coast. Later passing the Kwinte buoy one sunken destroyer and another badly down by the stern were passed.

At 1000 ship secured alongside Margate pier and disembarked troops. Although no exact counting of troops was possible, about 450 in all were landed, including approximately 50 stretcher cases and 100 walking cases.

The arrangements for disembarkation of troops at Margate were most efficient.

At 1107 Wednesday 29th. May slipped and proceeded back to Dunkirk, being joined by *Lydd* at North Goodwin light vessel. At 1315 *Lydd* reported a submarine to starboard, although not observed by *Pangbourne* a warning was broadcast at 1321. Between 1645 and 1715 just off Nieuport bank several air attacks were directed against *Pangbourne* and all ships in the vicinity. Immediately after this two British soldiers were picked up in an exhausted condition, apparently having been blown from the deck of some small ship. At approximately 1730 several enemy bombers appeared to be about to attack *Pangbourne* but passed overhead, and were distinctly observed to attack a hospital ship about a mile on the Starboard beam for a considerable period without registering any direct hits. Just before passing the Nieuport Bank buoy a large lifeboat containing some thirty Belgian soldiers was picked up and the boat taken in tow for use on the beach.

On closing the beach I was ordered to proceed alongside the *Clan MacAlister* lying at anchor and embark the crew. This ship was on fire aft, and the ammunition round the aft gun was continually exploding. The Master reported to me that there was no chance of saving the ship as all hoses were cut and the steering gear out of action. The crew, including some 30 Lascars, and several Naval ratings, – crews of motor boats – were all embarked. I then proceeded and anchored about half a mile off the beach opposite the Sanatorium. All available boats were lowered and sent inshore in charge of Lieut. W.K. Tadman R.N.R. and Mr. S.S. Rabbitts, Boatswain R.N. Between 1800 and 1900 the ship was subjected to numerous low diving bombing attacks, although no direct hits were made there were several near misses. The hull was holed on both sides above and below the water line and the D.G. coil cut in several places.

It was during this period that all the casualties occurred, resulting in the death of seven ratings and six Belgian soldiers, and wounding of seven ratings and two officers, and two Belgian soldiers. During a lull in the bombing attacks the cable was slipped, the capstan being out of action, and the ship got under way, the troops by this time coming off in various boats were picked up, and the boats abandoned as they were holed and boats' falls shot away. As both compasses were out of action I decided to get clear of the sandbanks before dark. During the above attacks fire was opened on the bombers, but one near miss aft wounded or killed the 12 pdr. gun's crew. The majority of Lewis gun pans in ready use racks were pierced by bomb fragments and caused several jambs. The spare 12 pdr. gun's crew was closed up, but by this time the bombers appeared to be concentrating on the harbour although several high bombing attacks were made along the coast.

On clearing the Nieuport Bank the paddle-minesweeper *Gracie Fields* asked for assistance. She had suffered direct hits and was out of control, steaming at about six knots with her helm jambed, with 15 degrees starboard wheel on. I proceeded alongside and took off about eighty British soldiers. After this, as she appeared to be a danger to navigation, I took her in tow leaving the ship's company on board. *Kellett* passed and at my request led me as my compasses were still dead.

At 0130 Thursday 30th. May the *Gracie Fields* reported that she was sinking. I slipped her and went alongside, took off the ship's company, four badly wounded soldiers, and abandoned her and broadcast her approximate position (51 degrees 20 minutes North, 02 degrees 05 minutes East). By this time *Kellett* was out of sight and visibility was poor. At 0646 the South Goodwin Light Vessel was sighted and I was led into Dover by H.M.S. *Mosquito*. I secured alongside disembarking jetty at 1000 and landed troops, wounded and dead.

After disembarkation ship proceeded to Submarine Basin and was taken in hand for temporary repairs by *Sandhurst,* and remained out of action until 2000 Saturday 1st. June. By this time the D.G. coil was functioning but the compasses were still out of action.

After leaving harbour I was ordered to proceed in company with *Halcyon* and ordered her to rendezvous at North Goodwin. On arrival at North Goodwin I patrolled in the vicinity, but saw no sign of *Halcyon,* and I heard on return that she had not left harbour. As all shipping going towards the beaches had now ceased, I decided to proceed to the eastward with a view of assisting any ships returning in difficulties. T buoy was passed at 0532 and course altered to westward. Off S buoy A/V *Stella Regal* closed and transferred 23 British troops whom she had picked up some time previously. Returned to Dover by 1030 and landed troops. At 2000 proceeded to Dunkirk in company with *Halcyon* and *Speedwell* by West Pass, entering the breakwater at 0030 Monday June 3rd. On entering I was ordered by R.A.D. to wait outside as there were no troops waiting embarkation.

At 0200 a lifeboat with 43 French troops and 4 Officers came alongside and embarked. They stated that they were from a French vessel which had run aground on a sandbank. Whilst getting this party inboard I was ordered by R.A.D. to return to England. As *Albury* was leaving harbour at this time I followed her out clear of the channel and then proceeded to Folkestone and disembarked troops, then proceeded to Dover and coaled as I had only 15 tons of coal remaining. Owing to being unable to leave Granville Dock until 2130 *Pangbourne* did not take part in any further operations.

On 10 June 1940, whilst Pangbourne *was docked at Grimsby, Commander Douglas-Watson sent a further report to Vice-Admiral Commanding Dover:*

Lieut. MacClelland, R.N. who although wounded continued to carry out his duties and remained in the ship until completion of the evacuation.

Lieut. Tadman, R.N.R. who took charge of the boats on the beach and by his coolness under severe bombing was mainly responsible for getting some 100 military other ranks on board.

Mr. S.C. Wiltshire, Com. Engineer who in addition to his normal duties as E.O. and repair officer was of great assistance in embarking badly wounded stretcher cases from the west inner mole at Dunkirk.

The following two ratings who have since died of wounds are specially mentioned for their devotion to duty and it is by the general wish of the ship's company that their names are forwarded:

Petty Officer William G. Hoare. P/J 80058.

Ldg. Stoker Thomas Richards. D/K 65339.

All hands behaved in the usual service manner during action and it is extremely difficult to pick out any individual, but the following names are submitted for their general bearing and example during the period in harbour whilst carrying out temporary repairs, when the nervous strain was increased by temporary inactivity and uncertainty.

C.E.R.A. H.C. Warren. D/MX 46398.

P.O. Cook. T.C. Waterhouse. D/MX 49073.

Yeo of Signals. F.J. Robertson. D/JX 131329.

Ldg. Seaman A. Reid. D/J 110480.

Ldg. Stoker K. Robb. D/KX 83589.

A.B. F. James. D/J 83299.

S.P.O. F. Luff. P/K 65656.

Sig. F.J. Stanley. D/JX 142926 (on dangerous list in R.N.H. Chatham).

A.B. E. Fitzgerald. M/DX 2882.

Ldg. Steward. W. Goodlip. Maltese. E/LX 22306.

The latter was my personal steward and was killed while attending to wounded in my cabin.

Whilst not an Admiralty account, the following graphic description is again considered worthy of inclusion as an addition to Commander Douglas-

Watson's official report. The first part was published in The West Australian *on 9 June 1945. The introduction stated: 'This vivid personal narrative of the epic evacuation from Dunkirk was written by an officer of a British naval vessel which took part in the operation. It was written – not with a view to publication – when the officer was lying in hospital at Leeds in June, 1940 and was received recently by a friend of the officer in Western Australia':*

This is the story of Operation *Dynamo* as I saw it. It is not complete. The full story could only be told if every one of the thousands who were there were to write his own part and the whole collection were welded together by some master writer. I make no excuse therefore that what follows dwells mainly on me. It is true of so many that it is at the one time both personal and impersonal. Our memories are all too short; we so easily shut out from our mind the unpleasant things in life, but these last days must never be forgotten. Dunkirk has been a retreat and the fact cannot be denied, although when we know more of the details it may be excused. But it has been a magnificent retreat, and never was I prouder that I am British.

I am a sub-lieutenant on HMS *Pangbourne*; the ship is half-leader of the 5th Flotilla and they call us the Fighting Fifth. I used to think that it was just alliteration, but now I know different.

It is the night of May 25 and we are berthed alongside the quay at North Shields. I'm duty officer, the Captain is aboard and the others with half the ship's company are ashore. We have been at sea sweeping mines since three o'clock this morning and I'm feeling pretty tired and wishing I could turn in, when the quartermaster comes to me and says the Old Man wants me in his cabin.

I go up top and knock on his cabin door. When I enter he is standing in the middle of his floor in pyjamas about to retire, and in his hand is a signal. He looks up and greets me in the bluff good-natured way that makes him popular with everyone from Jimmy the One down to our newest ordinary seaman. "I want everyone back on board by midnight, sub – we're sailing. Get in touch with the police and have the pubs and cinemas informed."

I shift down those ladders as though old Nick is after me, and get on to the police station. It's a pretty tall order to recover sixty men in a town the size of North Shields. I meet the duty "boy" from HMS *Gossamer* at the phone. He is there for the same purpose; it's the whole flotilla that is needed. For an hour I pace up and down the quarter deck, and then the men start to trickle back. Another hour and only ten more men to come. Eleven-thirty and every man has returned. I didn't believe it could be done.

The quarter-master pipes "Hands to stations for leaving harbour. Stand by wires and fenders." I go for'ard and one by one the ships of the flotilla slip from the jetty, and in line ahead we sail between the breakwaters and head for the open sea. I go up to the bridge. The Captain tells me we are bound for Harwick [*sic*], but he doesn't know why – or else he knows and won't tell. I have the middle watch. God, I'm tired! Roll on four o'clock. It's pitch black and I can scarcely see the ship ahead. I put up the revolutions a bit and next thing, there she is right under my bow. I curse and sheer off to starboard, reduce speed a little and bring her back. Why the hell doesn't she burn a brighter light? But it helps to prevent me feeling too sleepy.

"Up two turns. Steer 168 degrees" – "down one turn" – "down two turns" – "steer 170 degrees" – "steer 172 degrees" – "nothing to starboard" – "up one turn" – "boatswain's mate go down and boil the cocoa" – "port ten – midships – meet her – steady on 130 degrees – up two turns." The watch wears on and reluctantly it seems the clock points to four. Jimmy comes up and relieves me. I tumble down and fall asleep on my bunk.

It is eleven o'clock next day and we have berthed at Harwick; for the past two hours I have been bundling up the confidential books, for on arrival orders were received that all of them are to be deposited at the Naval Base. It smells like trouble. They only give orders like that when the ship is likely to be sunk in enemy orders. I'm in the front seat of a base car with the books piled in the back on my way to the Navy offices. The Wren driver asks me what is brewing. I tell her I don't know. She doesn't believe me. She says she hopes I'll be all right. I hope so too.

By two o'clock fuelling is complete, stores aboard, and the Captain, who had been to a conference, returns with the navigator. We go to harbour stations, and the flotilla steams out. As we leave I look back across the River Stour and I can see the red roof of my home. They don't know that I have been in the harbour. I look at it until it dips below the hill. I wonder. The Captain wants all officers on the bridge and we congregate by the flag lockers. He breaks the news.

"We're going to Dunkirk, gentlemen, to evacuate a very great number of people. We may have to make several crossings and we shall meet opposition. In half an hour's time we shall go to action stations and we shall remain there until the job is finished. The command of this ship will pass to executive officers in order of seniority in the event of anything taking it out of my hands. You are each to make yourselves familiar with courses and navigational marks between Dunkirk and Ramsgate, and be prepared to fight the ship as long as she floats. Good luck."

The order is given to the ship's company to change into clean underclothes; wounds turn septic easily enough, without contributing. No heroics – just a cold sober statement of the facts and a reminder of our duties as officers. We go to the chart room and make our own notes from the chart. The navigator gives us the compass deviation and variation and degaussing settings. We collect and load our revolvers and put on our ammunition belts.

The klaxons blare. Hands to action stations! I am in charge of the solitary ack-ack gun, a twelve-pounder on the quarter deck. I have a first-class gun's crew, all active service men who have practised for this time and again. I give the order to load HE and the gun is reported all ready. We wait. Six o'clock comes and no attack has developed. A peculiar smell is in the air. I know it from my days in the Merchant Service. It's burning oil fuel and there on the horizon ahead is a black cloud – smoke from the burning tanks of Dunkirk. It is flat calm now, and the wind has dropped, and as we draw nearer the eastern sky glows from a million fires.

We round Nieuport buoy and turn to the southward; I turn my glasses on the beaches. The silver sands are stained with black. I look again. The stain is a packed mass of people. Thousands upon thousands of them, looking to seaward to watch the flotilla arrive. And now I can see something more – something which my bewildered mind is unwilling to believe. The people are soldiers in British khaki! Can things be going so badly for us that we are evacuating our army? This is no regiment or division; it is an army of considerable size. I don't understand. A lamp winks from the shore. We are to go inside the mole to load evacuees. We turn to port and creep in ahead of a hospital ship.

No longer is there any doubt. We tie up and they swarm aboard us. Dirty, ragged, weary soldiers, with a forced smile on their white faces and a cheery word for the sailors although they are dead on their feet. They come without coats, some without shoes or socks – but few without some sign of an unbeatable spirit. We stow them wherever there is an inch of space, and they flop down as they are and relax. They seem to think because they are aboard a ship danger is past. And now we have received a message that we must shift berth into the inner harbour, where an ambulance convoy is waiting with stretcher cases. It is quite dark now, about 9.30 I think, and the Germans have started shelling the harbour. It is a 5.9-inch battery at Nieuport a mile or two to the northward. We find our way with great difficulty to the inner harbour and secure to the dockwall again. The stretchers come aboard. Poor devils. One asks me if it's rough outside. I tell him it's like a millpond and give him a smoke. He seems more concerned about being seasick than about the left arm they amputated this morning.

The shelling has intensified and is dropping about two hundred yards over us, but the tide is low, and although it makes it difficult to get the wounded aboard, we have the protection of the wall against the shrapnel. We are crammed to capacity and not another man could we take. The telegraph rings and we shove off. Now we are on our own. The other ships of the flotilla have found themselves work like ours, but as each is filled it moves off independently. We steam out of the harbour and turn north. It is nearly half-past twelve. I am on the bridge now staring into the blackness with the other officers to find the Nieuport buoy with its flashing green light. There is the pulsating note of motor boats in the distance – enemy motor torpedo boats. My eyes are smarting from the prolonged use of my prismatics.

Suddenly we see it. A tiny green light away out on the port bow. Funny thing it being there; it should appear right ahead. The captain orders an alteration of course to port and at the same instant that friendly little green light disappears. Then quite suddenly the ship lurches and we are thrown forward; a sickening, grinding noise mixes with the shout of "Full astern both engines" from the Old Man. It's too late, we are aground on a sand bank and we don't know where the hell we are. I've felt like this as a kid when I've lost sight of my parents in a crowd. The same thought is in the minds of all of us on the bridge – "What is the tide doing – rising or falling?" somebody thumbs through tables by the shaded light of a torch. "Full tide at three o'clock." He announces. Thank God! There's a good chance of backing off on the flood, provided those damned torpedo boats don't poke a fish into us first.

The engineer officer comes up to report that we are making no water and there is no serious damage below. From somewhere hot cocoa and sandwiches have arrived on the bridge and we all sit down and tuck in. The soldiers, blissfully unconscious of the danger, are mostly sleeping. Three o'clock comes and the engines churn the water into foaming soap suds as they strain to pull us off and we all sigh with relief as the ship starts to move, slowly at first and then quicker until we slide back into deep water. The navigator believes he has located the sand bank on the chart and suggests a course of 020 degrees. I could kiss him.

Ten minutes later when the dark shape of the buoy looms ahead. The light has been extinguished – shot out presumably by the torpedo craft. Now we are on the road home however and spirits are high again. Somebody tells the story of the Wren that sat on the Admiral's knee – we all know it but we laugh just the same. There is no question of getting any sleep – our cabins are bulging to the doors with soldiers and not a square inch of deck is left uncovered. Dawn breaks and with the first light we see the English coast again.

Soon we are at Ramsgate and the pongos refreshed after their few hours' rest, and wild with joy at being home file over the gangway singing and shouting. By now there are hundreds of ships and boats on the ferry service and the instant the last man steps ashore we let go and make room at the pier head for the next ship to discharge.

The second instalment of this account was published in The West Australian *on 16 June 1945. 'Last week's instalment told of the vessel's first visit to Dunkirk and its return to Britain with its full complement of exhausted and wounded soldiers. The narrative is resumed at that point':*

We Go Back. I work out the date. It is May 27. We have none of us slept since the 25th, and we are getting past it now; midday brings my relief to the bridge, and I go down to the ward room. There is no cooked lunch, but the stewards have knocked up platefuls of sandwiches and coffee. I eat some, but they have no taste. My lips and tongue are sore with smoking countless cigarettes, but I light another and sit back in an easy chair. The engineer officer and the boatswain are there too. The letter passes some remark about making a will. It started as being humorous, but we all three find that none of us has made a will, so we drag the table into the centre of the wardroom and sit down with pen and paper and make them out there and then. We witness each other's, place them in the wardroom letter box and sit back again.

A few minutes pass in silence and then a giant with a hammer smashes his weight against the ship's side four times in rapid succession. This is it! The storm is breaking. The klaxons scream their warning, and before they stop I am at the gun. There high above us are the planes – Heinkels and Dorniers – and the bombs are screaming down. I bring the gun on to a Heinkel IIIK that has started his bombing run in, and for the first time in my life give the order "Open Fire!" the shells are bursting short, and I order a change of fuse setting. The shooting isn't bad at all, but the plane still comes in. I see the bombs leave her – one, two, three, four, five, six, seven, eight, and take up their flight. They are over. I can see they are going to miss. I shift target right. A second Heinkel is coming in at 10,000ft on the starboard quarter. He is high enough to make me feel quite safe, and as the gun bangs away I feel that I am a spectator at a show, so dispassionate do I feel about the human life at stake. It is a grand game of shooting down the aeroplane – it is not the grim fact of using your skill and training to destroy five Germans in their flimsy craft.

I glance at my watch and see it is five o'clock. How long has this cat-and-mouse chase been going on? We must be getting close to the beaches again now. Will these damned planes never stop? They drop their bombs. They miss. They go away, and as quickly as they go others take their place. How much longer before they hit us? The gun's crew are sweating with the exertion and the deck is covered with the rejected charge cases. Not a stoppage on the gun so far. I cross my fingers.

Suddenly there is a silence. The aircraft have gone. Only temporarily I know, but how wonderful the respite from that inferno of sound! Everyone shouts when speaking; we are all gun-deaf. I had not noticed that we are back near where we went aground last night, and the sea is a mass of boats and debris. A destroyer on fire is being towed out on one side, and gaping holes in her side show where the bombs went home. Men are struggling in the water all around us, and we are stopping to pick them up. There is Jimmy and some of the hands helping them over the side. One is an RAF pilot in a great yellow Mae West. If only the British planes would come! Where are the fighters?

What is that on the port quarter? – it looks like a tiny cloud. I strain my eyes through the glasses. It's Jerry again. I give the orders mechanically, and the gun swings on to the bearing. They come relentlessly on like great black vultures. No use opening fire yet; they are not yet within range. These are a different kind, with queer wings and fixed undercarriages. I rack my brain to think what they are.

Suddenly the penny drops. They are Stuka dive-bombers. They wheel round in a circle and peel off one by one. Each has selected his prey, and here comes ours. In a screaming vertical power dive he is tearing down towards us at four hundred knots. The noise is terrifying. I am shouting ranges at the top of my voice. Surely to God nothing can stop him crashing on our decks! – he'll never pull out of this. He starts to spit fire at us, and the tracer shells from his cannon blind me as I watch for the bombs to fall. Our machine-guns are chattering back at him, and the red tracer bullets seem to be passing through his wings. My head will burst with noise soon. Part of my mind is acutely alert, watching and waiting for the moment when it is useless to load the gun; that point where before the round can be fired the target will have passed overhead. Yet another part of me is praying fiercely that he will miss us, with such an intensity of prayer that no words form part of it. Stupid things crowd through my mind – the dome on the big building on the bank of the Suez Canal at Port Said – the electric sign for Bovril in Piccadilly – the faulty switch on the electric fire in the lounge at home – the Wren driver whispers furiously at me "I hope you'll be all right – what's brewing? – I hope you'll be all right – what's brewing? I hope you'll be all right –"

"Take cover!" everyone goes flat. I press myself into the hard wooden deck. I saw the big bombs leave the fuselage between the spats of the undercarriage and two smaller ones from each wing follow it and gave the order. I heard the "Take Cover" and almost immediately realised it was my voice that gave it. The scream of the bombs is masked by the roar of the diving plane as it sweeps the masts. The world goes mad. The ship leaps in the air and cold salt water souses me as I shrink into the deck. The spanging of bullets and flying shrapnel is added to the explosion of the bombs. The breath is knocked out of my body and then for a brief moment there follows a stillness broken only by the retiring plane.

I stagger to my feet and gaze at a picture of utter horror. Blood and flesh is everywhere; mutilated bodies that ten seconds ago were men I knew personally, are flung in grotesque heaps all about me. The gun is pointing drunkenly at the sky, knocked completely from its bearings. Three of my seven men are standing with me stunned by the desolation around them. I climb with difficulty to where the gun layer is lying, his neck and stomach torn open and his hand blown away. We have no doctor – none could help him anyway. He is still breathing and moaning faintly. I slip a morphia tablet under his tongue and move across to the breech worker. No need for morphia here; he is dead. The loading number is lying with his eyes open and looking at me. I kneel beside him before I find what is wrong. A shrapnel splinter has fractured his jaw on the side away from me. He will be all right. I give him a tablet and cushion his head on a life jacket.

I wonder who is left on the bridge. I pick my way through the carnage, slipping in blood and on red flesh to the bridge ladder. The captain's steward is lying there without a mark, but the trickle of blood from his nose and mouth betray that his lungs have been ruptured by blast. On the bridge is the Old Man smiling beneath his enormous tin hat. I think to myself: it is the biggest tin hat I have ever seen. He asks about the gun. I tell him.

The Engineer officer comes up. He says there are hundreds of holes below the water line. His staff are working like slaves to plug them and there is a chance the pumps will keep the water down. Apparently all five bombs exploded close alongside but we have not suffered a direct hit. I ask where the other officers are and learn that they have taken the boats ashore for more soldiers. They have been gone nearly three-quarters of an hour. I am about to wipe my face with my hand when I see it is covered in blood. I look down and find my left trouser leg wet with blood. So that's why I'm limping. My shoulder is stiff too. I turn round and the Old Man tells me there is no back to my jacket. I slip off what remains of it and learn there is a neat slice carved out of my back. I investigate my left leg. I slip my trousers off and am standing in only my underpants doing a contortionist act to see where three small pieces of shrapnel have entered my thigh, when the drone of a plane changes suddenly to the crescendo of a power dive, and a second Stuka is plunging towards us.

There is nothing we can do. We are defenceless now, and there is no cover on the bridge. I feel quite naked and crouching down behind the mast suddenly think it terribly funny that I very nearly am. Never was the expression "caught with his pants down" more true. I wonder if this damned German pilot can see me and if he is laughing too. There is a sickening repetition of the cacophony of five minutes ago, but maybe my nerves are dulled, for this does not seem so bad. Down come the bombs – thank God well clear. Maybe he was laughing too much to aim accurately. Things are becoming confused. I am seeing with difficulty and voices are distant. Somebody is tying a field dressing on me and I'm no longer on the bridge. I'm floating about in the captain's cabin and there are a lot of people there with me. Against the forward bulkhead I can see a blanket spread over something that wasn't there yesterday. I realise what it is.

Jimmy comes in and speaks to me. I'm not floating now, I'm lying on my side in the Old Man's big easy chair. Jimmy tells me that he was on his way back to the ship when the first Stuka attacked and when the columns of water subsided he was amazed to see us still afloat. He says we are on our way back to England; that the pumps are gaining on the leaks and that air attack has ceased for the moment. He tells me that on his way back to the ship he saw the *Golden Eagle* take a bomb down the engine room skylight which blew her to pieces and covered the sea with fuel oil, and before any boats could reach the survivors the oil caught fire. I shudder and am surprised that anything can still shock me.

We are still talking when the telegraph rings and we reduce speed. We both go up to see what is happening. It is nearly dark but we can make out a big paddle steamer on the starboard bow. It is the *Gracie Fields*. She has been bombed and wants us to take her in tow. She sends her survivors over in a boat and we make fast a heavy wire and start to tow. The blind leading the blind. She is a fine ship and is almost new. I remember the fuss they made over her maiden voyage when *Gracie Fields* herself went aboard her and sang to the passengers. She is leaking badly now and is so heavy that our speed is reduced to about five knots. We tow her till midnight but she is sinking lower and lower in the water. Regretfully we realise that she is not going to see England again and we cast her adrift.

Dawn breaks over the misty horizon and there is the breakwater of Dover harbour in the distance. Soon we are secured alongside again, and the heart-breaking job of sending ashore our dead and seriously wounded begins. How long it takes! How desperately tired we all are! Today is May 29 and we have not slept since May 25.

At long last I step ashore. I expect to be able to get a dressing and return on board. I take nothing with me. The army doctor examines me and puts me in the care of an RAMC orderly. I am taken to the hospital train. I protest bitterly. They are stupid and not inclined to argue. Twelve hours later the train arrives in Leeds, and we are brought here. Thank God for the patience and gentleness of nurses.

ROSS
Hunt-class Minesweeper
Pennant Number J45
Official Rescue Total: 1,096

Built by Lobnitz in Rendrew Glasgow, HMS Ross was launched on 12 June 1919. It was originally intended that she would be named Ramsey, this being changed during completion. HMS Ross was also serving in the 5th Minesweeping Flotilla when she was called upon for Operation Dynamo. Until 28 May 1940, HMS Ross has been captained by Commander John Pollington Apps RN. Injured in the first trip across the Channel, Apps was replaced by Lieutenant Arthur Gadd RNR. It was the latter who subsequently wrote the following account, which is dated 7 June 1940:

On May 28th. 1940, at 1210 H.M.S. *Ross* left Harwich in company with Flotilla less *Saltash*, and secured alongside at Dunkirk East Breakwater at 2140 and commenced to embark troops. 353 troops were embarked in just over one hour, when ship slipped and proceeded to Margate by route Y.

29th. May, at 0606 *Ross* secured alongside at Margate Pier and disembarked troops, slipping at 0828 and proceeding to rendezvous with H.M.S. *Gossamer* at North Goodwin Light Vessel.

Gossamer and *Ross* then proceeded to Dyck buoy and commenced a sweep of channel from Dyck buoy to Middelkerke buoy. This operation was completed without incident at 1530, no mines having been found. Both ships then proceeded to position off W buoy and commenced Double Orepesa sweep along route X towards N. Goodwin Lt. Vessel. This sweep was completed at 2100 without any mines having been swept. *Gossamer* and *Ross* then proceeded by route X towards Dunkirk.

On 30th. May, at 0210 off 11W buoy in Dunkirk approach channel *Ross* closed S.S. *Normania*, which had been bombed and was sinking by the stern and took off 53 survivors including 43 troops, afterwards proceeding to anchorage off Bray at 0405. At 0630 a further 410 troops had been embarked so anchor was weighed and ship proceeded by route X towards Margate and anchored there at 1032 to await berth, finally going alongside at 1240. At 1420 on completion of disembarkation of troops, *Ross* proceeded to Sheerness to coal.

31st. May, at 0248 slipped and proceeded in company with *Sutton* and *Lydd* to Dunkirk beach by route X. At about 0815 the Captain slipped on the bridge and fell heavily breaking a rib, so 1st. Lieutenant took command. At 0910 ship anchored off Zuydcoote and commenced to embark troops.

An improvised jetty had been constructed by the army, of motor lorries and other vehicles, but unfortunately the wind had got up during the night causing a sea of about 3 which made boat work difficult and several boats were damaged when going alongside the jetty by striking under water projections of the vehicles, consequently after two hours only 121 troops had been embarked, so *Ross* proceeded alongside *Lydd* and transferred them, and then proceeded in company with *Sutton* and *Lydd* by route X. At 1553 *Ross* anchored off Margate where the Captain was landed by boat and taken to hospital. At 1930 weighed anchor and proceeded in company with *Albury* to rendezvous at W buoy with Group 1.

1st. June, at 0110 anchored off Le Panne and awaited arrival of troops. At 0350 commenced embarkation of troops by ships boats. The whaler suffered damage and was leaking badly, so that embarkation was carried on with motor boat and skiff only. At 0515 after embarking 92 troops weighed anchor and proceeded to Bray and continued to embark a further 168 troops. During this time machine gun aircraft made several attacks but no casualties were suffered.

At 0709 ship proceeded towards Dunkirk and at 0741 a bombing attack by five enemy aircraft was made when abeam of Dunkirk harbour. 16 bombs were dropped but there were no direct hits but the hull was holed by shrapnel splinters in several places above the waterline on the port side of the forecastle. The boiler brickwork also collapsed through concussion of bomb exploding port side amidships and the steering gear was put slightly out of line.

H.M.S. *Ivanhoe* about half a mile on the port bow was attacked at the same time and suffered a direct hit amidships.

When approaching 5W buoy occasional rounds from a shore battery were observed falling between 5W and 6W buoys so ship was turned inside 5W buoy leaving it on port hand.

At 0855 after passing W buoy a machine gun attack was made by a single enemy aircraft, when one stoker was seriously wounded and has since died. During the bombing attacks only one casualty was suffered, an ordinary seaman receiving a splinter wound in the foot.

Another A.A. gun forward would have been a great advantage as many of the attacking aircraft approached from that direction where of course the 12 pounder was unable to bear.

It is believed one enemy aircraft was brought down by *Ross*'s gunfire but it cannot be said for certain as other vessels were firing in the vicinity. The 12 pdr. guns crew was extremely keen and the eye shooting of the layer and trainer after the first few rounds became very good.

The establishment of H.A. ammunition for the ship seems hardly adequate as after the last encounter only eight rounds out of a total of one hundred were remaining.

The Lewis gunners also showed exceptional keenness, too much so at times, so that they were opening fire at too great a range.

The total number of troops carried was 1066 not including 121 transferred to *Lydd*.

In his covering letter, Lieutenant Gadd had pointed out that 'the whole of the ship's company behaved extraordinarily well whilst under fire, so that it is made very difficult to pick out individuals for special recommend'. However, he did go on to add that 'the following Officer and ratings are recommended for mention in dispatches':

Lieutenant David Croom-Johnson, R.N.V.R. for the cool way in which he controlled and encouraged the 12 pdr. guns crew during fierce machine gun and bombing attacks;

Ordinary Seaman Theo Norman Pasfield, P/JX176952, and Leading Signalman Edwin Charles Atkins, P/JX152931, for exceptional keenness and disregard of personal danger whilst Lewis gunner and supply at port Lewis gun.

Both these ratings, when they heard that *Ross* could not sail on Saturday night 1st June, immediately requested to return to Dunkirk in another ship.

SALAMANDER
Halcyon-class Minesweeper
Pennant Number J86
Official Rescue Total: 1,161

Ordered from J.S. White at Cowes on 5 February 1935, HMS Salamander was launched on 24 March 1936 as the eleventh Royal Navy warship to carry the name. She was deployed at Great Yarmouth for mine clearance work on the convoy routes in the North Sea when she was diverted to participate in Operation Dynamo. *On 7 June 1940, Lieutenant Commander Lionel James Spencer Ede provided the following 'report of proceedings':*

At 2000/26/5 I left the Humber under the orders of *Sutton* in company with *Sutton* and *Fitzroy*.

Arrived and anchored in Downs at 1510/27/50.

At 1540/28/5 weighed and proceeded under orders of *Sutton* in company with *Sutton* and *Fitzroy* via R.S. & T. Buoys to Dunkirk Roads. Rendezvous-ed with *Halcyon* and *Skipjack* by S. Buoy and proceeded in company, anchoring off La Panne at 2130.

Using motorboat and whalers embarked 150 men during the night.

In the morning I was ordered by *Calcutta* to close her and transfer to her military personnel as she could get no closer to the shore.

At 0705/29/5 I weighed and proceeded to *Calcutta* and at 0900 I transferred troops.

Proceeded back to La Panne and began loading troops using own boats and small shore pulling boats. A bombing attack by Junkers 87 was carried out in the forenoon and *Greyhound*, as well as several small ships, was hit about one cable from me.

At 1730 I weighed and proceeded via Dunkirk Roads and another high bombing attack was carried out. Observed Dunkirk and neighbouring beaches to be subjected to heavy bombing attacks.

Proceeded via T.S. & R. Buoys in company with *Sutton*, arriving and anchoring off Dover in thick weather at 2320.

Reported magnetic mines laid by aircraft during night vide my signal to V.A. Dover. 2345/29/5.

At 0600/30/5 weighed and proceeded alongside Admiralty Pier and at 0740 disembarked 289 men. Proceeded to ammunition ship and store ship at Eastern Arm. At 1610/30 slipped and proceeded to Dunkirk Roads via U, V. & W Buoys and anchored off Bray by 2100/30/5.

Embarked 397 men during the night and was ordered close *Shikari* for two Staff Officers. Embarked Brig.-Gen. Holden and another Staff Officer and the transferred motorboat to *Icarus* who had no powerboat.

Proceeded to Dover via W, V. & U. Buoys and went alongside Admiralty Pier at 0810/31/5.

Disembarked personnel, proceeded and secured to Eastern Arm to ammunition ship, etc.

Then proceeded in accordance with my attached narrative of events, dated 5th June, 1940.

Two days before the above had been written, Lieutenant Commander Ede wrote the following 'narrative of events which took place on Friday, 31st May, and Saturday, 1st June, 1940'. Unfortunately, the appendices to which he refers are no longer in the Admiralty files:

At 1800/31/5 I left Dover in company with *Halcyon* and *Skipjack* to rendezvous with the remainder of the minesweepers at W buoy by 2200 in accordance with V.A. Dover's 0357/31/5.

Here I took *Fitzroy* under my command and followed astern of the other two groups through Dunkirk Roads, past Dunkirk, to a position off Bray. I was the ordered by *Niger* to anchor one mile to his Eastward, to avoid magnetic mines laid near No.8 Buoy. This was accomplished by 0015/1/6.

The beach at Bray was under shrapnel fire from inland enemy batteries, and as no boats closed me I lowered a whaler with a Volunteer crew to land for soldiers (See appendix No.1).

The boat returned in about half an hour with one hand and a message from General Montgomery to inform all ships that he intended moving Westward to Dunkirk at once as the beach was becoming untenable. This message I passed to all ships in V/S touch.

The pontoon pier had been hit by shell fire and no troops seemed to be embarking at all, so I weighed and kept under way closing the beach as much as I could.

When a little light appeared, however, boats began to shove off from the beach and come to me. R.A. Dover now ordered all ships to embark men in boats and move Westward to Dunkirk at dawn. A continual stream of boats came off with military personnel, and by 0600/1/6 I had embarked about 450 men, including 29 wounded of whom 11 were stretcher cases. Attacks by aircraft took place on all ships and salvos of bombs were dropped, no ships being hit. We were the attacked by front machine gun fire from Messerschmitt 109's, and one casualty was sustained. L.S.A. Gullett was hit in the hand by a bullet. I then moved Westward astern of *Keith* and *Skipjack*.

At 0820/1/6 an air attack took place on all three ships, and *Skipjack* was sunk, and *Keith* hit and set on fire. *Keith* abandoned ship, and I closed her and sent away both whalers as lifeboats. (See appendix No.2). Whilst rescuing survivors I was again attacked by Junkers 87 dive bombers, and a salvo of four bombs fell about 50 feet ahead of the ship. They exploded under water when two bombs were approximately abreast the bridge. The ship lifted bodily and heeled to starboard, and settled down with a list to port. She then sunk about a foot, suddenly. I feared she was in danger of sinking, so I ordered the S.P's on board to be jettisoned. This was done in a weighted bag (See appendix No.3). I stopped engines and waited reports from the Engineer Officer and Executive Officer.

The Engineer Officer and First Lieutenant ascertained that the ship was still seaworthy, although she had gained about 1 foot of draught forward, and had flooded compartments amidships comprising the cold and cool rooms, gunners stores and canteen store. I about a quarter of an hour steam was got on main engines again. (See attached Engineer Officer's report).

A further air attack now took place, and a salvo of bombs fell on the port quarter about fifty yards astern. A heavy concussion was felt. I then decided to proceed as far as possible whilst the fan engines could be kept running. I left the whalers to assist picking up survivors from *Keith* and taking them to a tug standing by. I saw the Captain D 19 on the bridge of this tug, and he asked me to fire H.E. at the Asdic dome of the *Keith* which was listed heavily to port. Having none left I fired two rounds of S.A.P and destroyed her dome.

Having now 480 men in addition to my ship's company, I proceeded at full available speed to return via Dunkirk and W, V. and U buoys. We were again attacked by aircraft off W buoy, but a combined 0.5" and Lewis Gun fire of the ship's company, and Bren gun and rifle fire of the soldiers on board, kept the machines from pressing home their attack, and no further damage was sustained. 219 rounds of 4" H.E.H.A were fired in all during the morning and forenoon.

One fan engine now finally broke down, and we proceeded on one boiler at about 7 knots, reaching Dover at 1530/1/6.

The behaviour of the ships company was exemplary, and the morale of the soldiers in unusual circumstances was beyond praise.

I further beg to report that of the eight ratings who formed the lifeboats' crews five are still missing, as noted in appendix 2, and I especially wish to call attention to the behaviour of the ratings mentioned in Appendix 4.

In respect of the air attack on 1 June 1940, T.K. Reynolds, Salamander's engineering officer, writing on 5 June 1940, provided the following summary on 'the action taken to remedy urgent defects sustained':

The defects were caused by delay action bombs, exploding near the port side of the ship in the region of 34 station. At the time of the occurrence the whole of the messdecks and waists were crowded with soldiers standing up, and a number of wounded were on stretchers on the mess tables. Approximately 450 soldiers were on board, including about 20 stretcher cases. This rendered passage between the Engine Room and Boiler Rooms extremely difficult.

The first effect was to throw the ship heavily to the starboard side, at the same time apparently lifting her out of the water about two feet. She then rolled to port, and eventually took a slight list to port.

The effects on the machinery were as follows: The steam dynamo came off the board, putting the ship in darkness, and began vibrating badly. Steps were immediately taken to start the Diesel dynamo and lights were available in less than three minutes.

In the mean time steam pressure had fallen, as the forced draught fan in each boiler room had stopped. It was found that both fan oil sumps were cracked badly round the base, and the oil had drained into the fan flats. In addition the impellors were fouling the casings. The fans had been running about half speed at the time. The after fan was first of all restarted, after shoring it aft with wooden wedges to keep the impellor clear, and a chain of Stokers sent for oil to keep replenishing the sump to prevent the fan seizing up. Steam was raised for slow speed, and the ship got under way about 15 to 20 minutes after the explosion. The cylinder was then shored down from the deck above to keep the crankcase from fracturing completely.

A similar action was taken with the forward fan, and afterwards attempts were made to plug the cracks to help stem the flow of oil. Both fans were used for leaving Dunkirk, but when clear of Dunkirk Roads the forward fan was stopped owing to the danger of fire from the quantity of oil flung into the boiler room. The draught marks were sighted as soon as possible, and it was observed that the ship had gained approximately a foot forward, which remained constant. It was found that compartments forward had taken in small quantities of water, and compartments 32 and 37 had flooded up to the lower deck. In view of the fact that the ship had been under almost continual attack for about three hours, and that this was the third heavy attack in four days at Dunkirk, the morale of the Engine Room ratings was excellent.

The following ratings were exceptionally steady in carrying out their duties:

E.R.A. C.H. Andrew, M28768. In starting up the Diesel engine and restarting the auxiliaries and main engines when steam was available.

Leading Stoker A. Hussey, D/KX62678. In assisting E.R.A. Andrew
Stoker Petty Officer T. Rochford, D/KX 61034. By restarting the
damaged after fan, and raising steam in the after boiler.

Stoker H. Rogers, D/KX 82058. By his coolness in No. 1 Boiler room
when on watch during and after the explosion.

Stoker H.J. Thompson, D/KX 93732. Consistently volunteered to man
the whaler during his off duty watches.

The following two soldiers volunteered to go down to the forward
boiler room shortly after the explosion and helped to clear the loose
gear, such as deckplates, which had been thrown out of place on to the
pumps:

T78316 Driver G. Ronson, R.A.S.C.
385379 Private T. Willingale, Loyals.

William 'Young Bill' Stone was a member of the crew of HMS Salamander.
A veteran of the battleship HMS Hood, *his account of the minesweeper's work
at Dunkirk is carried on the HMS Hood Association's website,
www.hmshood.com, from where the following is quoted:*

We did five trips to Dunkirk in all, rescuing 200 to 300 men each time.
Things got worse each trip we made. Our final trip was on 1st June by
which stage there was the wreckage of sunken ships all around and
burning oil tanks by the dockside. Lines of troops were all marching
towards the sea. We were anchored off the beach with one of our sister
ships, the *Skipjack*, only about fifty yards away. At about 8am the
German dive bombers came over and attacked *Skipjack*. One of the
attacking planes was shot down but *Skipjack* was badly hit and capsized.
She must have had about 200 men on board. I had to say "God, help
us." I believe to this day that He did.

During our trips to Dunkirk, I was often stationed on the quarterdeck
helping men get aboard *Salamander* as they swam out from the beach.
Other groups of men had managed to find boats and row out to the
ship. On one occasion I had a rope around a badly injured soldier who
had bones sticking out of his trousers. Just as I tried to pull him in, the
ship went ahead and I lost him. I don't know what happened to him.

Unknown to me, on our way back on the final trip, we were attacked
by a submarine that fired a torpedo at us. When we got back to Dover
the Coxswain and the Able Seaman on the wheel said to me "Chief, we
held our ears today and waited for the explosion. Jerry fired this
torpedo that was coming straight for us amidships." *Salamander* had
been saved by her shallow draft – the torpedo had passed straight
underneath us …

In all the years since Dunkirk I had never come across anyone whom we had rescued in the *Salamander* until the summer of 1999. It was then that, whilst at a reunion of the Henley Branch of the Dunkirk Veterans Association, a chap came up to me and said, "What ship were you in at Dunkirk, Chief?" "*Salamander*," I replied.

"You saved my life," he said. He told me that he had broken into a boat shed at De Panne in Belgium with some other soldiers and pinched a rowing boat. They had started to row home when we picked them up … Following Dunkirk *Salamander* was put in to the Royal Albert docks in London to undergo repair to the damage that had been sustained during the evacuation.

Guardsman 2616563 Frank Fletcher DCM was one of the many rescued by HMS *Salamander. His account,* Dunkirk Evacuation: A Young Guardsman's Story, *can be seen on the BBC People's War website (www.bbc.co.uk/history/ww2peopleswar):*

About 2am the moon came out and it was possible to see where we were going at the final crossroads. The RSM, Cyril Sheather, stood checking and counting how many men had made it to the beach. He was never seen again presumably killed carrying out the final order.

The sand dunes gave a certain amount of cover from the shelling and all we could do was wait for daylight to see if the navy was going to rescue us. The light improved, the tide came in and destroyers appeared off shore. Spirits rose among the troops in the sand dunes. Before the destroyers could collect their quota, the Germans gave them the full treatment, one received a direct hit and sank in a few minutes The second was hit on the starboard side blowing a large hole in its' plates but it didn't sink. The troops standing on the port side were up to their knees it water. With one of her propellers out of the water, she turned around and crept away doing about 3 knots.

Next two minesweepers appeared, the troops left on the beach were mainly guardsman, Grenadiers and Coldstreams, the remains of a Scottish regiment and a few stragglers who hoped someone would get them home.

A Corporal and myself swam out and salvaged a Carey Life float; it held 4 of us and we tried to get out to nearest ship. (I later discovered that the life float was made in Frome at the Notts Industries Works!) With the tide coming in we didn't make a bit of progress but a lifeboat full of Scottish Troops commanded by a CSM who obviously fancied himself as a sailor threw us a line. We made it to the nearest minesweeper, the *Salamander*, the other being the *Speedwell*. We later described the *Salamander*, one funnel, one gun and one hope to get back.

The German planes returned to give us the full treatment, a stick of bombs dropped between the boats, nearly capsizing the *Speedwell* and causing steam to come out of the *Salamander* through holes that were never on the Admiralty drawings. However they were built of strong stuff and lived to fight another day. The hoist to the 4.5 gun went up in smoke and the shells had to be manhandled to the gun deck, the empties were dumped over the side burning and blistering the hands.

The morning wore on and we cruised up and down the beach taking on board any of the troops that made it to the nets slung over the sides. The 4.5 kept banging away helped by several Bren guns taken on board by the troops. I did ask the Petty Officer in charge of the gun whether we would get back. He said and I quote, "Son, I volunteered for this ship, the British Navy has never lost a *Salamander* yet through enemy action". As it survived several Russian convoys later in the war his confidence was not misplaced.

The Germans were still trying to sink us. One ME 110 received a direct hit above us and dived into the sea. The final few shells were being manhandled to the gun deck, a few more planes flew over but for once they were ours. The troops on deck gave them a cheer and toasted them in Navy cocoa. It was thick enough to cut but as the first hot drink for several days there were no complaints.

Having loaded our quota we turned and headed to the open sea and the white cliffs of England.

SALTASH
Hunt-class Minesweeper
Pennant Number J62
Official Rescue Total: 800

Built in Glasgow, the Hunt-class minesweeper HMS Saltash *was launched on 25 June 1918. Serving throughout most of the Second World War, including the D-Day landings, a fictitious HMS* Saltash *appears in Nicholas Monsarrat's famous novel* The Cruel Sea. *On 4 June 1940, her captain, Lieutenant Commander Thomas Randall Fowke RN, penned the first of two reports relating to the evacuation:*

During the operations off Dunkerque the following Officer and men have shown perseverance and courage, I have the honour to submit their names so that suitable action may be taken.

1. Lieutenant T.E. Williams R.N.R., First Lieutenant of H.M.S. *Saltash*. On the night of Friday, May 31st, he was loaned to H.M.S. *Hebe* but he was not required. On his way back in a motor boat he went in shore to pick up soldiers; not finding any he took two sailors and, pulling a whaler behind them, he made his way along the beach to see if he could pick any up. La Panne was being bombarded the whole time he was ashore. He knew that I thought he was aboard *Hebe* and that the C.O. of *Hebe* thought he was aboard [with] me so that he could not expect any ship to wait for him; both pontoons were destroyed while he was ashore. Eventually he returned to *Hebe*, and when he came back to me on Sunday night was perfectly ready and fit for more. He found only dead men, & must have been ashore two hours. While *Saltash* was rescuing survivors from S.S. *Brighton Queen*, and was in a precarious position alongside her bridge and on her deck and might have had to move any time (there was also intermittent bombing & machine gunning).

2. Brian Gaughan, Sto.1, C/KX79268,. stripped and swam with a line to two men a ¼ mile away, finding the line a hindrance he discarded it, and, unaided, rescued these two men. After a short rest he continued to swim out lines to men closer to the ship. Bombing and machine gunning was going on in close proximity to Gaughan.

3. Frederick Hutter, S.B.A. X7183. (R.N.A.S.B.A.), with the aid of two or three untrained assistants, succoured ninety eight (98), repeat (98) casualties, ten of whom required artificial respiration, several of the others were serious casualties. There was no Medical Officer on board and only two men of the 98 died. Hutter worked till he collapsed.

4. Thomas Cranstone A.B., B22751 (R.F.R.), swam out with a line and orders to ships skiff which was in difficulties, rescued this party and a party on a raft. Neither party could have reached the ship unaided for some time. Distance swum about 200 yards.

Lieutenant Commander Fowke's second report, 'on proceedings from N. Shields (29th. May) to Sheerness (3rd. June)', was dated 6 June 1940. Each of Fowke's entries were numbered; for the sake of clarity these have been deleted from the following:

29th. May.
A.M. Compasses were adjusted badly and at 1230 on the 29th. I sailed from the Tyne (encountering fog on the way) to Harwich.
Tyne to Harwich.
At 2025 and in approximate position 53° 56½' N. 0 19' E. four sharp jars were felt and it was thought that the vessel had hit a wreck. Twenty

minutes later five more jars were experienced and an explosion heard. Two vessels were in the vicinity, one making Pt. 68 on her siren [*sic*], and I decided that the bumps were probably due to patterns of depth charges fired by these vessels. On passage my compass showed itself very inaccurate.

30th. May.
Harwich.
At 1300 on 30th. I arrived off Harwich; my identification signal, although correct, was not accepted for about twenty minutes – reason not known. Coal and provisions were taken on board, ship was swung to obtain new deviation card. Tracks to Dunkerque were put on the charts, but no orders were received until 2225. At 2227 I sailed for La Panne. No communication or operational orders were received, so W/T watch was kept on 138 kcs and routine

31st. May.
Lost in Knock Deep.
The weather was very thick, but the trawler in position 51° 47′ N. 1° 48½′ E. at the bend in the channel was sighted. About ten minutes later orders were received from F.O.I.C. Harwich to use QZS 33. The obvious intention of this order was to avoid using the direct channel. This necessitated using Knock Deep channel, in my opinion, an extremely hazardous navigational passage at night and in thick weather, especially as my compass still appeared inaccurate. I proceeded down the Knock Deep taking continuous soundings. Eventually I ran into shallow water and tried every direction until I ran into 2½ fathoms, could not get out. At daylight a buoy was sighted (my deviations were still erratic, but the weather had cleared considerably).
La Panne.
About 1000 vessel was off La Panne and about the same time V.A. Dover's orders were received to rendezvous at position W. at 2200 and to amend programme accordingly. At this time I had not appreciated that ships were working independently and was expecting to meet M.S. 5 and the rest of the Flotilla; it also seemed that there would not be time to embark troops and return to Margate, discharge them into tugs there (I did not know that ships were going alongside the Pier – according to the chart there is not enough water) and return to position W. by 2200. I turned West again, but there seemed there would be a waste of time so, I decided to turn East again and report myself to *Hebe* (who had informed me was Senior Office, La Panne) and assist in embarking troops aboard other ships. Circumstances made it necessary to embark

100 troops aboard myself, no opportunity arising to put them aboard any other ships.

Dunkerque Roads.

Later I was ordered to proceed in execution of previous orders (I left one boat with *Hebe*). Just West of Bray I passed the Admiral and reported to him that I had 100 troops on board. He told me to join him and I followed him back to La Panne. While lying off there a further raid commenced and he ordered me to go West at full speed. It was during this raid that one aeroplane was brought down by the 12 pdr. gun at maximum range. The raid was nearly over and the Admiral out of sight by the time I was West of Dunkerque, so I returned to look for him and was told to return to La Panne, and embark troops after dark.

Dunkerque Roads.

At La Panne an R.N.V.R. Signalman reported to me that *Hebe* wanted an officer badly, the wording of the signal sounded as if the Commanding Officer wanted someone capable of relieving him for a period. This appears to have been wrong, and may have originated in a verbal message from the C.O. or the Commodore of the motor boat alongside. At any rate, I sent over my 1st. Lieutenant, he found he was not required in *Hebe*, so took the motor boat ashore to look for more troops. Finding none, he, with the aid of two sailors, walked along the beach pulling the whaler with them to see if they could find any. The whole time the place was being bombarded. (*Hebe* was signalling at times with a bright light). He eventually returned to *Hebe*. I consider his actions worthy of reward, as he could easily have returned to me at once.

Dunkerque Roads.

In the meantime I had taken a further 300 or so troops on board and was nearly full and, as the officers amongst them told me there were no further troops on shore, I reported this to *Hebe* and was told to return to Margate, not knowing my 1st. Lieutenant was ashore, but thinking him in *Hebe*, I did so.

I had now been between Dunkerque and La Panne for about 13 hours, several times passing the burning Clan Line steamer when she was being shelled and during frequent air raids. Ships Company had been continuously at action stations, or taking on troops, without proper food; also they had been vigorously employed almost continuously since leaving the Tyne 60 hours before but, as yet, showed no signs of strain. I was short of two seamen and the only officers were myself, Lieutenant H. Sobey R.N.R., and Temporary Lieutenant A.R. Patton, R.N.V.R., who, as yet, is not sufficiently experienced to be left as O.O.W., except under the most favourable conditions, and the Engineer Officer. There was very little H.A. ammunition left.

1st June.
Margate to Dunkerque. H.M.S. Havant.
Immediately the troops were discharged at Margate I sailed again for Dunkerque. On the way there I passed H.M.S. *Havant*, in distress behind Dyke Shoal. *Havant* was on fire for'd so I jettisoned my depth charges, placed my stern under her bows and took her in tow on my sweep wires. Only very slow speed could be made as her helm was over and she paravaned over to the side and pulled my stern over. During this time the ship was subject to frequent and heavy bombing and machine gun attacks – at one time there were 40 aircraft overhead. Many salvoes of bombs fell near to the ship mostly on the starboard quarter and port bow, some were within 30 feet of the ship. Most of the bombs were small but some were large. Splinters from the bombs and spray from their splash fell on board frequently. It was very noticeable that nearly all the splinters were very small and far too light to do damage, although the force of the explosion burst open the wheelhouse doors and shattered the windows which are protected by splinter mats. I believe most of the larger splinters passed over the ship, their trajectory presumably being nearly vertical on bursting, then fanning out and going further than the light ones. This bombing completely upset my compass. Machine gun attacks were also experienced, also from the starboard quarter and port bow. These were attempts to rake the ship fore and aft, but were all aimed too high; very few bullets were found on board afterwards, all being misses over.

The enemy made three mistakes during each attack. 1. He estimated the course on a line through *Havant* and *Saltash*. Actually *Havant* was about 10° on the quarter. 2. He overestimated the speed. 3. He overestimated the height of our decks above water.

Had he been correct in 1. he would have scored many hits with bombs, and if correct in 2. would have caused many casualties on deck. No casualties were experienced and no major damage was done. During this time I believe the *Havant* was also subjected to attack. I had now only two rounds of H.A. high explosive left, a few shrapnel and six pans of Lewis gun ammunition. 4 in. L.A. gun was used against low flying aircraft, but without any noticeable affect. 12 pdr. and Lewis gun seemed to disturb the enemy.

Later the Commanding Officer of H.M.S. *Havant* decided to abandon ship, as she appeared to be going to turn over at any moment. In my judgement, also, she was bound to capsize shortly and then would inevitably sink, as she had several large holes in her side near the deck level. As, after capsizing she might possibly drift towards the channel and sink in a dangerous position, or, more probably towards the shore, where she might have been salved by the enemy if she sank in shoal water, I asked the Commanding Officer if I should sink her where she was. He agreed and I cut my sweep wires and sunk her.

Rescue from Brighton Queen.

Five minutes after this the *Scotia* and *Brighton Queen* were sunk. I made a report and proceeded to rescue survivors. My whaler had been damaged and I only had a skiff left. One bunch of survivors were picked up and I then put the ship alongside bridge and mast of the *Brighton Queen* and partially on her deck, and took off men clinging to her. These men were mostly French Colonial troops and most reluctant to let go of what support they had, it was sometimes necessary to make a line fast to them and pull them off. A carley float and skiff were used to assist in rescue work, no other boats were available. While *Saltash* was alongside and on board *Brighton Queen* she bumped a little on the bilge, but it was not believed that any damage was done. German aircraft bombed and machine gunned men in the water. My skiff was machine gunned.

Rescue.

The work of S.B.A. Hutter at this time is worthy of mention. He, with the aid of untrained assistants, including Ldg. Sto. Crowley, dealt with 98 casualties, including 10 resuscitation cases and only 2 died. He worked most successfully until he collapsed. Also worthy of mention is B. Gaughan, Sto. 1. who swam about ¼ mile from the ship, when the ship might easily have had to leave him.

Rescue.

I had picked up 350 to 400 survivors by now, many of them serious casualties, there were no more survivors in the water so I returned to Margate. On the return journey I closed three trawlers and took on board the Commanding Officer and crew of M.T.B. 175, these included three serious casualties and one dead rating. I took the M.T.B. in tow and arrived at Margate at 1835.

At Margate and to Dunkerque.

About 2000 I left the Pier and about 2200 sailed again for Dunkerque with boats in tow, one motor boat and two small skiffs. I had some difficulty with the tow which delayed me about half an hour. Before getting to the green light buoy I ran into thick smoke (from Dunkerque) my compass being very unreliable, I had to rely very much on the hand lead (all the tubes for the machine had been used in the Knock Deep) which made my progress slow and I got too far East.

Dunkerque Roads.

Orders for this night said that all sweepers had to be clear by 0300 and the destroyer evacuation would commence at 0400. About 0200 I heard the whistle buoy and at 0245 was off the Breakwater at Dunkerque. The other sweepers passed me on the way out, so I followed them as I did not feel justified in breaking orders about being clear by 0300, even if I had an empty ship. During the return journey a small craft reported having seen a mine, I turned back along her course and found an object which I mistook for a mine, but on closer investigation, proved to be a kitchen utensil with broken handles. These broken handles may have appeared to the small craft as horns.

2nd. June.
Margate.
I anchored at Margate about 0800 and was told to wait instructions. As I understood that this was the final evacuation I did not trouble to make any special signal about shortage of coal. Myself, my officers and men had all been continuously on service for several days now, officers being only myself Lieutenant Sobey R.N.R. and Temporary Lieutenant Patton, R.N.V.R. Later, orders for this night were received. I weighed and proceeded to Sheerness at maximum speed for coal. There was just time if the orders were similar to the previous night.
Sheerness.
There was a trawler alongside the coal hulk when I arrived but she moved off, never the less, this, and tiredness of myself, officers and men delayed me an hour. (Myself and all officers and men were extremely near collapse now). My 1st. Lieutenant joined me as I was sailing out of harbour.
Sheerness sailed and returned.
Shortly after this, orders were received to be in position at Dunkerque at 2100, instead of 0100 as I had hoped. This was impossible, but thinking that I might be of use for rescue work outside if there was any bombing, I sailed and reported the position. I was ordered back to harbour.

3rd. June.
Sheerness sailed and returned.
Monday, 3rd. I arranged for compass adjustment. Time stated was 1500, I went to the swinging buoy at 1330 hoping that the time might be advanced, anyhow, I should be no worse off – I still had no H.A. ammunition. While going to the buoy a boiler feed check valve joint blew putting one boiler out of action for several hours, but I decided to start one boiler, hoping for the second one before arriving at Dunkerque.

No further orders were received and swing was commenced. The boiler stop valve spindle seized in a closed position then, putting that boiler permanently out of action. My Ldg. Tel. reported sick (mental) and, this, I expect, accounted for my not having received orders earlier.

I considered I might be as useful as smaller craft, even with one boiler, so I sailed and asked for orders to be re-transmitted to me. Commodore in Charge cancelled my sailing.

With reference to the Ldg. Tel. and his breakdown – I consider him very highly of mention. He had been in charge and continuously on watch and watch since 1230 Wednesday, 29th. decoding in his watch below and his breaking down was not surprising.

I should also like to mention continuous and unstinted work on the part of my other three officers. Lieutenant H. Sobey, R.N.R. – hard at it all the time and an invaluable navigator. Temporary Lieutenant A.R. Patton, R.N.V.R. – cyphering most of the time and ready for any call. Mr. J.T. Mathews – keeping these old engines going in spite of trouble with bearings and keeping his department going too.

After completion of this operation I discovered in conversation with another Commanding Officer and my new Ldg. Tel. that other ships had been keeping watch on 1700 kcs while we had been on 138 kcs. (Dover port wave), except for the time when ordered to set watch on 500 kcs (and this order was not received until 4 hours after the time stated to commence). No orders were received to set watch on 1700 kcs. and I consider that this is the probable reason why all operational orders were received late and none at all for the first day (Friday) I was with the Force.

SHELDRAKE
Kingfisher-class Patrol Sloop
Pennant Number L06
Official Rescue Total: -
Included in the 1935 building programme, HMS Sheldrake was laid down at Woolston by Thorneycroft in April 1936 as a Kingfisher-class Patrol Sloop, these vessels having been designed for coastal convoy service. After a refit at Chatham, during which Sheldrake was fitted with additional anti-aircraft armament, in April 1940 she joined the 1st A/S Striking Force as part of the East Coast Escort Force based at Harwich. On 2 June 1940, Lieutenant Commander Arthur Edward Tolfrey Christie submitted the following account to the Flag Officer in Charge, Harwich. Each of Christie's entries was numbered; for the sake of clarity these have been deleted from the following:

Operations in which *Sheldrake* has been involved during the evacuation from Dunkirk has enabled certain officers and men to distinguish themselves in H.M. Ship under my command. The circumstances are outlined below so that the necessary action may be taken by you should you concur.

Sheldrake was ordered by C-in-C. Nore. to proceed to the Kwinte Buoy and destroy the Asdic Apparatus of one of our destroyers wrecked in the vicinity.

On arrival *Wakeful* was found to be lying completely capsized with her stern resting on the bottom and only the forefoot visible, which appeared from oil marks on the waterline to be semi buoyant. A boat under the command of my First Lieutenant, Lieutenant Hugh William Mackenzie Rose, R.N. was sent over and placed a berthing wire running from the bull ring round the keel, to the bull ring the other side. It was intended to hang depth charges on this 'necklace' and countermine them with other depth charges, using Bickfords fuze.

For the second trip with two depth charges, it was necessary to tow the whaler to the wreck on the end of a grass and to pump out oil fuel from *Sheldrake* to counteract the effects of ground swell and strong tide, which made operations difficult, particularly on the weather side. Good seamanship and stout hearts succeeded in placing one charge on either bow in the required spot without damage to the boat. Throughout the operation all were acutely aware that we were only 10 miles from Dunkirk with aircraft of both sides passing the ship at intervals, and that a bomb in the vicinity of a boat would have countermined the depth charges that they were placing.

On the whaler's return to the ship for the demolition charges, C-in-C. Nore's signal "Cancel my 1044 area now mined" was received. It confirmed our own fears that we had been working in a mined area. It seemed a pity to leave the job half done and it was decided to sink the wreck by gunfire using D.A. fuze as near the required area as possible, and if the ship sunk before the charges placed had been exploded, to fire them with a countermining pattern of depth charges. She sank inside ten minutes, and using the escaping bubbles from the punctured stem as an aiming mark, a pattern was dropped, of which the centre charge produced a plume that told us that the desired effect had been achieved. The only damage to *Sheldrake* was a few light fittings on the Stokers' Messdeck caused by the capstan engine 'whipping' on the light deck above.

In addition to Lieutenant Rose I wish particularly to mention Acting Petty Officer Albert Edward Jackson, Official No. C/JX/125587 my Chief Boatswains Mate, whose energy on the whaler was largely responsible that the depth charges were placed.

The second incident which I submit should receive recognition for those concerned was the rescue of the survivors of H.M. Trawler *St.*

Achilieus, which had been mined. After a night spent dodging M.T.B. torpedoes with H.M.S. *Widgeon*, aircraft closed, and informed me that survivors were in the waters bearing 340 degrees; I wish particularly to stress the efficiency of this flight of three aircraft in leading me to the scene. After passing the signal most expeditiously, two aircraft continued to circle over the area while one of their number flew past the ship indicating the course to steer. This manoeuvre was repeated continuously. As the aircraft showing the way arrived in the position, another of the flight broke away to repeat the manoeuvre.

On arrival a number of men were found clinging to wreckage and rescued by the whaler while *Sheldrake* was manoeuvred to drift down on single men in the water. A net made in accordance with A.F.O.s. proved invaluable on one occasion. Able Seaman William Bond (no official number) Patrol Service, a Fleetwood fisherman, enlisted for hostilities only, displayed conspicuous bravery. A survivor was a few yards from the net on which Bond was standing, he was completely exhausted. I 'sung out' for someone to jump in, and hold him up for the few minutes it would take before the ship drifted down upon him. Able Seaman Bond complied and I have discovered since that he was unable to swim. He was however able to move the man the few feet necessary to the foot of the netting. I regret to add that the man rescued, although he revived for a time with artificial respiration, subsequently died on board.

In connection with the rescue work, I also wish to mention Officers Steward Morris Charles Donno, Official No. C/LX/22343, who repeatedly dived to assist in the recovery of other survivors and subsequently worked continuously for some hours without a break rendering artificial respiration to one or other of the five men being so treated while *Sheldrake* was returning to harbour.

I wish also to draw attention to the outstanding work of Petty Officer Albert Vincent Sears, Official No. C/J/104779, my Coxswain, whose first aid work was particularly commented upon by the Medical Staff on arrival. Of the eleven survivors rescued only two were able to walk ashore, four were cot cases and four men were found to be dead by the Medical Officer on arrival in harbour. All those who died had shown signs of recovery, but it has been ascertained that they died, not from drowning, but from the effects of a depth charge placed to blow up the Anti-Submarine apparatus, which exploded after the crew were in the water. This produced internal injuries and shock.

In addition to Petty Officer Sears, Able Seaman John Anderson, Official No. C/JX/125676, and Able Seaman Drummond Jackson Ryder, Official No. C/SSX/18252, were outstanding in the unflagging energy in trying to bring the apparently drowned men to life. It was once more demonstrated that no man, however apparently dead, should be given up until rigor mortis has set in. All those who died subsequently died as the result of shock and not from drowning, though they were apparently lifeless when in the water.

It was also reported by the whaler's crew that men wearing inflatable lifebelts only, appeared to float when unconscious or dead, with the face submerged. Those wearing cork life belts were half on their back with the mouth free to breathe. I feel that, while the rubber lifebelt is ideal, in that it can be worn whenever at sea, there is a distinct advantage when time permits in wearing a cork lifebelt in addition, and that this should be promulgated.

The day after the above account had been written, Lieutenant Commander Christie submitted a further report to the Commander in Chief, The Nore:

Sheldrake sailed from Sheerness at 1615 with an additional demolition party of 12, with orders to destroy the asdic gear in *Basilisk* ashore off La Panne. On passage zig zagging was employed where submarine attack could reasonably be expected.

Routed via T Buoy (2005), Oostdyck (2053), Middlekerke (2128), Nieuport Bk. (2224) Buoys I closed the shore in stages as the light failed, and was able to identify *Basilisk* by 2131 and then waited till 2230 for darkness before closing in. She was awash up to her FX deck in position Latitude 51 degs. 08 mins. 20 secs. North. Longitude 2 degs. 34 mins. 50 secs. East., 2 miles off shore.

The demolition party was immediately placed aboard, while *Sheldrake* lay off about a cable from the wreck. A few minutes after midnight the fuzes were lit, and the whaler hoisted at 0017. The officer in charge of demolitions has submitted a separate report as to the location of charges, which were lowered as far below water level as possible. The ship appears to have already been pretty well gutted by fire forward, and her bridge wrecked. He was unable to make his way aft, but reports that her back had apparently been broken by an explosion in the vicinity of the engine room. One empty C.B. chest was found.

Throughout the operation I was apparently not located though a few enemy aircraft were seen. Severe fighting was taking place ashore up till midnight, the right of the enemy line appearing to be on the beach abreast the ship, with her gun batteries on the left and Dunkirk illuminated by fires (as usual) to my right. This fighting died down as the repeated bombing of gun positions by the R.A.F. took effect. I regret it was not possible to close the reported position of *Crested Eagle* on the beach as *Sheldrake* would undoubtedly have been illuminated by our own parachute flares. I had also hoped by placing depth charges to complete the destruction of the ship, as had been done to *Wakeful*, in addition to the internal demolitions, but this was not possible: nor would a Mk.VIII. charge fired from the throwers have operated in the shallow water in which she was lying.

Apart from tide, there were no navigational difficulties, as the buoys were lit.

Having re-embarked the demolition party at 0017 I remained inshore between Nieuport Bk. GP. Occ. and Trapegeer GP. Occ. R Buoys until 0230 with the intention of waiting until enemy M.T.Bs. had either left patrol, or with a faint hope that I might surprise them on their return journey by appearing from the eastward with sufficient half light to be able to engage. None were met, and the dawn patrol of aircraft had not been established before I was clear of the area.

In submitting the above report I would like to add my own experience with M.T.Bs. during the last few days, in the hope that from such scraps of unexplained evidence a complete picture of their methods of operating may be built up.

During the night of Thursday 30th. May. I was stationed on one bow of *Vega* and *Blyskawica* [*Błyskawica*], with *Widgeon* on the other bow, patrolling between S Buoy and the West Hinder. At 2330 I was examined closely by a Seaplane (floats) fitted with a radial engine. No attack was made but at 0120 the French destroyer *Siroco* was torpedoed by M.T.Bs. within 2 miles of us. Four pairs of red flares had been observed at 0119 and a rocket at 0147.

During the night of Friday 31st. May. I was patrolling under the orders of *Widgeon*, stationed on her quarter, between R and S Buoys. At 2335 an M.T.B. was observed keeping station at 15 knots on the port quarter of *Sheldrake*, distant about 3 cables. Before fire could be opened I heard the 'plop' of the torpedo at 2336, and realising I was too close to turn and ram and would expose my beam dangerously I turned away to comb the track. The torpedo passed a ship's length under my stern and up the starboard side. *Widgeon* had seen the attack, and speed was increased to 20 knots. Corvettes have no searchlight which makes attacks on these small targets difficult, as they cannot be pointed on to the guns in the beam of the light, and are only visible through night glasses from the bridge.

At 2340 I opened fire with small weapon and turned to ram an innocent small boat which I managed to illuminate with the 10″ before doing her any harm. At 0030 an aircraft passed, out of range, at 2000ft. burning navigation lights, course West. At 0037 aircraft returned, course N.E. at 0040 flares were seen astern and *Widgeon* turned to investigate.

I followed. At 0041 a torpedo track passed down my port side, and two more torpedoes were heard to be fired. At 0055 and 0100 *Widgeon* sounded an alarm by siren, but I saw nothing. At 0135 one aircraft passed overhead, course S, at 2000ft. At 0303 one aircraft passed overhead, course 130degs. 2000ft. burning navigation lights. There were no further attacks, but I spent a hectic night following the continuous zig-zags of *Widgeon* till daylight.

Points that emerge from the above are:- (a) attacks are not always made by lying in wait ahead of the target and stopped. (b) small flares may sometimes be used at the moment of attack. (c) aircraft co-operate and have, I am certain, been greatly assisted by the marked phosphorescence of the water, which gives ships away to aircraft, particularly at high speeds.

On the night of Sunday June 2nd. *Sheldrake* was 2 miles off La Panne, and from 0115 to 0200/3. almost continuous flares were observed on a bearing which varied from 350degs. to 005degs. at an estimated range of 5 to 7 miles, height 1000ft. Each flare burnt for about 3 minutes (timed). Another was lit to replace it when it burnt out. The peculiarity of these flares was that they did not appear to be carried by aircraft, and they did not lose height: of this I am certain. One only did fall, and it was immediately replaced by another burning at the steady height.

SUTTON
Hunt-class Minesweeper
Pennant Number J78
Official Rescue Total: 1,371

The Hunt-class coal-burning minesweeper HMS Sutton *was ordered from MacMillan of Dunbarton in May 1917 and laid down on 6 July 1917. In the days leading up to the evacuation from Dunkirk,* Sutton, *captained by Commander (Acting) Grenville Mathias Temple RN, was taken off its normal duties of patrolling the East Coast and assigned to 'Special Duties'. On 24 May, for example,* Sutton *was one of the vessels involved in Operation EF, this being a plan to place blockships across the harbour entrance at Zeebrugge. Having returned safely to Harwich, within days* Sutton *had been reassigned to Operation* Dynamo. *In his report, Commander Temple takes up the story. His account is worthy of note for his repeated references to the presence (or perceived lack of) of the RAF:*

Sunday 26th. May.
Raised steam and unlocked from Royal Dock, Grimsby. Sailed at 1900,

Salamander and *Fitzroy* in Company. *Sutton* as Senior Officer. Fresh N.W. Wind, slight sea.

On passage several Aircraft seen and heard, mostly friendly. Passed by *Galatea* and destroyers.

Monday 27th. May.
Light breeze, calm sea, maximum visibility. Anchored in Downs by orders of V.A. Dover at 1600. *Skipjack* and *Halcyon* anchored nearby. Destroyers full of Troops continually passing at high speed.

Tuesday 28th. May.
Calm, some rain, visibility one mile.

1545. Weighed and proceeded to Dunkirk, Fourth M.S.F. in company with *Salam* [*Salamander*], *Skipjack*, later joined by *Halcyon*.

1730. Steering jammed, reduced speed and proceeded under hand steering.

1750. 5th, M.S.F. coming up astern, steering repaired, proceeded at 15 knots.

1825. Kwinte Bank Buoy abeam, Ship sinking in vicinity, rejoined 4th. M.S.F. Hurricanes passing overhead.

2030. More Hurricanes, sighted Dunkirk fires 10 miles, weather clearing, *Fitzroy* detached to investigate boat.

2050. Turned towards beaches and proceeded East, parallel. Observed large numbers of troops at intervals along beach near Dunkirk, with more scattered and decreasing groups towards La Panne. Desultory gunfire. No aircraft in sight.

2125. Anchored off beach about four miles East of Dunkirk, in four fathoms. No troops visible, owing to smoke and approaching darkness. Motor boat and whaler sent ashore to contact troops. Troops appeared from sand dunes in disorganised parties, mostly R.A.S.C. and R.E.'s who had lately been engaged on demolition of bridges, ammunition dumps and railheads. Troops were rather shaken by constant air attacks, with machine guns. They had been waiting on the beaches for 30 hours before contacting ships. Very critical of lack of Allied air support during whole of retreat, but were cheerful and disciplined. Rather exhausted after forced marches of 20 to 30 miles. C.O. reported no embarkation organisation or control ashore. The clean shaven and comparatively fresh appearance of the troops and the condition of their equipment, contrasted increasingly as the evacuation progressed, with the evidence of strain shown by Ships companies of H.M. Ships.

103 troops embarked between 2130 and 0200, in batches of 25, mostly with rifles and equipment. Beach good for embarkation, shelving sand and calm weather.

Wednesday 29th. May.

0300. Moved to another position further East commenced bringing off troops but motor boat broke down, and after dragging anchor into shallow water where by now a considerable surf was running, managed to get a line into a Dutch scoot, and was towed back to ship. Embarked small detachment of Leicestershire Regiment.

0730. Proceeded alongside *Calcutta*, who was anchored some miles off shore, and disembarked all troops, *Salamander* following.

0830. Returned to beaches, contacted 350 troops of R.A.S.C. and R.A.O.C. detachments, including Lieutenant Colonel and officers. With assistance of 150 troops, large ship's lifeboat was pulled down beach and successfully floated to assist embarkation, but after removing gear, air tanks did not give sufficient buoyancy to compensate for stove in garboard strake.

Serious lack of boats, reducing embarkation rate to about 30 per hour with own boats only. 227 troops embarked remainder being sent off to *Salamander* and destroyers. Some difficulty experienced through persistent attempts of large masses of French troops to intercept boats and demand passage. Assisted by British troops in heading off French swimmers by rifle fire from 50 yards further along beach. Dunkirk burning with much smoke. Maximum visibility, slight cloud. No R.A.F. support sighted all day.

1600. Level bombing attack on *Sutton*, *Salamander*, *Greyhound* and paddlers from 5000-10000 feet. One salvo pattern bombs without result. One salvo of H.E. straddling *Sutton* and paddlers, no hits. One dive bombing attack on *Sutton* and *Greyhound*, near miss started fire in *Greyhound* amidships. One line of 5 bombs close to G.H.Q. on sea front, on a line starting from centre of the town down beach and into sea, final two bombs falling each side of *Sutton*. Comparatively small bombs used, with several incendiaries, one of which set light to a drifter ½ cable from *Sutton* which was sunk by paddlers gunfire. No R.A.F. support visible. Few small machine gun hits on *Sutton*. *Greyhound* badly damaged by bombs and riddled with machine gun fire.

1706. Proceeded to Dover, leaving La Panne during further air raid of less intensity, in company with *Salamander*. No R.A.F. support visible on passage.

2300. Arrived off Dover, calm, mist. Air raid in progress, anchored. Observed plane at about 1500 feet drop three magnetic mines about 2 cables ahead, sounds of mines striking water clearly audible. Parashutes [sic] seen by several separate observers. Signalled position of mines to V.A. Dover.

Thursday 30th. May.
0600. Proceeded into Dover, discharged troops.
1052. Proceeded Sheerness with one boiler. Drew fires in other boiler to make repairs to brickwork, damaged by bomb explosion.
1632. Arrived Sheerness, embarked coal and ammunition.

Friday 31st. May.
0205. Left Sheerness in company with *Lydd* and *Ross*.
0400. Compasses suddenly produced 20 and 30 degrees of deviation, *Ross* assumed lead of division, later compass deviation improved and *Sutton* re-assumed Lead.
0812. Arrived Dunkirk, proceeded east parallel to beaches passing 4 planes wrecked on the beach west of Dunkirk, two with French markings.
0929. Passed Dunkirk harbour distant 1 cable. Harbour wall intact and little damage apparent from seaward except huge fires. Continual gunfire, some from beach close west of Dunkirk.
0835. Hurricanes and Spitfires overhead, proceeding homewards at high speed. One cargo ship sunk alongside east pier of harbour, 2 French destroyers and several cargo ships sunk east of Dunkirk. Long columns of troops marching into Dunkirk from east, scattered groups on the beach. Continuous column about 1 mile long along beach 3 miles east of Dunkirk.
0906. Anchored off La Panne. Wind N.W. force 3, freshening, sea slight but considerable swell. Commenced loading troops with Motor boat towing whaler and two army pontoons. Since previous day pier had been constructed by driving out lorries at ebb tide in line and securing planks on top, considerably expediting loading of boats, though embarkation rate was slowed considerably by lack of control at shore end of pier to move troops along and by natural reluctance of troops to venture along pier without being relieved of part of their heavy equipment. Some difficulty experienced in loading tow of 4 boats without smashing up against pier in swell, and in handling pontoons in tow in prevailing conditions which tended to reduce embarkation rate. Boats available quite inadequate, large open motor beach boats

required, together with vessel anchored broadside or sunk at head of pier to give a lee if necessary with oil slick provided. During embarkation *Sutton* collected soldiers from overturned pontoon. Allowed to broach in swell. Three believed drowned mainly due to lack of foresight of shore authorities in allowing troops to embark with full equipment and overcoats in deteriorating weather conditions. 120 troops embarked mostly R.E., R.A., R.A.S.C. with a few infantrymen and guards, morale was very good but very critical of lack of R.A.F. support and Belgium treachery behind lines. Country said to be filled with spies, night positions during retreat seen to be signalled by flashlight to planes, bombed within half an hour of being established. Surprising speed of advance of Germans against positions being prepared and defencelessness against dive bombing also important factors.

1137. Weighed anchor and discharged troops alongside *Lydd*. Wind and sea increasing slightly, rather low cloud.

1150. Proceeded North Goodwin Lt. Vessel to await time for next rendezvous. *Lydd* and *Ross* proceeded to Margate to discharge troops.

1538. Anchored at North Goodwin Lt. Vessel.

1855. Weighed and proceeded to Dunkirk in company with *Niger*. Passed great number of small craft, as well as destroyers and paddlers.

2115. Passed Dunkirk Harbour distant 1 cable. Heavy gunfire from beach about 2 miles west of Harbour, apparently enemy shelling town. Fires in Dunkirk more extensive.

2147. Anchored off beach between La Panne and Dunkirk. No sign of boats as expected.

2235. Boat from shore reported troops further to eastward, only boat available run aground. Moved 1 mile eastward.

Saturday 1st. June.

0100. No troops yet contacted. No boats except *Sutton's* available. Several minelaying aircraft overhead, observed parachute mines descending about 3 cables ahead and 1 cable astern. Mines reported dropped all over fairway.

0130. Commenced loading troops with our own motor boat and whaler and ship's lifeboat found off beach. Later assisted by motor yacht. Troops mostly R.A. and infantrymen including Guards, E. Yorks., and machine gun detachment. No R.A.F. assistance before or after dawn. Opened fire on occasional reconnaissance aircraft at dawn.

One level bombing attack at about 5000 feet followed by machine gunning whilst embarking wounded from pontoons alongside, one casualty receiving wounds in the back whilst being helped over the side. This machine gun attack undoubtedly would have been pressed home causing very heavy casualties but for concentrated Lewis gun and Bren gun fire from troops, who manned ships M.G. armament. Detachment of Guards also offered to provide Bren gun defence for the large ship's lifeboat against occasional low flying aircraft, but this was declined in order to utilise maximum space for embarkation. No R.A.F. machines observed engaging enemy at any time. Battery of two guns believed French 5.7″ firing continually on beach parallel to *Sutton*. Observed heavy and accurate shelling of La Panne beaches and main street and pier constructed previous day from lorries.

0600. Weighed and proceeded, leaving Dunkirk Roads close inshore to reduce possibility of encountering numerous magnetic mines laid during night.

1130. Alongside at Dover, discharged troops.

1810. Proceeded from Dover in company with *Niger*.

2121. Passed Dunkirk Harbour and arrived off beach, met by R.A. Dover in C.M.B. and ordered to proceed into Dunkirk to load at eastern pier. Proceeded into Dunkirk Harbour and made fast at seaward end of eastern pier by shore instructions.

Embarked 725 troops with two brows, about one third French. Enemy artillery very active and apparently still concentrating on back area of Dunkirk. Pier slightly damaged. Harbour area all quiet, embarkation completed in about an hour and a half without incident, but bombed about twenty minutes after *Sutton*'s departure by about 50 aircraft.

Sunday 2nd. June.

1207. Proceeded out of harbour for Dover, with speed reduced to minimise listing when turning, troops below trimmed to reduce listing and boats swung in. When abeam of FG Buoy received report that magnetic mines had been laid round buoy. When just abeam of W buoy, report again received that mines had been laid in the vicinity. AV buoy whole route reported mined. Later received report that Dover was being raided and mines dropped off entrance.

0306. At North Goodwin Lt. Vessel, aircraft, apparently enemy, passed close alongside flying low but presumably failed to observe ship in spite of exceptional phosphorescence.

0432. Entered Dover Harbour and secured alongside *Worcester* which had 45 killed and many injured in bombing raid on Dunkirk shortly after Sutton left. 7 survivors of *Keith* also arrived alongside with Captain D 19 in small motor barge, sunk in same raid.

Monday 3rd. June.

2010. Proceeded from Dover for Dunkirk, having embarked medical officer and orderly.

2052. Passing through the Downs, engines developed feed tank trouble, reduced speed. While attempting temporary repairs weather thickened rapidly reducing visibility to half a cable. Found impossible to arrive at Dunkirk soon enough for embarkation, in addition to unreliability of engines for manoeuvring required at Dunkirk.

2230. Signal made stating circumstances and decision to return to Downs to effect repairs. In turning in very thick fog to return, destroyer passed at considerable speed distant 5 yards.

2346. Anchored at North Goodwin Lt. Vessel.

Tuesday 4th. June.

0517.   Visibility improved, proceeded to Dover.

0720.   Made fast alongside *Niger*. Received signal, operation completed satisfactorily.

Having completed his report, Commander Temple went on to list a number of factors which he felt had obstructed the evacuation:

Low embarkation rate off beaches – at times less than 30 per hour caused by lack of control ashore for first few days; and absence of suitable boats.

No ship to beach communication to expedite loading, resulting in casualties caused by ships lying off beaches for hours in daylight.

No Medical Officers at beginning for attending casualties.

Apparently no R.A.F. protection whatever against level bombing and more particularly, dive bombing and machine gunning, except for last two days and a few short periods previously. This lowered troops' morale considerably.

Only one pier, built from lorries end to end, at position most open to enemy shell fire.

Sandbar off beaches preventing close approach, causing troops to hesitate to cross relatively deep water with full equipment to reach larger boats.

HA armament consisting of 12 pdr. and Lewis guns quite inadequate to produce barrage fire, or to discourage high or low flying attack.

No initiative shown by Army Staff in bringing into use local boats on beach.

Lack of foresight shown in allowing troops to embark with overcoats, packs, full equipment and rifles, (not held, but worn) causing hesitation on insecure pier, and difficulty in embarking into boats off beaches.

Insufficient boats at all times, and too few motor beach boats and shallow draft pontoons.

No apparent steps taken by Army to prevent low flying machine gunning off beaches by mounting Bren guns which were available.

Having considered those factors which he felt had obstructed the evacuation, Commander Temple then listed a number of points which had assisted the rescue work at Dunkirk:

Discipline and coolness of troops under fire on beach and in unfamiliar conditions in boats throughout evacuation.

Lifesaving nets rigged along ship's sides.

Assistance of Army Bren guns and gunners against low-flying air attack.

Calm weather and poor visibility.

Presence of HA light cruiser *Calcutta*.

Excellent physical condition of majority of troops.

Normal state in which all piers at Dunkirk were allowed to remain, which was invaluable in assisting embarkation of troops into ships.

Chapter 3

Auxiliary Minesweepers and Vessels

CRESTED EAGLE
Official Rescue Total: -

Built in 1925 by J. Samuel White at Cowes, the General Steam Navigation Company's paddle-steamer Crested Eagle *was requisitioned by the Admiralty at the outbreak of war in 1939. Having initially been involved in transporting evacuees, along with two other paddle steamers HMS* Crested Eagle *was carrying out routine anti-aircraft duties with what was known as the Thames Special Service Patrol, when, on 25 May 1940, she was summoned to Sheerness. Three days later* Crested Eagle *sailed for Dunkirk under the command of Lieutenant Commander (Temporary) B.R. Booth RNR, being directed at first to the beach at La Panne and then to the East Mole. Booth's subsequent report is dated 31 May 1940:*

I have the honour to make the following report on the loss of H.M.S. *Crested Eagle*, under my command, on 29th May, 1940. The times are approximate only.

1000. Ordered to proceed in company with *Royal Eagle* to coast east of Dunkirk to embark troops. *Royal Eagle* had on board S.O.T.D.F., Commander Cordeaux, R.N.

1330. Approaching coast I received a signal from S.O.T.D.F., to proceed Dunkirk as it appeared to him that there were only Belgian and French troops on the beach at that time.

1430. Made fast on Eastern side of Dunkirk Jetty, outer berth but one, which was occupied by troopship *Finella* [*Fenella*]. On the opposite side was *Grenade* and several trawlers.

1500. First raid after arrival commenced in which some trawlers were damaged.

1530. onward. Bombing raids on the harbour and ships in the vicinity almost continuous now. *Grenade* was hit, and more trawlers damaged. Attack was so intense that my attention was given to what was happening in the immediate vicinity. Troops were trickling along between raids and boarding s/s *Finella*. I was in touch with Commander Clouston R.N. who was in charge on the jetty. After *Grenade* was damaged her survivors came on board *Crested Eagle* and W/T messages were passed by this ship to Dover, V.A.

1700. *Finella* was about to sail when a bomb dropped down her funnel putting her out of action. Commenced to embark troops from *Finella* to *Crested Eagle*.

1700 to 1800. Troops and survivors from the damaged ships were embarked and I was ordered to proceed by Commander Clouston who remained on the jetty.

Swung clear of the Jetty and steered an Easterly course, the ship was raided continuously until, as I learnt afterwards, five bombs dropped together, four of which hit the ship.

As the engines (paddles) were still functioning I held on my course for a little while, but I soon discovered that the ship was on fire, certainly from amidships right aft. The deck was up four or five feet and the sides were in.

The Engineer, Lieutenant Jones, reported on the bridge at this time (although badly burnt) to say that we should not be able to proceed far, so decided to beach the ship.

At this point all S.P.'s and C.B.'s were jettisoned in the steel chest by the P.O. telegraphist.

Ship's head turned to the beach where she brought up sometime later.

Fire steadily gained ground and with the wind aft in very few minutes she was on fire fore and aft.

It is difficult to estimate the number of men on board, under the conditions that they were embarked, I should sat round about 600.

As the lower decks were filled first, casualties from the bomb explosions must have been severe. After beaching I advised all hands to take to the water as their only chance, and probably 200 men could be sighted at one time in the water. I regret to say that they were badly machine gunned.

In less than half an hour owing to the ship being all wood, with the exception of her hull, she was blazing furiously fore and aft and I feel that I can safely say that any gear or instruments left on board would never withstand the heat and be recognisable afterwards.

The crew throughout behaved wonderfully well, the guns were kept going right up to the last, for which I specially commend the Gunnery Officer, Sub-lieut. R.M. Roberts, R.N.R. and Able Seaman Frend who was acting as Q.O.

Chief Steward Cooch (T.124) worked nobly in alleviating the wounded which was a terrific job. There were so many in such a small place. Apart from these it is difficult to single out, they were all so good, no one could have been served better in the hour of trial, for which I thank them.

The Senior Officer, Thames Local Defence Flotilla (Commander E.C. Cordeaux) attached a covering note to Lieutenant Commander Booth's report. In this he stated:

I have now interviewed Lieutenant Commander B.R. Booth, the Commanding Officer of H.M.S *Crested Eagle*, and have had a personal account of the loss of the ship at Dunkirk.

I feel that in his original account Lieutenant Commander Booth has hardly done justice to the splendid work accomplished by himself, his officers and ship's company.

The ship was machine gunned on her way into Dunkirk and under continuous bombing and machine gun fire for many hours before being hit and also later whilst on fire and whilst endeavours were being made to rescue the wounded.

I was particularly impressed by his account of the behaviour of Sub-Lieutenant R.M. Roberts R.N.R. who encouraged his gun's crews to keep up to their guns under continuous machine gun and bombing attacks – the guns and gun positions being entirely unprotected – and continued careful and controlled fire until practically the whole of the ammunition was exhausted.

Lieutenant Commander Booth considers that the accurate pom-pom was undoubtedly the reason that the ship remained un-hit for so long.

It appears to me also that the behaviour of Lieutenant Commander Booth himself, in his general handling of the ship and situation is deserving of great praise.

Of note is that an additional report by Sub-Lieutenant R.M. Roberts is also attached to Lieutenant Commander Booth's narrative:

I have the honour to report that during the intense aerial bombardment of the pier, and the subsequent bombing, beaching, and burning of the vessel, all men under my control remained steady at their posts and carried out their duties with great coolness. I should like especially to report on the following men, Tilbury A.B.; Frend A.B.; Plack A.B.; Patrick O.S., for their work in keeping the vessel alongside the quay and for assisting the wounded men to board the vessel. I have to report that an unknown A.B. or O.S., a survivor from the *Grenade* suffering from severe facial injuries, requested that he should assist to man the A.A. guns. Being short-handed I posted him as gunlayer and Captain of the gun at No.2 Pom pom. This gun he kept in action for 20 minutes after the bombing of the vessel.

Four German prisoners on board were of great assistance in rescuing wounded from the damaged compartments, these men were handed over to a French N.C.O. on reaching shore.

Engineer Sub-Lieut. Turnbull, R.N.R. was placed in hospital in a large hotel about 2 miles East of Dunkirk. He was badly burnt about the hands and face and suffering slightly from shock. Owing to the congested state of the beaches it was impossible to collect all survivors. All men seen were instructed to return to England by the earliest available boat.

Private B. Fox, attached to the 16th Field Regiment, Royal Artillery, had helped carry stretcher cases onto Fenella, *only to be forced to quickly abandon the sinking steamer:*

We then carried the wounded on to SS *Crested Eagle* which a few minutes later was attacked by enemy aircraft, the engine room being bombed, causing an explosion, following which the ship caught fire. The ship's course was then altered towards the Bray Dunes and was eventually beached there … the boat was now burning fiercely amidships …

Upon reaching the top deck, we encountered Mr. Nublat, [a] French interpreter attached to the unit, who was lying on the deck badly burned and scalded. We made him as comfortable as possible and lowered him into a naval launch, which had been sent to pick up survivors.

All rescue boats were filled with wounded and scalded men, and as it was impossible to stay on SS *Crested Eagle*, I proceeded to swim ashore.

Corporal P. Carman, with III Corps' HQ Signals, recalled that when Fenella *was hit, the men were ordered to 'drop everything and dash' to* Crested Eagle:

The boat finally sailed & had been under way about 10 minutes when we heard a stick of bombs coming, we knew they were ours & dropped flat, a second later a bomb seemed to burst right on the ship's bottom. The lights went out and there was a terrific scorching blast of hot air, then the room filled with choking fumes & smoke as though from the wrecked funnel. The boat kept going and was run aground in shallow water.

There was a first blind rush for the one stairway & a fight to get out until someone started singing 'Roll out the Barrel' & amazingly enough it had the effect of bringing common sense to bear [and] it wasn't long before we were all climbing out – only to find ourselves in another saloon now well alight. However, an axe was found by the sailors & through the aperture we clambered to find 'planes still overhead & the sea dotted with men.

Corporal Arthur Turner, 48 Provost Company, Royal Military Police, was on board Crested Eagle *when she was hit:*

We'd sailed perhaps half a mile, and then we were bombed again,' he later recalled. 'The bomb went straight into the engine room and there were spuds, carrots, meat [everywhere] – evidently the bomb hit the provision store, as well.

A motor mechanic stationed with the Military Police (to look after our vehicles) was on fire. He was screaming, screaming … We rushed to get a bucket of water and chucked it over him. As we put this bucket down, he was putting his arms in the water, but all his skin came off. Then the whole place was on fire …

Me and my mates were holding onto the lattice work where the guide for the wheels was, and everybody was treading on my bloody fingers with big army boots. Then an officer said, "Come on lads – let's swim for it". So we dived into the water and started to swim.

My full pack hit me under the chin as I dived and I smashed a couple of my teeth, but I started to swim and managed to get off my battle dress jacket, but I had khaki trousers and braces on and as I was swimming the braces were coming down. I swam for the shore, and gradually got rid of my trousers, and even my boots. I was a pretty good swimmer, but I tried I tried to touch the bottom and I couldn't – I just sank. With panic I surfaced and then I swam and swam. Then I managed to stand upright and walk to the shore – I was in vest and pants and nothing else except socks.

DUCHESS OF FIFE
Official Rescue Total: 1,801

Launched on 9 May 1903 by Fairfield Shipbuilding and Engineering, Govan, Glasgow, Duchess of Fife *was requisitioned on the outbreak of war and*

*converted to the auxiliary minesweeper role, being based at Grimsby and Dover.
Lieutenant (Temporary) J.N. Anderson RNR's account of HMS* Duchess of
Fife *during Operation* Dynamo *is dated 7 June 1940:*

I have the honour to report that *Duchess of Fife* arrived off Bray Dunes
at 0110 on 29th May. Ship anchored under orders of Senior Officer
(*Waverley*). Previously, at the Whistling Buoy, as we were swinging in
line, there had been a tremendous explosion. The world was lit up for
a moment in a flash of lurid flame, and with some bathos there came to
me two lines of a long forgotten poem, "There came a burst of thunder
sound, The boy, Oh! Where was he?" (Casablanca). It was a British
destroyer struck amidships with what I subsequently heard was a
torpedo from a German M.T.B.

There was no sign of troops coming off but we could hear them on the
beach hailing "Ship ahoy". At daybreak hove up, and closed the beach.
Lowered my sea boats and was about to send them away under my
First Lieutenant and Sub Lieutenant Freeborn when a motor launch
from H.M.S. *Shikari* ranged alongside requesting lubricating oil. While
he was being supplied I arranged with him to tow my boats in, in
addition to his two cutters. By 0900 I had a hundred British troops
aboard.

At 1000, finding myself in less than 2 fathoms with a falling tide, I
weighed and stood further out. At 1010 I considered *Fife* safely loaded
with 416 troops, who, with their equipment, seemed to be sufficient.
Weighed under orders to rendezvous at Keweit Bank, but on arrival
there, finding enemy aircraft busy, judged it advisable to proceed.
Accordingly carried on and, on request for instructions, was ordered to
Ramsgate.

Arrived at 9 pm, disembarked troops, filled up with water, and the
Chief Engineer, Lieut. W.G. Stronach, R.N.R. set his men transhipping
coal from the reserve to the main bunker. This is arduous work and was
backed up by help from the deck department.

Sailed at 1130 am 30th May and passing Nieuport was shelled by
shore batteries. They had the range to perfection, but their deflection
was not so good. Two shells pitched ahead of my stem and three in my
wake. I judged it advisable to turn away, show them my stern, and zig-
zag till I was out of range. Arrived at Bray Beaches 6 pm, lowered my
sea boats and sent them away under command of Lt. F.W. Gartell and
Sub Lt. W.G. Freeborn. To show the spirit that obtained, I was
approached by my junior engineer, Mr. V.N. Wood, requesting that the
13 foot skiff should be lowered and he would take it in with the second
engineer, Mr. A.R. Japp, if I could give them someone to steer.

Accordingly the skiff was sent away with my coxswain, P.O. Ed. Arthur Brassington P/V289953 Naval Pensioner, in the stern sheets. The skiff brought off 30 men in parties of six at a time.

At 8.15 pm I had 535 troops aboard, all British and sailed. Slowed down to 7 knots and made Ramsgate 0700 on 1st June. Proceeded Sheerness for coal, water and provisions.

Sailed from Sheerness at 4.30 pm 1st June under orders to rendezvous 1½ miles east of Dunkirk at midnight 90 miles. Engineer Lieut. Stronach so shook up his engines that we arrived at 11.10 pm. Lowered sea boats and sent them away under command of Lieut. Gartell and Lieut. Lennox (navigating Officer under T124). The boats returned reporting no one was on the beach and the shelling was hot. I was hailed and asked if I would take my ship inside Dunkirk. Accordingly lifted my boats, weighed, and proceeded inside and laid *Fife* alongside. The pier was stiff with French troops. They took my lines and then refused to come aboard. One of my men got one by the leg and hauled him down the brow, but none others would follow.

Accordingly I climbed the brow and harangued them in a strange language, which I doubt had little effect. But, as is my custom, I happened to be wearing a beret, and at sight of the familiar headgear some 25 of them followed me down the brow. Again there was a hold up and going on the bridge I hailed to inquire if were was a British Officer within hearing. At the third hail a man forced himself to the rail and replied, "Don't be so windy. What do you want?" I replied, "Damn you sir, I am not windy or I would not be here. Are there any British troops on the quay?" He replied that there were no British troops on the quay, that these "yellow bellies" would not board, and that I might as well let go my ropes and clear. (5th column?).

It seemed I could do nothing but land a party and drive them aboard, when I was hailed from up the quay to bring my ship 200 yards further ahead. Accordingly fleeted along and found Col. Winterton at the head of a detachment of disciplined British troops in threes who marched on board. Sailed at 2.45 am on the 1st with 550 men having suffered some shelling, men being wounded while in the gangway.

Arrived Ramsgate 9 am. Landed troops, watered and proceeded Margate Roads for coal. My men had to board the collier, bag the coal and heave it aboard.

Left Margate at 7.45 pm and arrived Dunkirk midnight on Saturday. The scene beggared description. The whole city seemed ablaze. We stood right in and laid her alongside. Again they were French troops and after loading 390 there were none left. I hailed the quay but could get no reply and so let go and proceeded out of the nearest approach to

Above: Allied troops on one of these beaches forming into long winding queues ready to take their turn to board small boats which took them to larger vessels, many of which were Royal Navy warships. (All images Historic Military Press unless stated otherwise)

Below: Evacuation ships of all shapes and sizes, naval and civilian, heading back to the UK with their human cargoes.

Left: Soldiers wait patiently in line, up to their necks in the sea, to be hauled aboard HMS *Oriole*, which had been beached at La Panne, 29 May 1940. Though this is one of the most widely published pictures of the evacuation, rarely, if ever, has the photographer, Sub-Lieutenant Crosby, been credited.

Below: A remarkable shot of the beach at La Panne during a German air raid. It was also taken from the decks of HMS *Oriole*, once again by Sub-Lieutenant Crosby; he had turned and captured the very moment that a pair of German bombs fell on the sands and exploded.

Above: The personnel vessel *Tynwald* passes the wreck of her Steam Packet sister, *King Orry*, as she approaches Dunkirk on 29 May 1940.

Below: The anti-aircraft cruiser HMS *Calcutta* – one of the largest warships to participate in the evacuation. Though her commander, Captain Dennis Marescaux Lees, described *Calcutta*'s involvement in the evacuation as a 'minor part', she remained in action, and under fire, for much of Operation *Dynamo*. (US Naval History and Heritage Command)

Above: There can be little doubt that the forty or so Dutch skoots (or schuits) which participated in Operation *Dynamo* played an invaluable part in its success. These vessels were a self-propelled seagoing development of the towed barges so familiar on European rivers such as the Rhine, Elbe and Danube. Close examination of this image suggests that it depicts the skoot *Hilda* en route to Dunkirk towing a collection of smaller boats. *Hilda* had been lying at Poole when she was taken over by a crew commanded by Lieutenant A. Gray RN. During her three trips she transported 835 men.

Below: HMS *Wakeful* pictured at speed off Dunkirk prior to her loss. It was at about 01.00 hours on 29 May that *Wakeful* was attacked by German E-boats, being hit by a torpedo fired by *E-30*. *Wakeful* broke in two and sank in just fifteen seconds. Such was the scale of the disaster that only twenty-five of *Wakeful*'s crew and one evacuee were saved.

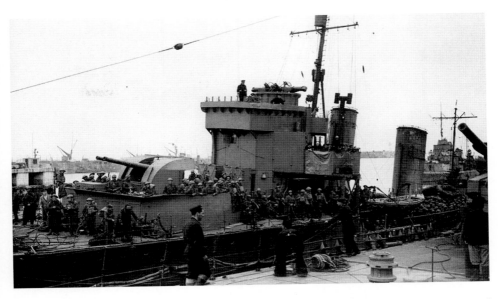

Above: The W-class destroyer HMS *Wolsey* pictured following her return from one of the crossings she made to Dunkirk under the command of Lieutenant Commander Colin Henry Campbell RN.

Below: Evacuated French and British troops on board ships berthing at Dover, 31 May 1940.

Above: A crowded and busy scene as destroyers loaded with soldiers of the British Expeditionary Force are pictured on their return to Dover during *Dynamo*. The warship in the background with the pennant number D-94 is the destroyer HMS *Whitehall*.

Left: A sailor assists a wounded member of the BEF ashore, followed by French soldiers, upon arriving at a South Coast port during the evacuation.

Above: Amongst the many 'Little Ships' at Dunkirk were the vessels of the Minesweeping Service. These men are pictured safe on the deck of the drifter *Fidget* during Operation *Dynamo*.

Below: A Royal Navy loss during *Dynamo* – the B-class destroyer HMS *Basilisk*. She sailed to La Panne on the morning of 1 June and was attacked three times by German bombers. One bomb from the first wave detonated inside the No.3 boiler room, killed all of her boiler and engine room personnel, fractured her steam lines and knocked out all her machinery. Near misses from the same attack buckled the sides of her hull and her upper deck. A second attack resulted in no further damage, but caused a French ship that had taken her under tow to drop the line. The third attack, around noon, sank *Basilisk*.

Above: British troops boarding the V-class destroyer HMS *Vanquisher* from the East Mole at Dunkirk at low tide.

Below: An aerial photograph of evacuation vessels of all shapes and sizes off Dunkirk during Operation *Dynamo*.

hell I have yet seen. The shelling was tense and aircraft were busy but Ramsgate had put 3 Bren guns and gunners aboard and they were very comforting.

In conclusion I would like to say that no Commanding Officer ever had such a ships company. Collectively and individually they were superb.

GLEN AVON
Official Rescue Total: 888

Built by Ailsa Shipbuilding at Troon, the paddle steamer Glen Avon *was launched on 30 May 1912. Having operated in the Bristol Channel throughout her peacetime career, the outbreak of war in 1939 saw her requisitioned as an auxiliary minesweeper. Assigned to the 8th Minesweeping Flotilla, HMS* Glen Avon *was commanded by Lieutenant (Temporary) B.H. Loynes RNR during* Operation Dynamo. *Having survived the evacuation, HMS* Glen Avon *was lost on 3 September 1944 when she sank at her moorings at Port-en-Bessin, France, during a severe gale. Loynes' narrative is dated 3 June 1940:*

We arrived Union Quay after sweeping operations at 1738/28 and commenced to coal, water and store for the passage to Harwich. At 2320 we left Union Quay for Harwich under the orders of Commander Biddulph, R.N. By 0005/29 the ships were in line ahead. I regret that on account of the bad quality coal supplied *Glen Avon* was unable to keep station and at no time during the passage were we able to obtain more than 95 lbs. of steam, even though seamen were employed to assist the stokers.

2. We arrived in berth at Harwich 0750/30 and immediately coaled and stored ready to sail at 1200. We left the Quay at 1340 and proceeded to the beaches 8 miles east of Dunkirk, arriving there and anchoring close inshore at 2225 and engaged enemy aircraft almost immediately. Boats were sent ashore while this was going on and first embarkation took place at 2245. We continued embarking troops until 0525/31 when we had on board 590 Officers and men of the B.E.F., including three French Officers.

3. The ship had been aground for just over one hour and we parted starboard cable in trying to get off. The port anchor we could not heave up. It had apparently fouled something on the sea bottom. We then unshackled at first shacle [*sic*] and slipped the port anchor. While getting off ground we engaged enemy aircraft which was making for the beach and we are of the opinion that we brought it down as he seemed to stop and wobble badly with smoke issuing from him.

4. We eventually arrived back at Harwich at 1520/31 and secured alongside H.M.S. *Snaefell* where we discharged the troops.

5. We then re-ammunitioned, coaled watered, and stored ship ready for sea again. This was completed, including two new anchors, at 2330/31.

6. At 1258/1 we were ordered to proceed to a position 1½ miles east of Dunkirk and leave at not later than 1400 to arrive there at 2200/1. We sailed at 1450, the delay being caused by having to wait for cutters and motor boat to tow over with us. On the passage over two cutters were lost; one having become waterlogged and the other having been broken up, and they had both to be cut adrift. We hailed a patrolling trawler to try to salve the waterlogged one. The passage to Dunkirk was uneventful until we were one mile west of Dunkirk Mole when a ship, apparently a trawler, was blown up. We did not stop to assist her as there were several other small craft in the vicinity. We arrived and anchored off the beach at 2245 and were immediately subject to shrapnel fire.

7. Our life boats were sent away and embarkation commenced at 2315. The motor boat towing two cutters failed to function half way between the ship and the shore, and it had to be abandoned. This failure seriously hampered the embarkation as only man power was available. We continued in this way until 0300/2 when I was ordered by a Naval Officer who had been in charge of beach operations, to sail. We then had only 295 Officers and men on board, and some of them wounded. The lifeboats which had been under continuous fire were waterlogged and had to be abandoned. I also had on board the aforementioned Naval Officer and 4 ratings who had been under his Command.

8. At 0303/2 we got under way and proceeded back to Harwich. At 0430 we encountered a small ship's motor lifeboat named the s.s. *Alphacca* containing 3 French soldiers and 24 Spaniards. We took them on board, searched them and placed them under arrest, afterwards sinking their boat. At 0530 we stopped, having applied to H.M.S. *Glen Gower* for medical assistance to try and save a soldier's life, and took on board one Army Surgeon. This effort however was unavailing; the soldier in question dying at 1015.

9. We arrived at Harwich and berthed at Parkestone Quay at 1145, where we landed our troops and the 27 rescued men.

10. I should like to call your attention to the conduct and unfailing willingness of Lieutenant Murphy R.N.R., Lieutenant Akitt, R.N.V.R., Lieutenant Dolby R.N.V.R., Sub Lieutenant Law R.N.V.R. and Sub Lieutenant Clark R.N.R., all of whom gave their utmost assistance to me in every way. The ship's company including T.124 ratings worked

unflinchingly under most adverse conditions and it is difficult to single any one man out for praise. One outstanding act was that of a trawler hand who had volunteered to sail with us. During embarkation operations this man, Seaman A. Farrow of H.M. Trawler *Anson*, saw an Officer of the Royal Artillery struggling in the water and immediately dived over the bow of the cutter, swam about 20 yards and took him aboard a motor launch which was nearby.

11. The ship suffered no casualties except myself, I having been shot through the hand on our first operation by a French Officer. This appeared to be an accident.

GLEN GOWER
Official Rescue Total: 1,235

Launched on 14 February 1922 by Ailsa Shipbuilding at Troon, having been requisitioned on the outbreak of war PS Glen Gower was sent to the Tyne. Commander (Acting) M.A.O. Biddulph, the Senior Officer of the 8th Minesweeping Flotilla, submitted his report on HMS Glen Gower's role in Operation Dynamo, to the Flag Officer in Charge, Harwich, on 3 June 1940:

I have the honour to submit this my letter of proceedings in connection with the evacuation of troops of the B.E.F. from Dunkirk.

2. During the forenoon of the 30th, May 1940, I was in receipt of a signal from V.A. at Dover to proceed to beaches 8 miles east of Dunkirk and evacuate troops, and to sail at noon. The two other ships of the flotilla under my command, H.M.S. *Glen Avon* and H.M.S. *Snaefell*, at present at Harwich, were in receipt of a similar signal.

3. As the ships had only arrived at Harwich at 0745 the same morning it was not possible to complete coaling, watering and provisioning by this time, and the necessary charts had to be drawn and the route obtained. All this was pushed forward with the utmost despatch however. Extra tinned beef, bread and butter were drawn for feeding the troops and the three vessels left at 1345.

4. I had spoken with the Commanding Officer of H.M.S *Oriole* which had arrived that forenoon from a similar expedition, and he was able to give me some valuable information as a result of his experiences. On leaving Harwich I addressed the Ship's Company and told them what we were going to do, and how I proposed to do it, at the same time informing them that any one's ideas would be considered and used if good. I also warned them that in view of the limited fresh water capacity of the ship and the fact that we must have plenty for the troops,

water must be used sparingly and that washing would be a punishable offence. This raised a cheer.

5. The flotilla proceeded in company but I made a signal to each ship to proceed independently at her utmost speed and to act in accordance with orders received, telling them briefly what I proposed to do myself. *Glen Gower* was soon left behind as she is somewhat the slowest ship and I felt rather like the Duke of Plaza Toro who led his regiment from behind, though not with the same intentions. I did not lose sight of them however.

6. By 1845 we had altered course into the main channel for Dunkirk and found ourselves in company with vessels of all types on the same errand while others were coming back laden with troops. The alarm was sounded several times in sighting or hearing aircraft but these all proved to be British.

7. At 2058 we turned to run along the coast past Dunkirk. Gunfire could be heard and a large fire was blazing in Dunkirk itself sending up columns of thick smoke which hung about like a pall over the beleaguered city. We passed Dunkirk light at 2117. At 2121 there was heavy H.A. fire heard ahead and the tracers from Bofers guns could be seen streaking into the sky. Bombs could be seen exploding on the beaches and in the water close to. The noise of aeroplane engines could be heard but at this we could not see the planes themselves. We passed a number of sunken vessels of various types and a burned out paddle minesweeper on the shore.

8. At 2124 an enemy aircraft was seen and three rounds were fired from the 12 pounder. As however no attack developed upon the ship I gave the order to cease fire, deeming it advisable to save our limited amount of ammunition for short barrage defence against dive bombing aircraft actually attacking the ship.

9. At 2137 troops could be heard shouting ashore, but we had not yet reached our destination. At 2140 more heavy H.A. fire was put up from destroyers and shore batteries.

10. At 2210 I came ashore in five fathoms off the beach approximately 8 miles east of Dunkirk. The tide was now ebbing. *Glen Avon* and *Snaefell* were anchored either side of me. The two boats were lowered and sent straight inshore, one with a party of ratings and one Officer, Lieutenant Johnson R.N.V.R., and the other with Lieutenant Chapman R.N.V.R., in charge. By this time it was completely dark. At 2330 the first boat came back laden with British troops followed closely by the second. The coxswains reported great difficulty in refloating the boats owing to the rapid falling tide and the very gradual slope of the beach. The soldiers were tired and disinclined to help to get the boat off. In view of the fact

that I intended to beach the ship soon after the turning of the tide at 0220 I decided to stop sending in the ship's boats for fear of getting them stranded. In the meantime however there was a more or less steady stream of troops arriving by local flat bottomed boats. Tea and sandwiches were served out to them as they arrived after which they mostly fell into the sleep of exhaustion.

11. Weighed anchor at 0205 and ran the ship into the beach taking the ground at 0220. The kedge anchor was laid out to prevent the stern swinging in. The idea of the beaching was that ladders and hawsers, hanging alongside, would be used by the troops to climb aboard with, after wading out to the bows. This idea proved to be impracticable, the ship being still some way from the water's edge, And the embarkation was continued by means of the ship's boats in charge of seamen coxswains, the two lieutenants being retained aboard to assist in the distribution and tallying of the troops. In the meantime the ship became hard and fast broadside to the beach due to the fact that the kedge anchor dragged. The stokers all assisted in the boats to relieve the seaman crews and the work of embarkation proceeded steadily by the ship's boats and flat bottomed craft propelled by soldiers themselves.

12. By 0425 we had embarked 530 troops. I then received orders from V.A. Dover, passed by a destroyer further out, and addressed to all paddle minesweepers, to proceed alongside Dunkirk pier. *Snaefell* in response to a signal from me towed my stern clear, and with the assistance of the engines the ship was soon afloat. *Snaefell* then proceeded. *Glen Avon* was at this time still aground but managed to refloat successfully. *Snaefell* proceeded direct to Harwich being filled to her capacity.

13. At 0520, having hoisted the boats, I proceeded for Dunkirk. The shore party who had come off and gone in again in a flat bottomed boat for another load were left behind, but I knew that they would make for the *Glen Avon* on our departure as she did not proceed until about half an hour later, by which time she was full and carried on direct to Harwich.

14. I entered Dunkirk harbour at 0600 and secured alongside the pier ahead of a destroyer and astern of trawlers. There was a sunken yacht outside the pier at the end and a sunken trawler astern of the destroyer. The pier had been badly damaged by bombs and shell fire. Opposite the ship a gap was bridged by a brow and near by was the body of a British soldier, killed presumably whilst embarking. A naval shore party consisting of two Officers and some ratings were engaged in the work of directing the troops to the various ships alongside. At the time of going alongside British troops were being directed into the destroyer astern.

15. Up to now things had been peaceful but at 0617 a whistling noise was heard and the sound of an explosion, followed rapidly by about 10 more. I saw from the bridge a mass of black fragments leap up on the fo'c'sle between the feet of Sub. Lieutenant N.A. Williams R.N.V.R., my Gunnery Officer, who was at his action station alongside the 12 pounder gun on the starboard side of the fo'c'sle. The other explosions occurred very close to the ship, following rapidly upon one and other. At first the idea in everyone's mind was that these were caused by bombs, but no aeroplane was seen. When the explosion ceased a hole was found in the fo'c'sle and I was informed that a shell had burst inside the ship on the stokers mess deck, killing five soldiers and wounding 7. Surg. Lt. Schofield R.N.V.R., immediately proceeded to the scene and the wounded were taken aft and cared for. Two were subsequently transferred to the destroyer before she sailed. The dead were laid out where they fell, and covered over with blankets. They belonged to the Cheshire Regiment. Sub. Lieut. William's escape was extremely miraculous, the shell having pierced the deck exactly between his feet. I proceeded later to the mess deck, which was a shambles of blood and brains. The structural damage was not extensive, though the deck below had been pierced by fragments, which included the fuze. An Artillery Officer identified the fragments, as those of an 4.2 long range howitzer.

16. Thereafter the ship was subject to periodical bombardment at intervals of about 20 minutes. The road to the eastward by which the troops were approaching was also bombarded as were buildings in the town, apparently by the same gun or guns.

17. The period of waiting under the bombardment was very trying for one realised that the ship might well be hit again and more loss of life bound to ensure due to the crowds of troops on board. All Officers and ratings preserved an admirable sangfroid and cheerfulness, and the troops accepted the situation with calmness. My feelings however and those of everyone else, were that it would undoubtedly be a good thing when we were full up and could leave this decidedly unhealthy spot. Though shells fell all round the ship some bursting practically alongside no more hits were registered. Some fragments fell on the sweep deck aft, but caused no structural damage.

18. The destroyer astern completed embarkation and left at 0650. We naturally expected that we would be filled up next, but this was not to be. We could see troops advancing in large numbers by the road, but they were directed to the two funnelled channel steamer at the head of the pier. Worse still 4 motor craft arrived alongside and started taking away some of the troops already aboard but that was discouraged and we only lost about 50 in this way. By this time the tide was running in

strongly and I decided to take advantage of this to turn the ship round and to occupy the billet vacated by the destroyer, pointed already for the departure. We commenced the operation at 0700 and were bombarded whilst swinging round but again miraculously avoided being hit.

19. At 0810 troops at last started coming aboard, including 13 wounded stretcher cases. A final bombardment from the howitzers occurred at this time, shells as usual falling close. At 0822 a German plane appeared diving low and was driven off by Lewis gun fire. By 0831 I judged that we were as full as the safety of the ship permitted, and I prepared to sail, but just before casting off a solitary and elderly colonel of Ordnance appeared footsore, weary but indomitably cheerful, shouldering an anti-tank rifle. At 0836, with a sigh of relief, I gave the orders to slip and we proceeded for Harwich.

20. At 0855 Spitfires were seen in some numbers which gave us a comfortable feeling. The ship was crammed with soldiers, all available space below being taken up and the upper deck swarming as well. The troops having eaten and drunk mostly slept all the way.

21. The voyage back was uneventful. Large numbers of craft of every description passed in the opposite direction, bound for Dunkirk to evacuate troops. The ship arrived alongside Parkstone Quay at 1715, and disembarkation proceeded promptly. The dead were removed later in the evening.

22. The ship was in a shocking state of mud, wet coal dust and rubbish etc., but the military authorities sent a party on board to clean up and as soon [as] possible the ship was put out of routine, all hands were sent to the canteen to feed, and the stokers, whose mess deck was uninhabitable, were provided with accommodation ashore. A guard was put on the ship and everyone else retired to sleep the sleep of the just, having had none at all the previous night.

23. June 1st. Ships of the 8th M.S.F., were ordered to proceed at 1400 for a second trip, this time to the beaches 1 to 1½ miles east of Dunkirk. On this occasion boats were taken in tow, *Glen Gower* having a motor boat belonging to H.M.S. *Gallant*, and two cutters and a pinnace from Shotley.

24. Ships preceded independently, *Glen Gower* leaving at 1430. The voyage over was uneventful except for the usual alarms for aircraft. At 1855 heavy firing could be heard to the southward. At 1930 Spitfires and British Bombers were seen, the Spitfires going homeward, while some bombers were doing the same, others proceeding for France.

25. At 2123 the fires could be seen at Dunkirk blazing furiously. Flashes of gunfire could also be seen. At 2150 two new wrecks were passed, a large vessel on her side still burning and a vessel close by with two

funnels and a mast out of the water, afterwards known to be the wreck of the H.M.S. *Brighton Queen* of the 7th, M.S.F.

26. Dunkirk and environs now appeared an inferno. Hugh flames were shooting up from fires in the town and the noise of gunfire and of bursting shells was terrific. At 2245 just after passing Dunkirk a very heavy explosion took place astern which seemed to lift the ship out of the water. Looking aft we saw a big column of water go up round a small coaster which we had passed some time previously. When this had subsided the vessel had disappeared. The explosion was obviously due to a magnetic mine which we had fortunately missed.

27. At 2250 a M.T.B. hailed us and I was told that I was now in the correct position and to go inshore and anchor, which I did in 4 fathoms at 2355. From now on we were continually under fire from what appeared to be 5.9in. shrapnel which was spraying the beaches and the ships. Shells were continually bursting overhead, but the ship was very lucky and was hit only occasionally by pieces of shrapnel which did no damage. Occasionally another type of shell of the "Whizz Bang" variety arrived on the scene. These appeared to burst in the water, shaking the ship considerably. I understood however that there were a good many casualties among the troops on the beach. At first the inclination of most of us was to lie down flat when the shells burst but very soon we grew accustomed to being under this form of fire and ceased to worry about it.

28. I had hoped to be able to lay out a kedge ashore and keep the stern towards the beach, running grasses to the shore for boats to pull themselves back by. This was, however, impracticable owing to the distance involved. I could not anchor closer owing to a falling tide. The two ships' boats were therefore sent in under oars with a shore party under the charge of Lieutenant Chapman R.N.V.R., to work in liaison with the soldiers. Instructions were to obtain a party of soldiers to surround each boat as it filled, and keep it afloat on the rapidly falling tide by pushing it out gradually. This scheme worked admirably, the soldiers being regulars of better quality than the first, and no boats were left aground with the exception of the pinnace. One cutter had to be cut adrift as it was found to be waterlogged. This left the motorboat and one cutter in addition to the ship's boats.

29. At 0210 the M.T.B. hailed us to proceed at 0300. I embarked as many troops as possible, and collected the shore party and hoisted the ship's boats, taking the remaining cutter and the motor boat in tow. The motor boat on its last trip was hit by shrapnel, fortunately without loss of life, while in tow and was cut adrift.

30. Weighed and proceeded at 0320. As daylight approached we kept a wary eye open for dive bombers but none appeared to our relief. We

had about 500 troops aboard and from what we heard there were still about 2 to 4 thousand left. I presumed we were ordered to leave at 0300 with the idea of getting away with what soldiers we had rather than risk the certainty of being bombed at anchor and sunk with heavy loss of life. We were the last vessel to leave in our vicinity.

31. The embarkation on this occasion was a very trying period, in what was undoubtedly a very hot corner. Sight and hearing were almost overwhelmed by the ruddy glow of flames, the flashes of gunfire, the shrieking of shells all around, and the noise of their explosion as they burst, and it says much for everybody that the work was carried out calmly and steadily.

32. The voyage back was fairly uneventful. We had a Brigadier aboard whose staff were all scattered and he only had his French liaison Officer with him. *Snaefell* and *Glen Avon* appeared in company and on request of *Glen Avon* I transferred at 0527 a military doctor to deal with a badly wounded soldier aboard, who, however, died of his wounds.

33. On arrival in harbour at 1135 the Brigadier somewhat embarrassingly but very kindly called for 3 cheers for "the Captain, Officers and men of H.M.S. *Glen Gower* who have rescued us in our hour of peril". We responded with three more for him and his men. The work of disembarkation was soon completed and the same procedure adopted as before. We were all very weary, but happy to think we had managed to bring back some 1300 Officers and men of the B.E.F., and proud to know we have been able to assist in the greatest evacuation in history. At the moment of writing, 3rd, June, we have had a day in harbour and are awaiting orders to go back and carry on with the work of evacuating French troops.

34. To conclude the narrative with a few remarks. The troops embarked upon the first occasion were mostly very young and appeared exhausted, which is not to be wondered at. On both occasions the embarkation Officers and men were very wet from wading to the boats and our Officers and ship's company were indefatigable in collecting their clothes to dry in the engine room and boiler room and lending them dry clothing and woollens in the meantime. The wardroom at one time presented the appearance of a Roman feast, with military Officers garbed in togas from the curtains, and girded with the undergarment of blanket round the waist.

The second lot of soldiers appeared to be steadier and more disciplined, being older on the whole, but both bodies were in good heart and ready to go and fight again. Their one complaint was that they had had no chance to stand up to the Germans, having continuously to fall back, and that they had nothing adequate to deal with the continual bombing and machine gunning from the air, which to them appeared to receive little or no opposition from our own Air Force.

Finally I would like to place on record for the favourable notice of their Lordships the conduct of the Officers and men whose names are given hereunder. It has proved not the least difficult of my tasks to single out individuals where all conducted themselves so admirably, with a coolness, courage, skill, and energy in accordance with the highest traditions of the Service. I am proud to command such Officers and men.

At the end of his report Commander Biddulph made specific mention of the following men:

Lieutenant in Command F. Brett. R.N.R., H.M.S. *Snaefell*.
By skilful seamanship successfully towed *Glen Gower* into deep water as she lay aground and saved her from the consequences of being left behind stranded at the mercy of enemy dive bombers.

Tempy. Sub Lieutenant R.A. Snell R.N.V.R.
This Officer is acting as 1st Lieutenant. During the whole period under review he was indefatigable in his efforts to organise the successful embarkation of troops under very trying and very difficult circumstances.

Tempy. Sub Lieutenant N.A.F. Williams. R.N.V.R.
As gunnery Officer organised the ship for defence with what remaining hands he had during embarkation and showed an example of courage and coolness, when narrowly missed by a 4.2 in howitzer shell, which was a pattern to all.

Tempy. Lieutenant L McShedden R.N.R.
Navigating Officer. He relieved me of much of the cares of navigation being as always utterly efficient and trustworthy and allowed me to give more time than I might otherwise have been able to have done, to the general direction and supervision of preparations whilst under way. Whilst at anchor and beached he was untiring and devoted in helping with the embarkation, seeming literally to be everywhere at once.

Tempy. Lieutenant (E) E.A. Rees R.N.R.
Chief Engineer. A pattern of cheery courage. When his duties did not keep him in the engine room he was continually on the upper deck,

assisting troops out of boats, organising parties of soldiers to assist the ship's company in hoisting boats, and making himself generally useful wherever his services might be required. He appeared quite unmoved by the 4.2in. howitzer fire and his example was undoubtedly an inspiration to others.

Tempy. Paymaster Sub Lieutenant D.G. Johnston R.N.V.R.
My secretary. His important duty was to keep a meticulous timed record of events by night and day. This he did most successfully and in the first night went ashore in one of the boats to record his impressions. Though often under fire he went on recording and produced an admirable and accurate record.

Tempy. Surgn. Lieutenant A.L. Schofield R.N.V.R.
Carried out his duties with devotion and skill which could not be surpassed, and did not spare himself until the wounded were treated and made as comfortable as possible.

Leading Seaman J. Darby. R.N. Off. No. JX. 139835.
On both nights was coxswain of one of the boats and gave a magnificent example of leadership and determination, inspiring his flagging crew to their utmost efforts in repeated trips.

Able Seaman J. Fleming. R.N. Off. No. DJX. 140199.
Coxswain of one of the life boats on the second night. Took most excellent charge of his boat under fire and made repeated successful trips to and from the beaches, maintaining order and showing himself fully worthy of higher rating for which he is being recommended.

Able Seaman L. Travers. R.N. Off. No. JX. 133139.
Coxswain of a boat both nights. On the second night showed himself utterly fearless, and was an encouragement to all his crew by cracking jokes as the shells burst near by and pretending to knock the bullets away with a piece of wood which he held in his hand.

Ordinary Seaman J.F. Stokes. H.O. Off. No. SSX. 23129.
Was blown into the air whilst on the beaches assisting with the embarkation but remained incorrigibly cheerful. He said that he thoroughly enjoyed himself and was undoubtedly one of the outstanding figures on the second night, and must have cheered the flagging spirits of the exhausted soldiers. He worked unceasingly in assisting soldiers into the boats.

Assistant Steward T. Matthews. T.124.
Another outstanding figure. Went away as a member of the boat's crew on both nights though he had done very little pulling before and when relieved, practically exhausted, then carried on with the distribution of food and drink to the Officers and men of the B.E.F. His cheery figure seemed to have an inspiring effect on them all.

Ldg. Stoker T Nieve. T.124.
The behaviour of the merchant service stokers as a whole was beyond praise. In addition to their ordinary duties at the boiler they unanimously volunteered to form boat's crews at varying times and at the end of operations were "all in", but they carried on as long as there was anything they could do. I have singled out the above named greaser as being particularly outstanding, as when he had completed a turn as a member of a boat's crew, though scarcely able to stand with fatigue, volunteered for any sort of job in which he could be of any use.

GOLDEN EAGLE
Official Rescue Total: 1,751

A First World War veteran, PS Golden Eagle *(built in 1909 at Clydebank) was called back to service in 1940, being based at Sheerness. Interestingly, the report on HMS* Golden Eagle *during the Dunkirk evacuation states that it was submitted by 'The Officers in Command', i.e. in the plural. As well as Commander E.C. Cordeaux (the Senior Officer Thames Local Defence Flotilla), this seemingly included Lieutenant J.C. Newman MBE, RNVR (listed in some official records as the Captain) and Lieutenant W.L. Lucas RNR. Newman's and Lucas' account is dated 4 June 1940:*

On May 29th about 1045 ship received orders to proceed to position 9 miles East of Dunkirk and embark troops.

Ship sailed at 1140 and arrived in position south of Quint Bank buoy about 1820 where a number of men were seen swimming in the water. *Golden Eagle* picked up all that remained in the water (some 285) and it was realised that two trawlers were also present picking up men. A French destroyer was present but left without taking any part in the rescue work.

It was ascertained that these survivors (British soldiers) were from H.M.S. *Waverley* who had been sunk by bombs about an hour previously. Ship then proceeded straight back to Margate and anchored at 0035, May 30th.

At 0445 went alongside and disembarked survivors.

At 1000 proceeded from Margate by route "Y" and arrived at the Dyck buoy at 1322 when a signal was received saying that ships were to use route "X". Ship was turned about and proceeded by "X" route to "W" buoy, when the Commanding Officer did not seem sure of his position and returned to "R" buoy and then finally returned to Margate where ship was berthed at 2137.

The Commanding Officer had previously made a signal to say he was unwell and on arrival was seen by a medical officer on the pier and was sent ashore.

Golden Eagle then shoved off and proceeded alongside H.M.S. *Guillemot* at 2359 and filled up with oil.

[Friday 31st May]

At 0430 in the absence of any orders it was decided to leave for Dunkirk. Proceedings were then as follows:

0742 Passed close to Dunkirk harbour entrance. Tried to get in touch with pierhead but failed.

0807 Anchored in position 2¼ miles N.E. of harbour. Dunkirk High Lighthouse bearing 224 deg. 2.4 miles. Lowered two boats and embarked about 40 troops from the beach. Received information that more troops were further East and owing to great number of boats and facilities in present position decided that *Golden Eagle* would be of greater assistance further East.

1005 Weighed and proceeded.

1035 Observed large number of troops waiting by Zuidcoote Sanatorium and no boats or ships in immediate vicinity.

1040 Anchored in 2½ fathoms in position Dunkirk High lighthouse bearing 237 deg. 3.25 miles. Established communication ashore by using ship's ropes secured ashore and by using two ship's boats and two small boats salved from beach, ferried troops from beach to ship. Owing to falling tide, shallow water and inshore swell operations were difficult and troops had to wade into 3 feet of water to keep boats afloat but by changing the boats crews for every trip – about 60 troops per hour were embarked. During this time bombing, shelling and aerial machine gunning took place, and gun's crews were continually on the alert and in action and embarking operations continued without a break. Embarked about 340 troops.

1645 Ship's position now untenable and recalled boats.

1720 When boats returned with last load, weighed and proceed close inshore to avoid shell bursts.

1840 Arrived Dunkirk harbour and proceeded in stern foremost.
1850 Berthed alongside East Pier and embarked about 870 troops. During embarkation continued air attack and shelling took place, ships guns were frequently in action.
2058 Cast off and proceeded with about 1250 troops on board.

Saturday 1st June
0115 Anchored in Margate Roads.
0608 Alongside Margate Pier. Disembarked troops. The Commanding Officer now returned on board.
0800 Cast off from Margate Pier and anchored in Roads.
1140 Went alongside H.M.S. *Gallant* for oil.
1935 Proceeded towards Dunkirk and at 2235 sighted unknown obstructions in the vicinity of No.7. Dunkirk Roads busy the weather was very hazy and thick smoke from Dunkirk obscured everything, and it was decided to cruise between "FG" and "W" buoys until daylight 2nd June:
0315 2nd June proceeded back to Margate arriving at 0545.
1114 Left for Sheerness where ship arrived at 1320.
The Senior Officer of the Flotilla then came on board and took command of the ship, sending the Commanding Officer ashore on leave.

In connection with the proceedings on the beaches we would like to emphasise the excellent work done by the whole ship's company. It is difficult to single out anyone for special commendation but undoubtedly the leadership of C.P.O. (Pensioner James S. Seaman O.N.C/J 3192) was of the greatest assistance and the individual work done by Edward C. Utton Sea, RNR X 1961a on the beach itself was outstanding.

As the Senior Officer Thames Local Defence Flotilla, Commander E.C. Cordeaux also provided a report under the title 'Report of Proceedings of A/A Ships of Thames Local Defence Flotilla, May 31st – June 3rd':

On completing discharge of the Military Units at Sheerness on May 31st H.M.S. *Royal Eagle* proceeded to a buoy and reported ready to proceed.

On June 1st at 0800 a signal was received from V.A. Dover, that all paddle minesweepers and minesweepers were to proceed forthwith to the beaches and I at once went on board *Royal Eagle* and after having embarked extra lifebelts and some rafts from the North Wall at Sheerness the ship proceeded to the beaches via route "X" at full speed.

When half way across a signal was received from V.A. Dover ordering *Royal Eagle* to Ramsgate to await instructions so the ship was turned and anchored off Ramsgate. No instructions were received but an Examination Vessel called alongside with a set of directions to minesweepers and paddle minesweepers to proceed to a point 1½ miles East of Dunkirk at 2200 to embark troops. I endeavoured to obtain confirmation that *Royal Eagle* was meant to be included in the signal – but not obtaining this I signalled that I intended to proceed and left at 1530.

Royal Eagle was the first ship to arrive off the beaches at 2200 and I directed the Commanding officer to anchor a full 1½ miles from the breakwater so as to leave room for the ships coming on to anchor astern. On arrival a French drifter with some French soldiers arrived alongside and disembarked them but by 2320 I had seen no sign of any boats although by then some six or more sweepers had arrived and I made a signal to V.A. Dover to this effect.

A signal was received that all sweepers were to be underway and clear of Dunkirk by 0300, and I presumed that this was on account of the shelling which was fairly continuous, though in the dark not very accurate.

It seemed as if the enemy had registered on a wreck a few hundred yards away from *Royal Eagle* as most of the shells fell between *Royal Eagle* and the wreck or just around the wreck. *Royal Eagle* was spattered with shell splinters and I kept the ship's company below the upper deck as much as possible.

A little before 0300 *Royal Eagle* commenced to weigh but two boats were sighted inshore with no ship near them and they were closed and their occupants picked up as well as two seriously injured men from a power lighter which was manned by naval ratings. *Royal Eagle* eventually left the beaches about 0330 being the last but one ship to clear. Owing to the absence of boats only some 120 French troops and half a dozen British had been embarked.

Royal Eagle returned to Sheerness and owing to a boiler defect was put at immediate notice for steam for half speed only.

H.M.S. *Golden Eagle* arrived at 1320 and I at once transferred to her and finding that her Commanding Officer was in a rather overwrought state I sent him on leave and assumed command of the ship myself. Orders were soon received for *Golden Eagle* to proceed to Dunkirk to arrive at 0100/3 and take off troops from the Mole. I sailed at 1725.

Whilst crossing by route "X" near "FG" buoy I sighted a motor torpedo boat which, after passing at some distance from me, came up astern and kept station on me although I reduced speed to see what the effect would be. I felt it possible that the boat was an enemy keeping astern of me ready to attack one of the homecoming troop ships. I did not consider the single letter auxiliary vessels challenge satisfactory so asked the M.T.B. her number and the name of the Commanding Officer; even then I did not feel satisfied so I ordered the M.T.B. to come up alongside my port side to be recognised or otherwise I should open fire. Visual examination at close range showed her to be friendly but I would submit that where our own M.T.B.'s are working in areas where enemy M.T.B.'s may be expected there should in future be very definite instructions as to their behaviour and should not follow astern of our own ships without definitely making themselves known and stating that they are going to pursue some such course.

I had some difficulty in finding my way to Dunkirk in safety owing to the many wrecks, several of which were uncharted and not known to me through having come through this area in the *Royal Eagle* on the previous night; also on account of the number of ships passing along the restricted channel in different directions in the dark. *Golden Eagle* arrived off Dunkirk at 0055 and before long there were some seven or eight ships all waiting to enter Dunkirk and manoeuvring to avoid wrecks and each other. A signal was intercepted to the effect that there were plenty of ships but no men to embark. At about 0210 a launch came round and ordered all minesweepers back to their bases but told me in *Golden Eagle* that I could enter harbour but was to be clear by 0250. I had considerable difficulty in entering as not only the ships outside but also several from inside the harbour were leaving and I had some narrow escapes from collision.

Before going alongside I turned over the handling of the ship to the navigator, Lieut. Lucas R.N.R., who had far more experience in handling this difficult type of ship than I had and had also been into Dunkirk once before and had some idea of the position of the wrecks and general situation. *Golden Eagle* proceeded to the Eastern Arm but was again checked by a ship shoving off just ahead of her.

It was 0240 before the ship was able to approach the Mole and, on getting alongside, there was no one to take our lines but all that could be seen was a line of French soldiers hurrying along the pier, not one of whom could be persuaded upon to take a line or even to stop. Eventually with the assistance of a British officer on the pier, who seemed to be doing magnificent work under very great difficulties, a bow line was got on and the bow hove in, a ladder was put up to the Mole but only one French soldier could be induced to come down it and none of them would stop to haul up the brows; about this time the bow wire parted and the ship swung off. It was now about 0300 and I was hailed by an officer in a motor launch and ordered to get out of it as soon as possible; and at about the same time a block ship entered the harbour and hailing me told me somewhat emphatically to get out whilst I could.

By this time the ship had drifted up against the Mole with a wreck just astern and it was essential to get her stern out in order to move out of the harbour. A short spring was improvised by securing a length of hemp between the sponson and one of the supports of the pier and this proved just sufficient to get her stern full astern – the time then being about 0320. Ships of this class will not steer astern unless the bow rudder is in use and there is considerable way on the ship, and, although the bow rudder had been connected up, it had no time in which to take any effect and I consider the ship to have been most fortunate in making the entrance.

During the whole of the time the ship had been manoeuvring near the wall fairly heavy shelling was in progress and one rating was slightly wounded by a splinter. On arriving outside the harbour I found the port paddle had many fathoms of hemp round the bearing – so as soon as I was just clear of the wreck at the entrance to the port, I stopped and got a number of hands on with knives to clear it. The bearing was practically cleared and I was able to proceed though only at half speed. In the increasing light the ship was shelled from a gun position to the west of Dunkirk, but was not hit. Soon after leaving the coast I picked up a service motor launch and also a lifeboat and towed them back to the North Goodwin.

HMS CRESTED EAGLE

I have not yet seen the report from the Commanding Officer of H.M.S. *Crested Eagle* but from the evidence of a survivor it appears that, after I had ordered her to Dunkirk on May 29th, she proceeded alongside the eastern side of the East Mole at Dunkirk and embarked troops and casualties including many from H.M.S. *Grafton* and a transport which had both been sunk alongside by bombs. Heavy bombing and shell fire was experienced but *Crested Eagle* was unhit until the evening when she had just left the Mole to proceed home with her load of troops and casualties and was hit by a bomb in the engine room. A fire was started and it appeared that as the engines were still working slowly the Commanding Officer decided to beach the ship. Before or after she was beached it is believed she was hit again by two bombs. It is thought that only a small proportion of the ship's company were casualties but that many of the stretcher cases who were accommodated in the wardroom and after part of the ship were lost in the fire.

HMS GOLDEN EAGLE

I would like to add the following remarks in respect of the report of proceedings forwarded by Lieutenants Newman and Lucas. Although

221

technically Lieut. Lucas is second in command of the ship (as an R.N.R. Officer – Lieut. Newman being an R.N.V.R. Officer), Lieut. Newman has carried out the duties of First Lieutenant and there is no doubt that the initiative and good work done by the ship during the absence of her Commanding Officer was due almost entirely to Lieutenant Newman who took upon himself the command and was loyally supported by the two R.N.R. officers – Lieutenants Lucas and Dent, who did excellent work once Lieutenant Newman had decided what was to be done. Lieut. J.C. Newman is 54 years of age and quite inexperienced in Naval matters – but I consider that the part he played in these operations is worthy of the highest commendation and I am convinced that had it not been for his leadership and initiative *Golden Eagle* would not have taken any active part in the proceedings.

I would like also to mention the good work done by Lieut. Lucas R.N.R. who handled the ship with great skill, and on the occasion on which the ship was in Dunkirk harbour at night. I consider that the fact that she got out safely was in a great measure due to his personal efforts on the springs, etc., as well as his handling of the ship.

To the list of men recommended I would like to add Fredk. J. Shirley, Acting Leading Telegraphist R.N.V.R. C/WRX84, whose efficiency and extreme devotion to duty has been of the utmost assistance to me as Senior Officer of the flotilla and also that of Able Seaman Scott S.T. TD/X1406, who was the only man I could rely upon to take the wheel with any degree of competency during the night visit to Dunkirk. I thoroughly endorse the recommendations given to C.P.O. Seaman and Utton, Seamen R.N.R.

KING ORRY
Official Rescue Total: 1,131

By the end of September 1939, the Isle of Man Steam Packet Company's King Orry, *a First World War veteran, had been commissioned as an Armed Boarding Vessel, or ABV. On 22 May 1940 she was taken off her regular duties and prepared for work assisting the BEF. Captained by Commander J. Elliott, RD, RNR, HMS* King Orry *was first damaged on 27 May, and then lost on 30 May. Elliott's account of this hectic period is dated 4 June 1940:*

Proceeding in accordance with your orders on the afternoon of the 29th May, I arrived in Dunkirk Roads at 0730. The voyage was without incident.

On rounding No 6 Buoy and approaching Dunkirk it was evident that considerable aerial activity was in progress and one of H.M.

Destroyers appeared to be making a smoke screen.

I proceeded along the channel and was subjected to a direct attack from a dive bomber when about half a mile West of the West Breakwater end. Six bombs straddled the bow – two to Port and four to Starboard. My thought at that moment was that we were fortunate to be missed, especially as two bombs bounced off the water on Port side – but as it happened, all the bombs exploded under water at the time the ship had passed into their zone. This shook the ship convulsively, but as no damage was reported or seemed evident at the time, I proceeded towards the harbour.

There was a continuous attack on the harbour and vicinity in progress. Two ships were in sight sunk at the East Pier on the inner and outer sides and one of H.M. Destroyers was burning furiously in the Western Basin. A Drifter was alongside about half way down the East Pier. There was no sign of anyone on the pier, nor was any boat moving in the harbour.

I now endeavoured to get alongside the East Pier on inner side but failed to turn ship head out at first attempt owing to strong set away from the Pier, so I drew off to try again. Unfortunately at this time we again came under heavy bombing attacks, which appeared at the time to be continuous. The ship was violently shaken and the steering gear was put out of action. All instruments, woodwork, etc. were shattered.

It seemed essential to get the ship alongside the quay and this I proceeded to do, but in closing the pier damaged same considerably. I do not think the structure could have been very strong as no damage was done to the ship, and my impression was that the ship merely pushed hard – there was no shock or rebound whatever.

We were now attacked again but no direct hits were made – bombs falling so close, however, as to give the impression of direct hits, especially as various debris flew up at every explosion.

I now resolved to secure the ship and shelter the crew ashore till we could examine the damage under cover of darkness. An immediate withdrawal from the harbour did not seem practicable without steering gear. Even although the engine room was intact it would take some little time to discover all damage, and I was not at all confident from previous experience that the ship with her small propellers would manoeuvre with engines alone in a tideway in the narrow waters, and might become a serious obstruction if she grounded.

Having secured the ship by the bow I made along the quay towards the drifter and placing the wounded in her, stood by for a short while, noting developments. But as the attack had ceased I returned to the ship and prepared to repair the steering gear, etc.

A Naval Commander from Headquarters ashore now came along and I consulted with him as to general position and as to steps to be taken if it were found necessary to leave the ship.

An examination of the ship showed that she was holed below the water line forward in two or three places and aft in the starboard Fireman's sleeping quarters. But this damage did not seem so serious as the fact that the steering gear was out of action and that the steam which prevented us from getting into the steering flat could not be cut off the boilers – there apparently being no stop valve accessible.

A fire had broken out in the Steward's quarters on the starboard side, but I was able to put this out without much trouble. The holes made forward were of a jagged nature, from three to four inches at greatest width, and also a number of rivets were blown out. Some damage to an oil bunker was apparent, as oil fuel was coming into the seaman's sleeping quarters forward in considerable but not heavy quantity. The worst hole in the stokers' quarters was caused by the blowing in of a completely deadlighted porthole.

All leaks were eventually stopped that were visible, and the pumps seemed to be coping with any influx successfully. Owing to the darkness it was difficult in some parts of the ship to fully ascertain all damage or possible hidden weaknesses.

I went ashore to discuss the situation with the Senior Naval Officer and had to report that I did not anticipate the ship being seaworthy before dawn, and that she was certainly not in a fit state to take on troops.

The ship had in the meantime been secured alongside, bow in.

It was considered from information now gained that the ship would again become subject to attacks at dawn, and would then most probably be destroyed. The Senior Naval Officer instructed me to either proceed to sea or endeavour to ground the ship on the East side of the pier, where she would be useful as a breakwater.

Soon after 0300 on the 30th May I decided to leave the berth, as the ship was aground and might be difficult to get off later. I also decided that if the ship was sufficiently manoeuvrable to be grounded where required that she could also possibly be extricated either bow or stern first from Dunkirk Roads and possibly reach assistance.

I found, however, that she was not at all handy on her propellers, and whilst endeavouring to point her for the channel she began to develop a list to starboard which developed seriously. Water was reported entering the stokehold and I sent the First Lieutenant to investigate. Almost immediately, however, it became obvious that the ship was sinking, and I ordered abandonment. Ship was now clear of entrance over towards North side of channel.

Our one remaining available boat on starboard side was turned out previous to this but was submerged as ship heeled over. As we had two Carley floats and a large number of rafts this was not a serious loss.

At about 0200, or shortly before, the ship foundered.

I was on the bridge and was joined by the Chief Engineer, Mr. Cowley (Temp. Lieut. Engineer). The First Lieutenant, Lieut. J. Lee, R.N.R., was attending to abandonment generally.

The ship turned completely on her starboard side and I stepped into the water, being afloat near the forward starboard boat, now submerged. The Chief Engineer was with me.

After and during the following hour several ships, including H.M.S. *Vivacious* and H.M. Drifter *Lord Grey*, picked up survivors, but I regret to report that two Engineer Officers, T124, and seven other ratings were lost.

A complete readiness to carry out all orders was shown throughout by all officers and ratings. Steam was maintained in the engine room, and everything done to find some means to repair the steering gear.

Fire from the 12 Pdr. H.A. gun and Lewis guns was kept up throughout all attacks, and from my own observation, one aircraft was damaged – a piece seeming to fall off.

As I was required for duty at Ramsgate on the 31st May and subsequent days, I have not been able to report previously, and with regard to times – all records have unfortunately been lost.

All Confidential Books and papers were burned in boiler room as soon as danger to the ship was evident.

Whilst forwarding Commander Elliott's account to the Flag Officer Commanding Dover, Captain W.R. Phillimore, the Naval Officer in Charge Ramsgate, wrote the following:

I desire to bring to your notice that Commander Elliott landed here on 30th May, after his vessel had been sunk at Dunkirk.

2. He then expressed a desire to assist at this Base. After 24 hours stand-off he turned to on Pier duty on the East Pier, assisting in the handling of craft as they came alongside with troops.

3. When the hospital ship *Paris* was damaged, he proceeded out in charge of the two tugs *Sun IV* and *Sun XV* to render assistance. *Paris* was found without crew and a line was put on board. Both tugs were subjected to machine gun fire. At about 0200 on 3rd June, the tow was abandoned and both tugs returned to this Base at 0600.

4. Commander Elliott has now been sent on leave p.m. 4th June – to his home address.

225

MARMION
Official Rescue Total: 713

Requisitioned for war service, the paddle steamer Marmion *was stationed at Harwich. Having survived the Dunkirk evacuations, she was sunk by enemy aircraft at Harwich on the night of 8 April 1941. Lieutenant (Temporary) H.C. Gaffney RNVR's report on HMS* Marmion *during Operation* Dynamo *is dated 5 June 1940:*

May 24th.
In company with *Oriole* sweeping the Would when we got German mine in sweep. The usual methods were used to dispose of this without result, the mine still coming to the surface when the ship stopped. *Oriole* closed and sunk mine by gunfire but it was apparently still foul of sweep. I accordingly went to deep water, hove in as close as possible, cut sweep wire, lowered boat with volunteer crew in charge of Sub-Lt. Black, R.N.V.R., with C.P.O. Brotherton, C/J 20237, Pen.No.28760, and T124 personnel – salved float – lost otter.

May 25th.
Swept as instructed with double oropesa from No.7 buoy to position Lat.52° 23½' N Long. 1° 54' E and returned sweeping to No.7 buoy, distance 80 miles.

May 26th.
Swept with single oropesa the area between Caister N and Caister S buoys. Salved oropesa float. At 1215 received signals from A.S. Motor Boats S.O.1 ad S.O.4. – 'Ashore'. It is ascertained that they were ashore on the Scroby Shoal. Approached as close as possible – tide ebbing and was unable to render assistance at that juncture. Yarmouth life-boat and tug standing by. Continued sweeping and on completion continued to the eastward of Scroby Shoal (upon orders of F.O.I.C. Yarmouth) and anchored as close as possible to the S.O.1 and S.O.4., their position being 52° 38.5' N, 1° 47.7' E. Life boats were lowered and manned by volunteer crews, Sub-Lt. Black, R.N.V.R. in charge of starboard life-boat and C.P.O. Brotherton, C/J 20237 in charge of the port one. Lines were taken ashore, one from *Marmion* and the other from tug *R.L. Barber* who was thus secured to S.O.4. which was the closer situated and almost on the edge of the bank – S.O.1 was some 70 yards high and dry on the bank.

May 27th.
At high water 0100. S.O.4. was refloated without much effort, at 0200

Marmion kept steady strain on S.O.1. and succeeded in hauling vessel 70 yards over the bank when tow parted at 0154. Vessel was then at eastern end of bank and in a position to refloat at next flood. Part of crews of both vessels had previously been brought aboard *Marmion* by the Yarmouth life-boat as a precautionary measure as the wind was backing to SSE and inclined to freshen, the glass reading 29.91. At 0800 resumed attempt to pass line to S.O.1. by the life-boat manned under same direction – a cross tide running very strongly – succeeded in getting rope fast. Tug *R.L. Barber* and another motor boat arrived 1040. Motor boat took wire from tug to within 50 yards of S.O.1 whereupon our starboard life-boat (Sub-Lt Black) took over and secured to S.O.1. She was observed to be floating at 1144. By this time the wind and sea had freshened very considerably and I consider that had the vessel not been refloated she would have been in great jeopardy. In conclusion I would say that the boat work in the tideway and the landing on the beach with ground swell reflects great credit on Sub-Lt Black, R.N.V.R. and C.P.O. Brotherton, C/J 20237and the boats' crews.

1320. Proceeded to anchorage Yarmouth Roads to await instructions. Short of coal and water.
1755 Orders to proceed to Lowestoft.
1925 Entered harbour.

May 28th.
Commenced coaling 0400 – cleared harbour 1103, rejoined flotilla at 1200 off Lowestoft – proceeding to La Panne.

May 29th.
0247 Picked up survivors from mined French Transport two cables from us. Signalled to French destroyer to stand by. Re-embarked survivors to French vessel, retaining six seriously injured French soldiers and Air Force Captain who were attended to by surgeon from near destroyer, *Esk*. Off Bray Dunes lowered starboard life-boat (Sub-Lt Black, R.N.V.R.) and port life-boat (C.P.O. Brotherton, C/J 202370) with volunteer crews mainly stokers and stewards – proceeded to embark troops – heavy surf running, starboard boat capsized, subsequently refloated. Later assisted by destroyer's motor boat and surf motor boat. Sub -Lts. Balfour and Patton later went in charge of boats.
1140 Proceeded as instructed by *Waverley* to land troops at Dover.
2040 Landed 339 British and French troops and wounded.

May 30th.
0230 Anchored outside harbour. Requested coal and water.

May 31st.

0400 Examination of vessel closed and ordered to proceed into harbour – secured to buoy 21.

1820 Proceeded to coaling berth. Took in 30 tons.

2255 Secured to buoy 34.

June 1st.

1621 Proceeded to Dunkirk arrived at anchorage in Roads at 2155 – Ship under fire and numerous hits by shrapnel – aircraft active. Port life-boat sent ashore with Sub-Lt. Patton in charge to locate troops.

June 2nd.

0200 Ordered into Dunkirk Harbour. Embarked French Troops and proceeded to Dover 0320. Disembarking 280 troops at 1035 thence proceeding to buoy.

1725 Proceeded to Dunkirk arriving Roads 2315.

June 3rd.

Vessel under gunfire – aircraft active. Entered harbour 0100. Vessel alongside mole – considerable swell – no troops for some time – much shelling. Embarked 204 troops and told to clear off as no more troops arriving. Port paddle fouled by floating rope. Cleared harbour at 0233 – proceeded to Dover. Disembarked troops at 0710 and later secured alongside extended arm of Prince of Wales Pier waiting orders – coal required.

Every effort was made to provide for the comfort of the British and French Troops whilst on board – Officers, Petty Officers and men surrendering their accommodation so that during the passage we had as few on deck as possible. This also ensured the better stability of the ship. Clothes, tea, cocoa and meals were provided completely exhausting our supplies.

In conclusion, the Officers and Men, the many under shellfire for the first time, acquitted themselves well and were at all times cool and cheerful under the somewhat arduous conditions and long hours.

Also on 5 June 1940, Lieutenant Gaffney submitted his 'recommendations of personnel', adding 'from these operations there emerge three very definite figures':

Sub-Lt Black, R.N.V.R.
In charge of starboard Lifeboat who made the initial landing when surf was running high – this officer came under fire for the first time. He was always in the forefront during divers jobs with calm and cheerfulness and providing a great example of a zealous and intrepid officer.

C.P.O. Brotherton, C/J 202370.
In charge of the Port Lifeboat at Bray Dunes made the initial landing in heavy surf. He was always at the wheel going alongside the mole at Dunkirk – there is no protection on the Bridge from shell or rifle fire – he was thus exposed for long periods when particular care and attention was necessary for steering and helm orders. He was a magnificent example to all, fearless and untiring – also, after leaving Dunkirk, he really 'fathered' the troops and ship's company.

Leading Stoker Thompson (T.124)
Made innumerable trips in lifeboats at Bray Dunes after coming off Watch in stokehold – rendered invaluable assistance when going alongside the mole on both occasions at Dunkirk. He scrambled ashore and hauled our lines under shell fire – an absolute glutton for work, he always managed to raise a laugh at the right moment. A really tight corner man, his conduct truly splendid.

I would like to pay tribute to the T.124 personnel (Stokers and Stewards) they volunteered to a man for boats crews and made an excellent show. They were lending a hand everywhere and everything they did, they did well.

MEDWAY QUEEN
Official Rescue Total: 3,064

The paddle steamer Medway Queen *was ordered in 1923 and entered service on the Strood-Chatham-Southend-Herne Bay route the following year. With occasional excursions elsewhere she served on the same route until the beginning of the Second World War. Requisitioned in 1939 and converted for mine-sweeping, HMS* Medway Queen *was assigned to the 10th Minesweeping Flotilla, which was based at Dover, in 1940. Her Commanding Officer during the Dunkirk evacuation was Lieutenant A.T. Cook RNR. His account is one of the briefest submitted to the Admiralty:*

[27th May]   Recalled from Downs and proceeded in company with *Sandown*, *Gracie Fields* and *Brighton Belle* to La Panne arriving at 2300hrs evacuated 600 British troops from Beach and proceeded to Ramsgate, ship attacked off North Goodwin Lt. by enemy aircraft opened fire and brought down one plane. Received S.O.S. from H.M.S. *Brighton Belle* sinking owing to striking submerged wreck. Proceeded alongside her and took off troops and all members of crew. *Brighton Belle* sank.

28th   At 2045 hrs [illegible] up and proceeded independently to Dunkirk, arrived at 2hrs and evacuated 450 troops returned to Ramsgate.

29th   1800 hrs [illegible] up and proceeded to beach at Bray, evacuated 450 troops and returned to Margate.

30th.   At 1900 left Margate and proceeded to Bray, evacuated 550 troops landed them at Ramsgate.

31st.   Sailing orders cancelled. Ship under 1 hrs notice to proceed.

1st. June   At 1100 hrs proceeded beach East of Dunkirk Defence at 1300 picked up open boat with 10 Spanish refugees, proceeded evacuated 700 troops, crews of *Aura* and *Fanta*. Ship attacked enemy aircraft west of Dunkirk opened fire and brought plane down on beach west of Dunkirk. Landed troops at Ramsgate.

2nd.   At 1800 hrs left Dover, at 0030 took off 625 French troops from East pier Dunkirk. Landed them at Ramsgate. Commander Greig of *Sandown* aboard.

3rd.   2000hrs proceeded to Dunkirk took off 400 French troops landed them at Ramsgate.

4th.   Evacuation complete returned to Dover.

One of the 139,997 French soldiers brought to the United Kingdom during the Dunkirk evacuation was Paul Dervilers. Speaking in 1989, at which point he was 87-years-old, he recalled his rescue at the hands of the crew of Medway Queen:

I was on the beach walking up the coast towards Belgium when I saw some Englishmen getting into a dinghy and I joined ten of them who tried to get aboard. But the dinghy became waterlogged. We all began bailing hopelessly with our helmets. Fortunately, half-way to an off-lying ship, we picked up an abandoned little skiff in good shape and we got into it. It was 2300 when we climbed up the ladder of the *Medway Queen*.

Private Henry Powell was a driver in the Royal Signals. His unit had been in France, as part of the BEF, since January 1940, being attached to 3 Corps' Medium Artillery HQ. His account of how he came to be rescued by Medway Queen *was written in 1998 and is quoted here from the BBC People's War website (www.bbc.co.uk/history/ww2peopleswar):*

On the surrender of the Belgian army we started to retreat, eventually getting to Poperinge [*sic*], where it all started on 24 May. While in Poperinghe we were heavily dive bombed and lost our OC, the officer commanding. We then started to drive towards Berques, but before we got there we were stopped at a crossroads by military police and told to get to Dunkirk. They told us it was every man for himself.

Further along the road we were stopped again and told to dump the lorry and go to the beaches at La Panne and proceed on foot. By this time our unit was gradually getting split up, so by the time we got to La Panne there were only four of us together in a chaotic situation.

On the beaches we huddled together in the sand dunes for protection from the constant bombing and machine gunning from the air. The bombing was ineffectual, just blowing up loads of sand, but the machine gunning was another matter.

Lying across the scene was a huge cloud of smoke coming from the oil tanks on fire in Dunkirk.

After a time, actually at dawn the next day, we were marshalled in groups of 50, under an officer or senior non-commissioned officer (NCO), and marched down to the water's edge. A beach master, who called each group in turn, maintained discipline there. I saw one group run out of line, and the person in charge was promptly shot by the beachmaster.

Owing to the shallow draft of the beach the embarking drill was to get into a rowing boat or whaler first, which took us to a launch lying a distance off shore. This, in turn, took us to the larger vessels lying further off.

On the way to the bigger ships the launch I was in was bombed. We didn't suffer a direct hit, though it was close enough to swamp the boat, and I found myself in the drink. It was a good job I could swim.

Having divested myself of my pack and so forth, I surfaced and looked around. I saw the ship was closer than the shore, so I struck out for it, a paddle steamer converted to minesweeper named the *Medway Queen*. After swimming approximately 50 yards, I arrived at the ship completely knackered and found myself hauled aboard.

Having only soaked fags, a squaddy came to my rescue and gave me a packet of army club. Later, one of the crew handed out cocoa, which was much appreciated.

When we had our full complement, we started to cross towards England. After a few scares from air attack, we arrived at Ramsgate. It was a good job it was a fine day because that way my clothes had been able to dry on me.

We disembarked and proceeded towards London with people cheering us on our way. We didn't deserve the cheers, but if anyone did it was the navy for getting us out. The Women's Voluntary Service (WVS) came to the rescue again, when we finally arrived at Devizes in the middle of the night on 2 June 1940. We were given two eggs and chips, and then kipped down in the gym on a mattress on the floor.

Having been threatened with destruction or demolition on a number of occasions since the Second World War, Medway Queen *was finally saved by the Medway Queen Preservation Society. Through their efforts, and with the support of organisations such as the Heritage Lottery Fund, this remarkable ship is being restored for future generations.* Medway Queen *is, at the time of publication, moored at Gillingham Pier where she can be visited. To find out about the Medway Queen Preservation Society's efforts to restore the paddle steamer visit: www.medwayqueen.co.uk*

MONA'S ISLE
Official Rescue Total: 2,364

Originally built for the South Eastern and Chatham Railway in 1905, this steamer was first named Onward. *After being purchased by the Isle of Man Steam Packet Company,* Onward *was renamed* Mona's Isle *in 1920. Requisitioned for service as an Armed Boarding Vessel, HMS* Mona's Isle *spent the first winter of the war patrolling the North Sea. In his book* The Ships That Saved An Army, *the author Russell Plummer writes that* Mona's Isle *'claimed to be the first personnel vessel to complete a round trip to Dunkirk and was already crossing when Operation* Dynamo *officially started just before seven in the evening on 26th May'. The following report was written by her Captain, Commander J.C.K. Dowding RD, RN:*

26th May.
2000   Anchored off Deal.
2116   Proceeded towards Dunkirk via route past Calais. Fine and clear.

27th May.
0115   Off entrance to Dunkirk. Signalled, no response. Being ignorant
       of conditions and harbour, attempted to enter <u>slowly</u>. Star engine

failed owing to wire round propeller. Considered entrance might be fouled so backed out. Propeller cleared itself.

0130 Proceeded down channel to interrogate several French craft as to position inside harbour, pilots etc. No satisfaction.

0250 Signalled V.A.D. for instructions. H.M.S. *King Orry* in similar position.

0321 Orders to enter at daylight.

0416 Entered and made contact with S.T.O. No tugs available, so swung ship and berthed at Quai Felix Faure, with all guns firing at enemy aircraft.

0530 Alongside. Commenced embarking. About 1500 men, approx.

0704 Proceeded out of harbour.

0730 Off Gravelines, observed several British small craft and Hospital ship being shelled some distance ahead.

0750 Heavily shelled and straddled by several [illegible] guns, approx. 12pdr firing shrapnel. Several hits of sorts and casualties.

0805 Considered it worth the risk of turning to N.W, being at the moment off Dunkirk A.W. buoy. Apparently got out of range.

0825 Six Messerschmitt appeared. Opened fire with 4" and 2 Lewis guns and 12 pdr. Aircraft carried out about four attacks, from the sun, invisible to us. From astern. Terrific machine gun fire, a great deal of which missed ahead, but many direct hits with cannon, especially round 12 pdr. whose crew under Sub Lt A.E. Neave R.N.R. stood up to it extremely well, but sustained casualties, including the sub lieutenant. The packed troops on the open deck suffered badly; had the shooting been accurate the losses would have been very much greater.

0835 Aircraft apparently out of ammunition and steered off. D.G. gear: W/T set; 10" signal lamp; steering gear; out of action. Speed maintained. Steered West to Outer Ruytingen Buoy No 7. by engines.

0900 Called H.M.S. *Windsor* (well to S.W of us.) asked her to report our condition to V.A.D. Steered W.N.W. approx.

0924 *Windsor* alongside. Put Doctor on board and escorted us to Dover.

1000 (approx.) Off Dover entrance; *Windsor* asked for tug. Reported the casualties.

1054 Tug *Lady Brassy* fast. Orders to wait for berth.

1156 Tug *Simla* fast with orders to enter, and go to Eastern arm.

1214 Entered harbour, and waited for berth.

1353 Berthed at Admiralty pier. Com'ced disembarkation at once.

1835 All ashore, including about 23 dead and about 60 wounded. All due to air attack. Remained at pier all night and berthed in

Granville Dock at 0520 28th May. To effect numerous repairs to all boats, steering gear, D.G. winding; electrical circuits; dynamo. Fresh and salt water tanks and services.

The behaviour of the entire ship's company under very trying conditions was magnificent, especially that of the Engine Room branch, whose work was considerably hampered by the congestion of troops and wounded round about the engine room, (on the Main deck).

The coolness, confidence, cheerfulness and courage of all ranks of the Military was a great incentive to all concerned.

The fear lest a 600 gallon Diesel Oil tank on the shelter deck should be perforated and take fire, being quite unprotected was the greatest concern.

1st June. Sat.
Ship in Granville dock. Repaired and ready for service.
0909 Left dock and proceeded to Dunkirk. By "X" route.
1305 Observed wreck of *Scotia* and another vessel, apparently on Dyck Bank, with H.M.S. H.15 alongside wreck taking off survivors. Closed as requested by H.15, in company with a great number of small craft proceeding to Dunkirk. Lowered 3 boats, maned by various ratings of all departments, and picked up a few survivors. All other craft doing likewise. Took some survivors from other craft.
1422 When no more could be done, proceeded towards Dunkirk. H.15 had left for Dover, crowded. *Scotia* was on fire aft and it was apparent that no more men were on the wreck itself, and very few alive in the water.
1448 Passed No 5 buoy. Heavily shelled and straddled by small calibre guns. No hits after about 4 salvoes.
1505 Between Nos 11 and 13 buoys, was straddled by two salvoes from Dive bombers. Bombs were very close, deluging the entire ship with water, but apparently no damage, though ship was badly shaken.
1540 Berthed at inside berth, Eastern arm, Dunkirk. S.N.O. wished me to go to Western arm, but tide being low there was insufficient water.
1550 Com'ced to embark British troops, and numerous stretcher cases.
1730 Ship full and very congested with about 1500 men. Advised S.N.O. I could not safely take more, being considerably worried about stability. S.N.O. strongly advised me to wait, under cover of shore guns, until 2100. when it was high water and getting dark for the passage across. This I agreed with; During this wait of nearly four hours, several dive bombing attacks were made by flights of aircraft on two wrecks outside the harbour, which seemed to indicate that they were anxious to get rid of their

bombs on anything that did not fire back. As an intense fire was maintained on them from our 8 Lewis guns and several Bren guns which the soldiers had rigged up in various places and worked for us. Several flights of aircraft passed overhead, apparently bombers, but whilst the R.A.F. were about there was peace. This long wait was trying to all concerned. A British Spitfire crashed outside the Harbour; the pilot rescued and put on board us where his coolness and help in identifying the aircraft was most useful. Both ships and shore batteries opened fire on R.A.F. machines more than once when recognition was difficult.

2100 Proceeded; a sunken trawler just inside the entrance made approach to the wharf difficult which must have been much more so after dark for the ships which came in after us. The enemy were apparently shelling the dock entrance from some distance whilst we lay there, but nothing came close to us.

2300 Passed North Goodwin L.V. The darkness was not deep enough to prevent ships seeing each other at some distance, or to pick up the wreck of the *Scotia* were [sic] she lay practically in the channel down to the No 5 buoy. I consider the navigation of all the numerous small craft to have been of the highest order, all things considered.

June 2nd Sun.
0150 Reported arrival off Dover to V.A.D
0300 Berthed at Admiralty Pier and com'ced discharging. Ship was then found to be making water in No 2 hold; stokehold. The main seam pipes joints were leaking in three places, and fracture is suspected. The L.P. turbine rings collapsed; the base of the bilge pump suspected fracture. The maintaining of a fairly good speed and working in the engine room on the passage back, with the escape of steam due to these defects was very creditable work. On this occasion as before the behaviour of the ships company was most praiseworthy; and conduct and courage of all ranks of the military was of the very highest order and an inspiration to all connected with them throughout these grievous times.

ORIOLE
Official Rescue Total: 2,587

Having been requisitioned by the Admiralty, PS Eagle III left the Clyde in early 1940, having been renamed HMS Oriole, for wartime minesweeping duties at Harwich. Lieutenant (Temporary) E.L. Davies RNVR wrote his report on HMS Oriole's *service at Dunkirk on 30 May 1940 (see also HMS* Plinlimmon):

Reference our recently completed trip to the Belgian Coast I think it my duty to draw both your own and their Lordships attention to the splendid manner in which every man of my ship's company acquitted themselves.

You are aware that except for the seven words ("You will be required to embark troops") in F.O.I.C. Harwich's 1016/28 I was entirely unaware of what was required of me and I could therefore only be guided by the outstanding facts that there were many ships in the offing and many destitute soldiers on the beach. We had no power boats and those ships that had power boats seemed to be lacking in a sense of co-operation, but it was early evident to me that owing to the considerable surf and shoal character of the beach boat work would inevitably be slow and cumbersome and not devoid of danger. Consequently, and well knowing the virtues of a paddler for such work, I deliberately ran *Oriole* ashore making a clearing station of her by inviting all ships in the offing to collect troops through me rather than waste further time with their own lifeboats.

I am aware that *Oriole* might have been utterly lost but I felt that I could satisfactorily answer such a loss. It is difficult to recount all that happened. The troops at first had to be held off at revolver point, but we soon initiated a modicum of organisation and then distribution went with a swing. Despite persistent bombing by the enemy I think we must have distributed some 2500-3000 troops between all types of ships in the offing and then as evening drew on I took on board *Oriole* the two or three hundred with whom I felt she would still float. As time for refloating approached I notified army officers that I would cruise about in the vicinity and would pick up all who could get out into nine feet of water by boats or any other means. I refloated about 6.00 p.m. and then cruised about in 8/10 feet of water until I had embarked an estimated 6/700 soldiers, nurses, mails, etc., the enemy bombing being simply torrential at this time.

I submit that machines of our Air Force should be in constant attendance on these beaches until operations come to a close. I do not suggest that the enemy will be deterred from attacking such a fruitful target, but I am absolutely confident that a knowledge that our machines were harrying theirs as they were harrying us would give us heart to feel that we had support from quarters where support was most desirable.

In all these operations the whole of my ship's company, without sleep, food or even water, used every endeavour to forward the work to the utmost of their abilities and consequently I would like to name every rank and rating as worthy of recognition. As however I recognise that to be impossible I submit attached a list of seven members of my Crew whose efforts on the Belgian Coast were of a very high order indeed.

On his return, Lieutenant Davies made the following remarks regarding the actions of some members of his crew:

Reference difficulties on the Belgian coast yesterday, operations being individual and without co-ordination between any of the services, and wherein *Oriole* having deliberately grounded for the purpose of forming a stable link between Army and Navy, and also wherein *Oriole* distributed some 2,500 troops to destroyers, minesweepers, and other auxiliary craft in the offing, I have the honour to cite the following names as worthy of marked distinction.

Harris, Roy S., Lieut. R.N.V.R., and 1st Lieutenant of *Oriole*
Although wearied prior to Belgian coast operations (the whole ship's company was equally wearied) was indefatigable in the intricate business of handling boats, lines, hawsers, etc in initiating and maintaining communications with the shore, etc, etc.

Crosby, John, Sub-Lieut. R.N.V.R.
On several occasions very gallantly and at his own obvious imminent peril dove into surf and tide (strong) to render assistance to soldiers in difficulties and was thereby responsible in preserving many lives.

Page, George, P.O. B/21629. R.F.R.
Was everywhere, did everything, for sailor and soldier alike. Page is the coxswain of the ship and therefore her housekeeper. The soldiers on the beach were clearly in a starving condition yet Page managed to keep some 700 in good heart by cleverly handling provisions designed to feed 45.

Giles, Jack, L.S. B/23499. R.F.R.
For making the initial trips to the shore, passing ropes, righting upturned boats and above all for creating organisation out of the chaotic conditions that prevailed amongst the troops.

Scothorn, William, Tel/B/Z/7560.
Gallantly maintained communication with the shore, having to swim the return journey several times at his peril. He assisted officers of

higher rank to board the ship and subsequently to get them away to other ships in the offing.

Grace, James, Seaman R.N.R.
Under L/S Giles passed ropes to shore through the surf, assisted in righting upturned boats, and was instrumental in maintaining order amongst the frenzied soldiers.

Bruce, William, Signalman/Militia.
Was indefatigable in getting signals and messages to ships in the offing for embarkation purposes. During enemy bombing attacks he displayed remarkable ability in spotting aircraft and his sixth-sense of divining which particular planes intended selecting this vessel as target undoubtedly helped in maintaining an efficient barrage.

The following transcript of a postagram, timed and dated as 18.00 hours on 2 June 1940, was attached to Lieutenant Davies' report:

Arrived evacuation beach Belgian Coast 1st June in accordance with instructions. Complete absence of transport facilities. Service ships using own motor launches and whalers at very slow speed. *Oriole* having no power boat was beached to embark soldiers. It would have been feasible to have filled the ship in half an hour but many hundreds of soldiers attempted to rush and it was necessary to haul off shore with about 200 on board and another fifty hanging to exterior protections all round the ship. Ship was taken to a more sparsely populated portion of beach, army officers were posted with revolvers to keep order and ship was beached again. Ship was again rushed by such numbers as to imperil her chances and chances of all then on board and she was therefore again hauled off shore with a total of about 470. Throughout enemy fighters attempted to machine-gun ship and soldiers in the water (no bombs this day) and with about 470 on board I deemed it advisable to return to base. We shot down one enemy machine. 1500/1 ends.

Dated 30 May 1940, Captain G.W. Heaton penned the following observations on his covering letter when forwarding Lieutenant Davies' narrative:

Oriole was deliberately beached and used as a pontoon for troops, over 3,000 being embarked over her into other vessels by this means. During the period she was ashore, although continually straddled by bombs and repeatedly splashed with water and sand thrown up by these, the work appears to have gone forward without hurry or fuss. In addition to the 3,000 troops saved by this means, she herself brought back to England a total of 2,591 on the two trips which she made.

I myself visited *Oriole* on her return to Harwich on the 30th May, and then had a long talk with Lieutenant Davies, R.N.V.R., and from what I heard and saw then, I find it most difficult to express in words my admiration for Lieutenant Davies' handling of an unprecedented situation and for the spirit shown by him and every Officer and man under his command.

There was no question of rest or anything else being required by them, but only a burning desire to get their ship coaled and turned round in order that they might get back to Dunkirk in the shortest possible time.

PLINLIMMON
Official Rescue Total: 900

Built by H. McIntyre at Alloa, HMS Plinlimmon *was launched in April 1895, her name originally being PS* Cambria. *Requisitioned in the First World War as HMS* Cambridge, *this paddle steamer was based at Grimsby and on the Tyne. Her return to peacetime duties ended in 1939 when she was again requisitioned. Converted to a minesweeper she was given the name HMS* Plinlimmon. *Lieutenant G.P. Baker RNVR's report of her role in Operation* Dynamo *is dated 9 June 1940:*

In accordance with instructions from F.O.I.C., Harwich, *Plinlimmon* left Harwich at 0455 on 31/5/40 for the beach at La Panne, where, on arrival at 1225/31, anchor was let go close in. Before boats could be lowered shells commenced to drop all round and orders were received from a Fleet Sweeper to weigh anchor. A motor boat with 30 soldiers on board, and with one disabled engine, was taken in tow, the soldiers eventually being transferred to *Plinlimmon*, and the motor boat advised to proceed independently on one motor.

At 1330/31 orders were received from a Flag Officer in a destroyer to proceed into Dunkirk, and at 1415/31 *Plinlimmon* moored alongside East Pier, immediately to the Southward of a sunken trawler. Brows and ladders were rigged and soldiers embarked, but it was not until 1600/31 that they commenced to arrive in sufficient quantities to complete the number required, although officers were sent along the pier from time to time to endeavour to collect them.

At 1740/31, having embarked approximately 900 Officers and men, *Plinlimmon* cast off and proceeded. At 1755/31 a German Messerschmitt aeroplane was shot down and nose dived into the sea about 1¼ miles on the starboard beam, and a pilot was observed coming down by parachute some distance ahead. He struck the water about 300 yards on the starboard bow, the ship was manoeuvred alongside & the pilot hauled on board. He proved to be Pilot Officer Verity, of Biggin Hill Aerodrome, Kent, who had shot down the above mentioned Messerschmitt, but was himself simultaneously shot down by another Messerschmitt.

Margate was reached at 2100/31 and the troops landed.

Plinlimmon was then ordered to coal and return to Dunkirk, but on proceeding at 1115/1 was ordered by visual signal to stop. It subsequently transpired that as she had not been degaussed she was debarred from further participation in the evacuation.

We lay at anchor in Margate Roads until 0900/3, when an Officer came onboard and asked if I would take my entire Ship's Company over to another paddle minesweeper, H.M.S. *Oriole*, whose ship's company were exhausted, and take her to Dunkirk for the final night evacuation. I instantly assented, the transfer was effected, the ship was coaled, and we proceeded in accordance with orders at 2000 on 3/6/40.

On arrival at Dunkirk at 0015/4 I proceeded into harbour, but was ordered to leave and await orders to the Eastward of the entrance.

I waited there until 0220/4, during which time I picked up 30 French soldiers, and 2 Dutch Naval Officers and 7 Dutch Naval ratings from small boats. I then left for Margate in accordance with previous orders, taking two temporarily disabled motor boats in tow.

At 0234/4 two men from one of the motor boats were swept overboard by the tow rope of the other boat whilst she swerved to avoid a buoy. I immediately slipped one motor boat, whose engine was then again in running order, diverted another passing motor boat to assist, and remained stopped in the vicinity in case any further assistance was required.

I proceeded at 0258/4 to Margate where, at 1305/4, the soldiers were disembarked. I then transferred back to *Plinlimmon* and sailed for Granton [sic] at 0655 on 5/6/40.

With regard to recommendations for decorations, it is considered that it would be invidious to select any one name, where everyone carried out all orders, arrangements, and improvisations with admirable smoothness and efficiency.

PRINCESS ELIZABETH
Official Rescue Total: 1,673

The paddle-steamer Princess Elizabeth *was built in 1927 by Day Summers of Southampton for Red Funnel Steamers. She operated for most of her career between Southampton and Cowes on a mixture of excursion and packet sailings from Southampton and Bournemouth. She was requisitioned by the Admiralty in September 1939 to serve as a minesweeper. After Operation Dynamo, her role changed in 1942 to that of an Anti-Aircraft Vessel, being returned to her owners in 1944. She continued to sail until 1965, when she became a floating casino, then a restaurant and pub in the River Thames. She then went to Paris, becoming an exhibition and conference centre, before returning to Dunkirk for the last time in 1999, where she serves today as a venue for city events and festivities. Her service during the evacuation is recounted by Lieutenant C.J. Carp RNVR:*

The Vessel was in the Basin undergoing boiler cleaning 26th-28th May, undocking p.m. tide 28th May and swinging for compass adjustment for D.G. a/m 29th.

We sailed from Dover at 13/00 29 May for La Panne Beaches via Q.Z.C.60, arriving there 2013/29, and lowered both ship's boats. Until dark we were constantly engaging enemy aircraft who were bombing the troops and boats. At 2103/29 I was ordered by M/S10 to proceed to the assistance of the *Gracie Fields* off the Middlekirke buoy, later, however, on receipt of a signal from the *Gracie Fields* that she had been taken in tow and did not require our assistance, I returned to La Panne and resumed operations with the ship's boats.

Sub-Lieut. J. Tomkins, R.N.V.R. who was in charge of our boats, rounded up three [illegible] and took them in tow. He reported that he had had great difficulty in getting the troops down the beach to the boats owing to the surf and the fact that they were tired out, he continued to tow this flotilla to and fro between ship and shore until ordered to get his boat hoisted.

At 0536/30 May weighed anchor and proceeded via QZC60 to Margate, arriving there and disembarking about 450 troops at 1420.

Whilst at Margate we took on board four small boats for beach work and were supplied with four ratings to man them by the N.O.I.C.

At 1518/30 I left Margate for La Panne Beaches via Q.Z.C.60, arriving there and anchoring at 2223/30.

Boats were sent ashore at once proceeding to embark troops. I was loaned a motor boat by a Fleet Sweeper during this period and she was voluntarily manned by H. Coalbran, Coxswain, and E. Baker,

241

Stoker (T.124). They continued running this boat and towing more small boats until we were loaded when the boats were turned over to *Essex Queen*.

The situation ashore was now showing signs of organisation, although our embarkation was necessarily slow owing to the majority of the troops being wounded.

At 0645 I left La Panne for Margate via Q.Z.C.60, arriving there at 1325/31 and disembarked about 400 troops.

At 1435/31 I left Margate and proceeded to Bray Beaches by X route, arriving there at 1950. When passing Dunkirk the Vessel was attacked by a large number of enemy aircraft and opened fire on them. It was necessary to open fire on many occasions whilst embarking the troops. During the night operations the troops and boats at the beach were under ceaseless shell fire.

Leaving Bray at 0115/1 June by X route for Margate the ship arrived there at 0735/1 and anchored whilst awaiting turn at Pier. At 0921/1 went alongside pier and disembarked about 400 troops. Before leaving Margate we received one Ldg. Seaman and 4 ratings from N.I.O.C. to assist in the boats.

At 1035/1 Vessel left Margate for Sheerness for ammunition and coal, arriving Sheerness 1415 and secured to No.4 Buoy awaiting berth. At 1750, having completed ammunitioning and having sufficient coal for another trip, I left Sheerness for Bray Beaches. After leaving "W" Buoy I ran into fog and dense smoke and could not make the entrance buoys at the Channel in time to enter and clear during dark hours. Having been ordered to return to Dover, I arrived there at 1033/2 June, docked for coal on a.m. tide and undocked p.m. tide, reporting Vessel as ready for sea; Ordered to remain at Dover.

Following instructions from V.A.D., slipped buoy at 1703/3 June for Dunkirk by X route. Arriving off Dunkirk harbour entrance at 2330/3, I berthed at East Pier 0015/4. After embarking about 380 French troops, I was ordered by the Pier Master to cast off and clear the harbour at 0220/4 June. Arriving at Dover 0700/4, troops were disembarked and the Vessel secured to buoy.

In the earlier operations we lost much valuable time through the lack of information. There seemed to be no Army officers ashore to take charge.

For their conduct during the whole of these operations, I can speak with the highest praise of all ranks and ratings who so ably assisted me to carry on. Although short-handed, the crew continued their duties with unstinting energy and cheerfulness. A particularly laudable feature was the manner in which every man, with a complete disregard of personal comfort, was willing to, and did, take over another's duties. These factors enabled me to accomplish our task with success and without the occurrence of a single serious accident either to the troops embarked or to the ship's company.

Attached to Lieutenant Carp's report were a series of separate letters bringing the following men to the attention of the Admiralty. For clarity, these letters have been condensed into the following list:

William King, Lt. (Tempy.), R.N.R. (T.124):
His conduct and bearing, during the operations, was most outstanding. His courage, coolness, and ability was so marked, that the crew were inspired by his own devotion to duty. He was on the bridge with me the whole time at sea, & during the operations was always to hand in the right place to help.

Mr. David Kinlock, S/Lt, R.N.R:
For the very efficient manner in which he conducted himself, and the gunnery of the ship, during the evacuation operations. He had so well trained his crew's that upon engaging the enemy aircraft, his crews worked with a smoothness & precision, that reflects the highest credit upon him. He was most helpful in all things & branches of the operations, never leaving the deck, day or night until the job was completed.

James Tomkin S/Lt R.N.V.R. (Tempy):
For the very excellent work he did while in charge of boats. He was most thoughtful, original, and ingenious, and always working to make the work easier for everyone. His courage and gallantry under the ceaseless shell fire & bombing on the beach was most marked and outstanding, and his tenacity, and leadership, in getting his boats loaded and off to the ship, under the very adverse circumstances in which he had to work & the material he had to work on, created such an impression upon me that I can with confidence recommend him, as the most outstanding officer or rating engaged on these operations.

Mr. Cyril Lavington, Lt.(E), R.N.R. (T.124):
For the very excellent way, he kept his engine room department functioning throughout the whole of the operations. During the embarkation of the troops, he was also at hand to help unload the boats, showing great coolness, and indifference to his own discomfort, that his bearing was a definite tonic to the morale of the Engine room

department, who worked throughout with a cheerfulness & tenacity that enabled us all to complete the work satisfactorily.

Coalbran, Harry, P.O.:
For conspicuously hard work, zeal, and efficiency; his general bearing, conduct & ability, in so many different ways, so helpful, and his coolness and courage and leadership in controlling others made him outstanding. He did most useful work, in getting the motor boat away & at work towing off large numbers of smaller beach boats, without any damage or loss.

Baker, Ernest. Stoker (T124):
For his zeal & hard work. Coming up from the Stokehold he at once volunteered to go away in the boat & did so, & continued to form the boats' crew upon every subsequent occasion. He also to charge of the engine of a motor launch we were loaned, & made a very efficient engineer for her.

Padfield, Arthur. Tel., R.N.V.R.:
For his zeal, devotion to duty, & the promptitude and skill with which he would receive and decode messages earns my highest praise. He was on W/T watch continuously during the whole of the operations and his cheerfulness was a decided asset.

Savidge, Ernest, Sig. R.N.V.R.:
For the very valuable work he did, volunteering to make up a boats crew. Although he was crushed between two boats and badly bruised, he continued his work, with a cheerfulness & total disregard for his own comfort. His conduct & bearing were praise worthy throughout the whole of the operations.

SNAEFELL
Official Rescue Total: 981

Built in 1907 as PS Barry *for the Barry Railway Company, this paddle steamer was renamed* Waverley *in 1926. Requisitioned the day before war was declared, after conversion to the minesweeper role* Waverley *was renamed* Snaefell *to avoid confusion with the Clyde paddle steamer* Waverley *which had also been taken into service. Assigned to the 8th Minesweeping Flotilla, HMS* Snaefell *was commanded by Lieutenant (Temporary) Frank Brett RNVR. His report is dated 4 June 1940:*

30/5/40

Departure from Harwich 1345 under the orders of the Senior Officer M/S 8, H.M.S. *Glengower* [*Glen Gower*]. It was decided at 1800 that, having encountered fog, the three ships of the Flotilla should proceed independently and take such action as was found necessary on arrival at our destination.

2102. Arrived off Dunkirk. It was apparent that the enemy was taking steps to prevent the accomplishment of the effort being made to rescue our comrades of the Army. Repeated bombing attacks were made on us by many aircraft.

2120. *Snaefell* in action. Our gunnery was excellent and although bombs were dropped ahead and astern of the ship no damage was sustained, despite the fact that I was unable to manoeuvre the ship owing to the many wrecks in the narrow channel.

2140. Enemy aircraft again made a bombing attack. *Snaefell* promptly replied, and aided by the gunfire of other H.M. vessels in the vicinity, the enemy was driven off.

2200. The tide now being 2 hours ebb, I decided that any effort to beach my ships was too hazardous, accordingly ship was anchored in 4 fathoms off La Panne, 8 miles East of Dunkirk.

Ships lifeboats were immediately lowered and manned by eager volunteers from the ships company for embarkation of the troops now seen on the beaches, and aided by several small craft, tired and wet soldiers of all ranks were ferried in safety to the ship.

Throughout this operation the enemy was firing along the whole stretch of beach. Several soldiers were found wounded but their courage never wavered and, although their disabilities in many cases hampered the efforts being made to rescue them, all were safely brought on board.

The Wardroom was converted into a Sick Bay and here first aid was efficiently rendered by Sick Berth Attendant W.E. Griffin of H.M.S. *Glengower* whose services were made available to me by the Senior Officer, 8th M/S.F.

Problems were now encountered. The continuous stream of officers and soldiers arriving with their equipment, wet and tired, all desirous of shedding their garments and to find a place to rest their weary bodies, was overcome by the skeleton crew on board, first by providing them from ships stores with hot food and clothing and turning the Engine Room and Boiler Room and Stokehold into a drying room.

The Mess Decks of Petty Officers, Seamen, Stokers were readily turned over to the troops. My own accommodation provided a resting place for 15 Officers, the Officers dining room being used by the remainder, about 30 in number. Passages on the lower deck were speedily filled, the upper deck, minesweeping deck, chart room, being used by the remainder of the troops unable to find covered accommodation.

31/5/40

0445. My ship now being filled to capacity and observing that other ships which had arrived during the night, I decided to weigh anchor.

0500. Anchor weighed and with all speed course was set for home.

1235. Entered Harwich and at 1305 ship was safely berthed at Parkeston Quay where troops were speedily disembarked.

1330. The ship now presented a scene of desolation, Flanders dirt and sand, discarded clothing was everywhere, but the Military authorities having sent a working party on board, the cleaning process now began, being completed at 1600.

The ships company, officers and men having had no rest since our departure from Harwich on the 30th I decided that as much sleep as possible should be obtained so as to fit us for another adventure on the following day.

Saturday 1st June, 1940.

During the morning fresh provisions, medical supplies, ammunition, etc. were delivered to the ship and, four cutters having been provided steps for departure were now made.

1450. Departed from Harwich and with all speed course was set for Dunkirk, towing 4 cutters. During the passage over we were this time further encouraged by sighting squadrons of the Royal Air Force planes which evidently kept at bay enemy aircraft for none were encountered.

2145. Arrived off Dunkirk and here our reception was met with bursts of shrapnel from enemy guns, which however fell short.

2155. Anchored 1½ miles East of Dunkirk in 4 fathoms.

2200. The 4 cutters and our own lifeboats, manned by the ships company, now set out for the beach and having landed Lieut. Smyth steps were taken to round up troops who had secured temporary sanctuary amongst the sand dunes and shattered houses of Dunkirk.

Here my report must emphasize the greatly increasing hazards of our adventure. Throughout the night the ship was constantly under fire from enemy guns, and although shells exploded within

50 yards of the ship no direct hits were registered, although *Snaefell* bears honoured marks of shrapnel. Ships boats with their crews were also attacked, shrapnel spraying them frequently. Several soldiers were slightly wounded.

2nd June, 1940.
0330. The ship now filled to capacity, bursts of enemy gunfire becoming more unpleasant, my ships company all safely aboard, anchor was weighed, and with full speed course was set for home, towing the four cutters.
0415. Overtook a Royal Engineers ferry in command of Lieut. T. Ponsonby, R.N.V.R. loaded with troops, and this Officer considering his service would be more useful at Dunkirk, he returned there having landed the troops he had rescued on board my ship.
0600. Enemy aircraft sighted, but whether from prudence and the fact that we were now able to bring into action 14 Bren guns and hundreds of rifles in addition to our own armament, no direct attack on us was made.
1100. Arrived off Harwich and 1130 safely moored at Parkeston Quay where disembarkation of the troops was speedily accomplished and the four cutters returned to base.

In concluding my report I would like to say that the behaviour of officers and ratings of all ranks was worthy of the highest praise.

WESTWARD HO
Official Rescue Total: 1,688

Launched on 7 April 1894 by S. McKnight at Ayr, Westward Ho served as a minesweeper in the First World War. It was a role she returned to after 1939. Lieutenant (Temporary) A.L.U. Braithwaite RNVR completed his narrative on 11 June 1940, pointing out in his covering letter that 'the memorandum [requesting the account] was not received on board Westward-Ho till after I had gone on leave':

May 31st.
7th Minesweeping Flotilla arrived at Harwich. I was ordered to coal and proceed independently to La Panne. I arrived at Dawn and in the first place attempted to put the ship ashore close enough to embark troops by wading. This proved futile as the water on this coast is so shallow

that the ship was aground over a mile from the beach. I then sent the boats in but there was a ground swell which was breaking too heavily on the beach for the boats to get off without immense difficulty.

The boats were repeatedly swamped and matters were not made easier by the reluctance of the troops to wade out. Some of my crew managed to assist a Motor Boat which made several trips towing the lifeboats but the engine seized up & this too drifted ashore and capsized.

Both my lifeboats were by this time hopelessly waterlogged and damaged but a Naval Cutter which was adrift was picked up and made two trips. On the second of these such difficulty was experienced in getting the heavily loaded boat clear of the beach that I was seriously afraid I should loose the crew, and when the cutter finally arrived alongside I decided that the risk was too great, and that I would shift the ship nearer to Dunkirk in the hope of finding better conditions. It had been necessary the whole time to manoeuvre the ship as the tide was falling and the boats were being swept down the coast as they pulled off, a grass rope streamed to assist them being useless as it was carried away by the tide. In all 150 troops were got aboard. About this time the Admiral Commanding made a signal to proceed to Dunkirk and embark troops from the Pier. This signal was almost immediately cancelled and I was ordered to stand by to Beach my ship to act as a breakwater. This too was cancelled and I proceeded to Dunkirk, went alongside outside the Pier and embarked 602 troops. I was then ordered to return to Margate as a heavy bombardment was in progress and there were no more troops on the pier.

In all 752 were taken off on this trip.

June 1st.

I returned to Dunkirk arriving about 1400, went inside the harbour and was ordered into the lock entrance to embark French troops – I turned the ship round ready to make a quick getaway if we were attacked. Nine hundred troops including a French General & staff were embarked. I considered it would be unsafe to take more as the ship listed very easily and if one Sponson gets in the water it renders steering most uncertain. I cast off about 1600 and made for the entrance, immediately 12 Bombers attacked the ship diving on her and letting go salvos of bombs some of which barely missed and seemed to almost lift her out of the water, a leak was started but was not serious.

In this connection I wish to point out that a wireless signal was sent entirely without my knowledge stating that the ship was sinking and in need of immediate assistance. I was not aware that any signal had been sent, except the one I authorised, until we were back at Margate. The impression that the ship was sinking was probably due to the fact that she took a heavy list to Port, her Sponson was submerged and the Port alleyway filled up, she became almost unmanageable & would not answer the helm hardover. This was an extremely serious matter in the very narrow channel at low water, and I at once ordered some of the troops over to Starboard which brought the ship upright and the helm at once began to take effect, but it was an extremely narrow shave of running aground, and the destruction of all on board.

The attack continued without ceasing for about half an hour and it is believed that 90 bombs were dropped, the ship was also being machine gunned. Killing 6 and wounding 21, this must be considered very slight under the circumstances and I regard it as a miracle that we escaped at all. Two Lewis guns, one Bren gun and the 12 Pounder were firing continuously, three planes were shot down and as no other ship was engaged at the time, and none of our Air Force were there, we are entitled to claim them as our 'bag'. Arrived back at Margate about 2000 and on arrival the French General decorated P.O. Wilcox, and O.S. Banner with the *Croix-de-Guerre* for bringing down the planes.

June 2.

We again crossed to Dunkirk arriving about 2300 but were ordered to lie off the harbour entrance. While doing so a C.M.B. was in collision with another vessel and was said to be sinking. She came alongside and about 50 French troops, the French Naval Attaché, and the Flag Commander on Admiral Taylors' Staff came on board.

There seemed to be great difficulty in getting the Frenchmen to come aboard and there was most unreasonable delay. My ship was slowly forging ahead and was obviously going to ram a destroyer which was hemmed in by various other ships so after giving four warnings I gave a kick astern on my engines which pushed the Motor Boat away but she came alongside again and all were taken on board. The Commander then rushed up on the bridge and soundly abused me for trying to murder him. I submit that as the C.M.B. was still afloat some considerable time afterwards I did not endanger him and that I took reasonable precautions for the safety of my ship. Soon after this I was ordered back to Margate so only brought off the 50 from the C.M.B.

June 3.

It was discovered at Margate that *Westward-Ho* was not De Gaussed and I was ordered not to make another trip. I have been asked to submit the names of Officers and Men who specially distinguished themselves during these operations but I feel that it would be unfair to single out any Officer or Man, the entire Ships Company were beyond praise and I consider it an honour to Command them.

In an earlier report dated 4 June 1940, Lieutenant Braithwaite made the following observation on the actions of his crew:

It would be unfair to single out any specific Officers or Ratings for special mention. My entire crew has been beyond praise, especially on June 1st when my ship was very heavily bombed and machine-gunned by 12 planes while leaving Dunkirk with 900 French troops on board. On arrival the French General saw fit to decorate two of the gunners with the *Croix de Guerre*. I feel that, although it is of course impossible, every member of the crew should also have been decorated.

Chapter 4

Personnel Vessels

BIARRITZ
Personnel Vessel

A First World War veteran, the Southern Railway steamer SS Biarritz
*operated on the cross-Channel routes for much of the inter-war period. She
continued sailing between Dover and Boulogne as a leave ship between
December 1939 and April 1940. Though* Biarritz *was immediately available to
Admiral Ramsey at the start of Operation* Dynamo, *her involvement would be
short-lived – as her master, Captain W.A. Baker, revealed in his 'narrative of
events' dated 7 June 1940:*

26th May
Standing by for orders.

27th May
Left Dover about 4.30 a.m. en route to Dunkerque at approx. 05.40,
whilst steaming along the French coast 6 miles E.N.E. of Calais, enemy
batteries opened fire. A considerable number of shells exploded near
this vessel and as far as can be ascertained, she was struck by 4,
sustaining the following damage:
  Shell plating (port & starboard) pierced in way of forward boiler
room; Steam pipe and various fittings in boiler room damaged; Shell
plating (starboard) pierced in way 1st Class Smoke Room; Damage to
woodwork and fittings in Smoke Room, main deck flat and Chief
Steward's cabin.
  Bulwark plating (starboard) amidships pierced twice. Shells
exploding in starboard lounge deck wrecking interior of state cabins A
and B, and severely damaging cabins Nos. 9 & 10. Cabin casing, lounge
deck, windows, decking and woodwork in vicinity badly damaged.

No. 4 boat, stern post fractured and boat planking split.

A number of smouldering life jackets jettisoned.

The following members of the crew were injured: Albert Phillips, Fireman – left thigh and shoulder; Archibald Crofts, 2nd Steward – wound in back; John Groves – slight wound in leg.

The ship was turned and headed back to Dover, having to cross a mine field to get out of range of the enemy gunfire.

The vessel was berthed alongside the Admiralty Pier, No.1 berth at 09.11, and two of the wounded, A. Phillips and A. Crofts, were taken to Dover Hospital where A. Phillips died the night of 27th May.

At 17.00 this vessel was towed into the Granville Dock by the tugs *Cordia* and *Brassey* [*Lady Brassey*] Temporary repairs carried out.

29th May
Temporary repairs carried out.

30th May
07.15 Cleared Granville Dock, and proceeded to Southampton to complete repairs, docked Inner Dock, Southampton 19.40.

1-4 June
Under repair at Southampton.

N.B. This vessel with the *Maid of Orleans* was under heavy enemy shell fire when off Boulogne on 23rd May, but sustained no damage.

As well as providing a narrative of events, Captain Baker also penned a report on the 'Conduct of Personnel while under fire off Gravelines, Monday, May 27th, 1940':

While passing Gravelines en route to Dunkirk we engaged the attention of enemy artillery on shore. The first shell entered the forward boiler room, piercing first a large diameter oil fuel vapour and overflow pipe and then the auxiliary steam pipe to forward. The nose passed through the further side of the hull on the water line while various minor damage was done by fragments, one entering the starboard wing fuel tank and another passing through the left thigh of Fireman A. Phillips severing the main artery, and causing great loss of blood.

Steam at full boiler pressure was entering the boiler room in great quantities. Further shells were hitting the region of the first hit and danger of severe scalding and of an outbreak of fire were the conditions under which Fireman Phillips then found himself. Notwithstanding, he made efforts to close the oil fuel supply to the furnaces of the two forward boilers. That he was unable to do so will occasion no surprise. As it was, he retained sufficient strength to climb two flights of ladder out of the boiler room where he was met by myself and he reported that he had been unable to shut off the fires. He then collapsed.

Fireman A. Phillips died on the night of May 27th as a direct result of his wound. In this connection it must be stated that 4th Engineer E. Terry, who was in charge of the forward boiler had left the room in pursuance of his duties only a minute or two previous to the event.

Meanwhile in the after boiler room Mr. Crockart in charge, on hearing the explosion of the shells and the subsequent escape of steam, sent his two firemen on deck to ascertain the happenings and to assist if required. He closed the supply of fuel to the forward boilers and then began to encounter very great difficulty in maintaining steam pressure and water level in boilers.

Due to the necessity of keeping way on the ship to get out of range and to avoid stopping in the mine field into which the ship had to be turned, it was imperative to keep fires under the three after boilers in spite of the fact that at times the water could not be seen in the gauge glasses. It was impossible for a time to even locate the damage in the forward boiler room.

Mr. Crockart also attempted to enter the compartment through the water-tight door, but escaping steam made this impossible.

It was also the cause of others being unable to enter by the main deck entrance.

Fireman Phillips showed a high level of courage and devotion to duty.

Mr. J. Crockart, Third Engineer, also showed great courage and determination under trying circumstances.

ISLE OF GUERNSEY
Hospital Carrier

Another Southern Railway vessel, the steamer SS Isle of Guernsey *had been requisitioned from civilian service in September 1939. The following account of HMHC* Isle of Guernsey's *part in Operation* Dynamo *was provided by her master, Captain E.L. Hill:*

Having received orders from Dover at noon, we proceeded towards Dunkirk in company with the Hospital Carrier *Worthing* and Transport *Mona's Queen*, following the route given by the Naval Authorities.

253

At approximately 4-0 p.m. as we approached Calais, which lay in ruins under a heavy pall of smoke, two British destroyers crossed our bows, hove to and commenced shelling the Shore Batteries who promptly returned the challenge. To avoid this No Man's Land we were forced to deviate, as our proper course would have taken us between the combatants. Whilst carrying out this manoeuvre, enemy planes appeared and commenced bombing the convoy but none of the three vessels were struck, although the bombs fell very close.

Arriving off Dunkirk, which was under an even heavier pall of thick black smoke than Calais, we manoeuvred our way inside through the various wrecks of vessels which had been struck by bombs and the *Worthing* having been made fast to the Quay we moored alongside her. A few moments after our arrival streams of motor ambulances arrived threading their way through the columns of troops who were not so seriously wounded and were able to walk. Loading was commenced immediately and every member of the ship's crew assisted in stretcher bearing so as to facilitate loading.

By 9-55 p.m. *Isle of Guernsey* having 346 cases on board, and as her number of cots is only 203, many of these cases were accommodated in between the cots on the deck along corridors, in fact wherever it was possible to put a stretcher. The voyage back to Newhaven, via Dover passed without incident and was completed by 4-53 a.m. on the 27th May.

At 11-47 a.m. on the same day, unloading having been completed, water, provisions and oil fuel taken aboard, we proceeded to Dover for orders.

May 29th 1940
At 5-16 p.m., having received orders, we proceeded towards Dunkirk, following a course which took us well clear of Calais. At 7-12 p.m. we stood off for a while because of an engagement between aircraft and a British destroyer immediately in our track.

At 7-30 p.m. an airman was observed descending by parachute close ahead of us and the vessel was stopped to save him. One of the seamen went down a rope ladder to assist the airman, but before he reached the bottom, 10 enemy planes attacked the ship with bombs cannon and machine guns. By a miracle none of the bombs struck the ship, although considerable damage was done by the concussion, shrapnel, cannon shells and machine gun bullets. British fighter planes drove off the enemy and we proceeded towards Dunkirk with a terrific air battle taking place overhead.

Arrived off the port at 8-20 p.m. we found it was being bombed and shelled, and we had orders from the shore to keep clear. Returning along the channel in company with two destroyers, we later received orders to wait until darkness had fallen and then return to Dunkirk.

At 11-30 p.m. we entered between the breakwaters, the whole place being brilliantly lit up by the glare of fires, burning oil tanks, etc., and managed to moor up alongside what was left of the quay at 12-30 a.m. Loading commenced at once and by 2-15 a.m. we had taken on board as many as we could numbering 490. All the crew and R.A.M.C. personnel behaved splendidly throughout, carrying on with their duties and doing their utmost to load the ship as quickly and as fully as possible, although the ship was shaken every few minutes by the explosion of bombs falling on the quay and in the water.

Leaving the quay at 2-15 a.m. we proceeded out of the harbour and just outside we found the sea full of men swimming and shouting for help, presumably a transport had just been sunk. As two destroyers were standing by picking these men up, we threaded our way carefully through them and proceeded towards Dover. It would have been fatal for us to attempt to stop and try to save any of these men, as we made such a wonderful target for the aircraft hovering overhead, with the flames of the burning port showing all our white paintwork up. Everything was comparatively quiet on the way across, except that just before we got to Dover, a patrol boat headed us off as we were heading straight for a recently laid minefield. Arriving off Dover at 7-0 a.m. we received orders to proceed to Newhaven and arrived at that port at 11-15 a.m.

No further trips were made to Dunkirk, because by the time our damage had been repaired, the evacuation was completed.

Appended to *Captain Hill's report is a short note which, dated 10 June 1940, was written by HMHC* Isle of Guernsey's *Chief Officer, Mr R.F. Pembury:*

During the aerial attack on this Vessel, mentioned in the above report, J. Fowles, A.B. showed great courage in climbing down a rope ladder to assist a British airman who had baled out of his plane. He was wounded by machine gun bullets and shrapnel, assumed mortally wounded and lost, but was later saved by another vessel.

For their part in the evacuation, Captain Hill was awarded the Distinguished Service Cross, as was the Chief Engineer, Mr D. Robb. Able Seaman John Fowles was awarded the Distinguished Service Medal, whilst Mr Pembury was Mentioned in Despatches.

MAID OF ORLEANS
Personnel Vessel

Originally laid down as a cross-Channel ferry for the South Eastern & Chatham Railway, Maid of Orleans *was requisitioned by the Admiralty for duty as a troop transport and completed in August 1918. She was returned to her owners the following year, being transferred to Southern Railway in 1923. The author of the following account is not known:*

On 26th May, this vessel received orders to proceed to Dunkirk. Prior to leaving 6,000 (2 gall) cans of water were put aboard for use of troops at that port, together with other stores, cases of maps etc. A detachment of troops, 250 in number, consisting of details of A.S.C. Signals etc. were also embarked.

Left Dover at 1100 and proceeded to Dunkirk, taking the short sea route. Came under fire from a battery near Calais. Shells although falling close, registered no hits on this vessel.

Arrived off Dunkirk, but did not enter port, but returned to Dover, arriving off that port during the afternoon.

Received orders to return to Dunkirk, this time with an escort and arrived about 5.30 pm. Entered Dunkirk and berthed alongside *Mona's Queen* at the Gare Maritime.

The latter vessel was already loaded with troops and this vessel could not discharge until the *Mona's Queen* had pulled out, thus allowing this ship to go alongside the quay to land the water and stores.

There was no interference from aircraft, probably due to the fact that a thick pall of smoke covered the ship from the burning oil reservoirs nearby.

All hands then collaborated in discharging the water. This was done by forming a chain from the Well deck to the gangway. This work proceeded until an order from the quay was given to stop. The water supply being considered sufficient.

Troops were then embarked and the ship left about 3.0am.

Some difficulty was experienced on leaving owing to the low state of water and the port propeller was slightly damaged.

Were attacked by enemy plane which dropped two bombs, but did not succeed in touching this vessel. The total number of troops carried on this trip were 988, including 8 civilians. Arrived at Dover at 0600 and discharged. The same afternoon (May 27th) this vessel returned to Dunkirk, but, on arrival at the Roads received orders from the S.T.O. Dunkirk (Conveyed by S.S. *Canterbury*) not to enter, so returned to Dover and anchored in Harbour. On the morning of 29th May, at 0437 this ship returned to Dunkirk and berthed alongside the East Mole, as far in as possible. Shifted ship three times as tide ebbed making inner berths at pier untenable.

Vessel was alongside about five hours, during which time the pier was shelled. On leaving, passed through an area where a submarine hunt was in progress. Vessel subjected to bombing attacks. Arrived at Dover and discharged the 1372 troops carried and which included a number of stretcher cases.

Left again for Dunkirk at 2145 on May 30th, taking the long route and arriving at the East Mole at approx. 0100. The only berth now usable being the one at the extreme end as the pier had been subjected to heavy damage from shell fire and bombs. Embarked 37 off. 1216 O.R. (including 42 stretcher cases). The latter were made as comfortable as possible in the Restaurant and Saloons. The discipline of the troops was exemplary.

Subjected as usual to attacks from bombing planes but which did not touch this vessel, which returned to Dover on the morning of May 31st.

Proceeded again to Dunkirk at 0030 on the 1st inst. arriving just before daybreak berthing at the end berth of the East Mole. Low water and wrecks making berthing more difficult. Two destroyers berthed alongside and were loaded over the deck of this ship.

This ship then embarked 1856 troops (including about 400 French troops). By this time it was daylight and enemy bombers became more active, both when the ship was alongside and after she had left to return to Dover, at which port we arrived during the morning.

On the evening of the same day orders were received to proceed to Dunkirk and this vessel left at 2030.

While leaving Dover Harbour, H.M.S. *Worcester* collided with this ship, holing shell plating and causing damage too serious for this vessel to proceed to sea. Returned to anchor in Dover Harbour.

The ship left for Folkestone on the evening of the 2nd June and berthed in the Inner Harbour where the damage was inspected and the ship made sea-worthy preparatory to leaving for Southampton.

During Monday the 3rd inst. work proceeded and the ship left for Southampton on Tuesday afternoon, the 4th June, and arrived at the latter port at 2100.

The total carryings for this vessel from Dunkirk was 5,511.

Serving in the Royal Army Ordnance Corps and attached to the 1st Battalion Oxfordshire and Buckinghamshire Light Infantry, Lionel Tucker was one of the men rescued by HMT Maid of Orleans. His account is another quoted here from the BBC People's War website, www.bbc.co.uk/history/ww2peopleswar):

257

We were dug in at a place called Cassel and under heavy attack by the Germans when orders were given to do what we could to immobilise all our vehicles to prevent the Germans from making use of them as they were hard on our heels. After the job was completed we then set out on a march to Dunkirk which was about 21 miles. From then on things couldn't have got much worse as we under attack mostly from the air the whole way, and on reaching Dunkirk it didn't let up …

After spending a day trying to get aboard a boat of any kind without success, an officer with a pistol in his hand ordered a large number of us to leave the beach and make our way to the Mole which we found already packed with hundreds of troops. The trek to the end of the Mole was disastrous – Jerry came over and made a direct hit causing many casualties, also a long delay in proceeding any further along. Eventually the gap was bridged and we were able to proceed, at that point I decided to remove all my webbing and equipment into the sea in case I had to swim for it.

Eventually our savour was in sight, a fairly large ship which I learnt later was the *Maid of Orleans*. By this time I had lost any idea of time and was thoroughly exhausted, [so] got on board, flopped down on deck amongst the others and fell fast asleep. I remember nothing about the journey until I had a friendly kick from someone saying 'On your feet mate, we are in Dover'. I really couldn't believe what I was hearing was true; this was 0945hrs on the 1st of June 1940.

MALINES
Personnel Vessel

The last ship built for the Great Eastern Railway, Malines *was completed in 1921. Two years later she was transferred to the London & North Eastern Railway. Her Master during the Dunkirk evacuation was Captain G.H. Mallory. The following account, addressed to the Principal Sea Transport Officer at Dover, is dated 11 June 1940:*

Ordered from Southampton, we proceeded to Dover and received instructions to go to Dunkirk by the Northern route from the North Goodwin Light Vessel. As events proved, it would have been better if my instructions had been more detailed and if I had been supplied with the large scale charts. These latter had been promised but not delivered.

However, the necessary daylight to navigate the shoals remained, and I had had some experience of the locality, so *Malines* proceeded at 16 knots to arrive off Dunkirk just after dark.

To my astonishment the whole port seemed to be in flames, and, although it could not be exactly determined, the work of destruction appeared still to be going on. The masts and funnels of ships could be distinguished by the light of the flames, but whether sunken or afloat I did not know.

Morse signals were ignored, and an attempt to enter the harbour was met by gunfire from the Western breakwater, so, determined to find out the true condition of affairs, I patrolled along towards Gravelines, where a Pilot station was supposed to be established. Although I hailed several craft, I could get no replies, and returned to Dunkirk. An attempt to enter by our consort, H.M.T. *Scotia*, was also greeted with gunfire, so that I decided to go eastwards to meet friendly co-operation.

The dim shapes of vessels inshore could be determined, but my draught being more than 15 feet, and no chart to hand, I hesitated to deviate from the Channel. Here my lack of information is now apparent, as, from later events, I judge that these ships were removing parties from the beaches. No doubt my signals to attract attention were a source of extreme annoyance to them, who preferred to be unobserved by the enemy.

One large vessel, recognised later as a Clan liner, moved out of the port, and I was on the point of returning to question him, when he was attacked and sunk completely across the fairway.

Therefore, I resumed the patrol to the Eastward, seeking better contact, and encountered a destroyer, who signalled "Follow me". Turning in his wake and following, I ran aground, and soundings showed a depth of only 12 feet all round the ship, an alarming position, as no navigation marks were visible to enable me to fix my position, or to determine where the deep water channel lay. It was two hours later, on the rising tide, that I succeeded in getting afloat, no doubt with disastrous effect on the propellers. Being now completely bewildered, I worked back towards the Nieuport Bank Buoy to get a definite departure and await daylight.

Just as dawn was breaking the sounds of an engagement were heard, and flashes seen in the North-East, and when we reached the locality, shouts for help were heard from all directions. Stopping to lower three boats, I was then interrupted by S.O.S. Signals from an undetermined craft a mile or so to starboard. Leaving the boats to their rescue work, I steamed alongside what proved to be the destroyer *Grafton*, who, in company with H.M.S. *Wakeful*, had been torpedoed by enemy motor torpedo boats. One of the latter craft, still in the vicinity departed on my arrival, possibly misled by the appearance of my two-funnelled ship.

With some injury to my port bow and superstructure I was able to hold position alongside *Grafton* and embark over a thousand survivors of the troops and ships' companies. Unfortunately, many had been killed and injured, including the Captain of *Grafton* and Military Officers, when the ship was torpedoed. At this point, H.M.S. *Ivanhoe* came to assist and completed the work of rescue, demolishing the wreck by gunfire.

Recovering my boats, except one which had been damaged when *Ivanhoe* picked up my 3rd Officer and boats' crew, I proceeded direct for Dover. Having no Medical Officer and very little equipment, I regret that the injured could only be given amateur attention, but the best was done for them. Great credit is due to my Purser, Mr. Walter Messenger, who, with the help of a single R.A.M.C. orderly whose name, unfortunately I do not know, worked under unpleasant conditions and with limited means on behalf of the injured men.

At Dover the survivors were landed and the ship re-conditioned. A Medical Officer and two orderlies were appointed, and a troop of soldiers with Lewis gun equipment attached to the ship. Charts were obtained, and the ship sailed for Dunkirk, this time by the "X" route over the Sandettie Bank.

At Dunkirk more havoc had been wreaked overnight, and the enemy pressure was more intense. Wrecks littered the fairways and harbour, but the quay was still available, and after some confused ordering, I was able to get alongside and embark a thousand troops despite the shelling from tank guns and the diversions of two air raids, in which our gunners were able to participate. The low level of the water and my deep draught compelled me to limit the embarkation to a bare full complement, although I should have liked to take the complete army. Other ships were, however, available, and so I returned to Folkestone.

At Folkestone there was difficulty in obtaining coal stocks and I was detained overnight. The crew, by this time, were showing signs of strain. Some of them had been bombed out of S.S. *St Denis* at Rotterdam, and my own men had survived very unpleasant experiences there. Some of the weaker spirits were failing, and the Medical Officer certified three Engineers, the Wireless Operator, the Purser, a seaman, and several engine-room hands unfit for duty. Here I refer you to the enclosed copy of a report submitted to the P.S.T.O., Southampton, to which port I was compelled of necessity to return.

Except for this one unpleasant incident, my gratitude goes to the men who assisted in the very difficult operations, particularly to the Medical Staff and soldiers, who adapted themselves to the unfamiliar conditions remarkably well. The gunners performed good work in four aerial attacks, and have, moreover, excelled themselves recently by destroying an enemy 'plane at Cherbourg.

The following is the transcript of the report, dated 2 June 1940, which was submitted by Captain Mallory to the Principal Sea Transport Officer at Southampton:

I report herewith on the circumstances which compelled me to dispute the instructions of the S.T.O. at Folkestone and abandon the operations of rescue work at Dunkirk.

Those operations had been of a highly dangerous and arduous nature, the situation at Dunkirk being much worse than is generally known. The quays have been continually under shell fire for the past two days, and bombing attacks by aircraft very frequent. In addition, the enemy is employing fast motor torpedo boats which are accounting for heavy losses among our ships.

Seven of our consorts are sunk in the vicinity and when, finally, out H.M.T. *Prague* was bombed and badly damaged, the weakening morale of my crew was badly shaken. The Wireless Operator, Purser, three Engineers and several other hands were already in a state of nervous debility and unfit for duty, while many of the crew were not to be depended upon in an emergency.

I would point out here that their unpleasant experiences during the attack on Rotterdam are more than a contributory cause, and they have been co-operating loyally under a heavy strain ever since.

When, finally, the crews of the Manx steamers refused to sail, it was evident that my crew was on the edge of revolt. After consultation with reliable witnesses, both marine and military, I considered the odds against a successful prosecution of another voyage too enormous, and the outcome too unprofitable to risk the ship. My draught does not permit me to reach the beaches at Dunkirk, and the quay appears to be untenable.

This ship having suffered damage while rescuing the crews of two destroyers, and having grounded and damaged the propellers in the shoals around Dunkirk, I have decided, on my own initiative, to return to Southampton, and if possible, dry-dock and put the ship in condition for further service, especially as we cannot now maintain a speed of more than 14 knots.

In any case, a few days relief from tension are necessary to the crew, and I appreciate their services too well to risk their coming into conflict with the Naval Authorities. Also, the missing members are much easier to replace from our own staff at Southampton than from any other place.

I attempted to signal this decision to the Authorities at Folkestone, but was unable to gain the attention of the Signal Station after repeated trying for two hours.

Trusting that I have acted in the best interests of all concerned, and awaiting your further instructions.

Serving in the 9th Army Field Workshop, Royal Army Ordnance Corps, Tom Perrin was one of those who would, no doubt, recall the work of Captain Mallory and his crew with much gratitude. His unit's retreat to Dunkirk had begun at the small Belgian village of Oestvleteren near Ypres; by 25 May, he found himself on the beaches near Bray Dunes. Perrin soon encountered a small rowing boat which took him a short way out to sea where he was transferred to HMS Doggersbank. *In turn,* Doggersbank *handed him across to HMS* Grafton. *His account, quoted here from the BBC People's War website, www.bbc.co.uk/history/ww2peopleswar), details what followed:*

For some reason even when there were no other people to come aboard we waited and waited and waited until it was dark. Eventually we began to move eastwards parallel with coast for some distance before turning towards England ...

About thirty minutes later just as our ship got under way there were two huge explosions as the *Grafton* was hit by two torpedoes, which blew off the stern of the ship. I was standing by a fan inlet which had a high pitched whine, and in the silence after the noise of the explosions I remember the fan running down and the pitch of the sound getting lower.

We lay, wallowing in the channel swell praying that the bulkheads would hold. If they had gone there would have been few survivors for there were no life jackets and most of the lifeboats and rafts had been damaged in the explosions. Everyone was ordered to keep still and to keep silent. I still remember the eerie silence, 1,400 men making no sound, only the slap, slap as small waves lapped against the ship ...

Out of the morning mist appeared a destroyer escorting a cross channel steamer the S.S. *Malines* which tied up alongside the *Grafton* and in single file we crossed from the bridge of the helpless Royal Navy ship to the deck of the steamer. It took quite some time before everyone was off the *Grafton* as there was a considerable number of wounded, some of them stretcher cases, but eventually the last person left the *Grafton* and we pulled away on what we sincerely hoped was the last part of our Channel crossing. When we were well clear H.M.S. *Ivanhoe* torpedoed the hulk of the *Grafton*, which disappeared quickly below the waves.

Under escort we finished the crossing and entered Dover harbour, tied up and disembarked. All I had when I walked down the gangway was my battledress and rifle, the rest of my kit was on the *Grafton* now at the bottom of the Channel.

MANXMAN
Personnel Vessel

Launched in 1904, TSS Manxman *was a turbine steamer that had been built for the Midland Railway for operation between Heysham and the Isle of Man. Having seen service as a Royal Navy seaplane tender from 1916 to 1918, on the outbreak of war in 1939* Manxman *was again taken up for duty, this time by the Ministry of War Transport as a personnel ship.*

Manxman *served alongside seven of her Steam Packet sisters during* Operation Dynamo. *In all,* Manxman *evacuated 2,394 men. Her captain during the evacuation was Master P.B. Cowley:*

Monday 27th June
Ship laying in Southampton. Received orders to proceed to Dover. At 15.35 we sailed.

Tuesday 28th June
02.15 Arrived off Dover – received orders to proceed to anchor at Downs and await instructions.
18.35 Sailed for Dunkirk. Grounded 22.50 on Smal Bank in company with three other vessels; precarious position in view of the early rising moon and the possibility of enemy bombing planes. The cause of grounding – two buoys marked "lighted" on charts, actually extinguished (cause unknown).

Wednesday 29th
02.30 Refloated – no apparent damage and proceeded to Dunkirk.
06.00 Arrived off Dunkirk awaiting berth. Whilst there *Mona's Queen* (same Company's vessel) was blown up by magnetic mine at approximately 1,000 feet astern of us and sank in four minutes. Two destroyers anchored close by sent two boats off very quickly to the rescue. We had previously passed over the same spot.
08.40 Berthed at Dunkirk Mole.
10.30 Let go and proceeded to Dover for orders. Gunfire and bombing by enemy whilst at the Mole, which was replied to by our destroyers and A.A. fire. We had approximately 2,000 troops on

board, as we had disposed of all our lifebelts which number over 2,000. Nothing to report on the passage.

16.15 Arrived at Dover. Received orders proceed to Folkestone.

17.35 Arrived at Folkestone and disembarked troops.

Thursday 30th

20.42 Took our departure for Dunkirk. Nothing to report on the passage.

Friday 31st

05.14 Berthed at Dunkirk Mole; embarked approximately 1,700 troops of which 100 were stretcher cases. We were three hours at the Mole; whilst there, heavy bombing and shelling by enemy (we had three attacks in all) but our ship escaped damage, our Naval vessels having replied vigorously and driven off the aircraft.

08.15 Sailed from Dunkirk – voyage without incident.

13.20 Arrived at Folkestone and disembarked troops.

Saturday 1st June

07.06 Backed out from Folkestone to anchor awaiting orders. Shortly after backing out, a sweeper exploded a magnetic mine not far from the Pier, and in the track which we had previously crossed. This and the *Mona's Queen* incident evidently proved that our "Wiping" by the French at Cherbourg was effective.

10.05 Sailed for Dunkirk.

Sunday 2nd June

05.06 Arrived at Dunkirk Mole. To our surprise, no Naval vessels of any description were present. Approximately 200 troops amongst whom was Brigadier Massey of the R.A. were on the Mole. These men moored us, and then embarked. As the visibility was poor I twice sounded the ship's siren to attract the attention of any more troops at the head of the Mole. A few soldiers carrying one wounded man came, which party were taken on board. A German bomber appeared and launched one aerial torpedo which fell 200 feet on the East side of the Mole.

This bomber was chased away by three of our aircraft. As there was no person left on the Mole to let go ropes, we cut them and backed out and proceeded down the East channel in case any small boats might be coming off with troops. None came and I deemed it prudent to get out. One mile from Dunkirk Mole we picked up a small boat containing five soldiers. We proceeded on out through the West channel and escaped to sea. Luckily visibility was only ¾ mile, and the enemy could not see us from the shore. It transpired later that all craft had orders not to enter the Port, but as I did not receive any message, they had evidently missed me in the dark and haze. I consider that we had a very lucky escape. We were only armed with a Bren gun manned by two Army gunners and an improvised Lewis gun manned by two of our sailors.

Nothing further to report on the passage.

10.43 Arrived at Dover and disembarked troops.

23.30 Sailed from Dover, for Dunkirk.

Monday 3rd June

04.30 Arrived off Dunkirk and received orders from a destroyer to return to Dover without entering Dunkirk.

08.50 Berthed Dover – no troops on board. Ship ordered to be ready for sailing but sailing orders cancelled later.

On Tuesday, 4 June 1940, Manxman *sailed for Plymouth, arriving at 12.15 hours the following day. During the journey she came under fire again, being fired on by a small guard boat that had obviously not been alerted to her arrival.*

It is possible that one of the men described by Cowley to have manned a Bren gun during the return crossing on 2 June was 22-year-old Lance Corporal James Wareing of the 5th Battalion Border Regiment.

Wareing takes up the story following his arrival at Dunkirk (his account is also quoted here from the BBC People's War website, www.bbc.co.uk/history/ ww2peopleswar):

We were so tired we were almost asleep on our feet. We tried to get some kip but there was no rest for us as the enemy kept bombing continuously.

The first morning we were there we found out that there were several small boats coming in to save us. We were then lined up along a wooden pier. Again the Bosch foiled us.

We were lined up on the mole or harbour wall five abreast (three columns of French and two British) and that was how we were to be loaded on board and we were ALL coming to England. While we were on the mole waiting to be checked in, the man in front of me said that when the Red Cap asks you which regiment you were from, you told him you were from the same unit as the man in front. Corporal Light was asked this question and he answered Border Regiment, which was not the regiment of the man in front. The Red Cap stood and told Light

265

to get out of the queue, as he should not be there. There was an argument and the Red Cap drew his pistol and was going to shoot if Light did not get back. Poor Lightfoot did not get home that night.

By this time I had had enough. I told my pal Lance Corporal Hartley we would try to get some sleep on the mole as it was safer there. I had just dropped off to sleep when I was awakened by the noise of running feet. Looking up I saw several officers running to the end of the pier. So off we went to join them. When we got amongst the officers we found that there was a little boat tied up to the pier. There was no one on board until a General appeared who seemed to be in charge. The boat was the size of a large lifeboat.

It was then I scrambled down the wooden pier and jumped on board … I picked up some rope and started to coil it. The General saw me and asked if I knew anything about sailing. 'Yes Sir', I replied and carried on coiling the rope. 'OK Corporal, carry on', was the reply. I was afraid that an honest response, as I had never sailed, would have got me ordered off the boat.

About ten minutes after that the officers who were still on top of the pier shouted to the General that there was a big ship coming in. I dropped everything and started to climb my way up through the woodwork of the pier. The General climbed up using the ladder at the end of the pier. By the time I got to the top the boat was nearly in, so I jumped on board and called to my friend Hartley to join me. To cut the story short we were both on board and ready for sailing. The two of us had spent two nights around the mole waiting to get away after a march of several days from Belgium and we were finally sailing home.

We got clear of the harbour and into the English Channel all within half an hour. During this time I saw a Bren gun and tripod on the bridge so I started to assemble the tripod and place the gun in position just as the General came up again. I was packing equipment around the gun and putting it in good working order. The general seemed pleased with his inspection and said, 'Good, carry on Corporal' …

We arrived at Dover tired, weary and hungry but the Salvation Army was there to help. We were sent into a park for a night before boarding a train. The Salvation Army provided sandwiches and drinks at many stations en route to Northallerton where the regiment regrouped.

The participation of Manxman *was discussed in the following report on the part played during Operation* Dynamo *by seven personnel vessels drawn from the Isle of Man Steam Packet Company. Included in the Admiralty files alongside the first-hand accounts, this report is unfortunately undated and anonymous:*

These were *Mona's Queen, Manxman, Tynwald, Manx Maid, Fenella, Ben My Cree* and *Lady of Man*. Of the 29 personnel vessels employed in the operation, none of these 7 came through with a clean sheet. *Mona's Queen* was sunk by a mine on her second voyage so is excluded from the comments which follow. *Fenella* likewise was sunk in Dunkirk harbour on her first voyage.

Tynwald
Transported 7534 troops in 5 voyages. Should have completed 6 voyages. When due to commence her fourth voyage ... refused to sail and did not sail again until 1945/2. On a written enquiry from the S.T.O., Folkestone, on the 2nd June, whether or not the ship would sail for Dunkirk if required, the Master, W. Qualbrough [*sic* – actually Qualtborough], replied by letter as follows:

> Dear Sir,
>   Your letter received. I had a signal from the master of the *Malines* last night to say him and the master of the *Ben My Cree* had considered it hopeless to proceed to Dunkirk. Our crews have been continually on their feet all the week and especially the deck officers who have had to be on their feet for so long. I myself have had 4 hours rest for the week and am at present physically unfit for another trip like what we have had. If it is absolutely necessary to go I will abide with the masters of the other ships decision.
>   P.S. There is two more of the crew going ashore now absolutely nervous wrecks and certified by the naval doctor.

Meantime relief crews had been sent for for the *Tynwald* and an armed naval guard was placed alongside at Folkestone where the ship lay. The crew did not attempt to leave the ship but contented themselves with shouting abuses at the sentries. Relief crews arrived at 1950/2 and the old crew were then allowed to leave. Complete list of their names and addresses were taken and given to the S.T.O., Folkestone. Those who stayed of the old crew were the Chief Officer as Master, Second Officer, Purser, W/T Operator and Carpenter.

A naval officer and 10 naval ratings were put on board as moral stiffeners and the ship sailed at 1925/2. Completed a round trip which was repeated next day without incident.

Manx Maid
Never completed a trip. Should have sailed on 3 separate occasions. On the last occasion, at 1745/2, she produced an engine breakdown

as excuse. Was given up as hopeless and other ships made use of instead.

Ben My Cree
Transported 408 troops in 2 trips. Should have completed 4. The master was evidently in league with the masters of the *Tynwald* and the *Malines*. On failing to sail during the night 1/2nd June, in reply to a written enquiry from the S.T.O., Folkestone, whether or not he would sail, George Woods, Master, replied in writing – "I beg to state that after our experience at Dunkirk yesterday, my answer is 'No'."

At 1850/2 *Ben My Cree* came alongside Folkestone. Naval guards were placed on the gangways and abreast the ship. As the ship was berthed the crew were demonstrating and shouting that they were going to leave the ship and on the prow being run out, they attempted to do so with their kits. Leading Stoker Booth ordered his men to come on guard and advance up the prow. The crew thereupon returned on board at once, where they remained until the relief crew arrived. The Captain and crew left the ship, the Chief Officer stayed as Captain, together with 3 greasers and the W/T Operator. Otherwise the ship was manned with the new crew. Unfortunately on sailing, at 1905/2, *Ben My Cree* was in collision and did not complete the trip.

Lady of Man
Carried out 4 trips and transported 2902 troops. One trip was abortive through no fault of the Master, as the ship was ordered back from Dunkirk before entering that harbour. The last 2 trips were carried out with a Naval officer and 10 Naval ratings on board as an insurance, but there is no suggestion that the *Lady of Man* did not attempt to play her part.

Manx Man
Transported 233 troops in 3 voyages. Should have completed 5. On her fourth trip, due 2115/2, *Manx Man* [*Manxman*] refused to sail from Folkestone. New crew was put on board, the engineers remaining.

She started a trip but failed to make Dunkirk. On return, the original Captain rejoined with some of the original crew. She should then have sailed at 2010/3, but the Captain reported 3 engineers short at the last minute. It was not considered necessary to wait for the engineers and the Master and crew disembarked and the new crew provided. Before use could be made of her, however, the evacuation terminated.

PRAGUE
Personnel Vessel

Built in 1929 for the London & North Eastern Railway, the SS Prague *was commanded by Captain Cliff Baxter during Operation* Dynamo *(both Baxter and his Chief Engineer, Bill Oxenham, were awarded the Distinguished Service Medal for the part in the evacuation). Baxter's subsequent account was written 'off Deal' on 6 June 1940:*

May 27th

2015 In accordance with orders received the ship left the Old Docks Southampton, where she had been in port since the 24th, at short notice for steam, and proceeded to Dover via the route given by the N.C.S.O. Southampton.

May 28th

0448 The ship made Dover and orders were received to go to anchorage in the Downs. This was done and the ship lying with the South Foreland Lt. Ho. 261, 3¼ miles by 0512. During the same forenoon the Examination Officer visited the ship and gave me two small scale charts of the Dunkirk district, and promised to return with a large scale chart of the Dunkirk district when he had obtained one, but this was evidently not possible and the ship made all her passages across and return on small scale charts only.

1700 Orders to proceed were received and a departure time of 1830 was fixed. In accordance with these orders the ship weighed and proceeded in company with *Manxman* and Hospital Ship *Paris* via Route "Y".

The weather was drizzly and misty, the visibility shortening as the coast of France was approached. The draft of the ship was something over 16ft. and in view of the meagre information about the Zuidcoote Pass which was procurable from the small scale chart, it was decided to allow the other two ships, both of considerably less draft than *Prague* keep ahead, the ships being roughly in single line.

The great majority of the buoys were unlit, and as remarked above the visibility poor, and when very near to the Zuidcoote Pass all three ships ran ashore, it is estimated very near to No. 2. E. Buoy, and presumably on the Smal Bank.

Prague and *Paris* came off immediately, but *Manxman* stuck for some hours. Meeting one of H.M. Sloops, whose Captain very kindly sent a boat with advice of the district and a chart marked in some more detail than our own, we realised that it was hopeless for a ship of our draft to attempt the Pass at that state of the tide, and accordingly returned to the vicinity of the Nieuport Bank Buoy and anchored to let the tide rise a few feet. *Manxman* joined us here a few hours later and afterwards acted in concert with us.

May 29th

0355 Got under way again and proceeded via the pass to Dunkirk, and when ordered to enter the port made fast just inside the end of the Eastern jetty. Embarkation started almost immediately, the Naval Beachmaster very kindly realising our difficulties and loading us up in time to return through the Pass before the tide fell too much as our draft when loaded with troops was estimated to be in the neighbourhood of 17'6".

0735 The ship left Dunkirk and proceeded home by the same route, signalling Dover at 1230 the same day and receiving orders to proceed to Folkestone, which port was reached by 1300 and berthed by 1330. Troops were disembarked and the vessel coaled and watered and prepared for the next voyage.

Generally speaking, as regards this voyage the only serious difficulty encountered was the navigational one, there was plenty of enemy action but there was no direct attack upon the ship, by air or sea.

May 30th

1200 The ship proceeded to anchorage off Folkestone, weather dense fog.

1700 In accordance with orders received, the ship got under way and proceeded to Dunkirk by route "X" in company with numerous craft large and small, naval and merchant. Certain minor departures from the official route were made necessary by the draft of the ship, but the weather was fine and much clearer, and *Prague* arriving off Dunkirk at 2030 berthed well inside the outer harbour alongside the Eastern jetty.

Troops were embarked immediately so as to clear the ship before the tide went, as the low water depth alongside was only ten feet, but despite this, with a full load of troops when ready to sail, the ship was well on the ground and it took the combined efforts of two tugs and both engines working at full power to get the ship afloat which was eventually done by 2245 when the ship left for England again. While in Dunkirk there were air raids in the vicinity but no attack on the ship. There was however a considerable amount of shellfire, and several projectiles estimated as 4" and 6" fell and burst in the water about a hundred yards from the ship.

The voyage back along the western part of the Dunkirk Roads was made at slow speed but was otherwise uneventful, the ship arriving back in the Downs at 0600 on the 31st. whence she was ordered to Folkestone where she duly arrived at 0648 and disembarked her troops.

During this voyage considerable difficulty was experienced with the coal which was of a type unsuited to the ship's furnaces, and the speeds obtained were far below the ship's best.

May 31st
From 0800 when the troops were clear was spent in coaling and watering and preparing for the next voyage, after which the ship went to anchorage off Folkestone.

June 1st
0315 Orders to proceed having been received, the ship was got under way by 0335 and proceeded to Dunkirk by Route "X" again, where she arrived at 0715. From about 0700 onwards the ship was subject to intense air attacks in company with other craft, and we made what reply we could with one Lewis gun and one Bren gun whenever we judged that the hostile aircraft were within range.

Several casualties were observed among H.M. Ships, but we were too busy berthing the ship, and later shifting across the harbour, to take precise notice of what was happening in this direction. The ship finally berthed at the Western side of the outer harbour, close outside the locks and then proceeded to load about three thousand French troops it is estimated.

0903 Having completed loading the ship, left for England once more and proceeded down the Western Roads. At the end of the channel in the vicinity of No. 6. W. Buoy, the ship was subjected to a considerable amount of shellfire from the shore. The great majority of the shells fell short, and none hit the ship, and apparently after passing the buoy and altering course to the northwards, we passed out of range and the firing ceased. Ships passing us on the opposite course were warned of this where it was possible.

1009 Buoy "W" just past the Ruytingen was passed and the ship making along the homeward route towards Buoy "V", another

271

intense air attack by dive bombers developed. Heavy fire was opened by all ships in the vicinity against these aircraft (estimated to number about half a dozen) and the ship kept continuously under helm. Suddenly an aircraft appeared out of the clouds almost directly overhead, and swinging round, dived on the *Prague*.

Releasing three bombs together while still at a considerable height, the aircraft escaped without coming into effective machine gun range, and the bombs fell very close to the stern of the ship which was swinging hard round to starboard. The force of the explosion was terrific, and the ship seemed to be lifted almost out of the water.

Although not actually hit, it was evident that the ship was very badly damaged aft. The stern settled down considerably and the starboard engine had to be stopped immediately as the shaft was bumping round in the stern very badly. The watertight doors were closed at the time in accordance with wartime procedure, but the force of the explosion had evidently made them considerably distorted, as the ship filled up to the after engine room bulkhead and the water rose to the level of the maindeck. There was a certain amount of leakage into the engine room through the bulkhead, but the ship's pumps managed to slow down the rate of the rising water to a reasonable amount.

The only presumable casualties to personnel were one fireman missing, presumed to be blown overboard. Two French soldiers were also seen in the water and as small naval auxiliaries were seen making in their direction, it is hoped that they were picked up, but no reports have come in up to date.

From the time of the explosion, 1025, the ship was kept going ahead as fast as it was possible to do on the port engine which was the only one left in service, craft in the vicinity were warned and several naval auxiliaries agreed to stand by us and the ship slowly progressed homewards.

It was evident however that the water was gaining, and such measures as getting as many troops as possible forward to ease the weight on the after part of the ship were giving only temporary respite, so it was decided to try and transfer the troops while the ship was still under way, so as to lose as little time as possible. H.M. Destroyer *Shikari*, and a sloop and a paddle minesweeper whose names we were unable to obtain came alongside in turn and very skilfully managed to transfer all except a hand full of troops while the ship was steaming as fast as possible towards the Downs. This being completed it was possible to concentrate all efforts on saving the ship by getting into as shallow water as possible before we found ourselves unable to control the inflow of water.

By 1331 the ship was well inside the Downs and the Tug *Lady Brassey* made fast. Dover was signalled and orders were received to anchor in the Downs. On receipt of these the ship proceeded to the Small Downs and entered the Ramsgate channel.

Having arrived at a spot slightly North of the ruins of Sandown Castle, about a mile North of Deal, the ship was gently beached, an anchor laid out and all active participation in the evacuation of Dunkirk ceased by 1730 June 1st.

Of the ensuing period there is little to say except that the ship was boarded by the Admiralty Salvage Officer first thing next morning and the ship examined as thoroughly as possible the next low water.

Each time the after part of the ship drained out with the tide, all the visible leaks both in the shell plating and in the bulkheads were stopped as effectively as possible with the materials at hand, and three salvage pumps were rigged in the after 'tween decks to deal with whatever water which leaked past the plugs.

These operations were still in progress on the 4th June which is the end of the period about which you desire this narrative of events.

ST SERIOL
Personnel Vessel

Launched in March 1931, the steamer St Seiriol *was operated by the Liverpool and North Wales Steamship Co. on its Isle of Man routes. On 5 June 1940, the Admiralty wrote to Captain R.D. Dobb, the Master of* St. Seiriol, *through the head office of his employer, requesting an account of his vessel's part in Operation* Dynamo. *The company's secretary replied stating:*

We have to inform you that Captain Dobb is away from home and under Medical Treatment. We attached a report signed by the Master dated 8th June, and addressed to this Company with the intention of it being forwarded to the competent authority. We have also received a report from the 2nd Officer and we enclose extract of same. We also attach an extract from the report which was forwarded to the Director of Sea Transport on the 7th June and signed by the Chairman of this

273

Company. We are expecting a report from the Chief Officer – J. McNamee and Purser D.D. McMahon, which will be forwarded on to you within the next two or three days. The Master of the vessel left the ship by order of the Medical Officer on Thursday 30th May.

The following is the account provided by Captain R.D. Dobb:

On Tuesday the 21st May at 7.30 pm, while entering Calais, my vessel was attacked by three enemy bombers but they failed to make a hit. While alongside more attacks were made but we managed to get away at 8.30 pm, and proceeded to Dover and then to the Downs to Anchor.

On Monday 27th May at 1.30 pm., we proceeded to Dunkirk in company with the *Channel Queen* arriving Dunkirk about 8.0 pm. alongside the Mole, but were ordered to go to the beaches to pick up troops, using our lifeboats. While the lifeboats were away I was asked if I could go back to the Mole by a destroyer as there were a very large number of troops there. It was now about 10.0 pm. and dark and heavy bombing and gunfire all around.

I got alongside the Mole in a very short time and embarked 600 soldiers and left the Mole at about midnight. I went back to look for my lifeboats but as they were being used to convoy troops from the Beach to other craft I proceeded to Dover via the Calais route as ordered by a Destroyer. During the passage I was again attacked by Aircraft but got away without being hit. On arrival at Dover I was ordered to Folkestone to disembark.

The M.V. *Channel Queen* was bombed and sunk.

On Wednesday 29th May we left Dover at 12.30 pm for Dunkirk to embark troops. Arrived off Dunkirk in heavy bombing and shore gunfire and proceeded to go alongside the Mole, when the Mole was bombed, also the *Fenella* which was alongside and the *Crested Eagle*. I could not make a landing. There were no troops there so I proceeded to the beach to embark troops following the S.S. *Crested Eagle* which had a compliment of troops. The bombing was now terrific. The *Crested Eagle* was hit and went on fire, and we lowered our only lifeboat and rescued 150 men from the burning ship under very heavy fire from the air.

Arrived Dover about 6.0 am and disembarked. (Thursday 30th May).

The account by Mr Birss Jones, the 2nd Officer of St. Seiriol, was written at his home at Bangor on 10 June 1940 and included the following:

The Night of the 27th May

We arrived at Dunkirk between 7 and 8.0 pm and as soon as we got alongside the Pier the bombing started from all directions, so the

Captain had orders to go out again and get all the troops he could get from the beach. The bombing was still going on but we were lucky, so we dropped anchor and the Captain ordered boats to be lowered and manned and to go ashore and get as many troops as we could. I took charge of No.3 Lifeboat with J. Wishart Greaser, and H. Roberts. A.B.

The night was dark but the burning buildings ashore lit up the beach, so I managed to get the boat full of wounded soldiers and when I got out again I could not find the *St. Seiriol*. While I was ashore the Captain got order to go back to the Pier and load troops, so I took my load to a destroyer and put them on board there and I went for another boat load and back to the destroyer. It was getting about half past eleven, so the Lieutenant told me and my men to go on board and cast the boat adrift as they were leaving at midnight. Just before we left the *St. Seiriol* came close and hailed the destroyer that he had three of his men ashore, so he was told that we were on board. We proceeded with the destroyer and arrived at Dover and I joined the *St. Seiriol* at Folkestone midday on the 28th.

The Night of the 29th May
We got to the Pier at Dunkirk about 7 o'clock, after Jerry had been trying to bomb us all along the Coast. The first thing we saw was the S.S. *Fenella* alongside the Pier and P.S. *Crested Eagle*. The *Fenella* had been bombed and disembarking the troops and her crew to the other ship. After the *Crested Eagle* left the Pier she was bombed and on fire so the Captain run her ashore. We had orders to man the boats. Of course we had only two boats left. I took charge of No.5 boat and the Chief Officer took charge of the other, so we managed to get some on board, wounded, scalded, burned and half drowned. It was hellish there and bombs dropping all around.

On the evening of 6 June 1940, the Minister of Shipping, the Right Honourable Richard Cross, delivered a broadcast on the BBC to thank the Merchant Navy and its men for the vital part they had played in the Dunkirk Evacuation. The broadcast painted a realistic, if inspirational, picture:

'The men on these ships worked till they dropped,' Cross said. 'Without sleep, often without proper meals, for days on end they passed to and fro across the Channel, under attack by enemy batteries on the coast, by enemy aircraft with bombs and machine-guns, by enemy submarines and motor torpedo boats.'

The Minister of Shipping made particular reference to deck and engine room officers who responded to the appeal for experienced men: 'We could promise them nothing but fatigue and danger, but the response was immediate. Within a few hours, we had the received the names of about 350 volunteers ... There was one factory at Ramsgate, on which we called for volunteers. The appeal was 'You are going to hell. You will be bombed and machine-gunned. Will you fetch back the lads? There was no hesitation. Tools were thrown down and the engineers went straight down to ships they had never seen before and within twenty minutes had sailed for the bomb ridden waters of Dunkirk.'

During the broadcast Cross also singled out a few individuals. These included 'a young fifth engineer who had only been four months at sea. After a long series of bomb attacks, he came up from the engine room to get a breath of fresh air. An officer suggested that he man a Bren gun for a short time. A German bomber swung round to repeat the attack. The young engineer released a short burst of fire and brought the bomber down into the sea.'

Mr Cross also talked about a man he described as an elderly chief officer, 'well past the prime of life': 'Three of the four boats on his ship had been blown away by bombs. He spent the whole of one night in the remaining boat, picking up survivors from another ship which had been sunk. He and his boat's crew rescued 150 men. He became partially paralysed in the legs, but was perfectly ready to make another trip if called upon.'

This story inspired the nation and people demanded to know who this tough old man was. B.E. Bellamy, on behalf of the Director of Sea Transport, wrote to the Vice-Admiral Dover on 26 June 1940, providing the answer:

With reference to our telephone conversation of last week concerning the "elderly first officer", referred to in the broadcast made by the Minister of Shipping, I am enclosing for your consideration, copies of letters received from the General Secretary of the Mercantile Marine Service Association [A. Wilson], and Captain N.A. Moore of the Shipping Federation Limited.

The General Secretary's letter is dated Friday, 14 June, 1940:

It has been my good fortune to meet the "elderly Chief Officer" mentioned in your broadcast in connection with the Merchant Navy's part in the Dunkirk evacuation. I refer of course to Mr J. McNamee, the Chief Officer of the North Wales Steamship Company's S/S *St. Seiriol*. I had to force the story from him, and really was impressed by the simple narrative of a very splendid act of courage.

By the way, he is rather amused over the reference to his being past the prime of life, and although his legs are still affected, he hopes to be back in harness again soon.

My object in writing, however, is to ask you whether this very fine example of bravery is to be recognised. I know there must have been hundreds of similar cases, but to me Mr. McNamee's case is outstanding.

In his letter of 24 June 1940, Captain Norman A. Moore provided more detail:

I can do no better than relate as accurately as possible the whole story concerning the relief of the *St. Seiriol*'s crew.

Early on Thursday, May, 30th., I was informed by the P.S.T.O, Dover, that the crew of the *St. Seiriol* has complained they were no longer fit to continue their duties and, if it was considered necessary they were to be relieved as soon as possible.

I immediately went on board to investigate the complaint and it was only as a result of my inquiries, that I became fully aware of the prevailing conditions and the arduous tasks the men concerned with the evacuation were performing. The *St. Seiriol*, a small, unarmed coasting passenger vessel, had already made several trips to Dunkirk in circumstances, which as you know, would be most trying to crews of warships.

I found most of the crew in a very fatigued and nervous state, even though many of them were quite young and of good physique.

After interviewing several of the men I consulted the ship's Adjutant and Army Doctor to ascertain their views. They were slightly doubtful about the necessity of relieving some of the younger men but they had not the slightest hesitation in saying that Mr McNamee would have to be relieved immediately as he was suffering from a form of nervous paralysis from the waist downwards, which rendered him incapable of standing for any length of time. The Doctor then informed me that in his opinion Mr McNamee's condition was entirely due to the excellent work he had been performing during the night. Apparently, the *St. Seiriol* had made contact with a vessel which was sinking from the result of enemy action and went to the rescue.

Unfortunately, only one of the *St. Seiriol*'s four lifeboats remained at the time. This was quickly launched and Mr McNamee took charge of it. Throughout the period, in which a large number of men were rescued, he worked untiringly, directing the operations and assisting in pulling the survivors from the water into the lifeboat which, apart from anything else would impose a great physical strain on him.

To sum up, I quote the actual words used by the Doctor, a young Irishman, who I should say, would not be inclined to exaggerate or to give any praise without it was really merited, having been engaged in evacuation work throughout the operation: "This is no case of a man shirking or getting the wind up. That man has guts."

Chapter 5

Dutch Schuits, Trawlers and Coastal Craft

ARLEY
HM Trawler

Built in 1904, the 304-ton trawler Arley *was commanded by Lieutenant G.W. Robinson RD, RNR during Operation* Dynamo. *His account is dated 2 June 1940:*

On arrival at the entrance of Dunkirk on Wednesday May 29th at 1430, I received orders from H.M.T. *Fyldea* to proceed up harbour and turn, whilst he took the transport steamer *Loch Garry* in tow out of harbour. After turning head to seaward I was ordered to tow transport out, as I had then gained the most favourable position for the manoeuvre.

I took the stern rope from *Loch Garry* and after towing her stern clear of destroyers, commenced pushing ahead while the steamer came astern with engines.

This operation would have taken the vessel out of harbour all clear stern first, but for some reason, which I cannot explain, she reversed engines and went ahead, causing the towing hawser to be slacked away to prevent parting.

On resuming pushing operation on *Loch Garry*'s starboard quarter, my boat deck pressed on to D.G. wiring of her, causing it to take fire. This was caused by the lengthened towing hawser allowing my ship to go too far ahead, a position which I had no time to adjust, as the tide was carrying us both very close to Western Pier head, and I was compelled to go full speed ahead to clear us both.

Having completed this manoeuvre I re-entered harbour, and took up position astern of H.M.T. *Fyldea* and moored to Eastern arm, with H.M.T. *John Cattling* and *Calvi* berthed outside of me; H.M.T. *Calvi* being the outside ship. Soon after mooring, heavy bombing commenced by

278

German Aircraft, and although every ship in harbour put up full anti-aircraft barrage, the bombs were dropped either side of the Eastern arm.

Several raids were carried out at short intervals, and during one of these a bomb dropped very close to *Polly Johnson*, wounding several of her guns crew. During a later raid the Destroyer *Grenade* was hit, also H.M.T. *Calvi*. The *Calvi* was hit by a bomb on the port quarter, and soon commenced to settle down, taking a very heavy list to port – at the same time H.M.S. *Grenade* commenced settling down.

The next raid was directed more on the harbour, and shore end of the Eastern arm causing a delay on the troops coming along the pier. At this period the position became serious, and it was decided all trawlers should clear harbour.

Owing to the serious position of *John Cattling* being fouled by *Calvi* sinking alongside of her, I kept *John Cattling* moored to me, whilst I towed her astern clear of *Calvi*, I then hove ahead, again close to pier, and embarked as many soldiers as possible; the remainder of the troops going to the paddle steamer berthed on the eastern side of the pier.

I then passed ahead inside of H.M.S. *Grenade* and cleared harbour astern of H.M.T. *Polly Johnson*, *Brock*, with H.M.T. *Fyldea* leading.

When clear of harbour I closed on H.M.T. *Polly Johnson* who informed me by megaphone that she was unable to proceed any faster owing to trouble in the engine room and would I keep close to her. I took up position about ¾ of a mile ahead of her as she reported all her charts had been shattered. We were by then reduced to slow speed, and I informed H.M.T. *Fyldea* that *Polly Johnson* was in difficulties and could not proceed any faster. I received orders from *Fyldea* to stand by *Polly Johnson*, which I did, keeping about ¾ of a mile ahead of her. Although I was only proceeding at slow speed, the *Polly Johnson* still dropped astern.

I then received a message from H.M.T. *Fyldea* that if *Polly Johnson* could not proceed I was to take her crew and scuttle her clear of the channel and act independently. I ordered this message to be sent to *Polly Johnson* as relayed from *Fyldea*. By this time we had reached a position half way between Nieuport Buoy, and Middlekerke Buoy, and I stopped engines until *Polly Johnson* came within hail. During this period several more raids were carried out by German Aircraft on the Destroyers and other craft close to us.

When *Polly Johnson* closed on me, the Skipper informed me he was already to abandon ship; his confidential books etc., were packed ready to pass to me. I then closed on her and lashed alongside until the two stretcher cases and all the other members of her crew and passengers were safely on board. I then cast off and moved away from her.

The Skipper of *Polly Johnson* – Skipper Lieutenant Lake R.N.R. (ret.) informed me that the water in engine room had gained up to the platforms, and in the stokehold the water was about to put her fires out.

After leaving *Polly Johnson* I requested one of our Destroyers to sink her as she had been abandoned, but as I received no satisfactory reply, I returned to her and fired two shots of common shell into her at waterline.

As I had by now about 90 men on board, including several wounded, I decided to make all speed for Dover. The tide was setting to East North East, and assuming the *Polly Johnson* would drive away from the channel, I left her, the Skipper agreeing that she would sink in about two hours.

Soon after leaving *Polly Johnson* I received an S.O.S. from a Paddle Steamer who had been badly bombed whilst I had been taking off from *Polly Johnson*. I decided I could not take all her men, so I steamed and intercepted one of the scouts, and two French trawlers, and directed them to go to the paddler, which they did. There was also one drifter standing by her and one of our destroyers heading for her, so I decided nothing further could be done, and returned to harbour forthwith.

A further account of Arley's *role at Dunkirk, and that of her sister ships, was provided by Lieutenant Robert Bill RN in a report entitled 'Operations with M/S Trawlers at Dunkerque':*

I have the honour to submit the following report in connection with operations by M/S Trawlers at Dunkerque on Wednesday 29th May, 1940.

Before sailing I collected all Unit Officers and explained what we were going to do, issued and explained their routes, and impressed on them that they must act independently in the case of an emergency. I then instructed them to sail independently and meet me in the vicinity of the Gull Buoy by 0400.

Ladders were embarked off Ramsgate by 0430 and we proceeded in company to Dunkerque, arriving at 1330.

On arrival I hove to and signalled to S.N.O. through *Grenade* requesting permission to enter harbour. The reply came back "Wait – you may enter harbour after 1600". I then signalled – "Can I be more use off the beach", as there were already three destroyers and the transports alongside the wall. I then received the signal – "Enter harbour and pull off *Loch Garry*, trawlers may then take her berth".

I then signalled *Arley* to follow me in and we pulled *Loch Garry* from the wall, and proceeded to take her berth. The remaining four trawlers then entered harbour and berthed alongside us as directed by the Piermaster (Commander at about 1420).

I landed and reported to the Piermaster and asked for instructions. I was instructed to wait and to fill up my ships after the transport *Fynella* and *Grenade* had completed. Ladders were rigged up the wall and the ships were prepared to receive troops.

Up to this time practically no troops had appeared at the far end of the pier, and *Jaguar* was nearly full and *Fynella* about half full. *Canterbury* was also nearly full and was embarking wounded which completely jammed other traffic along the pier. Sketch "A" [below] shows positions of ships at this time.

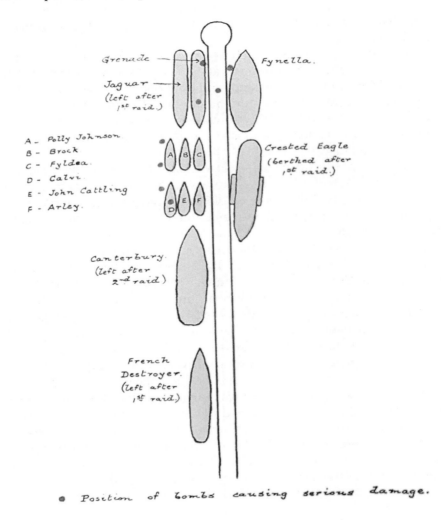

281

The first raid occurred at about 1530, by about six or seven bombers. All ships opened fire and a fairly effective barrage was put up. About 20/30 bombs were dropped, but they were mostly wide.

There were near misses on *Canterbury, Calvi, Polly Johnson* and *Jaguar* and a number of men received shrapnel wounds in all these ships.

Fighters then appeared and the raiders were driven off. One was shot down by fighters and I think one by *Jaguar*. *Jaguar* left harbour, and the remainder of ships attended to their wounded. I arranged to place all wounded in the *Canterbury* and got the assistance of the Surgeon Lieutenant from *Grenade* for the more serious cases.

I inspected *Polly Johnson* and although damaged I considered she could make the return journey and instructed the Skipper not to embark more than fifty men, and if damage became more serious to transfer them to *Brock*.

During this lull more wounded troops were embarked in *Fynella* and *Canterbury* and a few other troops wandered up the jetty. I was then told that I could try and fill up my ships and I stationed Officers abreast each ship and instructed them to order all unwounded men down into the trawlers. They were mostly unwilling to embark in what they considered "fishing boats" at first and made various excuses to try and get to the larger ships.

As the rate of filling up was so slow I asked the Piermaster if I could send the four outside ships to sea to wait their turns and decrease the target, but I was told that there would be a large number of men ready as soon as the wounded had been embarked and that the ships were to remain alongside.

I was then asked by the Piermaster if I would place a trawler alongside the Western Jetty and light some smoke floats, and he suggested that I might like to volunteer for the job. I said that I was quite prepared to do the job by boat, but that I did not consider it possible to place a ship alongside the jetty as the foundations of the pier were shewing when I entered the harbour, and that my trawlers were all drawing over 15 feet while the rise and fall on that day was only 11 feet.

Jaguar completed and left harbour during this period, and a large paddle steamer (I think *Crested Eagle*) berthed ahead of *Fynella*.

At about 1630 the second raid was carried out, but this was a rather half-hearted affair. All ships opened fire as before, and no damage was done to the ships alongside. About 20/30 bombs were dropped as before but they were divided between three targets – *Jaguar* leaving the harbour – the ships alongside, and two French destroyers on the opposite side of the harbour. The *Jaguar* was damaged.

Fighters again appeared and the raiders were driven off.

The *Canterbury* completed and left harbour, and a destroyer came in to take her place.

After this raid more troops started to come down the pier and although traffic was still hampered by the wounded and stretcher cases quite a large number were embarked in the trawlers.

At about 1800 the third raid started. This was a very much more determined attack, and the bombers came over in waves at a few minute intervals – fire was opened but fighters appeared and it was impossible to tell if they were enemy or not and it hampered the firing to a great extent.

About 100 bombs were dropped, and the attack appeared to be directed entirely on the pier and the ships alongside.

The *Calvi* and *Grenade* received direct hits and sank immediately. *Calvi*'s masts and funnel were above water and her ensign remained flying from the foremast. There was a direct hit on the pier close to the end and *Fynella* was damaged. A certain amount of panic ensued and men started climbing out of one ship into another, and some attempted to run back towards the shore.

At this time I was with the Piermaster and he instructed me to draw my revolver to quell the panic and to load up with survivors and troops and to get the ships out as quickly as possible. As the wreck of the *Grenade* was drifting down on the trawlers, I instructed *John Cattling* to attempt to pull her clear and to follow the other ships out. *Polly Johnson* and *Brock* picked up troops and survivors, got clear, and proceeded out of harbour at full speed. *Arley* was clear and *Fyldea* under way.

The Skipper of *Fyldea* kept his ship close to the wall and several more troops and survivors jumped on board. I was further up the pier trying to find the Piermaster again for further instructions, but I failed to find him and just managed to jump on board as she was leaving. This was at about 1815.

Lieutenant Reake – the First Lieutenant of the *Grenade* – then told me that the Piermaster has also instructed him to get the ships clear of it and to go round to the beaches. I therefore took the four remaining ships towards the beaches and signalled to the ships there asking if there were any troops available for me. After three unsuccessful attempts to obtain further troops to fill up to capacity – all ships replying that they were themselves having difficulty in completing – I received signals from *Polly Johnson* and *Brock* stating that they were damaged. I ordered *Arley* to stand by *Polly Johnson* and to remove her crew and sink her if necessary.

With *Brock* in company I then proceeded towards the *Jaguar* who was anchored in the vicinity of the Nieuport Bank Buoy with her troops on board and another destroyer alongside her, and asked if I should take some from her. I was told to escort her as she had no boats and I therefore told *Brock*, whose damage was slight, to proceed independently. I proceeded with *Brock* for about two miles to exchange the necessary signals and satisfy myself that she was capable of making the journey and then returned to *Jaguar*. By this time she had weighed, and I followed astern of her and signalled my maximum speed.

At about 1930, five German Dive Bombers passed on our port side at about 2500 feet, in the direction of the *Jaguar* and started to make an attack. We opened fire with the 12 pounder and one plane detached itself from the formation and made an attack on us. As the plane straightened up to attack I gave the order "hard-a-starboard" six bombs were dropped which fell about 40/50 yards on our port beam. We then straightened up and proceeded on our course.

The other planes attacked the *Jaguar* who replied with her multiple pom-poms and zig-zagged, and no hits were registered, although all attacks appeared to be very close to her.

After this attack she increased speed and she was soon out of sight.

Having been left by *Jaguar* – who was taking a different route I set a course for the Dyck Buoy and followed "Y" route.

Between "T" and "S" buoys I overtook *Brock* and she signalled that she could only steam at half speed and that she had three serious cases on board. I signalled her to heave to and went alongside her and transferred her survivors and troops to *Fyldea*.

I then proceeded at full speed and arrived back at Dover at 0300.

During the bombing raids and the periods between, the situation was so tense that it would have been almost impossible to realize any passage of time, so that the times in this report may be in error to a considerable extent.

The bombs dropped during the raids appeared to be of a heavy type. They could be quite easily seen as they fell and looked about the size of a 15" shell. The bombers attacked in waves of about two or three, releasing two bombs at a time, which prolonged the period and disorganised the embarking and tended to cause panic. Most of these bombs fell within 70 yards of the trawlers. The ships were also attacked with "cannon". This was not noticed at the time due to the intensity of the bombing, but ½ inch iron shells were picked up afterwards.

The behaviour of all Officers and men was at all times exemplary, and at no time did I notice any man shew any disinclination to do his utmost or shew any sign of panic even when others were panicking. I would like to mention Skipper Lieutenant Lake, whose ship was badly damaged. He retained complete control of his men and assured me that he would take his ship back to port if it was possible. This afterwards proved to be impossible, and her crew were taken off by *Arley*, who fired two rounds into her and left her to sink clear of the channel. *Arley* was not able to fire again as she was attacked by bombs.

Lieutenant Warde and Sub. Lieutenant Roberts R.N.V.R. were also of the greatest assistance. They supervised the placing of the ladders of the foremost group and throughout the whole period remained cheerful, and encouraged their men.

I subsequently discovered that the *John Cattling* was detained in Dunkerque by the Piermaster and remained there until dark, where, in spite of further bombing, she carried out the most useful work.

I authorised provisions and rum to be issued in moderation to survivors and troops, and morphia to the seriously wounded, at the discretion of Commanding Officers.

CARIBIA
Dutch Schuit

There can be little doubt that the forty or so Dutch schuits which participated in Operation Dynamo *played an invaluable part in its success. A collection of Dutch motor coasters collectively known as schuits, they were a self-propelled seagoing development of the towed barges so familiar on European rivers such as the Rhine, Elbe and Danube.*

In The Ships That Saved An Army, *Russell Plummer noted that 'despite considerable variation in both size and age, almost all were flat bottomed, designed to take the ground at low water, and had operated along the coasts of the Low Countries, mostly owned and crewed by a single family who made their home in accommodation above the engines right at the stern. A large number of these craft crossed to England following the fall of Holland and were moored either on the Thames or in Poole Harbour. Their potential, initially for transporting supplies, was not lost on Captain J. Fisher, director of the Ministry of Shipping's Coastwise and Short Sea Department. As early as 20th May he arranged for 40 of them to be commissioned by Royal Navy crews, and the British personnel quickly translated the Dutch title of "schuit" to "skoot!" Chatham crews took over 22 craft lying in London's river and the remaining 18, at Poole, were manned from Portsmouth, mostly with RNR or retired list officers placed in command.'*

Caribia was one of the schuits that had been lying at London. During her time off the French coast Caribia *transported 701 men. Though some sources state that she had been commanded by Lieutenant M. Morais RN and then, from 29 May, Lieutenant G. Williams, the following report, dated 8 June 1940, was written by Lieutenant Donald H. Swift RN:*

The draft left Chatham at 0800 on the 26th May and took over the ship from the Dutch crew at Tilbury at 1500. In the afternoon victualling stores were embarked and the ship was then "wiped". This was satisfactorily completed at 0315/27.

The ship was then ordered to proceed to Southend for compass adjustment and to Sheerness for storing and fuelling. Southend was reached at 0630 and during the forenoon the ship was swung for compass adjustment. On arrival at Sheerness at 1300 the ship moored and fuel and water were taken in and later naval stores and special stores embarked.

The ship was then ordered to proceed to Southend for orders. At 0800/28 orders were received to proceed to Marte les Bains [*sic*]. On approaching Dunkirk at 2230 a drifter with 120 troops on board was closed. These troops were embarked and the drifter returned to the harbour for more. As these had not arrived after one hour the ship entered the harbour and secured alongside the eastern pier. The ship was then filled with a total of about 320 troops and at 0400 slipped and proceeded.

At 1300/29 the North Goodwin examination vessel was hailed and orders were received to proceed to Margate. The troops were disembarked at Margate Pier at 1600 and provisions and stores were embarked. Orders were then received to proceed to the beaches east of Dunkirk, with *Zeus* [another schuit] in company as the latter's compass was unreliable. The ships slipped and proceeded at 1930/29.

The ships anchored off Bray at 0500/30 where troops were waiting on the beaches. They were embarked with the assistance of boats from the shore and at 1000/30 the ship was full with approximately 350 troops. Between 0900 and 1000 shells fired from the direction of Nieuport were falling in the vicinity of the ship.

As *Zeus* was also ready to proceed, the ships weighed and proceeded at 1000. From 1015 for 45 minutes the ship was shelled from the direction of Nieuport. Avoiding action was taken and no direct hits were received. The firing was very accurate in view of the poor visibility prevailing.

The ships arrived at Ramsgate at 2000/30 and troops were disembarked. The ship was then ordered to anchor in the roads.

In the afternoon of 31st May orders were received to proceed to Dunkirk but to arrive before midnight as this was understood to be the final evacuation. The ship weighed and proceeded at 1500. About 2000 the ship was bombed but there were no direct hits and no damage was caused.

The Dunkirk western channel was entered at 2230. A ship, full of troops, was hailed to establish where the embarkation was being carried out. Information was received that the troops had been obtained from the eastern pier of the harbour. This was reached at 2230 but after waiting for 30 minutes no troops could be found. There was considerable air activity and gun fire at the time. At midnight the ship proceeded out of the harbour and eastward inshore along the beaches. No troops however could be found and at 0130, in view of the warning before sailing, the ship returned to Ramsgate, which was reached at 0900. In the afternoon of the 3rd June orders were received to be prepared to proceed to Dunkirk but these were later cancelled.

In the evening of the 4th June orders were received to proceed to Tilbury. At Tilbury on the 5th June orders were given to destore at Royal Victoria Yard, Deptford, and to proceed to Surrey Commercial Docks. The dock was entered at 1530 and the ship handed to the Port of London Authorities.

DOGGERSBANK
Dutch Schuit

Another schuit taken over by the Chatham personnel was Doggersbank, *which was lying at Gravesend at the time, though it had been working at London. Under the command of Lieutenant D. McBarnet RN, she made three crossings to Dunkirk, in the process rescuing at least 800 men. For his part in the evacuation, McBarnet was awarded the DSO, his Engine Room Artificer, E. Horne, the DSM. McBarnet's report is dated 7 June 1940:*

In accordance with verbal instructions received from the Commodore's secretary R.N. Barracks, Chatham, I have the honour to make the following report of proceedings of H.M.S. *Doggersbank* for the period Sunday 26th. May to Wednesday 5th. June, in connection with the evacuation of military personnel from Dunkirk beaches.

I took over the Dutch Scoot *Doggersbank* from her owner captain at Gravesend and commissioned her with a crew of one other Lieutenant R.N. and 9 ratings. We sailed P.M. for Sheerness where we secured alongside at about 2000. Stores adequate in quantity and description were all ready to be loaded into the ship on arrival, the whole organisation being extremely good. Ship was swung at 0930 next morning and we sailed at 1600 for Dunkirk, anchoring in the Thames estuary during the hours of darkness.

We arrived at Dunkirk about noon on Tuesday 27th. And were told to proceed to Brai [sic] Beach where I grounded the ship with a kedge anchor payed out from astern. Our draught (6ft.) proved however to be too great to enable the soldiers to wade out to us so the life-boat and lifesaving raft were hoisted out and used to ferry the men from beach to ship. The boats were immediately mobbed on arrival inshore and swamped. They were righted and bailed out but considerably difficulty was experienced in preventing to many men trying to embark each trip. Later in the day the Army officers ashore organised their men and military police prevented the men rushing the boats and shot anybody who attempted to do so. This very much expedited the embarkation. By about 2000 I had embarked some 450 men most of whom had been on the beach 3 days without food or water though a great many had water bottles full of Whiskey. Our stores and fresh water were consequently finished within an hour.

At this time there was a great lack of boats on the beach so I considered that I would be most usefully employed going as close inshore as I was able, collecting a full load and then transferring them to bigger craft further out which I accordingly did, collecting water and biscuits when alongside Destroyers.

About this time I managed to pick up some abandoned boats but had not got the hands to work them so I joined all my lines together, sent one end to the beach where I had it hauled up beyond high water mark, the other end I secured to my life-saving raft which I anchored as far out as my length of lines would allow me. We then proceeded as close inshore as we could, picked up the grass and used it as a warp between ships and shore. The soldiers were very reluctant to wade out to the boats after dark so embarkation became slow despite the guest warp. I had however collected another load by the morning and as there were no Destroyers or other larger craft near the beach I was on I had to take my load up to La Pan [sic]. As far as I could see the beach I had left (opposite the sanatorium) was the only one which was properly organised and where troops could consequently be embarked much quicker than elsewhere, so I boarded H.M.S. Codrington and explained the situation asking if a Destroyer could be sent down with me. The Codrington came down herself and ordered another Destroyer to join her. After this the Sanatorium beach was well attended by larger craft.

Whilst I was reporting to Codrington I sent my boats inshore to bring off some of the Frenchmen who were assembled there. They immediately mobbed and capsized the boats, threatening my sailors with revolvers when they tried to evict some. I sent in another boat with an armed party and rescued three of my four seamen the other being taken off by a Destroyer's motor boat. Later in the day I saw the French soldiers still crowded in my boat which was then high and dry.

I transferred another load of soldiers to Destroyers during the day and was much assisted by *Codrington* leaving her boats with me. During the night at 1½ hours before low water I ran the ship aground as by this time my crew who had all worked continuously since our arrival were almost at the point of collapse and could no longer work the boats. The soldiers were able to walk out to the ship for about ½ hour either side of low water and during this time I collected a full load of between 300 & 350 men. About two hours after low water I managed to float off and as by this time there were plenty of pulling boats and motor boats to tow them I decided to take my load to Margate where they were disembarked at about noon on Thursday 30th. On arrival all gear left behind by the evacuees was cleared out of the ship and quantities of stores placed onboard. I was very much impressed by the efficient organisation of the Pier staff.

After refuelling and filling my fresh water tank I sailed for Dunkirk where I arrived that night and embarked another load with which I sailed next morning. On arrival at Margate P.M. on Friday I was told to remain there till further orders. At about noon on Sunday the second I was told to tow four motor boats to Dunkirk. On the way across we were waved back by some ship whose name I could not see but decided to go on in fulfilment of my orders. I found a number of Frenchmen on the beach but very few would embark as they said we would be bombed, this was probably due to the fact that we were the only ship working on the beach and therefor the only target for aircraft who came our way, most of them however dropped their bombs on a French gunboat which had been grounded opposite the harbour. I tried two or three places along the beach but without much success, I did however manage to collect some British soldiers from boats which they had salvaged. I then proceeded towards Dunkirk but when I saw there was a paddle steamer secured alongside and only a few men coming down to her at considerable intervals. I decided to return with what men I had. There were no other ships moving in the channel on the way back so we received the undivided attention of 18 German aircraft who carried out high level bombing attacks on us in groups of three for forty minutes without getting any salvos very close. They were driven off by 7 British fighters. I can only surmise that the Germans were amusing themselves at our expense as they were dive-bombers who did not once carry out a dive-bombing attack despite the absence of A.A. fire.

On arrival at Margate A.M. on Monday the 3rd. I was again told to anchor and await instructions. P.M. on Wednesday 5th I was told to proceed to London where I arrived next day and paid off ship, the crew returning to Chatham.

FREDANJA
Dutch Schuit

Previously lying at Poole, HMS Fredanja *was captained by Lieutenant Commander K. Stewart during the evacuation, in which the vessel rescued 1,002 men. This report, believed to have been written by Stewart, is dated 26 June 1940:*

I have the honour to report that on our first visit to Dunkirk we arrived in the approaches to the harbour at about 2330 and asked another ship, which had been to look at the beaches, whether we were required there. Hearing that we were not needed there we proceeded into the harbour and went alongside the Eastern Arm at about 0015

We had orders to sail not later than 0330 but s we were not full of troops at that time we remained alongside until 0415 when we had about 400 soldiers onboard. The reason we were so long is that they were filling larger ships at the outer end of the pier before us, and also the troops were only arriving on the jetty at irregular intervals.

A German aircraft was sighted shortly after we had sailed but did not attack. We returned by Route 'Y' to Dover where we secured alongside Admiralty Pier to disembark at about 1415 on May 28th.

During the night of May 28th-29th about 20 tons of stores and fresh water were put onboard and at 0800 on May 29th we again sailed for Dunkirk, proceeding by Route 'Z' in company with H.M.S. *Jaba*.

We anchored as close to the beach as possible about one mile to the Eastward of the Eastern Arm at 1400 and immediately lowered our two skiffs to land the stores and embark troops. It was soon found, however, that the embarkation was getting ahead of the discharge of stores so the remainder of these were transferred to *Jaba* who landed them by putting her bows on the beach.

Having got between 400 and 500 soldiers onboard by 1830 we weighed and stood by *Jaba* for half an hour until she had got afloat again and then proceeded to Ramsgate by Route 'Y' with H.M.S. *Amazone* in company.

Between the Nieuport and Middlekirk buoys we were attacked by a German aircraft which made two low level bombing attacks at about 300 feet, dropping two bombs in each attack. The first pair fell about 40 feet from the ship on the starboard side and on the second attack the bombs were considerably closer, the nearest being between ten and fifteen feet away on the port side. Both attacks were made from almost right astern and with all the bombs there was a very noticeable delay between their striking the water and their exploding.

The shock of the explosions lifted the engines from their bed, stripping the threads of the holding-down bolts and breaking one in half. Other damage consisted of breaking most of the fittings aft, throwing the compass out by about 20° and internal damage to the gear-box.

The aircraft carried out two more attacks with machine guns only, wounding six men. First aid was rendered by the First Lieutenant and Coxswain.

As the plane delivered his attacks I altered course to Starboard and opened fire with the Lewis gun. This was hit in the ammunition pan on the third attack and a double feed resulted. It is possible that the enemy rear-gunner was hit as his tail gun was not in action on the last attack.

H.M.S. *Amazone* was asked to stand by me during the night as there appeared to be every possibility of the engines breaking down.

The crew behaved excellently under fire and I especially wish to mention Thomas A. Willing, Petty Officer, P/J100988, who showed great coolness and efficiency in keeping soldiers calm during the attacks and in rendering first aid afterwards. Also Jack S. Ambrose, a/E.R.A. 4th Class (number not known), who did excellent work in the Engine Room during and after the attacks in keeping the engines going and in repairing the gear-box, especially as this is his first ship.

We disembarked at Ramsgate at about 0830 on May 30th, after which we anchored outside the harbour to have temporary repairs made.

On completion of Operation *Dynamo* we were ordered to Poole to pay off but the engines broke down off Newhaven. We were towed into the harbour to be repaired and at 2000 on June 14th we sailed for Saint Malo under orders from Commander-in-Chief Portsmouth.

FRISCO
Dutch Schuit

One of the schuits that had been lying at Poole, Frisco *was commanded by Lieutenant George Symons RN during* Dynamo. *His report, which fails to mention that his vessel also rescued some 1,002 men, is dated 9 June 1940:*

Sunday 26th May.
At Portsmouth – ship was being wiped, swung and generally prepared for service.

Monday 27th May.
Sailed from Portsmouth at 0500. Arrived Newhaven at 1315.

Tuesday 28th May.
Repairs were effected to for'ard Capstan. 2100. Sailed for Dover.

Wednesday 29th May.
0900. Secured alongside Submarine Basin Dover. Watered and provisioned ship.
1230. Sailed for Dunkirk towing a pulling Boat. During the passage every endeavour was made for receiving and embarking troops. My crew worked continuously at improving ladders and guest warps, and preparing the holds.
2330. Entered Dunkirk Roads. I steamed as close to the Beach as possible from about 6 miles to the East of Dunkirk right up to Dunkirk, but was unable to see any signs of troops. It appeared that *Frisco* was the first skoot to arrive in the Roads.
0030. Entered Dunkirk and secured alongside the Mole. I then started embarking troops until the skoot *Sursom Corda* secured alongside me when I transferred them across. At about 0130 I decided to commence filling my ship alternately with *Sursom Corda*. Between 0130 and 0300 several skoots endeavoured to come alongside *Sursom Corda*, I instructed the Commanding Officer of *Sursom Corda* to tell them to berth further up the Mole. I left the Mole at about 0315 having got onboard about 350 men and 4 officers. I arrived at Dover after an uneventful trip at about 1500 Thursday 30th May.

Having provioned [*sic*] and embarked water tins I sailed again for Dunkirk at about 2100. This time I proceeded by the Calais Channel. My crew worked extraordinarily well clearing up the hold and preparing it again for more troops. Although we were in the Beam of Calais Searchlights for about 2 hours it appeared that we remained undetected.

Friday 31st May.
At about 0245 I observed what appeared to be a fairly large derelict two funnelled ship with a slight list to port. As I approached her a voice shouted for Help, and at the same time the ship took up a violent list to port and appeared to be sinking. I considered lowering a boat and searching for the man, but as I might well have endangered the Boat and Boats crew, both urgently required for the evacuation I regretfully proceeded. The ship sunk just after I had passed her.

I understand that *Sursom Corda* who was some way astern of me did lower a boat but was unable to find the man. Shortly afterwards I observed a flare on the water some 400 yards ahead of me, almost immediately afterwards a bomb fell about 250 yards on my starboard bow. At about 0415 I entered Dunkirk Harbour but as the Mole was completely deserted and the place was being shelled I left hurriedly. I then proceeded along the coast until I saw dense columns of troops on the beach where I anchored and then veered as much cable as necessary so as just not to ground, I lowered my Boats and started to load up. An Air Raid occurred at about 0630 but no damage was done to ships in my immediate vicinity.

During the morning one of the Beachmasters came off to me and endeavoured to persuade me to beach the ship so as to load quicker, pointing out that two other smaller skoots (*Hebe* & *Sursom Corda*) were doing so very successfully. As it was now a falling tide with an onshore wind I refused. For this I was later very glad as both other skoots shortly afterwards became stuck on the beach and were unable to get off. (*Hebe* came off at the next high water).

During the forenoon I hailed a large motor driven pleasure boat, got him alongside me and transferred 250 men to him. By about 1230 I had onboard 648 men and space was extremely cramped. I had delayed my departure hoping that a destroyer or other fast craft would appear and take my load from me so that I could fill up again. However as another skoot appeared I slipped my anchor (the capstan being again defective) and sailed. Just as I was about to leave Dunkirk Roads I was hailed by a Fleet Minesweeper and ordered to tow a Drifter full of troops to Dover. By 1330 the Drifter was in tow and we were proceeding at about 5 knots.

At approximately 1400 a Heinkel appeared out of the low cloud and at a height of 350 feet released a large bomb, probably 500 lbs, and as he passed over he opened fire with machine guns. The bomb fell on my Port quarter between me and the Drifter. Luckily the Bomb exploded below the surface and beyond violently shaking both ships no major damage was done. The force of the explosion caused my compass to jump out of its gimbals. Certain damage was done to Auxiliary Machinery in the Engine Room. After we had been proceeding for about half an hour we were shelled by the Nieuport Battery. As the third salvo straddled us I decided to risk the navigational dangers and cut across the sandbanks so as to present the minimum target and to open the range as fast as possible. Luckily the Enemy never found the range again. Thick fog was encountered at about 1830.

On making the North Goodwin Light Vessel I discovered that the shaking up had caused a 30 degree error in the compass. During the passage through the Downs the tow parted on several occasions due to the wash of fast moving vessels.

At about 0100 on Saturday 1st June I was about 1 cable from the entrance to Dover Harbour when I was bombed again. This time it was only a very small bomb, which although a very near miss only wetted the troops on the port side aft. There were no casualties from machine gun fire.

At 0130 I secured alongside Admiralty Pier Dover. At 0230 we shifted billet and secured for the night for which I was very grateful as we had been running continuously for over three days and I had had no sleep for 90 hours. On Saturday temporary repairs were effected to the Engine and provisions and water embarked. At 1700 I proceeded to Ramsgate with *Hebe* in company arriving at 2000, where as I could not anchor I secured in the Inner Harbour.

On Sunday and Monday 2nd & 3rd June respectively permanent repairs were effected to the Engine and Capstan. When all skoots were brought to immediate notice in case they were required again it was decided that *Frisco* was not sufficiently reliable and so was left in the Inner Harbour.

I cannot speak too highly of my crew who worked continuously, and on Friday were in the Boats for 7½ hours without a break. The only men being onboard at the time were my First Lieutenant one seaman and the E.R.A. and myself.

HILDA
Dutch Schuit

Hilda had been lying at Poole when she was taken over by a crew commanded by Lieutenant A. Gray RN. During her three trips she transported 835 men. Gray's narrative was completed at Chatham on 6 June 1940:

I have the honour to report the proceedings of H.M. Ship *Hilda* (late Dutch Schoot) under my command from Sunday May 26th to Wednesday June 5th 1940.

The ship commissioned at Tilbury at 1000 on May 26th. Necessary stores were placed on board and wiping completed.

Considerable difficulty was experienced with the engines due to inexperienced personnel, this delaying sailing until 0500 May 27th.

Ship was swung for adjustment of compasses A.M. May 27th at Southend and then proceeded to Sheerness where further necessary stores were placed on board.

At 1800 I proceeded to Southend for route instructions with orders to proceed to Dunkirk, and subsequently left Southend in company with *Doggers Bank* [*Doggersbank*] about 2030. I anchored at dusk near the Shivering Sand Buoy and proceeded at 0400 by the medium length route.

On arrival at Dunkirk about noon I went alongside prepared to embark troops, but was ordered to proceed to the beaches and there embark troops.

I proceeded to Bray Dunnes where a large concentration of troops was assembled and went close inshore let go storm anchor and got out embarking ladders over the bow. This method would have been fairly successful had I had time to secure the ladders firmly. The troops, however, waded out "en masse" and very soon surrounded the ship, overcrowded the ladders which were too steep for them to climb unaided, and got into difficulties by getting out of their depth.

It was only by superhuman efforts of the 1st Lieutenant (Lieut. Berry RNVR) and the ships company that the exhausted and water logged soldiers were hauled on board. Later a grass was passed ashore and manned by the troops which provided a quicker and safer means of embarking, but although the ship was kept aground for'ard all the soldiers arrived wet to the neck.

By about 1900 I had about 500 troops on board and proceeded to transfer them to a destroyer, and then went inshore again. About 100 were embarked by ships boat before dusk, when I grounded on the ebbtide and was unable to get off. By 0130/May 29 there was only about two feet of water round the ship, and 400 troops waded off and were embarked with great ease.

Shortly after 0400 the ship was refloated and I transferred the troops to a destroyer. On proceeding inshore again embarkation was very slow, and after receiving some very seriously wounded I proceeded again to a destroyer with only about 100 troops on board.

I then proceeded to La Panne beach and was ordered by *Keith* to transfer troops from a grounded paddle steamer to the destroyer. This proved impossible, and I anchored and used the ships boats. During the afternoon embarkation proceeded much more quickly with the help of flat bottomed canoes. The ships and beach were heavily bombed on two occasions, and bombs fell very close. No damage to *Hilda* was sustained except, the dinghy which was holed by splinters and abandoned. By 1900 I had nearly 600 troops onboard and proceeded to the eastward to look for a destroyer to which to transfer them. However at this time the only destroyers in sight were some miles to the eastward and being heavily bombed. Two were seen to be hit so I decided to proceed to Dover with my load, as I had practically no food left on board. I proceeded by the long route arriving about 0800 Thursday May 30th.

Lewis guns were fitted and stores received. Six Sub Lieutenants RNR and 25 ratings for boats crews joined and I was ordered to sail for Deal on arrival of six volunteer motor boat drivers.

These did not arrive until 0600 May 31st.

I discharged Lieut Berry RNVR ashore sick suffering from exhaustion.

I reached Deal at 0830 and placed myself under the orders of Captain R.R. Pim R.N.V.R. Six motor boats and 2 lifeboats were towed to Dunkirk and on arrival I was ordered to proceed to La Panne beach.

On arrival there at about 1600 the destroyers and beach were being shelled from shore. I therefore lay off for about 30 minutes meanwhile the destroyers got under way and shelling ceased. I closed the beach slightly to the westward of La Panne and Captain Pim went ashore to organise the embarkation.

This proceeded very quickly indeed and easily and by 2030 I had 600 onboard, which I transferred to the *Scimitar*. I then returned to the beach and embarked a further 100 troops when Captain Pim returned onboard and informed me that the beach was closed and any further troops had been instructed to proceed to Dunkirk.

On his advice I proceeded further to the westward and anchored opposite the French battery until daylight. During the night I shifted berth further to the westward to avoid "overs" from the German batteries shelling the French Fort.

At dawn June 1st I closed the beach again where some troops were seen marching towards Dunkirk. They showed no particular desire to come off and only about 100 stragglers were embarked, the main body continuing along the beach.

At about 0800 therefore I closed the *Keith* flying the flag of the Rear Admiral Wake-Walker. Captain Pim reported the situation and was ordered to close the beaches close eastward of Dunkirk, and if there were no troops there to proceed to England.

Shortly after this strong formations of enemy dive bombers appeared and *Keith* was repeatedly attacked until put out of action and abandoned ship. During this period I remained under way zig zagging as apart from *Keith* and *Skipjack* there appeared to be little else for the aircraft to attack.

I at once proceeded to the aid of *Keith*'s survivors and with the help of motor boats recovered a large number including two British Brigadiers and a French General. While this was taking place enemy dive bombers appeared again and sank *Skipjack* about half mile from me. As soon as possible I proceeded to their aid and picked up all the survivors except about 12 who were recovered by a tug. They were in a very piteous state being covered in oil fuel, and in some cases seriously wounded. By the time this was completed I had more than a full load, considering their condition, and proceeded for England. Dive bombers appeared again and finished off the *Keith* but by some oversight did not attack *Hilda* although she appeared to be the only craft left afloat in the roads.

I passed Dunkirk breakwater about 1130. Shortly after passing No 6 buoy I was overtaken and passed by *Scotia* and a paddle steamer homeward bound laden with troops. When they were about a mile ahead dive bombers once again appeared and both were hit and sank very rapidly. I proceeded at once to the spot and recovered a few survivors, but could be of little assistance being already overloaded. As soon as further help arrived I proceeded to Ramsgate arriving about 1730.

Later I proceeded to Dover to land Captain Pim, but did not arrive until after dark, and was not allowed to enter harbour. I anchored to the East of the South breakwater.

At about 0030/June 2nd a magnetic mine was dropped close astern of me in approximate position 4 cables E by S of the South breakwater. This I reported to the Examination vessel and shifted berth further inshore.

At about 0800/June 2nd I proceeded to Deal to land Captain Pim and received orders from Dover to proceed to Ramsgate.

At 1900 I was ordered to take two boats in tow and proceed to embark troops from the beach close eastwards of Dunkirk. Lieutenant Sidmouth-Willing of the Sea Cadet Training Corps was drafted to me as 1st Lieutenant. I cannot speak too highly of his keenness and efficiency during this operation.

I arrived off Dunkirk about 0130/June 3rd and sent the boats inshore under the command of the 1st Lieutenant. I remained under way between the jetty and sunken French destroyer. With an ebb tide I considered it impracticable to go further inshore. I was shelled intermittently but no damage was done. By 0330 there was no sign of my boats; dawn was rapidly approaching therefore I closed *Rika* further to seaward where I found one of my boats.

The Commodore then closed in his launch and confirmed that there were no troops on the beach and ordered me to return Ramsgate.

The Commodore subsequently picked up my other boats crew and 1st Lieutenant.

I arrived at Ramsgate about 0800 on Monday June 3rd and remained there until ordered to sail for Tilbury on Tuesday.

The ship was paid off A.M. Wednesday June 5th in Surrey Commercial Docks.

I cannot stress to highly the excellent behaviour of the ships company throughout, in conditions where they had virtually no sleep and very little to eat. In particular Acting Petty Officer Leslie Charles Curd C/3X 155644 and Able Seaman George Edwin Godfrey C/3X 144637 were outstanding in all they did.

Interestingly, a report by Captain R. Pim, R.N.V.R also exists and is part of the Admiralty files. This document is dated 2 June 1940:

Object.
Evacuation of military personnel at La Panne Bains and Bray-Dunnes.

Orders Received.
To take as many small motor boats, lifeboats, etc. as possible to the above- mentioned beaches and effect the evacuation of all troops found there. The operation was not to include Dunkirk beach, where evacuation arrangements had already been organised.

Action.
Arrangements were made by Captain G. Fraser. D.S.O., Sea Transport Department, Dover, for the requisitioning of motor boats and lifeboats at Dover, Deal and Walmer. These were inspected and arrangements made for their being manned and provisioned on the afternoon of 30th May. The preparation of these matters of detail in advance by Captain Fraser were entirely responsible for my being able to get together sufficient boats to send early the next morning, and subsequently for providing something in the way of food for the very large number I had on board.

31st May.
I sailed from Deal with 8 boats in tow for Dunkirk early on the 31st, and Captain Fraser undertook to despatch the remaining boats to Dunkirk as soon as they became available. I took 50 gallons of petrol in 2-gallon tins on deck for re-fuelling, the majority of these tins subsequently being jettisoned during the dive bombing east of Dunkirk. Several civilians at Deal desired to accompany the party, and five in fact did manage to get to Dunkirk and were of the greatest possible use.

On arrival off Dunkirk I was informed by the Senior French Naval or Port Official that I was to proceed to La Panne Bains and Bray-Dunnes beaches forthwith, and he confirmed that Dunkirk beach was properly organised. An M.L. came alongside and took four of my boats in tow to La Panne Bains.

The motor and lifeboats were sent away at 4.40 p.m. to work the beaches, which at this time were being shelled with shrapnel.

I found four additional boats at anchor and acquired these as reinforcements. I also requisitioned four lifeboats from a tug and three from a drifter.

I approached a number of trawlers and other small vessels which seemed to be getting under way for Great Britain and asked them to remain until I could fill them up with troops. It seemed to me that the orders which they said they had received to return to Great Britain were not bona fide.

I proceeded ashore and interviewed various military officers at as many of the beaches as possible. At the request of a senior military officer I agreed to assume the duties of Beach Master and arranged to continue the organisation until all the troops on the beaches were on board. I told them that if anything went wrong during the night we would return at dawn. I learned that some of the men had been in the dunes for two or three days awaiting embarkation, and they were obviously much cheered up to learn that they would get out that night. The flat-bottomed boats which the military had been using themselves were extremely dangerous in the surf which, although not very great, was sufficient to capsize these boots.

I found from experience that it was much quicker to run a load of troops in a single motor boat rather than to fill up one or more lifeboats and tow the   greater number. The dangers of controlling boats in tow when they were crowded both near the shore and alongside H.M. ships were considerable. During the night I acquired in one way or another five additional lifeboats, and in many cases the military themselves acted as crews.

The pontoon bridges which had been built by the military the previous day were extremely useful, and were largely responsible for the rapid evacuation of troops. It is interesting to note that a few moments after the last man had been taken off one of these bridges it was hit by enemy artillery.

All the troops that I could find were embarked by midnight and placed in ships which sailed for England. Just before midnight I went along certain of the beaches to look for stragglers. A Staff Officer informed me that no more troops would embark from these beaches but that they would march to Dunkirk, as it was anticipated these beaches would be shelled and would probably be in German hands the following day. This, as it turned out, was a correct forecast.

I estimate that from pontoon bridges and beaches approximately 5,000 troops were probably embarked.

The soldiers, though obviously extremely tired, made no complaints of the delay or of the wettings which they got in wading out in the surf to get into the motor boats, and were more than thankful for the kindnesses which were shown them in the various ships. One could not but be impressed by the amount of friendly cheering which occurred when H.M. ships passed the troop ships at sea. The great majority of the troops were carrying their rifles and side-arms, and I insisted that in no case must they be thrown away. I was impressed to notice that the military padres were always amongst the last to leave the beach in their respective parties.

Several of the motor boats had now broken down and between midnight and 3 a.m. complete repairs were done to these boats, which was most creditable to the R.N.R. and R.N.V.R. officers and ratings sent from *Excellent* and *King Alfred* to man them.

I found it necessary to shift my anchorage to the west during the night, as shells meant for the beaches were ricocheting over H.M.S. *Hilda*.

In accordance with my undertaking to the troops, I sent off all boats again at 3.15 a.m. to search the beaches, starting from the western end of Bray-Dunes. During the next three hours approximately only 250 men were taken off the beaches, and these in small parties; they were apparently stragglers. A large rear-guard party marching along the beach decided to continue to Dunkirk.

1st June.

At 7.30 a.m. approximately I closed H.M.S. *Keith* and reported the position to Admiral Wake-Walker. He told me to continue my search of the beaches and if possible transfer my troops to another ship, subsequently returning to England. Unfortunately, with the exception of *Keith*, *Skipjack*, one destroyer a considerable distance away and an Admiralty tug there were no vessels to whom I could transfer these troops, besides which, with the dive bombing and shelling, it would, as it turned out, have been impossible.

At approximately 8 a.m. H.M.S. *Keith* received a direct hit from a dive bomber and was abandoned shortly afterwards. I closed *Keith* and picked up some 50 survivors out of the water, including the Q.M.G. of the B.E.F. and other Staff Officers. At this stage I jettisoned all my spare petrol. The Admiralty tug went alongside *Keith* before she sank and took off the majority of the survivors. I then proceeded to the east to make a final inspection of the beaches and to see that no motor-boats had been left behind.

Half an hour later *Skipjack* received a direct hit from a dive bomber and sank immediately. I closed *Skipjack* and picked up some 60 or 70 survivors.

Dive bombing had been more or less continuous since early morning and the attacks went on while *Hilda* proceeded towards Dunkirk on passage home. British fighters were seen on two or three occasions, but during the greater part of the day the Germans seemed to be in complete control of the air.

At 10.30 approximately I sailed for England, being narrowly missed on several occasions by bombs, and after an hour's steaming, while in the vicinity of two of H.M. transports I saw the latter struck by dive bombers and sink.

As I now had some 530 troops on board my small vessel, many of whom were in an extremely critical condition or badly wounded, and as there were some 15 ships standing by to pick up the survivors from these transports I thought it better to continue my course to England, but succeeded in picking up a number of French survivors. I was impressed by the splendid action of one British army officer, who several times went overboard to tie lines round those in the water. I did not ascertain his name.

I passed a signal to V.A. Dover through a destroyer giving E.T.A. for Ramsgate and asking for ambulances.

I arrived at Ramsgate at 5.30 p.m. and landed all my British and French troops together with survivors from H.M. ships. One man had died and two others were in an extremely critical condition.

I telephoned a full report of the operations and of the final evacuation of the beaches to an officer on the Staff of V.A. Dover, and at 7.30 sailed for Dover. While on passage home I passed a number of motor boats being towed to Dunkirk, and after consultation with the Q.M.G. advised them to continue their journey and ask for instructions on arrival, as they might be of use to the Officer-in-Charge of the evacuation at Dunkirk beach. The only boats brought home by me were two which were completely out of order. The other lifeboats, whalers etc. were left at Dunkirk for further use.

Hilda arrived at Dover at 10 o'clock but was not permitted to enter. While at anchor outside, at approximately 11 o'clock a magnetic mine was dropped 50 yards south-east of the ship, and this was duly reported to the Examination Officer and sweeping operations carried out next morning.

2nd June.
Reported at the office of V.A. Dover the results of the operation which I had been ordered to carry out, and was told to submit a full report in writing.

General Observations.
The evacuation was carried out without injury to any of the troops, but a number were killed on the beaches by shrapnel while standing by or moving along.

I found that the crews of the motor boats, all young officers and ratings, were very steady both under shell fire and while close to dive bombing.

The great majority of the troops were carrying their rifles and equipment, and I was particularly struck by the fact that I heard no complaint at any time from these tired men, even when up to their shoulders in water in the surf. They appreciated to the full the efforts we were making.

Owing to the swell a number of boats capsized in the surf, which gradually subsided with continued good weather. The swell on the 31st had calmed down considerably by the morning of the 1st June.

The marksmanship of the A.A. machine-gunners in *Hilda* seemed to be very accurate, and they realised that it was essential to fire at bombers before they got into their dive. The dive bombers seemed to be extremely accurate in their aim.

Messrs. Hammond of Deal, who act as Admiralty agents, were most helpful in every way in finding suitable motor boats and lifeboats, in arranging requisitioning, and obtaining spare supplies of petrol at short notice.

I was much impressed by the good-nature of the ship's company in handing to all those who lost their clothing or were in sad condition owing to being covered in oil, any parts of their uniform or private possessions not in use. This applied equally to the soldiers, who were most generous in sharing their clothing of all sorts.

I must record the assistance given me by Lieut. Few, R.N.V.R. of H.M.S. *Sandown*, in bringing the troops from one of the piers. He made a great number of trips in a most expeditious manner and his cheerfulness was a decided asset.

I should like to bring under notice the efficient manner in which the Commanding Officer of H.M.S. *Hilda*, Lieut. Gray, and the coxswain, Petty Officer Curd, carried out their duties, and this applies equally to the whole ship's company. Many seriously wounded men were on board, and each of these received such careful attention as was possible.

I was much struck by the efficient manner in which H.M.S. *Hilda* was handled while rescuing survivors and also in avoiding dive bombing operations.

MASB 6
Motor Anti-Submarine Boat

Built by British Power Boats, MASB 6 was one of sixteen examples of the type (all subsequently converted to MGBs) constructed on 70 foot hulls and fitted with a pair of powered aircraft turrets mounted on the centre line, the latter being two quad 0.303-inch turrets manufactured by Boulton and Paul. Unfortunately, it has not been possible to identify the name of the Lieutenant RN who provided the following log:

May 23rd.
1329. Sailed from Portland for Harwich.
2152. Arrived Dover – fuelled.

May 24th.
0857. Sailed form Dover.
1316. Arrived Harwich.

May 25th.
Fuelled.

May 26th.
Fitted quadruple Lewis gun in place of port double.

May 27th.
1307. Sailed for Dover in company with S.O.7.
1753. Arrived Dover. Reported to V.A. Dover.

May 28th.
1100. Sailed with S.O.7. to search for Hurricane reported in the sea S.W. of Goodwins. Following air battle off Dover earlier.
1400. (approx.). Returned to Dover. Search unsuccessful.
2117. Sailed from Dover to find S.S. *Clan Maclister* [*Clan Macalister*] in the Downs to give her instructions.

2300 (approx.). Found *Clan Macalister*. Embarked two stretcher cases on deck.

May 29th.
0015. Collided with and sank small motor launch *Minekoi* with whaler in tow. Saved crew of three.
0255. Secured Dover.
0441. Sailed from Dover to turn back to Ramsgate all small craft from Thames Estuary. Took in tow six cutters and one whaler found drifting.
0630 (approx.). Recalled to Dover. Handed tow over to motor boat to take to Ramsgate. Fueled [*sic*].
1921. Left Dover for anti M.T.B. patrol.

May 30th.
0710. Secured Dover.
0901. Left Dover with Lt-Comdr. [illegible] to marshal and instruct all small boats arriving from south coast.
1335. Secured Dover. Fueled. Carried out engine repairs.

May 31st.
1140. Sailed for Ramsgate to rendezvous with small boat convoy.
1220. Arrived Ramsgate. Off-loaded depth charges.
1453. Sailed from Ramsgate escorting five tugs and five drifters all towing open boats.
1930. Off Reutigen Bank. General bombing attack on shipping.
2100. Arrived off Dunkirk. Took on board Lt-Comdr. Wynne-Edwards (from *Keith*). Instructed open boats where to operate.
2315. In collision with large yacht. Hole in starboard bow above water line. Some ribs broken.
2400 (approx.). Returned to *Keith* off La Panne. Took on board General Leese.

June 1st.
0030 (approx.). Crossed to *Hebe* to collect Lord Gort. On arrival found he had just gone over to *Keith*. Returned to *Keith*.
0304. Sailed for Dover with Lord Gort and General Leese.
0547. Arrived Dover. Fueled [*sic*] and carried out repairs to starboard bow.

June 2nd.
1201. Sailed from Dover to search for Drifter *Girl Gladys* reported

broken down 7 miles east of Dunkirk and soldiers in open boat 3 miles off Dunkirk reported by aircraft.

1330 (approx.). Collected occupants of two open boats off Dunkirk. Left 1st. Lieut. to sail Thames barge with approximately 240 soldiers to Dover.

1530 (approx.). Picked up 18 soldiers in open boat. Carried out unsuccessful search for drifter *Girl Gladys*.

1700. Abandoned search. Set course to intercept Thames barge.

1720. Dive-bombing attack by six or eight planes.

1730. Set course for Dover as now had wounded on board.

1922. Arrived Dover.

June 3rd.
Refuelled. Carried out repairs to bullet holes and engines. Fuel tanks and hull seams leaking.

June 4th.
1255. Sailed for Portland.
2057. Arrived Portland for docking.

Search for Hurricane.
At approximately 1100 S.O.6 and 7 were instructed to search for Hurricane reported in sea, position 5 to 10 miles S.W. of Goodwins. Course was set S.E. from Dover until Goodwins bore N.E. Boats then opened up to approximately 2000 yards and swept 10 miles S.W. Course was then altered to S.E. and again to N.E. and sweep carried back to opposite Dover. Much wreckage was examined but none that could have been aircraft.

May 28th. 1940, 2117, to May 29th. 0255.
Instructions were received to find the S.S. *Clan Macalister* anchored somewhere in the Downs and in conference with the Captain of the ship and the Commander R.N. in charge of M.L.V.s to decide the best course for *Clan Macalister* to land her boats and to instruct her to proceed accordingly. Subsequently to report to the Chief of Staff what action was being taken.

Serious difficulty was experienced in finding *Clan Macalister* owing to large number of ships in the Downs and absence of examination vessel. Contact was made however at approximately 2300. *Clan Macalister* had no charts of Dunkirk and consequently S.O.6.s were handed over to her. It was decided she could probably get within fifteen miles of La Panne, and she sailed accordingly. It would appear that she got very much closer and unfortunately is still there.

Two stretcher cases were taken off being members of the crew of the M.L.V.s who had fallen down the hold of the *Clan Macalister*. At approximately midnight S.O.6. set course for Dover, and shortly afterwards collided with motor launch *Minekoi* with whaler in tow. This occurred owing to the whaler appearing close under the port bow. Course was immediately altered to starboard and collision occurred with the launch which was previously not seen. The crew of three – Sub/Lieut. R.E. Blows, R.N.V.R., A.B. Stewart and Stoker Macgill – were rescued after difficulty owing to rain squall and slightly choppy sea. Able-Seaman Shuttleworth did good work by jumping overboard and supporting the one member of the launch's crew who could not swim. I believe the launch's crew subsequently sailed for Dunkirk in another launch.

Return to Dover was made at 0255 where the stretcher cases were dispatched by ambulance.

May 29th. 1921, to May 30th. 0710.
Anti-M.T.B. Patrol. Instructions were received to rendezvous with two M.T.B.s from Harwich at 2100 off the Quint buoy. S.O.6. proceeded there at full speed but was one hour late at the R.V. At approximately 2230 the two M.T.B.s arrived, and passed approximately half-a-mile from S.O.6. who could not connect with them owing to their superior speed. Contact was not made until approximately 0230 and this was done with due caution to avoid being mistaken for an enemy craft. Much of the night was spent with engines stopped when boats and planes could be detected by sound at a far greater range than visibility permitted. It is submitted that this course might profitably be employed during patrols.

May 31st. 1940, 1140, to June 1st. 1940. 0547.
Instructions were received to proceed to Ramsgate, rendezvous and escort small boat convoy to Dunkirk. The convoy sailed at 1453 approximately 3 hours after scheduled time. Opportunity was taken at Ramsgate to off-load all depth charges as it was considered inadvisable to continue carrying these. The convoy consisted of 5 tugs and 5 drifters each towing between three and fifteen small boats.

The convoy straggled somewhat on the way over and when the Reutigen buoy was reached the leaders were eased down to enable the convoy to arrive together. At this time a large force of German bombers and fighters were seen approaching. There were innumerable ships of all shapes and sizes in the vicinity and a general bombing raid was commenced. British fighters arrived at this time and the attack became disorganised. The bombers eventually disappearing inland.

The convoy arrived off Dunkirk at approximately 2110, S.O.6. embarked Lieut. Comdr. Wynne-Edwardes [sic] from *Keith* who directed the convoy to the various beaches as required. At approximately 2315 when returning to the *Keith* a collision occurred with what appeared to be a medium-sized yacht. S.O.6. was put into astern but the yacht's stern swinging round as she altered course to port stove in S.O.6. on the starboard bow fracturing several ribs and making a large cut in the planking above waterline.

While the damage was being inspected by the aid of a shaded torch fire was opened on S.O.6. from a German aeroplane. On arrival at *Keith* General Leese was embarked and instructions were given to collect Lord Gort from *Hebe*, and to return to England dropping General Leese in Dunkirk if Lord Gort approved.

On arrival at *Hebe* it was discovered that Lord Gort had crossed to *Keith*. S.O.6. returned to *Keith* and approximately three-quarters of an hour later Lord Gort also arrived there. He was embarked forthwith and he and General Leese taken direct to Dover.

Considering it was the first time that any of the crew had been under fire their behaviour left nothing to be desired.

June 2nd. 1940, 1201, to 1922.
Instructions were received to carry out a search for drifter *Girl Gladys* reported broken down 7 miles east of Dunkirk and for approximately 30 soldiers in an open boat about 3 miles off Dunkirk reported by aircraft. Course was set from Dover direct to the outer Reutigen.

It was then intended to proceed slowly towards the coast to search for the open boat, subsequently to put out to sea clear of land and make another approach to the coast approximately 10 miles east of Dunkirk to allow for the set of the tide from the time the report was received. Air escort had been promised and caution had to be exercised as no ships were operating off Dunkirk during daylight.

About half-way across a French trawler with an open boat in tow was hailed. He reported having picked the boat up with soldiers off Dunkirk and it was thought this might be the boat for which we were searching. To make sure we proceeded to Dunkirk where two open boats and a Thames barge with sail set were found approximately three miles from the coast.

The first open boat yielded five Spaniards, the second one about 6 soldiers, Belgian, French and English. We then went alongside the Thames barge at approximately 1330. This was found to contain about 220 soldiers including two Colonels and a Major of Artillery, and various wounded. They were endeavouring to sail to England but had made approximately three miles in 10 hours, see note below. Motor-mechanic Whittaker fitted a new piston to the air compressor motor while 1st Lieut. and myself trimmed the sails. They had no charts on board. The air compressor motor was made to run but all efforts to start the diesel failed.

I then left my 1st. Lieut., Sub. Lieut. De Hammel, with instructions to sail the barge to Dover, and proceeded along the coast having opened up the distance to search for the *Girl Gladys*.

About two miles to the east I found an open boat containing 18 soldiers who were embarked, after which we approached to within approximately three miles of the coast slightly to the eastward of La Panne. Visibility was good and no sign of the drifter could be seen, the search was therefore abandoned and course was set to intercept the Thames barge.

At approximately 1720 when out of sight of land we were attacked by either six or eight dive-bombers, 20 to 30 bombs were dropped and fell at distances varying from 10 to 50 yards of the ship. The bombers appeared to attack in pairs out of the sun and having released their bombs continued their dive firing machine-guns.

Course was altered frequently in an endeavour to miss the bombs. Some appeared to explode after entering the water, some on striking the surface and a certain number appeared not to explode at all. One exploded under the bow right ahead and the ship passed through the splash. A certain amount of discomfort was experienced by myself and members of the crew who were exposed to the splash in the eyes for the next twelve hours or so.

Able-Seaman Power was wounded in the leg when manning the port turret, also one of the soldiers in the fore peak. As I now had wounded on board I considered it advisable to return to Dover forthwith and to ask for assistance for the barge. A tug was sent out at approximately 2100 and found the barge sailing well about 10 miles from Dover. I consider Sub. Lieut. De Hammel performed a very creditable operation. The bombing to which the ship had been subjected had caused leaks to the hull and the petrol tank and the ship was not used again for that night's operation.

The career of the Thames barge before meeting S.O.6 is worthy of comment. From accounts it would seem that the 220 soldiers arrived at Braye dunes at approximately 0500 and saw the barge lying off-shore. They waded out and found she was aground. One officer examined the engine and when the ship floated with the rising tide, started the diesel. Unfortunately it was in astern and they again beached themselves. After some delay they floated off and again started the engines making sure it was in ahead. They came up all standing on the anchor. After ineffective efforts to weigh the anchor they ran it out to a clinch and let it go, by which time the air bottles were exhausted and they were unable to start the diesel. They therefore decided to sail, but due to the absence of anyone with sailing knowledge their efforts created nothing but slight leeway which was counteracted by the set. They were therefore stationary when discovered.

I cannot speak too highly of the conduct of all members of the crew during this somewhat trying time and it is difficult to mention anyone specifically.

Sub. Lieut. De Hammel's safe-conduct of the barge is worthy of note, while the tireless energy and keenness of motor-mechanic Whittaker and the efficient way in which he kept the engines running and dealt with unexpected contingencies was also a magnificent effort.

MTB 67
Motor Torpedo Boat

An example of the Thornycroft 55-feet-type class, MTB 67 *had been ordered on 26 February 1940 by the Finnish Navy. Requisitioned by the Admiralty on the same day,* MTB 67 *was commissioned on 19 April 1940, having been built at Thornycroft's yard at Hampton-on-Thames. She survived Dunkirk, only to be bombed and sunk by German aircraft at Suda Bay, Crete, on 23 May 1941. The following account of her part in Operation* Dynamo *was written by Lieutenant Charles Anderson RN on 1 June 1940:*

Monday, 27th May.
p.m.   Arrived Dover with 10th Flotilla in Company. Fuelled. Detached from flotilla and sailed for Nieuport taking Belgian personages. M.A/S. Boat No.8 [MASB 8] in company.

Tuesday, 28th May.
0300   Landed Belgian personages at Nieuport. Sailed for Felixstowe escorting MTB 22 with Admiral Keyes on board.

Tuesday – Friday
Employed in screening patrols for evacuation of B.E.F. Based on Felixstowe.

Friday, 31st May.
0600 Sailed for Dover with MTB 107 in a company. Fuelled on arrival

and sailed for Dunkirk with orders to report to V.A. Dover in *Keith* and, acting under his orders, to evacuate Lord Gort. Ordered by Admiral to bring off naval ratings from beaches two miles west of La Panne. Continued evacuating soldiers till MTB 67 went aground. Shelled whilst aground, necessitating use of main engine to refloat. This caused considerable damage to main engine. Remained in vicinity till petrol gave out and then returned home, arriving Dover 0010/1.

Saturday, lst June.
Proceeded to Portsmouth for slipping with M.T.B. 68 in company.

Damage to MTB 67.
At approximately 1900 on Friday, May 31st, 1940, H.M. Motor Torpedo Boat No. 67, under my command, was employed in evacuating the British Expeditionary Force from the beach two miles west of La Panne. Heavy surf was running at the time.

I approached the shallow water at dead slow speed, keeping my port auxiliary and starboard main engines running in order to give me immediate astern power when required. On my port bow was a jetty at the end of which I had been informed was deep water, but which I had been instructed not to use. Ahead of me were various small craft of about my own draught. These were not aground.

Soundings from the forecastle showed ample depth of water and the port engine was going astern when a wave caught the boat and carried it ahead causing the propellers and rudders to ground. The bow was afloat.

All around in the water were wounded and exhausted soldiers and as the tide was rising the worst of these were taken aboard.

As embarkation of these men was taking place however, a shore battery opened fire on the neighbourhood. It was therefore considered advisable to get M.T.B. 67 under way as soon as possible.

This was done by manual pushing, lightening the stern at the expense of the bow, and going astern on the starboard main engine. It is considered that this latter action is responsible for most of the damage.

MTB 102
Motor Torpedo Boat

MTB 102 *was designed (under the designation Vosper Private Venture Boat) by Commander Peter Du Cane CBE, Managing Director of Vosper Ltd., in*

1936. She was completed and launched in 1937, and ran trials on the Solent. When she was purchased by the Admiralty and brought into service she was named MTB 102 (the 100 prefix denoting a prototype vessel, making her the first MTB of the modern era). She was crewed by two officers and eight men. The following report of her involvement in Operation Dynamo *was written by Lieutenant C.W.S. Dreyer on 7 June 1940:*

Thursday, 30th May.

0530. Secured in Submarine Basin, Dover. Having received orders from the Chief of Staff, Dover, I sailed at 1300 for Dunkirk in accordance with those orders. On approaching No. A.W. buoy in the Dunkirk approach channel, I noticed some shell splashes between me and the land, and, therefore altered course and steered along the North side outside the channel.

At 1430 I came alongside the East quay in Dunkirk harbour. I disembarked, and my First Lieutenant, Midshipman J.F. Wilford, R.N.V.R. took the boat outside to await my return. I reported to Captain Tennant R.N. and received his orders to take Commander Henderson and Commander Elwood along to the beaches to La Panne to review the situation.

On passage to La Panne we were attacked by 3 M.E.110's in close formation from ahead. No damage was caused – own speed 2 knots.

At 2000 on completion of our tour of the beaches we returned to Dunkirk, disembarked Commander Henderson and Commander Elwood and embarked [illegible]0 British soldiers and sailed for Dover.

At 2115 about 10 miles S.E. of Dover I was stopped by Commander Le Mesurier in the D.C. Motor Boat and took him back towards [illegible] to pass messages to three tugs on their way to Dunkirk.

At 0030 secured in S/M basin.

Friday, 31st May.

At 0130 I received my orders for Friday, 31st May.

At 1100 I proceeded in accordance with those orders, arriving off La Panne at 1240. I went alongside H.M.S. *Keith* and reported to Rear Admiral Wake-Walker. He embarked and we took him along the beaches, being shelled of La Panne, and then back to H.M.S. *Keith*.

At 1445 went to pick up pilot of crashed Hurricane. Pilot was dead but parachute was recovered, leading to subsequent identification of the officer.

At 1500, returned to H.M.S. *Keith* and reported short of fuel.

1530. Towing boatloads of soldiers to various transports.

1640. Sailed for Dover, securing 1800.

Saturday, 1st June.

0600. Proceeded in accordance with signalled instructions from Vice Admiral, Dover.

0750. Arrived Dunkirk. Passed H.M.S. *Ivanhoe* being successfully bombed.

0755. Approached H.M.S. *Keith* who appeared to be not under control, she had just been bombed.

0800. Went alongside and took off Rear Admiral Wake-Walker and Staff and one wounded torpedo-man. Approached two tugs to order them to assist H.M.S. *Keith*.

0805. Thirty-five JU.87 dive attacking, many bombs falling close astern, nearest 10 yards, observed delay action of smaller bombs in the water.

0810. H.M.S. *Keith* again bombed – considerable damage apparent.

0830. Alongside Dunkirk – intermittent shelling in harbour and western arm of inner harbour.

0915. Sailed for Dover with Rear Admiral Wake-Walker and staff on board.

1100. Secured alongside H.M.S. *Sandhurst*.

Sunday, 2nd June.

Having been given 24 hours for Engine Room maintenance, I reported ready for service at 1530 and received sailing orders.

2035. Proceeded for Dunkirk.

2255. Secured alongside Eastern Jetty in Dunkirk harbour. Intermittent and accurate shelling of all quays and to the Eastward, some falling to Westward.

2310. Took on board a Brigadier. Captain Tennant R.N., Commander Elwood R.N., Commander Banks, R.N. his demolition party and one Flying Officer, R.A.F. dressed as a Belgian peasant.

2315. Sailed for Dover. On this night shelling was more intense and though this seems doubtful, if M.T.B. 102 was the target, more accurate.

0120. Secured in submarine basin in Dover.

Monday, 3rd June.

At 2015 proceeded with Admiral Wake-Walker and staff on board.

2200. Arrived in Dunkirk harbour. Proceeded on auxiliary engines under orders of Rear Admiral Wake-Walker who was directing disembarkation of French soldiers. Wreckage considerable and slight wind caused swell in conjunction with strong ebb tide.

0135. Large explosion just eastward of Eastern breakwater. Shelling continuous, heavy and not particularly accurate. Assuming piers to be target, mostly falling to the Eastward, some close.

0315. Operation completed. Past blockships and sailed for Dover. Slight shelling from beaches, inaccurate.

0505. Secured in submarine basin, Dover.

Wednesday, 5th June.
1000. Sailed for Portsmouth.
1545. Secured alongside H.M.S. *Hornet*.

Throughout these operations I received every assistance from my First Lieutenant Midshipman J.F. Wilford R.N.V.R. who navigated for me with skill and coolness under trying conditions.

Engine Room Artificer, Third Class George William Hymans, O.N.M.X. 49826 maintained and ran his engines continuously under difficult conditions. His services were invaluable.

Able Seaman Albert R.C. Stephens O.N. P/JX. 131369 displayed the greatest coolness throughout. He manned his guns permanently during each trip and his coolness and cheerfulness were of the greatest help in maintaining morale, whilst his skill with his gun discouraged the hostile aircraft that were encountered.

Amongst the other key moments in MTB 102's *wartime career was when she was used, in 1944, to transport Winston Churchill and General Eisenhower during their review of the ships assembled off the South Coast for the D-Day landings. Having been refurbished and used in the 1976 film* The Eagle Has Landed, *starring Michael Caine,* MTB 102 *is one of only a few Second World War Royal Navy vessels still afloat, and is thought to be the only Royal Navy commissioned vessel that took part in the Dunkirk evacuation which has survived. This unique vessel is supported by the MTB 102 Trust. For more information, please visit: www.mtb102.com*

MTB 107
Motor Torpedo Boat

Built by the Thornycroft yard at Hampton-on-Thames, MTB 107 was ordered on 6 April 1939, being described as a Thornycroft experimental-type. Some sources state that she was commissioned in June 1940, suggesting that she had barely been delivered when she was assigned to Operation Dynamo. Her

*Commanding Officer during the evacuation was Lieutenant John Cameron
R.N.V.R. His report was written at Portsmouth on 7 June 1940:*

Monday, 27th May.
MTB 107 proceeded from Portsmouth at 0800 on 27th May in company
with MTB's 67, 68, 104 and 106 for Felixstowe, arriving at Dover 1345,
remaining there overnight and proceeding the following morning to
Felixstowe, arriving 1200.

Tuesday, 28th May.
Left Felixstowe 1830 in company with other M.T.B's for patrol between
charted position of Wandelaar Light Vessel and Thornton Ridge Buoy.
Arrived on patrol line 2135. Stopped and remained on patrol until 0400
29th May. Thereafter returning to Felixstowe arriving 0810 29th May.
Patrol was uneventful.

Wednesday, 29th May.
At Felixstowe.

Thursday, 30th May.
At Felixstowe.

Friday, 31st May.
Left Felixstowe in company with M.T.B. 67 at 0600 for Dover, arriving
there at 1015. Left Dover in company with M.T.B. 67 for Dunkirk and La
Panne at 1600. On passage fired on by shore batteries between [illegible]
and Grevelines [sic]: no hits. Met H.M.S. *Keith* with Vice Admiral, Dover
on board in neighbourhood of Dunkirk at approximately 1745. M.T.B.
67 [contacted] H.M.S. *Keith* for orders. Thereafter proceeded to La Panne
for purpose of embarking certain naval ratings. Considerably [sic] shell
fire at La Panne, some very close, but no hits. Returned to H.M.S. *Keith*
on orders of M.T.B. 67 to inform Vice Admiral that all ratings were said
to be safely embarked. Rejoined M.T.B. 67 at La Panne. After rejoining
recovered 3 naval ratings from water in state of exhaustion. As M.T.B.
107 has only one engine and no reverse gear it was considered
inadvisable to run her on to the beach to embark troops. After picking
up these ratings closed a gunboat which was lying close into the beach
for purpose of transferring them to her, there being no accommodation
in M.T.B. 107, or any provisions of any kind. Having closed, gunboat
and come alongside was ordered to cast off. This was fortunate as
immediately thereafter shell burst at the spot where M.T.B. 107 had been
lying. Thereafter cruised in company with M.T.B. 67 until ordered to

return to harbour with M.T.B. 67. During this period beaches between La Panne and Bray appeared to be under fairly constant attack from gunfire and bombs. Whilst cruising in company with M.T.B. 67 an enemy aircraft was seen to crash in the sea. Stood by M.T.B. 67 on her orders while she endeavoured to pick up two of the crew who had come down in the sea. This attempt was not successful. On the return passage to Dover, again came under fire from same battery between Calais Grevelines. Shooting seemed half-hearted and inaccurate. Arrived Dover 2315.

Saturday, 1st June.
Left Dover 1100 with Admiral Hallett on board proceeding by way of Downs and North Goodwin Light vessel to Route X where a patrol was maintained under Admiral Hallett's orders until 1600. Thereafter returned to Dover arriving there at approximately 1830. No event of any importance except the surprising ineptitude of an enemy bomber which dropped one bomb at three ships which were lying stopped. The bomb missed by a large margin and no further bombs were dropped.

Sunday, 2nd June.
Left Dover, 1845. Proceeded to Downs where embarked Captains of blockships and transferred to H.M.S. *Vivacious*. 2020 proceeded in tow of H.M.S. *Vivacious*. 2230 Slipped tow and embarked Captain Dangerfield R.N. from H.M.S. *Vivacious* and proceeded to Dunkirk independently. Navigation was rendered difficult by spray obscuring vision and by unknown deviation on the compass which had never been swung. 2230 (approx.) Arrived off Dunkirk and entered harbour and cruised there. Considerable shelling in progress, particularly in vicinity of East Pier, alongside which M.T.B. 107 secured to land Captain Dangerfield. On his return left harbour and searched for blockships, two only being found, the third having been sunk in collision on the way. During this period M.T.B. 107 was alongside, she was crushed by large French fishing craft which were engaged in evacuating troops and were either unable or unwilling to keep clear. After closing the block ships followed first into harbour and received crew from her boat and transferred them to H.M.S. *Vivacious* lying outside, thereafter going in again and picking up the remainder of the crew of the second blockship. Thereafter left Dunkirk at 0345 with H.M.S. *Vivacious* and M.A/S.B 07 arriving Dover 0630 3rd June. Considerable difficulty was experienced in manoeuvring M.T.B. 107 in Dunkirk harbour on account of much heavy wreckage, her inability to go astern and her large turning circle.

Monday, 3rd June.

Left Dover 1735 and proceeded to embark Captains of blockships, transferring them to H.M.S. *Shikari*. 2030 Proceeded in tow of H.M.S. *Shikari* to Dunkirk in company of blockships. On arrival off Dunkirk slipped tow and employed taking messages to blockships. On blockships weighing at about 0245 attended leading blockship S.S. *Gourko* to follow her in and take off crew. During waiting period H.M.S. *Shikari* bombed without effect. Heavy shelling rifle and machine gun fire observed. As H.M.S. *Gourko* was proceeding to enter heavy explosion was observed on board her from mine, torpedo or bomb. At once closed her to render assistance and secured alongside. At about same time MA/SB 10 did the same and embarked part of her ship's company. S.S. *Gourko* sank rapidly, breaking one of MTB 107's lines in so doing. As MA/SB 10 had proceeded into harbour to follow the remaining blockship MTB 107 remained to rescue more of S.S. *Gourko*'s crew who had not succeeded in getting away. 8 were rescued, including the commanding officer, 3 being seriously and 4 less seriously injured. Very considerable difficulty was experienced in doing this owing to much heavy wreckage, the presence of the wreck of S.S. *King Orry* and the lack of manoeuvring power of MTB 107. When satisfied that no-one remained in the water, proceeded to search for H.M.S. *Shikari* to transfer survivors, as the small size of the boat and lack of any accommodation made this highly desirable. As no sign of H.M.S. *Shikari* or MA/SB 10 [MASB 10] could be found, and the blowing up of the remaining blockship had already been observed, and it was now practically broad daylight, the time being between 0350 and 0400, I decided to make for Dover independently at utmost speed. On passage thick fog was encountered and, owing to regretted error in navigation, MTB 107 became involved in the Goodwins. I thereupon anchored until the weather cleared, having no faith in my compass. The fog rapidly cleared, and I proceeded across the sands to the North Goodwin buoy, thence to Dover, arriving 0730, 4th June.

Tuesday, 4th June.
At Dover.

Wednesday, 5th June.
Proceeded from Dover to Portsmouth in company with D/C Boat and MTB 102.

Note of Proceedings of MTB 107.

31/V.
Left Felixstowe for Dover in company with 67 at 0500 arrived Dover a.m. Proceeded with 67, 1600, for Dunkirk and La Panne to bring off Lord Gort. On passage shelled by battery near Gravelines – shooting not very accurate. Met *Keith* near Dunkirk with V.A.D. on board, about 1800. Received order to proceed to La Panne to ensure embarkation of naval Ratings from shore. At La Panne recovered 3 ratings from sea. Considerable shellfire at La Panne, some being uncomfortably close. Continuous bombing of beaches. Returned to Dover arriving about 2000 – again shelled by Gravelines Battery – inaccurate in dusk.

1/VI.
Embarked Admiral Hallet proceeded 1100 to patrol transport line on Route from N. Goodwin L.V. to Dunkirk. Relieved 1800 (approx.).

2/VI.
Proceeded with blocking expedition to Dunkirk leaving at approx. 1900. In tow of *Vivacious* until 2230 when tow slipped and embarked Capt. Dangerfield. Proceeded to Dunkirk – entered harbour and proceeded to Inner Harbour. Landed Capt. Dangerfield and secured alongside E. Pier. Much shelling and bombing. Re-embarked Capt. Dangerfield and left harbour, thereafter searched for and found block-ships, giving them instructions. Followed block-ships in after all transports had left, at about 0330. Took off crew of 1st blockship and transferred to *Vivacious* lying west of harbour. Returned to harbour and picked up remainder of crew of 2nd block-ship and transferred to *Vivacious*. Thereafter proceeded in company with *Vivacious* to MASB '07' [MASB 7] to Dover.

3/VI.
Left Dover 1815 after ferrying blockship Captains to and from *Shikari*; taken in tow by *Shikari* and proceeded at 2030 to Dunkirk. Slipped tow off Dunkirk. Waited for transport to clear – block-ships proceeding inside – attending on leading block-ship when she blew up – probably by mine – near wreck of *King Orry*. Secured alongside to render assistance at about 0250. M.A.S.B. also came and took off part of crew. Ship sank rapidly breaking heaving line by which 107 was secured. Thereafter remained in vicinity to rescue persons in water – picked up 8 including Captain (3 seriously 4 less seriously injured). *Shikari* and M.A.S.B. not being visible and as no other survivors could be seen and it was now (0345-0400) daylight decided to proceed to Dover. On

returning ran into thick fog and grounded on Goodwins – anchored and when weather cleared proceeded to Dover arriving 0700 (approx.). Sailed for Portsmouth 1000 5th June.

Comment.
Great difficulty was experienced in handling 107 in confined waters and Dunkirk harbour owing to absence of any reverse gear, and very poor turning circle. Navigational facilities are almost entirely absent, and crew get very wet under almost all conditions at sea. These boats do not seem useful for anything beyond purely local defence purposes. During the time alongside Dunkirk Pier boat was severely crushed by French fishing boats and there was also great difficulty experienced in picking up survivors of block-ships owing to boats' unhandiness and presence of large amount of wreckage.

PASCHOLL
Dutch Schuit

Originally lying at Poole, the schuit Pascholl *had originally been commanded by Lieutenant T. Johnson during Operation* Dynamo. *Johnson was, however, transferred off the vessel on 2 June. Some sources state that he took over command of the paddle-steamer HMS* Portsdown, *though his replacement, Lieutenant J.N. Wise RNVR, in his report dated 7 June 1940, provides a different account:*

The above ship returned from La Panne to Sheerness on Sunday 2nd June. Her Captain immediately left her to return to his duties in Naval Control, Ramsgate. At 1230, on instructions from the Commodore's Office, I reported to Admiral Taylor and without further notice, was told by him to take command of the above ship, and take her to Dunkirk.

There being no routing orders available I was told instead to await the departure of H.M.S. *Reiger* and sail in company to Ramsgate. *Reiger* was unable to sail until 1630 and Ramsgate was reached at 2300. We anchored and went ashore for instructions which were to our intense disappointment; we were to be off for the night and await further instructions. With the exception of two of the ship's company, all on board complained that they were reliefs for the original crew and asked to be relieved, having done one or maybe two trips across already. It proved impossible to do this for them until Tuesday morning, but after they had been allocated definite jobs and posts during the operations and had been given a little verbal encouragement they settled down, gave of their best and did their duty in traditional manner.

At 1430 Monday, 3rd June, I was advised that the *Pascholl* would be sailing as flagship with four other Schuits. At 1500 Commander Hammond, R.N. came on board with his navigator, Lieutenant de Mornay, R.N. With great tact and understanding they assured me that they were largely passengers and in no way intended to interfere with, or supersede the Captain. My somewhat natural disappointment at the apparent loss, in spite of these assurances, of the opportunity of conducting the operations on my own initiative, was more than offset by company, guidance and encouragement they afforded to the two Officers of the ship.

We sailed at 1600 and promptly lost one of the five ships – *Reiger* which, to Commander Hammond's lurid disgust, went on the putty (Quern Sand). Overtaking a convoy of weird, but gallant little French fishermen, we arrived in Dunkirk harbour at 2300 after a most tame passage.

The town was blazing furiously and presented a truly memorable spectacle. The harbour was congested, some of the ships there being wrecked, and in cases already ablaze. Difficult navigation was intensified by our not being able to find the Nouveau Avant Port (no proper plan of the harbour being available), our peregrinations nearly putting us on the putty twice. In desperation we went alongside the Packet Boat Quay of the inner harbour, secured and got ladders aboard. Commander Troup, waiting on the quay immediately asked our capacity, and I foolishly but optimistically replied "Oh, between 500 and 1,000".

Poilus in reasonable order commenced to invade the ship and were embarked in an orderly fashion, each man being disarmed before being allowed to descend into the hold. The work of embarkation was supervised by the First Lieutenant (Sub Lieut. St. Aubin, R.N.V.R.) in a most creditable manner.

One of the most memorable and inspiring sights was that gallant old gentleman Commander Hammond complete with "Mae West" life belt, his Capt. Kettle beard sticking out from under his "battle bowler", rushing fearlessly up and down the jetty, helping here, advising there, and constantly enquiring of me "how many more do you think we can get aboard?".

Meanwhile some of the other Schuits had secured nearby, (one ran aground and was, I believe, abandoned). A destroyer came up astern and in securing hopelessly wedged us in, and carried some of our quarter deck gear away with her bow hawser. When the hold and deck was full of Froggies (not a tommy was to be had) we ceased embarkation but had to wait for the departure of the destroyer astern.

After about 15 minutes wait we got away without hitch, thanks to the efficiency of the ships company, who worked extremely well. The congestion at the time was chaotic, ships going astern into others coming ahead, French destroyers shrieking their sirens, small craft nipping here and there, rendering the exit most dangerous. Without mishap, however we cleared the piers or moles at 0030 Tuesday 4th and arrived without incident in Ramsgate harbour at 0830. During the passage there and back and the whole time we were in Dunkirk, we were not once troubled by enemy planes or shell fire at all. There was much shelling of the town whilst we were there and the blazing was intensified, but the operations on the quay proceeded absolutely undisturbed.

The whole affair seemed most tame to me, compared with what I had been led to expect, and indeed I was a little disappointed that there was not more "activity". We were also disappointed and surprised to learn that our estimates of our load of 500 troops was in excess by about 200. It was not possible to carry more than the approx. 300 that we had (which included about 10 Officers but no sick or wounded) especially as the Frog insisted on embarking with his bed, kitchen range etc.

Commander Hammond and Lieut. de Mornay left the ship on arrival and the crew, with one exception, was relieved by a new one later in the day. The next day, Wednesday 5th, we sailed at 0500 in convoy of Schuits for Poole; off Folkestone the *Ruja* (Lieut. Webster, R.N.) broke down. We took her in tow for the rest of the way, travelling entirely alone as the convoy, which never formed up properly, in any case, was consequently lost thereafter.

We reached Newhaven at 1900 and were admitted to the harbour at 2200. We sailed again at 0800 on Thursday 6th and reached Studland Bay – *Ruja* still in tow – at 2100. At 0030 Friday 7th a German plane (presumably) which was heard was reported to me by the anchor watch to have dropped a parachute (and presumably a mine) 70 to 100 yards away with a splash. I took bearing on the ships present to fix the spot (no land or lights being visible) and reported the matter to the pilot next morning. There were supposed to be so many mines there that we gathered the pilot to be little interested in this one addition to the flock and he took no particular note of the information.

We entered Poole harbour in convoy at 1000 on Friday 7th and paid off the ship.

RAF MOTOR BOAT 243

The following report, dated 4 June 1940, was provided by Sub-Lieutenant R. Wake R.N. for submission to the Commanding Officer HMS Lynx *(a shore establishment for coastal forces craft at Dover):*

I have the honour to submit the following report in regard to the passage of R.A.F. Motor Boats No. 243 and 270, in which the former boat was sunk.

The two boats left Dover under the command of Commander Clouston R.N. in R.A.F. Motor Boat No.243. The complements of the two boats consisted of the R.A.F. personnel and the Naval embarkation party on passage to Dunkirk, with two Naval French Officers and two French Petty Officers who were acting as liaison to the British Party.

At 1900, when about 6 miles off Grave Lines, eight Junkers 87 planes were sighted. These attacked us with machine-guns and small bombs. My boat avoided the first attack, but, on looking round, I saw that Commanded Clouston's boat had a "near miss" from a bomb, and was heeling heavily to starboard.

During the next ten minutes, I was fully occupied in navigating my boat to avoid the attacking planes. When I next had time to look round for the other boat, only her bows were visible, and the whole crew were in the water. I closed the position, and slowed down to pick up survivors, but Commander Clouston ordered me to leave them immediately and proceed at full speed to Dunkirk.

I increased speed, and was shortly afterwards attacked again, and, during this attack, my boat was repeatedly hit by incendiary machine-gun bullets, and my starboard engine was put out of action. The speed of the boat was reduced to six knots. I set the mean course for Dunkirk, and shortly afterwards, about half an hour after the commencement of the attacks, the enemy aircraft left us.

I proceeded to Dunkirk, arriving there at 2100, and reported the loss of R.A.F. Motor Boat No.243. To Rear-Admiral Wake Walker. Two destroyers alongside were warned to keep a good lookout for Commander Clouston and his crew, but I regret to report that Sub-Lieutenant Soloman R.N.V.R. and Aircraftsman Carmaham are the only survivors known to have been picked up. Aircraftsman Carmaham reported that he saw Commander Clouston dead in the water some hours before he was picked up.

In my opinion, if my boat had remained to pick up survivors, the extra load in the boat, which would have necessitated men being seated

321

on the top of the canopy, added to the fact that one engine was out of action and the boat was making water slowly, would have made our arrival at Dunkirk most unlikely.

I would wish to call to your particular attention the bravery and devotion to duty shown by the Coxswain of the boat Corporal Flowers R.A.F., who, during the whole attack, conned his boat in obedience to my orders with great speed and decision. And also of Lieutenant de Vaisseau Roux of the French M.T.B. No.24 [MTB 24] and of his Petty Officer Henri Kroener, who, in the face of continuous attacks, maintained a continual fire from the Lewis Gun, mounted in the open cockpit aft, to such good effect that the crew of one of the Aircraft were seen to leave it by parachute. Without doubt, the continuous and accurate fire by Lieutenant Roux saved us from almost certain destruction.

St. Clears
HM Tug

The Admiralty steam tug St. Clears *had been built in 1919 by Livingston & Cooper. During Operation* Dynamo *she was commanded by Master W.J. Penney, whose account, submitted to the King's Harbour Master at Sheerness, is dated 7 June 1940:*

The Tug *St. Clears* under my command left Sheerness, in company with *Sun V*, towing eleven naval cutters and with 70 naval ratings under Commander Hayward, R.N.R. on board at 1205 on 28th May.

After arriving at Dover route instructions were issued by examination tug in South Downs and both tugs proceeded and at 0015 on 29th May, *Sun V* was involved in collision with H.M.S. *Montrose*. I searched the vicinity for two hours but failed to locate same. I then proceeded as instructed by *Montrose*. When passing Gravelines we were surprised by fire from a shore battery in a position bearing 022° from Dunkerque C.W. buoy. We continued on our course for a short time until the firing became intensified shells falling very close to our stern some of which holed and sank two cutters in tow. I then ordered the helmsman to alter course to bring the battery astern of us, finally steering a course of 020° till out of range of guns.

The wireless operator was maintaining continuous watch so I was able to make an immediate report of the attack which I considered urgent in view of the possibility of other small craft following the same route. This warning was received and immediately re-broadcast by

North Foreland Radio. During the whole of this time the conduct of my officers and men was admirable, particularly that of Able Seaman Arthur Chawner who was at the wheel, he steered the ship with great precision and altered course efficiently when ordered to do so. We then proceeded on the course 020° until we arrived at position T where H.M. Trawler *Blackburn Rovers* was stationed.

After some delay I proceeded Northern route as instructed by trawler. When passing Newport, shore batteries again opened fire, shells falling very close, this battery was silenced by French Destroyers, but two cutters were lost in this action and a third cut adrift, this cutter was later picked up by H.M.S. *Crested Eagle* and towed to my position off La Panne. I proceeded with six remaining cutters and anchored off La Panne. Commander Hayward dispatched the cutters to the beach of La Panne and commenced embarking troops immediately. During the whole of the time at La Panne aerial attacks were continuous. Commander Hayward and his men showed great courage and endurance in working the cutters, continually transporting troops.

Our guns were manned, the foremost by a naval rating one of the relief crew of cutters, the after Lewis gun by myself, being supplied with ammunition by naval ratings. We fired both guns at any machine that came within range particularly at one machine which carried out a machine gunning attack. Under these very exceptional circumstances the crew behaved excellently taking shelter in alleyways and mess decks when ordered by me. During one bombing raid I hove in anchor. I proceeded to unknown destroyer which had been hit but was not required.

I was signalled to assist H.M.S. *Bideford* ashore. I transferred cutters to *Golden Eagle* and proceeded to assist. During this period I picked up 70 French troops from small local boats.

At 2200 Engineer reported defect to main engines. The defect was signalled to *Bideford* who asked me to report situation to H.M.S. *Hebe*. I closed *Hebe* and made necessary report then proceeded back to Sheerness at slow speed due to defect.

Strathelliot
HM Trawler

For its part in the Dunkirk evacuation, the trawler Strathelliot *was commanded by Sub Lieutenant W.E. Mercer RNVR. His report, addressed to the CO of HMS* Wildfire *(a shore establishment at Sheerness), is dated 5 June 1940:*

I have the honour to submit the following report of certain proceedings affecting H.M.T. *Strathelliot* on May 30th and 31st, June 1st and 2nd 1940.

Acting on orders received from P.M.S.O., Sheerness, I repaired on board H.M.T. *Strathelliot* at 10.30 May 30th with instructions to escort a convoy of motor cruisers to Ramsgate. The executive signal was received at 1410, anchor was immediately weighed and the convoy was picked up at 1430.

The route ordered was via 33 QZS, but as certain boats had proceeded into the Princes Channel, I ordered course to be laid through that channel so that we should not lose touch with them. At 1550 we hove to and took in tow two disabled boats – the *Skylark* and *Court Belle II* – proceeding at 1635. At 1800, we again hove to to await boats astern, and they coming up, we took in tow the *Mary Rose*, proceeding at 1840. At 1845 we were again compelled to stop, as certain other vessels were in trouble, but these being taken in tow by others, we got under way again at 1910.

Our orders were to close the Examination Vessel off the N. Goodwin L.V. for instructions, but, as we approached we received orders by R/T to proceed to Ramsgate and to report to the N.O.I.C. there. We arrived off Ramsgate about 2200 and came to anchor – ordering all motor boats to make fast to the trawler. I then went aboard motor boat *Forty Two*, whose officer was a Lieutenant R.N.R. in command of the boats and put off to search for three boats lost in the darkness. These were fortunately picked up near the Gull Buoy and escorted to the *Strathelliot*. I then went ashore in *Forty Two* and reported to the N.O.I.C. at 2305.

I was then ordered by him to escort the convoy to Dunkerque, but having received orders from Sheerness to return, I requested permission to telephone Sheerness for confirmation. This being given, I collected orders, route orders and charts, being ordered to sail immediately. I then returned to the *Strathelliot* and asked the Lieutenant R.N.R. to call all the officers in command of motor boats to the trawler. They were then given orders and charts so that in the event of their losing touch with the escort, they would be able to proceed alone.

I arranged to hoist a red lantern of low visibility in the trawler, so that boats could keep in touch with us in the dark and also arranged certain signals which were to be made on our siren to cause the convoy to heave to, to proceed or to ease down. I gave orders to be prepared to move off at 0200 and the officers returned to their boats. There were eight defective boats to be towed and arrangements were made as to which boats were to do the towing. In the darkness however, it was impossible to hold to these arrangements, but all the defective boats were taken in tow by others. Anchor was weighed at 0205 and the convoy proceeded to sea.

At the North Goodwins L.V. the convoy was hove to and all ships accounted for; course then being set vis U. V. and W buoys for Dunkerque roads. The seas had by this time become very heavy, due to a strong N.W. breeze and the boat's crews were suffering great discomfort. The towing was causing considerable damage to the boats, although speed was reduced to two knots and at 0640 the *Skylark*'s towing bollard tore away and she was taken in tow stern first – there being no other point forward at which the towing wire could be secured.

At 0730, the *Mary Rose* reported that, due to a following sea bringing her up against the trawler's counter, her stern was damaged and water was entering faster than it could be pumped and bailed out. I therefore decided that as she was unlikely to be of any use at Dunkerque – even presuming we could get her there – she should be abandoned and sunk. I therefore ordered the rest of the convoy to proceed under the Lieutenant R.N.R. We then took off the crew of the *Mary Rose* and fired one tray of Lewis gun ammunition into her water line, breaking her up by ramming her to prevent her becoming a danger to navigation. We then proceeded after the convoy and picked up another boat which was being towed.

At 0820, the *Skylark* sustained further damage to her stern due to the strain on the tow caused by the heavy seas, and, as she was in danger of foundering, her crew were taken off and a cargo of ladders and petrol and all serviceable stores aboard transferred to the *Strathelliot* – the boat being then cut adrift. We then closed a trawler *KO* and semaphored her to sink this boat which she did.

At 0845, we took in tow the *Malden Annie IV*, but at 0855 her Port mooring bollard tore away and the towing hawser was then secured to the Starboard. This was showing signs of parting, and finally tore away at 0940. The hawser was then secured to a small hook.

At 1000 we closed the trawler *Grimsby Town* and sent a message ashore by her reporting our position. A mechanic was put aboard the *Malden Annie IV* to try to effect repairs to her magneto, but this was found to be impossible. A hawser was then passed right round underneath her and was secured on deck, the towing hawser being bent to this. The hawser parted at 1215, when *Malden Annie IV* reported that water was entering due to damage received forward. A new hawser was passed and the vessel towed stern first. A great deal of damage had been caused to her superstructure by heavy seas crashing her into the trawler, but having lost two ships, I was loth to lose a third. The tow parted twice more in the course of the afternoon, but the vessel was eventually taken to Dunkerque. I would like to mention the conduct of the officer in command of the *Malden Annie IV* who worked extremely hard under very trying conditions to bring his ship to port.

At 1530 we were proceeding down the channel into Dunkerque when a destroyer came out firing on and being fired on by batteries ashore. It was impossible for us to steer out of her line of fire, due to our tow, but fortunately, although shells were falling close to us and planes were trying to bomb the destroyer, we sustained no damage – the nearest shell being about 70 yards on our starboard beam.

On two other occasions between 1530 and our arrival off Dunkerque beaches at 1620, we received salvoes of bombs intended for destroyers but sustained no hits. We came to anchor off Dunkerque beaches (as close in as our draft would allow) and eventually attracted the attention of a motor launch manned by Sea Scouts. They came alongside and we asked them to bring us some troops from the beach. We put our ship's boat over the side and she was towed ashore to assist. From this and another motor launch we eventually received a total of fifty-four French soldiers.

Although we waited for a total of two and a half hours we were unable to get any further boatloads of soldiers, and at 1920 we decided that, not knowing the state of the tide and being in danger of settling on the sand, we would weigh and proceed to Sheerness. Had there been any possibility of getting any more men, we would have waited but there were insufficient small boats to supply the ships there.

During our three hours there we were bombed continuously, five bombs falling all round us – within 50 to 70 yards at one time without doing any material damage. The crew behaved with great coolness and determination throughout. Anchor was weighed at 1920/31, and we set course for Sheerness, anchoring at 0005 June 1st off the North Goodwins L.V. and proceeding at 0300, arriving at Sheerness at 0830. The troops were landed and I proceeded ashore to report.

At 1223, acting under orders received, we slipped from Sheerness to escort a second convoy of motor boats to Ramsgate. At 1240 we picked up and took in tow motor launch *Empress* and a naval launch. The rest of the convoy proceeded via Gore Channel, but as we could not follow by this route, I ordered course to be set via the Princes Channel keeping the convoy in sight to starboard. We hove to off Margate and when the convoy came up, proceeded to Ramsgate where we arrived without incident at 1650. The motor boats went inside and we anchored outside. I went ashore in the launch to report to the N.O.I.C. I suggested to him that we might be allowed to tow the *Empress* and the launch over to Dunkerque where they could ferry for us and after loading both the trawler and themselves, we could tow them home. He agreeing; we sailed at 1805.

We had no trouble with the tow on this occasion, but on approaching Dunkerque we were endeavouring to pick up a buoy, which, (so we had been told at Ramsgate) should have been lit, but which, we afterwards found to be extinguished when we went ashore.

It was necessary to slip the tow in order to go astern and the *Empress* drifted ashore, although she had previously reported that one of her engines was running. We do not know what eventually happened to her. As we were succeeding in drawing the trawler from the shore, we blew a certain prearranged signal on our siren to call the *Empress*, but only succeeded in attracting thereby the attentions of a searchlight ashore which endeavoured to pick us up. After about ten minutes it was extinguished. I ordered the launch which had been assisting in getting us away to go to the assistance of the *Empress*, and later in Dunkerque harbour, the launch reported that he was going to assist on the beaches. Whether she had rescued the crew of the *Empress* or not, I cannot say.

We eventually reached Dunkerque at 2310 where we went alongside the inner jetty. The tide was very low and we had great difficulty in getting the men aboard and at 0115 on June 2nd the skipper reported that owing to the increase in draught due to the number of men aboard, we were in danger of settling on the mud. Consequently at 0130 we slipped and stood out of the harbour. During our two and a half hours there we were shelled incessantly – shells striking the cranes and buildings around the harbour, but no casualties or damage were sustained.

Outside the harbour there was only one buoy lit and we made a little too much across the channel before turning down it, so that owing to our draught we went aground again fortunately getting away again about 0215.

At 0340 we sighted a floating mine about 20 yards on our starboard beam and reported this to an escort vessel astern, asking her to report it as our R/T was out of order.

It was impossible to assess the number of troops aboard, but it was certainly in excess of three hundred and possibly three hundred and fifty – all French and including General Nicolle and his staff.

We arrived off Ramsgate at 0745 where the soldiers were landed. I went ashore for orders and was ordered to return to Sheerness where we eventually arrived at 1330 – coming to anchor on the West Shore. I then came ashore and reported.

During the whole of these operations, the crew have behaved with great coolness and energy despite their having been without rest for most of the time and under fire for the first time. No casualties have occurred and no damage done to the ship on her two groundings.

Sun IV
HM Tug

A steam tug of 200 tons, Sun IV *had been built in Hull in 1915. Lieutenant J.E.L. Martin RN submitted his report of its part in the evacuations on 18 June 1940:*

I have the honour to refer to Nore General Order 448/40 and to submit the following narrative of events:

At 0200 Friday, 31st May, 1940, the London tug *Sun IV* (Master Mr. Alexander, Manager of the firm), slipped from Tilbury Docks with 12 lifeboats in tow. A London Pilot was embarked and remained in the tug until the evacuation was completed. Ships' lifeboats were manned by half naval and half volunteer crews.

Southend pier was hailed at 0415/31 May, 1940, and the tug anchored. Provisions were embarked for boats' crews and the opportunity was taken to allow boats' crews a hot cup of tea in the tug.

At 0445 anchor was weighed and the tug proceeded to Ramsgate arriving at 1115, where she was armed with two pairs of Lewis guns mounted either side of the wheel house.

The tugs were sailed for Dunkirk at 1330. Commander Tyler came onboard as his tug had run out of coal and water. Lieutenant Wilkinson and a further party of seamen were also embarked.

At 1915 a high level bombing attack took place, but bombs all fell a long way from the tug.

A boat was capsized when the tug met a destroyer's wake and it is regretted that one Stoker was drowned. This casualty was reported on arrival in harbour by Commander Tyler.

At 2230 the tug was ordered to a position one mile east of Dunkirk by verbal orders from a motor torpedo boat. By 2300 the tug was anchored three quarters of a mile from the shore and the boats were sent in with Lieutenant Wilkinson and Lieutenant Fletcher, R.N.R., in charge. From 2300 to 0300 there was periodic shelling and one bomb from an aircraft, which was engaged by Lewis guns, was dropped about 100 yards from the tug.

At 0315/1 June, 1940, having embarked 88 soldiers both French and British, the tug weighed anchor. Only three boats had been able to get back to our tug, but the remainder of the boats' crews were either on board or were towed back by drifters to Ramsgate. At 0445 one boat was set adrift as it was filling rapidly with water; while this was being done a German fighter flew towards us and was engaged with Lewis guns.

0830/1 June, 1940, arrived at Ramsgate. Commander Tyler went inshore for orders.

Anchor was weighed at 1615 and tug proceeded with two boats in tow. A small trawler was seen to hit a mine south of the North Goodwin Light Vessel at 1645.

Three German bombers carried out a level bombing attack at 1830 from about 8000 feet. Ten bombs were dropped falling about 250 yards astern. British fighters appeared about a quarter of an hour later as three transports passed.

At 2030 the motor lifeboat *E.M.E.D.* hailed us and asked to be shown the way into Dunkirk. This boat remained with us for the remainder of the night. The Lieutenant R.N.V.R. in command was unfortunately killed by shrapnel during the night. This was reported by Commander Tyler on arrival at Ramsgate.

At 2100 a small motor boat informed us that there were no troops left in Dunkirk. Commander Tyler disregarded this and went into the harbour in the motor lifeboat with Lieutenant Fletcher.

At 2130 the tug was hailed by a motor torpedo boat and orders were received to use the boats to fill up minesweepers which were to arrive later.

At 2145 the motor lifeboat and one boat were sent in shore. The tug then towed the remaining boat as near in shore as possible. This boat then pulled for shore. The tug was then anchored about three quarters of a mile from the Eastern breakwater.

The pulling boat returned with the news that there were no soldiers ashore at 2230, and said that she had not seen the other boats.

2300-0100/2 June, 1940, fairly heavy firing over and short, chiefly shrapnel. All hands kept under cover, until the motor lifeboat returned at 0130. The tug then weighed and proceeded to Ramsgate.

At 0140 an M.T.B. again hailed us and we were sent back to fill up with soldiers, and anchored in position again at 0215. After waiting till 0330 for the boats the tug weighed and went further in shore to pick them up, but ran aground about a quarter of a mile off shore. The flooding tide and the use of engines astern together with physical jerks by the soldiers refloated her. Boats meanwhile had been secured. We then proceeded to Ramsgate with 142 soldiers on board and in the motor lifeboat, which we towed.

At 0415 we ran aground for the second time one mile west of the breakwater, but managed to get off after ten minutes. A slight haze gave us a peaceful passage home arriving at Ramsgate at 0745.

Commander Tyler left us A.M. and we were told the tug would not be required that night, but at 2000/2 June, 1940, we were ordered to weigh and proceeded to a position near position "W" to salvage the Hospital Ship *Paris*. At 0100 we eventually located her and the tug *Sun XV* with a Commander R.N.R., on board, attempted to tow her. We lay off until she had got secured, but unfortunately her first wire parted. About two minutes later a German machine dived down and machine gunned us. We engaged the aircraft with Lewis guns; both the ratings on the guns getting in bursts.

We were then ordered by the Commander R.N.R., in the tug *Sun XV* to leave after he had asked us what we thought of the situation. The hospital ship was in about five fathoms of water and was very heavily down by the stern. Both the Tugmaster and I considered that if we were to get her back safely we would require an escort. It would be very slow work to tow her as she was a twin screw ship. I think that she was already aground, but it was hard to tell. The tug arrived back at Ramsgate 0645/3 June, 1940.

At 1130/3 June, 1940, we were ordered alongside to water and get provisions. The opportunity was taken to fit sandbags on top of and around the wheelhouse. Due to the tugs large draft we could only remain alongside for about an hour either side of high tide.

Commander Le Measurer came on board at 1600 and four large motor boats were secured astern. At 1700 four tugs weighed and proceeded. Two motor boats were slipped at 1830 and came under their own power. British fighter patrols were observed during the evening. At position "W" two German floating mines were sighted. They were destroyed by minesweepers.

At 2130 one motor boat was abandoned after the tow ropes had parted, as its engines were broken down. It was, unfortunately, a boat only three days old.

By 2330 we were approaching the breakwater when a small boat filled with French soldiers hailed us. These soldiers were embarked. They told us that the Germans were in the town, but that the French held the coast for about one and a half miles to the westward of the breakwater. The tug was stopped to the eastward of the breakwater and we remained in this position until 0200/4 June, 1940, when we went inside the harbour to try and pick up more soldiers from the pier. H.M.S. *Malcolm* hailed and asked us to hold her stern up to the jetty. This we did. Between 0200 and 0230 there was periodic shelling outside the breakwater.

At 0230 the tugs had been ordered to leave and we proceeded with our one remaining motor boat steaming under its own power. One aircraft was engaged with Lewis guns at 0310, it did not retaliate. The motor boat was taken in tow about half an hour later. The tug was anchored in Ramsgate at 0730 after an extraordinarily peaceful passage home.

Lieutenant Fletcher and myself together with nine naval ratings left the tug A.M. on 5th June, 1940. Lewis guns and two Able Seamen were left on board until the tug arrived back at Gravesend.

Both the naval ratings, the civilian tug's crew, and the volunteers behaved splendidly.

In The Ships That Saved An Army, *Russell Plummer notes that during* Sun IV*'s rescue work on 1 June a total of 112 men were loaded. One of the soldiers plucked from the water turned out to be the brother of Wally Jones,* Sun IV*'s engineer.* Sun IV *survived the war, being sold to an Italian company in 1966 – at which point she was renamed* San Benigno.

Chapter 6

Shore Personnel

SENIOR NAVAL OFFICER AFLOAT, DUNKIRK
Rear Admiral William Frederic Wake-Walker

Rear Admiral William Frederic Wake-Walker CB, OBE's extensive account of his involvement in Operation Dynamo was completed in April 1941. There are a number of annotations, corrections or additions written in the margins of the original copy – including the date of each section. Where appropriate, all of these have been taken into our transcript:

On my return to the Admiralty from lunch on Wednesday, 29th May, I was told that I was wanted by Vice Admiral Phillips and I went to his room at 2.45. There I found him with the Naval Secretary and he asked me if I would like to go to Dunkirk to try and get some organisation into the embarkation there.

I said that I would be delighted. Some discussion then followed as to my appointment, as it was not intended that I should supersede Captain Tennant who was already the Senior Naval Officer, Dunkirk. It was decided that I should be Rear Admiral, Dover, and be in charge off shore at Dunkirk.

Vice Admiral Phillips told me that 70,000 had already been embarked and that a great effort was needed to get off many more. He suggested that I should fly my flag in a Trawler, and told me that Commodores Stevenson and Hallett were already over there in charge of certain beaches. He had no idea how long it would last but thought for not more than a very few days.

I immediately arranged for a car to drive me to Dover and told Lieutenant-Commander Wynne-Edwards and Commander Norfolk to come with me. My signal officer was unluckily away in Newcastle but I arranged with the Director of the Signal Division to tell off one of the signal officers at Dover for me.

Before leaving I saw the First Sea Lord who told me that it was thought that the French were not doing their full share and that I was to stress this on my arrival so that pressure could be brought to bear on them to send more ships. There was also the difficult question whether French troops were to be refused embarkation; it was obvious that our own troops had first call but it would be difficult to discriminate against Frenchmen. Actually it was not until Friday, 31st May, that a signal was made stating the Government's policy to give equal opportunities to British and French troops.

We all set off for Dover in a car about 4 o'clock with a suitcase apiece and a minimum of gear. Passing through Canterbury we stopped and bought a large supply of chocolates and cigarettes, and reached Dover about 6.0 p.m.

At the casemates in Vice Admiral, Dover's offices I was given some idea of the situation and shown a map of the coast to the Northward of Dunkirk; on this three beaches off La Panne, Braye and St. Malo had been optimistically numbered for embarkation of British troops, each beach being divided into three sections. I was told that the Army were coming down to these particular beaches and that certain others between St. Malo and Dunkirk were being used by the French. I received very little other information except that Dunkirk harbour itself had been heavily bombed, and *Grenade* and other ships had been sunk there.

I was also shown the three approaches to Dunkirk. One of them from the East could no longer be used at night as enemy M.T.B.s had sunk a destroyer there.

The Western one was being shelled from the shore in daylight and the centre one was none too easy to make for navigational reasons.

Captain Bush was in the *Hebe* and was in charge off shore until my arrival.

Two destroyers were ready to sail from Dover for Dunkirk and were to take over two lots of beach parties. One of these parties amounting to about 80 was made up of Lieutenants from the Gunnery and Torpedo Long Courses with Petty Officers and Men; they were intended to act as disciplinary parties on the beaches. In the earlier stages of the embarkation many of the troops were completely disorganised and had become a rabble, some throwing away their rifles and others lying on the beaches refusing to get into the boats. These disciplinary beach parties were intended to check this and an order was contemplated that no man would be embarked unless he had his rifle.

Actually by the time I got there things had improved and the fine bearing of the men, their discipline, and the way they stuck to their equipment was most marked.

Another party of 200 men were intended to act as beach parties to assist the embarkation.

The Vice Admiral, Dover, stressed that these Naval Ratings must be got away and must not run the risk of getting caught ashore at the end. I met the signal officer, Viscount Kelburn, who had been lent to me, and arranged that he should collect a party of Signal Ratings to accompany me.

I was also much surprised to meet Commodores Stevenson and Hallett, who arrived at Dover by train after I did; I thought they were already at Dunkirk.

I finally sailed in the *Esk* at 2000 with these two Officers, the disciplinary beach parties and my signalmen and staff. There was no news of the 200 men of the beach parties and I do not know to this day what became of them.

On the way over I arranged that Commodore Stevenson would take charge off La Panne, and Commodore Hallett off Braye, and at that time I intended to be off St. Malo and Dunkirk myself or to put Captain Bush in charge there. I also spoke to the officers in charge of the disciplinary parties and warned them not to get caught but said that it would probably be impossible to give them any order as to when to come off. It was thought that the embarkation could hardly go on for more than a day or two and each day we expected to be the last.

At this time I must confess that I had very little idea of what it was going to be possible to do or how to set about it. I knew that large numbers of craft of all sorts, Destroyers, Sloops and Minesweepers were fetching troops back, but I had no idea at all of local conditions – where they could berth, the possibilities of using the harbour – boat facilities for off shore transport – or what communications existed.

My general plan was to put an officer in some small ship in charge off shore at each of the main beaches and to try and organise the flow of ships to the beaches myself from some central position.

In the *Esk* we were kindly given some sandwiches, and after a short talk we made ourselves as comfortable as we could in the Captain's cabin and tried to sleep. I had hoped to get over to Dunkirk in daylight but the various delays in collecting men and so on made this impossible and it was dark when we got near. From a long way off the flames from burning oil tanks at Dunkirk [were] lighting up the sky, and a black pall of smoke above it, could be seen.

As we got nearer we could also see a ship on fire off shore, and this eventually proved to be the *Clan Macallister* at anchor off Braye. She continued to burn up till the end and there were occasional pops of small arms ammunition. She was deserted but played a very useful part as a distraction for the Germans who shelled and bombed her continuously instead of the ships nearby who were embarking men. Often as I passed her later on I thought of getting her towed away but there was no ship to spare from the more important work of saving men, and I expect she is still there.

Another deserted Merchant ship off the entrance to Dunkirk played a similar useful role and was the target for many bombing attacks.

May 30

We approached the Dunkirk beaches from the South and stopping off each we sent the beach parties ashore in the Destroyer's boats. All this took time and it was not till 0400 that we found the *Hebe* (commanded by my old shipmate, Lieutenant-Commander John Temple) off Braye and transferred to her. At the same time the two Commodores were put into drifters. It was difficult to see in the dark what the situation was, except that there were many ships, drifters and boats off the beaches, and they were joined by the two destroyers. It was flat calm. In the *Hebe* I found Captain Bush and heard more of the situation, and he spoke of the ghastly sight of the shore black with men standing in the water up to their waists. He had had to watch the terribly slow progress of embarkation which I had not then seen, but I did not feel that I could accept the note of despair which I seemed to detect in his voice.

In the *Hebe* we moved eastward to La Panne and there dawn found us and gave us some idea of the task ahead.

The coast here is a long stretch of sand dunes rising fairly steeply in places from a gently shelving beach which dries for 200 yards or more at low water. Off shore the water deepens very gradually and a destroyer cannot get nearer than half a mile. At intervals along the coast there are small towns, seaside resorts, which appear perched on the top of the dunes which slope there more gently to the beach. Such are La Panne, Braye and St. Malo – red brick houses, pretentious villas and the typical modern seaside architecture. But now the growing light showed a different picture – at the water's edge was a dark line of men and there were large groups of men all over the beaches. Off Braye the *Bideford* was ashore with her stern completely blown off by a bomb; the *Locust* – a shallow draft river-gunboat – was trying to take her in tow and eventually did so and got her off and back to England. Further down towards Dunkirk another ship was high and dry and burnt out on the beach – this, I think, was the *Crested Eagle* and there were also many boats of one sort and another broached to on the beach.

335

Lying off the beaches were Destroyers and Sloops, Drifters and other craft, and men were making their way off in whalers, motor boats and pontoon craft.

There was a slight swell which made landing difficult and many boats broached to and were stranded by the tide. The visibility was not good and overhead there were low lying clouds – a blessing for which we were greatly thankful, and which we were not always to enjoy. As soon as it was light I was able to get some clearer idea of the situation and conditions. The beaches were packed with troops, but they appeared to be orderly and under proper control. Off the beaches were a few ships as close as they could get and these were being slowly filled up by their own boats and a few local craft. Ships' motor boats were towing off the whalers assisted by motor launches, but these could not get very close in. Pontoon craft were being paddled off by soldiers but it was not easy to get then back inshore again, often they were left to float away empty. As soon as a Sloop or a Destroyer was full up she left and took her boats with her – the boats' crews were guns' crews and no-one wanted to be without them.

To anyone with an appreciation of the practical difficulties of embarking in small boats with a long pull to seaward, the sight of that beach black with troops was dismaying. The numbers increased steadily as more men filed down the sand dunes and at the back of our minds all the time was the question and fear of how long the defence line could hold and the weather remain fair.

The crux of the matter was boats, boats' crews and towage to and fro, and at 0630 I signalled the urgent need of these. Later, about 7.30, most of the ships had loaded up and were leaving and I asked for more ships and again stressed the need of boats.

About this time I moved down to Dunkirk to get in communication with Tennant and went in alongside the pier in response to a signal.

The outer harbour at Dunkirk (see plan [*missing*]) is formed by two breakwaters approximately at right angles, leaving a narrow entrance between. The Western arm is built solidly of stone, but the Eastern arm, or East Pier as it will be called, is only solid for a short part at the inshore end. The rest of it is built of concrete piles through which the tide flows and on which is supported a narrow pathway wide enough for four men walking abreast. Alongside the East pier is the channel to the inner harbour and docks. A short length of piling runs out parallel to the East pier and encloses the entrance to this channel which is about 150 yards wide.

A new series of docks under construction has an entrance opening off the outer harbour, and jutting out in the harbour by this entrance is the West quay.

The West quay was used entirely by the French and luckily for us they did not consider the East pier suitable for embarkation. It was from the East pier that all the British embarked and on the last two days a large number of French troops also.

The tide had a big rise and fall and at high tide you could step straight on to a destroyer's deck, but at low tide it was a fifteen foot drop. A lot of ladders were sent over and secured to the sides of the pier, but it took time to get soldiers with their rifles and packs down these ladders. On Thursday morning when I first went in [3 or 4 words are illegible] trawler (C) sunk alongside the pier and another ship (A) sunk outside the end. The trawler and drifter shown sank later, as also the block ships.

There were four berths alongside the East pier which could be used. The inner one (F) could only be used by small ships at low tide, but at high tide personnel ships could get into B, D and E.

The *King Orry* during a bombing attack on 29th May rammed the pier and made a large gap in it abreast E berth; until this was bridged the outer berths could not be used as the roadway along the pier was cut. The harbour was very shallow to the west of the West quay, and the place where the *Rouen* went ashore on the night of 2nd June when leaving the Quay is shown – also where the *Kellett* grounded on the night of 3rd June.

As soon as *Hebe* got alongside the East Pier I made my way up to the Local Naval Headquarters while the *Hebe* was quickly filled up with six to seven hundred men – some of them wounded.

The Naval Headquarters were established in a dug-out at the shore end of the East Pier. This area was not large and was separated from the mainland by a bridge over a canal. The surface was uneven and covered with heaps of rubble – there was a Bofors gun and a few ambulances, dust-stained dishevelled cars and wounded men. I was greeted by some of the staff of the S.N.O., Captain Tennant. This small band of Officers with a party of ratings did wonderful work controlling the embarkation and dealing with the situation ashore. They worked under constant shellfire and were short of sleep and food. While I was waiting there, shelling of the area began and we retired to the dug-out entrance – but were urged by a French soldier to go further down and round the corner as he said the direction of the fire was straight into the entrance. I did not see Tennant as he was away somewhere with the General, but I learnt that there were plenty of troops ready to embark at the pier and they would take all the ships that could be sent in.

At this time the gap in the roadway half way along the East Pier completely cut off the end, so that the only berths where we could embark were inside this point. Later this hole was bridged so that the whole pier could be used except where ships were sunk alongside.

It had been my intention to keep *Hebe* as my headquarters, and for this reason she had not taken any troops on board from the beaches. I did not feel I could refuse to fill her up at Dunkirk, and once this was done the question of their disposal inevitably arose. On leaving Dunkirk I returned to the beaches, sending in any ships to load at Dunkirk and from then on I had continually to try to hold the balance between keeping sufficient ships off the beaches and keeping Dunkirk supplied.

I also reported that until more boats were available for ferrying it was essential to concentrate on evacuating from Dunkirk itself.

It may be as well here to explain why Dunkirk was being so little used at this time while so much effort was being expended on the beaches. On 28th May, a heavy bombing attack was made on Dunkirk when the harbour was full of ships. *Grenade* was sunk and *King Orry* (on 29th/1700) and several other ships alongside the piers were hit. As a result of this a junior member of the Naval Party ashore, whose judgement had been affected by the events of the day, dashed off in a car to La Panne where he saw Lord Gort and telephoned to the Admiralty to say that further embarkation from Dunkirk itself was impossible. In consequence Dover was sending all ships over to the beaches and none into Dunkirk and it took us two days to overcome the results of this indiscretion, which had a considerable temporary effect on the plans.

As a result of a report from a destroyer that Dunkirk was usable Vice Admiral, Dover, asked me if ships should be sent there, and at 0830 I signalled from *Hebe* that destroyers could come into Dunkirk in succession and that troops were waiting close to the pier.

Off the beaches loading was proceeding slowly. Conditions were not bad, though there was a slight swell running in sufficient to make boats liable to broach to. At La Panne lorries were being driven into the sea to form a sort of breakwater, and this was also done at Braye.

About mid-day there was an air attack on ships and on La Panne, and later when it cleared a bit overhead there was an attack on Dunkirk. Several French destroyers came in by 'Y' channel, and were fired on from the north of La Panne, and there were some guns which tried to shell the beach between Braye and La Panne but the steep dunes protected it.

On my return to La Panne I met Commodore Stevenson who had transferred to a motor launch and was doing excellent work. He had landed and was wet to the waist. Ashore he had seen Lord Gort who was anxious to see me. As the conditions inshore were getting worse and I did not want to get stranded I decided to go into Dunkirk and drive to La Panne from there.

All this time the large number of men and wounded in *Hebe* had been on my mind. Feeling that I could not keep her any longer I decided to send her back to Dover with Captain Bush to explain the boat situation and point out the vital necessity of sending out boats and crews.

Accordingly at 3.30 I transferred my staff to *Windsor* and went into Dunkirk in M.T.B. 102 which had come at my request. I had felt badly in need of means of getting about quickly, and a fast boat of light draft would have been invaluable. The trouble was that when I did get one its endurance was so low that it had to return almost immediately to Dover.

On arrival at Dunkirk I found that Tennant was with Lord Gort and that to drive there would be likely to take a longer time than I cared to be away – so I decided that I must land from a boat after all.

The M.T.B. had not enough fuel to reach La Panne and return to Dover, so I boarded the *Gossamer* and took her up to La Panne where I transferred to *Worcester* at about 5.30 p.m. There I again found Commodore Stevenson and lent him my spare pair of trousers and underclothes as he got soaked through whenever he landed.

La Panne was in telephonic communication with England and sometimes I received messages by W/T from Dover about the situation there – as for instance one timed 1749 saying that ships were urgently wanted off La Panne – actually at 1900 there were four destroyers and one minesweeper at La Panne and the situation was constantly changing. G.H.Q. was in touch with Admiralty and Vice Admiral, Dover, and gave their views and criticisms of what was happening. This probably accounts for a signal from the First Sea Lord on this day asking if boats were distributed along the beaches to the best advantage. Actually of course practically the only boats that could get inshore except the pontoons and a few local craft were whalers and their distribution was dependent on the position of the ships they belonged to.

So far as was possible I kept ships off all beaches, but in doing so I was badly hampered by the lack of means of getting about quickly. Often when I was off La Panne ships would arrive and stop off the other two beaches, send in their boats and start loading, by then perhaps some off La Panne would leave and a redistribution might be desirable, but it was impracticable once ships had their boats away.

At 1900 small numbers of aircraft made attacks on La Panne and ships off the beaches and about this time a puffer, the *Tiny* (Skoot), loaded with ammunition arrived. She was told to beach herself at La

Panne, the tide being then high, this she did and was cleared as the tide went out, though I believe a good deal of her cargo was finally dumped in the sea.

At 2000 I started inshore again in *Worcester's* whaler on my third attempt to see Lord Gort. There was a slight swell and I got wet to the waist landing. I took in with me my Flag Lieutenant and a small party of signalmen to open visual communications with G.H.Q.

I was met on the beach by Tennant and General Lees and went with them to G.H.Q. which was established in the last villa but one on the south edge of La Panne. This was a pretentious house with a largish dining-room with French windows opening direct on to a road running along the top of the sandy slope from the beach.

I found Lord Gort and his staff about to have dinner and he insisted on my joining them. He was charming and seemed very cheerful and unperturbed and glad to see me. He had been told that a Rear Admiral was being sent to take charge of the embarkation and made me feel that that simple fact should have a great effect. I must confess I did not feel so confident of what it was possible for me to do. However, we did not really discuss matters till after dinner.

I shall not easily forget that meal. For one thing my trousers and seat were very wet and it seemed so strange to be sitting there sharing the Commander-in-Chief's last bottle of champagne and looking out across the beach to the sea. There were eight or nine of us including Tennant and myself. I forget what we ate except that the final dish was fruit salad from a tin and I felt that my extra mouth was robbing the others of their share. After dinner, Lord Gort and General Lees discussed the situation with Tennant and myself; it became obvious to me that they felt that they had successfully fallen back more or less intact on the sea in the face of great odds and that it was now up to the Navy to get them off but that the Navy were not making any real effort in the matter.

Very early in the discussion I stressed the difficulty, slowness, and dependence on fine weather of any large scale embarkation from the beaches and expressed the view that the bulk should move westward and come off from Dunkirk.

This brought from General Lees a disparaging remark which included the words "ineptitude of the Navy". I could not let this pass and told him he had no business or justification to talk like that.

At this time British troops were acting as a rear guard and were holding a line which came down to the coast a little to the north of La Panne. It was then the intention that they should withdraw from this line at midnight on the Friday – next day – and fall back on the beaches. These troops were some of the best and Lord Gort was very anxious that they should get away; there were about 5,000 of them. He had spoken to the First Sea Lord who had said that the Navy would make a supreme effort to get off the remainder during the next day and the rear guard the following night, and that details were being sent out to me by Captain Bush, who had gone back to Dover in the *Hebe*.

I must confess I felt daunted at the prospect and the seeming impossibility of the task. Apart from the rear guard there were tens of thousands of others to come off beforehand, and the thought of that rear guard falling back in the dark and being embarked with an enemy active in pursuit raised unpleasant pictures.

The plan made by the Admiralty, and Vice Admiral, Dover, had every chance of success, but it did not fall out as planned as I shall tell later.

I arranged with Lord Gort that he would embark from La Panne at 6.0 p.m. next day and that I would have boats and ships there for the purpose. If embarkation from there was impossible he would go into Dunkirk.

On my return to *Worcester* I told Commodore Stevenson of the arrangements for embarking Lord Gort and put him in charge of them. I intended at that time to be there myself also.

About 10 p.m. I started back to the ship. It was getting dark and as I left the house with Lord Gort an enemy plane came over and a Bofors gun opened fire on it. I said goodbye to Lord Gort and went down the beach with Tennant, General Lees and my Flag Lieutenant. Tennant asked if I had got a boat and I laughed and told him that I had got to make my own way off – boats were too precious to be kept hanging about. The tide was further out and there were a number of boats and pontoon craft stranded. A number of men of the 12th Lancers were trying to get pontoons afloat, and it was good to see them taking action to help themselves. Lying unused was a pontoon boat about 8 foot by 4 – flat-bottomed with sides about 18 inches high. I called over some soldiers and we got round it and carried it to the water's edge. I then placed four of them each side and told them to wade out with it and get in when I told them. As we waded out the sea was calm, but a small swell was coming in and as the water got deeper I got them into the boat two by two until only Flags and I were still wading at the stern with the water well over our knees. Finally we got in together and I started the soldiers paddling by numbers, rather like a racing boat's crew. They soon picked it up but I noticed there was already a good deal of water in the boat – the freeboard was about 3 inches and the wavelets were washing up to my stern as I sat on the gunwhale. I decided we should not get far before we [were] swamped, and finding by means of my paddle that we were still in fairly shallow water I told my crew to

341

jump out. Out we all got and returned with our boat to the beach and emptied it. Tennant and General Lees had been standing all this time watching and as we came ashore I could not resist the temptation of saying to the latter "Another example of Naval ineptitude".

Reluctantly I had to reduce my crew by two and off we set again. This time things went all right and the soldiers settling down to paddling in fine style with the aid of occasional "one-two-threes" soon brought us off to the *Worcester* again.

Having already lent all my spare clothing to Commodore Stevenson I had to fall back on Commander Allison for a change and I emerged from his cabin wearing an ancient pair of grey flannel trousers, dirty white gym shoes and no pants. Luckily it was fairly warm even at night, though at times I did feel rather lightly clad about the legs.

May 31

It was about 2230 when I got aboard the *Worcester* which was slowly filling up with troops and I remained there till 0100. By that time she was full up and I sent her back to Dover and transferred to the *Express*. Earlier in the day I had asked for a ship with two lines of W/T communication and had been told that *Keith* was detailed and was due at 2000. She did not appear and I remained for the rest of the night in *Express* which gradually filled with troops.

By this time I had been off the beaches for 24 hours and they had seemed very full ones. I don't know when I ate or slept though I have a recollection of lying down in the *Hebe* for an hour, and of trying to sleep sitting down on the bridge of the *Express* leaning against some instruments with very sharp corners.

The picture as I saw it then was briefly this: There were tens of thousands of men on or near the beaches and in and around Dunkirk – no-one seemed able to say how many. The rearguard were to be withdrawn at midnight the next night, i.e., 24 hours ahead, they were the best troops and must be got off. Dunkirk itself was the only place where rapid embarkation could take place and a large proportion of the troops were coming down to La Panne and Braye, 10 and 5 miles away from Dunkirk.

At the beaches the only boats available except for pontoons and a very few local boats were ships' boats which went away with their ships or were crewless if left. In many cases they had to pull in as ships' motor boats were often out of action, and towage was badly needed. Embarkation depended entirely on fair weather – an onshore wind of any force would have stopped embarkation completely.

I had stressed the vital necessity for more shallow draught boats and crews and knew that steps were being taken at home to do all that was possible.

During the day French destroyers had been coming in by the Northern passage and channel and had been fired at from the shore. They went into Dunkirk and loaded at the West quay. Otherwise no French ships seemed to be there.

Destroyers, minesweepers, paddlers and all manner of craft were arriving, loading and leaving the beaches and Dunkirk continuously, but there were often periods when no ships were at one place or another and loading had to wait.

Bombing of ships and beaches had so far been spasmodic – the day had been overcast, visibility was not good and you could not see from La Panne to Dunkirk. The sound of fighters out of sight overhead seemed to account for our freedom from air attack.

A report of aircraft dropping mines one mile north of La Panne was received at 0400 and planes frequently passed close overhead during the dark hours. With the dawn a wind from the N.W. sprang up right on the beaches, and when it was light many boats could be seen capsized or breached to and high and dry on the beach, including one at least of the local boats which carried a lot of men and could get close inshore. It was not a cheering sight and as the day aged the sky overhead cleared and visibility improved. We watched the sky anxiously for the protection of haze but it remained clear all day.

At 0730 I made contact at last with *Keith*. *Express* was by that time fully loaded and left for Dover as soon as I had transferred to *Keith*. Here I found that a flag had been procured and it was flown on my arrival on board; up till then I had used a red ensign to indicate which ship I was in.

As had been my intention with *Hebe*, *Keith* did not embark any troops and I moved up and down the coast in her doing what I could to keep ships distributed off the beaches and a flow of ships into Dunkirk. A signal made by me at 1035 gives a good picture of the conditions:-

"To V.A. Dover. Majority of boats broached to and have no crews. Conditions on beach are very bad due to freshening on-shore wind. Only small numbers are being embarked even in daylight. Under present conditions any large-scale embarkation from beach is quite impracticable. Motor boats cannot get close in. Consider only hope of embarking any number is at Dunkirk. Will attempt to beach ship to form a lee to try and improve conditions."

343

From V.A. Dover came a signal urging the importance of using the beaches as long as possible, and to emphasise the situation I made a further signal at 1105 to say:-

"Dunkirk our only real hope. Can guns shelling pier from Westward be bombed and silenced."

The successful use of Dunkirk depended on our being able to put ships alongside the Eastern breakwater and it was my constant fear that this might be so accurately shelled as to render it untenable.

I also signalled to the shore urging movement towards Dunkirk and as a result troops could be seen moving slowly westward.

From seaward, everything that happened on the beach could be clearly seen. Bodies of men marched along – some in good order, others in groups and knots. At one time a battalion in perfect order marched down through a winding road from the dunes to the shore and I was told later that it was the Welsh Guards, but I am not certain that this was so.

It must not be thought that embarkation from the beaches ceased – all the time slowly men came off and ships filled and left, but the largest numbers came from Dunkirk itself.

Commencing the day before and continuing on this Friday the army had been driving lorries down the beach to form a sort of barricade and breakwater. At Braye the R.E. had planked a gangway and made a handrail on these lorries so that motor boats could go alongside. Unfortunately the line ran straight out to sea and as the wind was directly on shore the breakwater gave very little shelter – still it did help.

During the forenoon I made contact again with Commodore Stevenson who by now had completely lost his voice. I sent him over to some paddle minesweepers which were off Braye to get one beached to act as a breakwater. This he eventually did and the next day she was high and dry at daylight. I do not know to what extent she was of use – the trouble being that no ship was long enough to cover the distance the tide ran out, and so could only be of value for part of the tide.

The *Hebe* returned at 1000 with Captain Bush and the plan for the embarkation that night. Briefly the plan was this:-

Large numbers of boats were now being sent over in tow of tugs and all manner of vessels. They were due to start arriving at 1500 and these boats were to be <u>kept</u> for the use of the rearguard for whom the embarkation scheme was planned.

To take the troops 11 sloops were being collected and were to rendezvous and proceed in company, their arrival being timed for 0130 on the 1st. They were given berths in which to anchor in three batches, one batch off each of the embarkation beaches.

A feature of this plan which I felt to be impracticable was that the small craft were not to be used except for the rearguard. It was asking too much to think that when our crying need was for inshore boats any such could possibly be held idle while so many men were on the beaches with ships ready waiting to bring them off.

The actual development of this plan was very different and the results will be told later.

After discussion with Captain Bush I sent *Hebe* up to La Panne with orders to be there at 1800 to receive Lord Gort whom Stevenson was to bring off. I intended to be there myself but was concerned to have a second string in case of mischance.

There was some shelling of the beaches during the day, but in most cases the shells landed on the dunes which had a fairly steep scarp and protected the beach. This shelling was principally to the westward of Braye and at one time a French battery 2 or 3 miles out of Dunkirk on the top of the dunes but close to the sea received a lot of attention.

About 1330 as I was returning to the eastward *Hebe* signalled that she had been shelled off La Panne at 1200 and had had to move westward a couple of miles. Later at 1430 I went up in *Keith* off La Panne to see if the battery could be shelled. As soon as we got there, shells began to fall and got gradually closer until I judged it wisest to move out of range. It was not essential to be so far east and there was nothing to be seen of the battery. The fire was being directed by an observation balloon away over by Nieuport which was plainly visible. I asked for it to be shot down, aircraft came over apparently for the purpose and at times it was hauled down but always reappeared. The shell bursts were fairly heavy and appeared to be 6 or 8-inch and they fell in salvoes of four.

Owing to the shelling of the anchorage at La Panne and the difficulty it might cause later in the day I urged Lord Gort to embark as soon as possible, but he would not leave before the time that he had arranged.

Soon after, I moved down to Dunkirk so as to be on the spot when the boats arrived. On the way a terrific air battle took place overhead and it seemed to go against us. I saw three Spitfires shot down, one went inland over the dunes, still under control, one came down towards the sea at a fairly gentle angle and when only one hundred feet or so up the pilot seemed to be pulled out by his parachute and came down in the sea with his parachute open – the plane went on for quite a way and then flew into the water. The third pilot baled out a good way up and came down a couple of miles away. An M.T.B. and a motor boat in sight went off to try and pick them up and the Captain of the M.T.B. told me later that the pilot they got to was shot to pieces and they salved his parachute for identification purposes. I am afraid the other was not found.

I waited anxiously off Dunkirk for the arrival of the boat tows and while I waited, came a signal from V.A. Dover to say that the Army wanted to start embarkation at 2000 instead of 0100. I replied saying that the boats had not arrived and the sloops would not be there then but that I would do my best. To anticipate – this had an unfortunate effect, because, as the sloops intended for the beaches could not be there in time I had to keep destroyers, minesweepers and other craft off the beaches which would otherwise have been sent in to Dunkirk during the night. As a result though many were embarked from the beaches very few ships went into Dunkirk where men were already waiting and full use of it was not made.

It was always impossible for me to do more than deal with the situation of the moment. I did not know what ships were coming or when – except for the pre-arranged plan of the sloops. Nor was it possible for Dover to give me much information. Ships got back there, unloaded, and were off again, the stream was constant but irregular and it was not possible to see any way ahead. My policy was always to keep only sufficient ships off the beaches and send all the others into Dunkirk, but the situation changed continually. When I was off La Panne I could not watch the other end of the line – I wanted to be in several places at once.

The first of the boat tows was due at 1500 but did not appear till a couple of hours later. I can well remember the first, a tug with what looked like half a dozen dinghies in tow. She was preceded by some useful motor yachts which came in company.

I could not wait off Dunkirk as I was anxious to get away up to La Panne for Lord Gort, so I left Wynne-Edwards in a motor yacht to direct the tows as they arrived, and to order a large number of hoppers and other craft that were lying off the Western beaches to beach themselves on the rising tide so that men could embark.

The embarkation of Lord Gort produced some odd incidents. As already related I had arranged with Stevenson to bring him off at six o'clock. If the weather was too bad he was to go into Dunkirk and embark from there.

I had ordered *Hebe* to be off La Panne at that time and was going up there myself in *Keith*. In the meantime Dover had been busy and had sent over four M.T.B.s and M.A.S.B.s to get him. The signal informing me of this, like many others, never reached me. During the afternoon two M.T.B.s came to me and said that they were to embark a party from a point two miles west of La Panne. This quite baffled me and I thought that they must have been sent to fetch off some of the Naval landing party, but I realise now that the party concerned was the H.Q. Staff.

Anyway, shortly before 1800 I was approaching La Panne when *Hebe* signalled to me "General on beach abreast you", and there I saw a group at the water's edge with a couple of cars and some signalmen. *Keith*'s boats were at once sent in, but to my surprise Lord Gort was not in the first boat and I learnt that he was in *Hebe* already. Three trips were necessary to bring off his staff and a heavy air attack took place while this was going on. One plane tried to bomb the boats and they had a miraculous escape. I saw one bomb burst between them as they were loading up and the motor boat returned covered in grey mud.

Many air attacks were made at this time on the ships and beaches, and *Hebe* shot down a Heinkel. There was also a great increase in shell fire off Braye, where the *Clan Macallister* was a valuable decoy. She was hit and bombed several times and started burning again. I got the impression that these guns were firing blindly into this area, as shells fell near the *Clan Macallister* and over her but not among the ships loading which were some way inshore of her. Later, however, these ships did come under fire, and *Vivacious* reported she had been hit twice and had eleven casualties, and two or three hundred troops on board. I ordered her to go into Dunkirk and fill up there.

General Lees was the Senior Officer of the H.Q. Staff and I thought it would be a good education for him to see something of what the naval problem was, so I kept him on the bridge with me. As Lord Gort was in the *Hebe* I felt that he was safe, and as the *Hebe* was doing good work embarking troops I did not send her back to Dover with him at once. Therein perhaps I was wrong, as I had not realized the anxiety of the Government to have him safe and sound at home but had felt he would sooner the ship helped to bring off more men rather than that he should land a few hours earlier in England.

During the day I made a signal to all ships with instructions for supporting fire against enemy tanks and lorries on the beach. The critical place was likely to be at La Panne after the line was evacuated, and I intended to be there myself in *Keith* at daybreak the next morning. I also kept *Basilisk* free of troops for the same purpose.

The weather improved gradually and at 1700 I was able to signal:-
"Weather off beaches now good. Many more boats should come into use again as tide rises. General movement of troops westward towards Dunkirk. No petrol supply yet and many boats are getting short off La Panne and Braye. Movement from Dunkirk continues. Great air activity."

Actually drifters with petrol arrived not long after at 1815.

After embarking the Headquarters Staff I returned to Dunkirk to see how the boat situation was getting on. There I found Wynne-Edwards who had been doing good work, and I saw for the first time that strange procession of craft of all kinds that has become famous – tugs towing dinghies, lifeboats and all manner of pulling boats – small motor yachts, motor launches, drifters, Dutch scoots, Thames barges, fishing boats, pleasure steamers. As the tows of boats appeared they were told to which beach they should go, and I was particularly anxious that there should be sufficient at La Panne which was farthest off. I directed several tows to go on to La Panne, telling them it was ten miles up the coast, and shortly after, as the light was failing, I decided to leave Wynne-Edwards in an M.A.S.B. to direct the remaining tows and go on up to La Panne myself.

Off Braye I saw what I had feared, that the tows I had ordered to La Panne were stopping at Braye and I arrived there just in time to warn *Codrington*, who was off Braye, to send them on further. I had General Lees on the bridge and I remember pointing out to him how easy it was to talk about distributing boats and craft at certain places along a ten mile stretch of coast, but that it was a very different thing to get it done in practice, in the dark, by craft which had not been there before and with no lights to help them. The inevitable tendency was to stop at the first place they came to where other craft were assembled.

However, in the end a pretty fair distribution was made and Wynne-Edwards, when he returned to me at about 2230, was able to tell me that there were a number of boats off La Panne.

It must have been on this evening that I saw two Transports go into Dunkirk and I was very nervous that they would be bombed. Just as it was getting dark they moved out and shortly after there came the sounds of very heavy bombing from that direction. I felt sick as I thought that these two ships were being attacked, but I learnt later that it was not so, and this bombing, I think, was from our own aircraft attacking batteries down the coast.

It was now dark and I remained off La Panne in company with *Hebe* and several other ships.

Once it was dark I did not feel that much could be done by moving about, so I stayed off a Panne during the night. I waited there wondering how things were going. Everything was black, ships and boats showed no lights though I had asked for a light to be shone seaward to guide boats inshore. So far as I knew the rearguard was falling back and it was a question whether it could get off before the Germans found out and could follow up. Shelling was continuous and by the sound some shells were falling among the ships at the anchorage.

What news I had was conflicting – a message from shore to say that thousands of men were waiting but no boats, messages from ships that their boats found no one on the beach. The truth of it was, I think, that the Germans had the range of the lorry breakwater and the beaches near it and they shelled them heavily. Boats went in there and found no one as the troops had moved further west clear of the shell fire. I do not know to this day what really took place there. Off shore one felt helpless, the ships and the boats were there and the troops ashore and one could do no more.

Aircraft passed close overhead flying down the anchorages and fairway, and *Malcolm* off Braye reported that a number of parachute mines had been dropped to westward of there and suggested that ships ought to leave by the Zuidcoote pass in the morning, as the passage to the West was so heavily mined.

The noise of M.T.B. engines could often be heard to seaward and eastward and added to my anxiety, though I thought they might possibly be our own patrol. About 2300 I received an urgent signal from Admiralty asking where Lord Gort was and why I had detailed the M.T.B.s sent for him to other work. As the M.A.S.B. had just returned with Wynne-Edwards, I sent it off at once to *Hebe* to collect Lord Gort. To my horror it came back almost at once to say that Lord Gort had just left *Hebe* in a motor launch. It was very dark and *Hebe* could not be seen though we knew where she was and I waited anxiously for the boat to arrive. Presently out of the dark a boat appeared and came alongside, still not the right one and I had a bad moment thinking of the possibilities of the boat getting lost. However, to my relief, after what appeared [to be] about half an hour, the right boat, in charge of Stevenson once more, found us at last. Apologising to Lord Gort for keeping him waiting so long, I transferred him to the M.A.S.B. and sent him off to Dover with General Lees.

June 1

My experience of the bombing the day before led me to request fighter protection at dawn though I had no doubt that this was already being arranged. At 0215 I heard that troops were moving Westward and came to the conclusion that embarkation at La Panne was no longer possible. *Malcolm* and *Harvester* which were off La Panne were ordered into Dunkirk in consequence.

I also made a signal telling ships to keep close to the fairway buoys as I hoped that they would thus avoid any mines which had been dropped in the channel. At 0235 I made the following signal to V.A. Dover and Admiralty:- "Yesterday ships off Braye were under fire. Today's shorter front will bring dangerous area Westward. For this reason and mining consider any beach work too costly and evacuation must be confined to Dunkirk. Small craft will be moved Westward at dawn."

To this V.A. Dover replied:- "While leaving this to your discretion it is essential that beaches should be used until found impossible."

My signal above was made before it was light but I had already pretty clear indications that La Panne was untenable and as it grew light about 0330 I anxiously looked ashore. The *Basilisk* was with me as I had kept her empty so as to be ready for any supporting fire against tanks or lorries along the beach. Up by La Panne the beach was deserted but for the lorry breakwater and scattered cars. The sea also seemed deserted unfortunately – the small boats had vanished, a few empty ones were drifting on the tide to the Westward. One or two motor launches were about and I told them to collect some of the boats adrift. Down off Braye there was a minesweeper ashore and also a paddle minesweeper. Ships were still loading off Braye and to the Westward and men were moving Westward along the beaches.

I moved down off Braye and hailed a tug which was on its way back with some soldiers on board and told her to go in and try to tow off the minesweeper. The Captain paid no attention and obviously was only concerned to get away. I finally trained a gun on him and told an R.N.V.R. Sub-Lieutenant who was on board to take charge, put the soldiers on board the *Sabre* who was nearby and go off to the help of the minesweeper. It was not nice to have to threaten these men who were really volunteers, but it had to be done. I could not risk ships and men for the sake of some volunteer's feelings and nothing else seemed to have any effect. The real trouble on this and another occasion later was that the tugs were told to go over with pulling boats in tow and load up and they regarded themselves as transports only. I was never informed of this or their orders and regarded them as tugs and for use as tugs.

All this time I had to move in waters which aircraft had been mining during the night, but I put my faith in the degaussing and also kept to the edge of the fairway when possible, and my faith was justified.

At 0400 it was misty with low clouds and I hailed these conditions with relief, but unluckily they did not last. Most of the ships were full. Those that were not I sent into Dunkirk for though there were still many men on the beaches, and some of the small boats were still there, the majority of small craft had disappeared back to England. Here again I did not realise that they had been sent over for the night and were making their way back as intended.

At 0625 I reported:- "Situation report at 0600 1st June. Troops are evacuating gradually to Dunkirk as Eastern beaches are untenable. I am directing all boats and small craft to vicinity and loading all ships at Dunkirk. More ships required. Heavy bombing on Dunkirk and fighter attacks on ships."

About this time I suddenly saw a Belgian fishing boat appear on the scene from seaward down the Zuidcoote pass. I was suspicious of her and ordered *Basilisk* to investigate. She turned out to be the first of a dozen such boats which shortly after appeared. They were on their way into Dunkirk to assist in the evacuation.

As the mists and clouds dispersed many aircraft appeared on the scene and fighters constantly came low over us. More often than not they were Spitfires, but our ships were not taking chances and nearly always opened fire indiscriminately on them. As this kept happening I hoisted 6 Flag – "Cease fire", and blew the siren to draw attention and try and stop the firing. In spite of this I can remember our own machine gun aft in *Keith* firing away regardless of the "cease fire" gong; once [they] started firing they could hear nothing.

Keith by this time was running very short of H.A. ammunition and had only about 30 rounds left for her H.A. gun. The 4.7's could be used for barrage fire only and had a limited elevation. I decided in consequence that I would shortly transfer my flag to *Basilisk* and send *Keith* into Dunkirk to fill up and return to Dover. Before I had time to do so a very heavy bombing attack developed, first of all in and around Dunkirk itself. I remember someone saying "a destroyer has blown up off Dunkirk" and I looked and saw a ship entirely enveloped in smoke just off the entrance. This was the *Ivanhoe*, but she did not blow up and a couple of hours later I saw her being towed back to Dover. In this attack the *Havant* was also sunk near the entrance.

I did not see the formation that made the attack, as we were some distance away and my attention was on the local situation. Not long after a compact formation of about 30 or 40 J.U.87's appeared from the South-West. Everybody opened fire on them and I watched the bursts which seemed to cover the whole area of the formation. As this happened the formation opened out and covered an ever-increasing area and the bursts spread out too. The fire seemed to be effective and I thought it was driving them away, so much so that I left the bridge for a moment. As I was returning I felt that speed had been increased and the ship was heeling over under helm. I got to the wheel house where everyone was lying down and the Quartermaster was steering by means of the lower spokes of the wheel. The ship heeled over suddenly and tea cups skidded across the deck. I had to hold on and tried to get up the bridge ladder, but there were a couple of men on it blocking the way. Then there were three loud explosions and the ship shook and heaved as if she was hit. All this took only a moment or two and by then I had got to the bridge. The ship was steaming fast and steering in circles and I heard that three planes had made a dive-bombing attack. One bomb had burst 10 yards astern and the helm had jammed. The others had missed close by. Orders were given for hand steering and before long the ship was under control again. The Captain gave orders for an anchor to be cleared away. I heard a man moaning abaft the compass platform and went to see what was the matter. One of the director's crew was holding on to the fingers of one hand and I could not see that he was hurt. I heard afterwards that he had a large wound in his thigh and was bleeding very badly, and he must have been hit by a stray splinter form one of the misses.

In a very short time three more planes came into the attack. I looked up as they dived at us, saw the bombs released and watched them as they fell. Everyone on the bridge was lying or crouching down but there was not much room and I could only find room to bend a bit.

It was an odd sensation waiting for the explosions and knowing that you could do nothing. When they came it was obvious that the ship had been hit. She shook badly and there was a rush of smoke and steam from somewhere aft. I made my way aft to see what the situation was and found a Chief Stoker shutting off stop valves in the steam pipe from the upper deck. He said that the Senior Engineer was lying dead on the floor plates. A man passed me carrying a wounded man on his shoulders from right aft on his way to the sick bay; his face was cut and covered in blood. Smoke and steam were coming out of the after funnel and the ship was listing to port, but I could see no signs of damage and learnt later that the bomb had gone down the funnel and burst below.

Thinking there was danger of fire the foremost torpedo tubes had been trained outboard and torpedoes were fired to get rid of them. As this was happening I looked over the starboard side and could see holes there just above water which must have been made by the bomb in the boiler room.

In the meantime the anchor had been let go as the ship could not steam and shortly after M.T.B. 102 came alongside. As I could do no good in the *Keith* I decided to leave her in the M.T.B., and my staff came down and joined me. The wounded man I had seen carried forward was also put on board.

In the M.T.B. I first went to two tugs which were not far away and sent them to the *Keith*, and then made for Dunkirk. As we left I saw another attack develop on her and once more watched the bombs dropping. One bomb hit her under the bridge on the port side. First there was a white splash and then the black smoke of the explosion.

When I last saw her she had a heavy list to port and her H.A. gun was still firing.

Keith was hit twice more and her men were taken off by a tug which also picked up men from the *Basilisk* and *Skipjack*, both of which were sunk at this time. Unluckily another plane landed a bomb in the tug too and sank her. About 30 men of the *Keith* were lost and the planes came down and bombed and machine gunned the men in the water.

On the way into Dunkirk we provided amusement for several dive-bombers, who bombed and machine-gunned the M.T.B. most of the way. The bombs could be seen coming and dodged in so small and handy a boat and we came to no harm.

We reached Dunkirk about 0915, and I landed with the intention of seeing General Alexander who was in command now that Lord Gort had left. He was, however, away, and so was Tennant, but I saw a Staff Officer and learnt from him that the plan was to continue the evacuation during the next night from the Western beaches and Dunkirk. The rearguard were to withdraw from their new positions at dawn and retire to Dunkirk. This meant continuing the embarkation for several hours of daylight, and the experience of that morning made me uneasy as I feared heavy losses under similar conditions.

The local headquarters on the pier looked much the same as when I had last seen it, except that now the open space was full of ambulances and wounded with doctors among them doing what they could.

While I was standing there I looked out to sea and I saw a destroyer pass the entrance in tow of a tug. I was told it was the *Ivanhoe*, and it was good to know she had a chance to reach home in safety, as she eventually did.

As all the ships which had not been sunk were now gone and there was no more I could do there, I decided to return and make contact with the V.A., Dover. I accordingly set off back in the M.T.B. and in spite of more bombing and machine-gunning reached Dover in safety at 1130.

It had seemed a pretty long day already when we made fast alongside the depot ship *Sandhurst*. While waiting there for a car, I was lent a clean shirt and a new pair of grey flannel trousers by Captain Gladstone to replace those, now rather the worse for wear, which I had borrowed from Allison in the *Worcester*. Soon a car arrived and drove me and my Flag Lieutenant up to the offices of the Vice Admiral, Dover. The others I dropped at the local hotel. I walked into the office, a rather untidy figure, and was greeted by Ramsay and Somerville. They had heard that *Keith* had been hit on the bridge and were pleasantly surprised at our safe return. After sending a telegram to my wife and arranging for a phone message to tell my Secretary to bring down a pair of trousers, shirt and shoes, I went up to the Vice Admiral's house in Dover Castle and had lunch with him. It was a lovely sunny day and the view over the channel seemed so peaceful, that, in spite of the large collection of ships, it was hard to believe that Dunkirk was so short a distance away.

After lunch I slept on Somerville's bed till about 1530 when I returned to the V.A.'s office to hear the plans for the night. The way led down a steep road with a fine views of the harbour and Straits and then by a tunnel into the hill below the castle. First down a steep slope with floor and walls of concrete, then into a wide passage through walls of chalk with layers of huge flints, dimly lit by an occasional lamp. This opened at the end into a large oblong chamber at right angles to the passage and divided up by boarding into a number of offices. Past these a narrow passage led to the end and the V.A.'s office. Here the chamber finished in a large window and door out on to a narrow railed-in platform on the sheer face of the cliff. Immediately below you looked down 300 feet into the chimney pots and gardens of houses on the foreshore, and beyond the harbour was spread out in clear view. No Naval Officer can ever have had a better view of his command.

One of the offices in this "casemate" as the chamber was called, was known as the "Dynamo Room", from the code word which had been given to the Dunkirk operation. Here the presiding genius was Captain Denny, who was responsible for the general details. With him there were about 20 or more Officers, soldiers, Naval Officers, Board of Trade and Sea Transport Officials, and the work they did was marvellous. They were controlling, organising, fuelling, supplying, not only men-of-war, but a variety of merchant vessels. Sometimes the crew of a merchant vessel would refuse to go to Dunkirk again – within a few hours the Sea Transport Officer had got another crew and the ship would sail. At Ramsgate, the Nore, and various other places besides Dover, ships and boats were collected and organised, but the head and control of the whole was in this room, where they worked continuously and tirelessly against time day and night.

Admiral Somerville had come down to assist Admiral Ramsey, and Captain Bisset to assist Captain Morgan, the Chief of Staff. This was absolutely necessary as at any moment in the day or night some decision might have to be made.

Here I went for information and to learn what was planned for the night. Briefly it was this:-

Embarkation was to take place between 2100 1/6 and 0330 2/6 and was to be from the 1½ miles of beach to the East of Dunkirk. For this large numbers of ships and small craft were being assembled and sent over. Personnel ships were to be sent into Dunkirk itself and to go alongside the pier. The Air Force were to concentrate their efforts between 1900 and 0700 over the period when ships would be on passage to and from Dunkirk.

The personnel ships were large fast passenger vessels of the cross-channel type which had been taken up for ferrying troops across to France. They were manned by their normal crews and had been going into the harbour and loading alongside the pier. They could carry large numbers, some as many as 3,000 men, and so were very valuable, but they were also large targets and were used with reluctance when bombing was probable, especially as several would only go into Dunkirk in daylight. This was now considered too dangerous, and in consequence Naval Officers were put on board to act as advisers to the masters and the crews were stiffened with seamen. For the rest of the evacuation they went in every night and did magnificent work.

Besides the personnel ships various other craft were to go into the harbour to load alongside, including French destroyers. The British ships were to use the East Pier where the British troops were and the French the West quay, where the French were.

If any large numbers were to come off from Dunkirk itself it was essential to be able to use the East Pier. This already had one gap in it made by the *King Orry*, but the gap had been bridged. I feared that the Germans would now shell this pier heavily and perhaps damage it or at any rate make it impossible to keep ships alongside. I accordingly asked if the R.A.F. could reconnoitre and report what the state of the pier was and whether it was being shelled. This was arranged and had an amusing sequel as will be told later. Before I returned to Dunkirk a report came back from the air reconnaissance giving an accurate description of the gap in the pier which we already knew about, but not a word as to whether it was being shelled.

It was arranged that I should go over in M.A.S.B. 10, one of the Motor Anti-Submarine Boats. These are large fast motor boats, rather like M.T.B.s, with a speed of 25 knots and armed with two twin machine guns and depth charges. A portable loud-speaker set was to be fitted in her, as I had found a similar set very useful in *Hebe* and *Express*.

In the afternoon my Secretary, Paymaster Commander Bailey, arrived down bringing with him some clothing which was very welcome, and I was able to feel respectable once more. I sent him back to London as there was nothing there for him to do.

I had arranged to leave Dover at 1700 and on my way down to the Naval Harbour I stopped in the town to buy a pair of pants and some food to take over with us. I picked up Wynne-Edwards and Norfolk at the hotel where they had managed to get a room and make up some of their lost sleep.

June 1, 1800
We clambered down an iron ladder at the Submarine base and across several boats to get on board M.A.S.B. 10. Here I found that a flag had been made for me out of a piece of cleaning cloth – the red stripe made one half of the cross and the other half and the balls had been added in red paint. With this flag flying we left the harbour on a lovely afternoon to the salutes of the ships we passed. The harbour was full of destroyers, sloops and minesweepers, many with signs of their strenuous time upon them – bent bows, holes and the evidence of bumps and collisions. Some were out of action altogether and all were enjoying the first few hours at rest in harbour that many of them had had for many days.

I think I put in an hour's sleep on the way over and I fancy that up till then I had had about 7 hours altogether in short snatches, but I felt quite fresh and fit all the same.

When we were some miles from Dunkirk we sighted two M.T.B.s coming towards us on the Port bow. They were not British and it seemed quite likely they were Germans. We had turned towards them but as I felt it was my business to get to Dunkirk and not get involved in a scrap with M.T.B.s I gave orders to go back to our course and go full speed. As we did so the others turned towards us and for a time it looked as if we could not avoid them, but we gradually drew away and they turned back to their former course. I think they must have been French as I don't fancy Germans would have left us alone.

The rest of the passage was without incident and we got into Dunkirk about 1900 and made fast alongside the shore end of the pier. From there I went to the "Bastion" which was the headquarters of the Army and the local French Naval and Military Command. From the foot of the pier it was a ten minutes' walk along a road which ran behind the old ramparts of the town facing seaward on the left hand. On the right were buildings and sheds, mostly roofless or damaged, that hid shipbuilding slips or shipyards. Mounted in one of the embrasures was a French field gun which was firing back over the town. The road was fairly clear but littered with lorries and cars the whole way, leaving little room to dodge others which careered along the road at intervals. Men straggled along the road and one Frenchman asked for directions, but there were very few troops to be seen as they were kept away on the beach behind the shelter of the wall except when ships were coming alongside.

The "Bastion" comprised several large earthworks and an open space, most of which was taken up with parked and battered cars.

French soldiers and marines stood about and guarded the entrances to various chambers inside the earthworks.

In one of these was the room which was Tennant's headquarters, and there I found him with General Alexander. It opened off a narrow dark passage and was lit by a single lamp – a bare small room about 10 feet by 8 feet. While I was there the lights went out and we waited in darkness for an air raid to pass. Then we discussed the situation. I told them what was arranged and heard with great relief that the French were holding a line in rear of ours and that the rearguard were to withdraw through this line which the French would continue to hold. After a drink with them I persuaded Tennant and Maund to come and have super with me in the M.T.B. As I came out of the door into daylight again I found my staff talking to Balfour, my proper Flag Lieutenant, who had been in Newcastle when I left London. He had followed me down to Dover and had then been sent off to Dunkirk the day after I left, with a W/T set and was looking out for the W/T and signal work there.

Back on the pier again I waited for Tennant who presently walked down. His tin hat had been decorated with the letters "S.N.O.", cut out of silver paper and stuck on with sardine oil – it looked very distinguished all the same. As we stood talking there a Lysander Army Co-operation plane came over very low and flew down the pier. It was fired at by several Bofors guns and Tennant said "I'm sure that damned fellow is a Hun – he has been flying over here all day". I then realised it was the plane sent over at my request to see if the pier was being shelled and felt rather sorry for the poor chap, though he seemed none the worse. I explained the situation and hoped I had calmed their fears.

After this excitement we returned to the M.A.S.B. and had some food. The party ashore had not had much to eat and the beer, fruit, some raisins and chocolate which I had brought over besides more ordinary food was much appreciated.

As we sat eating a figure in brown overalls suddenly appeared in the cabin saying "I am the sole survivor of the *Keith*". It was the Navigating Officer and he told how after the *Keith* was sunk most of the survivors were in a tug when she was hit by a bomb and also sunk. He had swum away and eventually got ashore whence he found his way to a battery on the dunes some distance outside Dunkirk. There he was given some clothes and he had then walked into Dunkirk. He thought that none of the others had been able to swim ashore. It gave me a great shock at the time, but fortunately it was not true as many men were picked up and only 3 Officers and 33 men were lost and 16 wounded.

Close to where my boat was made fast a drifter was moored to the pier; this was for Tennant's use, besides which he had a couple of decrepit old steamboats. The next day when I came in the drifter had been sunk where she lay, by a shell.

The Naval Party ashore consisted of about half a dozen officers and a number of men, used for berthing parties, messengers, signalmen, W/T ratings and so on. I fixed up with Tennant to collect some of them at 0200 but he would not leave himself and I remember his saying before we parted that night "Tomorrow we'll either be back in London, in a German prison or done for".

After leaving Tennant we went outside the harbour to meet the first ships arriving. It was about 2100 and beginning to get dark. The first ship was a sloop, followed by minesweepers, destroyers and tugs; they anchored off the beaches to the East of the pier and boats ferried men off. Before it got dark I had noticed 3 or 4 Thames barges anchored off the beach, they seemed to be deserted but men got off to them and away, and one barge was later met in mid channel full of soldiers who were trying to sail her home. A Naval Officer was put on board and she got back safely.

During the night I found that there were more ships lying off the beaches than could be loaded, and at the same time there was plenty of room at the pier, so I kept on the move between harbour and outside diverting ships from the beaches as necessary. Outside off the beaches there was not much to be seen except the shapes of darkened ships and an occasional boat full of men trying to find its parent ship. Actually the beaches were very heavily shelled but a lot of men came off in spite of it.

The pier was outlined against the glow of fires that were still burning somewhere to the Westward in Dunkirk, and the steady stream of men passing along it and the shapes of ships alongside were silhouetted against the glare. Inside the harbour there were numerous small craft passing up to the inner basins and navigation was always exciting. French T.B.'s came in and loaded alongside the West quay where, from the boat, the masses of French troops in orderly ranks with their characteristic helmets showed up against the fires beyond. There was the noise of continuous shelling which seemed to be concentrated on the beach and to Eastward of the pier, but inside the harbour the crack of bursting shells sounded very close and I often looked round in the expectation of splashes nearby but saw none. Shells were however falling inside the harbour and about midnight I saw two masts sticking out of the water with the masthead light still burning on one. It was a trawler which had just been sunk. There were casualties also in a destroyer alongside.

June 2

At 0200 as arranged we went up to the shore end of the pier to embark the base party. As we got alongside there was a violent outburst of shelling, which seemed to be very close to us, but the pier gave one a feeling of protection. There were no signs of the party so Wynne-Edwards went along to the dug-out and headquarters 200 yards away. I waited on the parapet for his return and watched the solid line of men making their way along the roadway to the pier. By this time they were Frenchmen who had cut into the flow of British troops by a converging route. As a result 5,000 British were held up or did not get off that night – instead a lot of French troops got away from the East pier in addition to those from the West quay.

Wynne-Edwards came back soon to say the party were on their way and at about 0245 we left the pier with the party on board.

By this time it was beginning to get light, and as the morning was very clear I decided to get the ships away at 0300 instead of 0330 as had originally been planned. Men were still coming down the pier, but it was no use running the risk of having ships sunk alongside and blocking the pier and harbour, so I reluctantly told ships to leave and followed the last out of harbour. This bare recital of events gives little idea of the conditions and background against which they took place. To me there were two contrasting aspects – darkness looking out to seaward, and landward dark silhouettes showing against the steady glow of fires and the occasional flash of bombs. To seaward lay the ships visible as dark blurs only, waiting off the harbour entrance for their turn to come in to the piers, looming up large and distinct as they drew near. Looking shoreward the whole town and harbour were shut in by a pall of smoke overhead, which was lit up by the glare of fires in several places inland. Against the glare the piers, harbour and town were sharply silhouetted, and on the piers and quays an endless line of helmeted men in serried ranks sometimes moving, sometimes stationary. The funnels and masts of ships showed clear as they lay alongside or went in and out of harbour, their hulls hidden and dark and invisible. There was not a great amount of noise, syrens [sic] hooted occasionally when ships moved, shells bursting with sharp cracks, distant crashes of bombs, machine-gun fire faintly heard and nearby at times when someone fired at a plane overhead, engines throbbing as a destroyer moved past, occasional orders and hailing of boats.

The French T.B.'s had an A.A. machine gun that fired a stream of bullets with coloured tracers, these and the ordinary tracers filled the sky with firework exhibitions in lovely curves of light.

The return to Dover gave me the chance to sleep but soon we slipped into the harbour and made fast alongside – broad daylight and a silent town asleep but the welcome sight of a car waiting for us. Up to the Offices for a few words with Somerville and then to the Admiral's house and a couple of hours on Somerville's bed. It was very convenient to have him on duty at that time of day leaving a vacant bed. I slept heavily and woke suddenly as two fellows came into my room – it was Berthon, Captain of the *Keith*, and his First Lieutenant. They were black with oil fuel and in the clothes they had been rescued [in] the day before but they had come to let me know they were safe. I looked at them only half conscious and dropped off to sleep again at once, with a feeling of thankfulness.

After a bath and breakfast and a few moments in the sun outside I felt fit for anything and made my way to the dungeon office again to discuss the next night's operation. There were still 5,000 of the B.E.F. to come and an unknown number of French, which was thought to be from thirty to forty thousand.

The plan was to use Dunkirk only, except for some French local craft which would embark from the beach immediately East of Dunkirk. The embarkation was to start at 2100 and go on till 0300 at which time blockships were to enter the harbour.

I had felt the previous night that more ships could have used the pier had they been available and I had sent additional ships there from off the beaches into the harbour. To make full use of the pier this night a programme was worked out of personnel ships, destroyers, minesweepers and sloops coming in at half-hourly intervals to different berths so that three or four ships should be alongside the East Pier continuously. Denny thought this impossible and liable to result in confusion but a scheme was got out which provided a carrying capacity of 37,000 men in addition to those that would get off in the small craft. I also asked for a couple of fast boats to act as runners for me, and two – I believe from the *Vernon* – were told off.

Besides the large ships there were tugs, scoots, drifters and all manner of small craft going over as well – some of them to lay off and be loaded by smaller boats and others to go right up the harbour past the large ship berths.

There was a large number of wounded in Dunkirk and orders had had to be given that fit men were to be got away in preference, as apart from anything else, embarking wounded would have taken up too much valuable time. In consequence it was decided to try and get some of the wounded away in daytime in Hospital ships in the hope that the Germans would respect them. Two were accordingly sent over but one was bombed and sunk and the other was so badly damaged that she had to return. The wounded, except those who could walk and get down to the piers, had to be left behind.

I went over again in M.A.S.B. 10, accompanied by Somerville and Goodenough and on the way we had a mild bombing attack and also picked up three Belgian soldiers who had got about half way across in a pulling boat. They were not too pleased at being taken back to Dunkirk but were later decanted into a destroyer.

Just outside the harbour we met one of the two fast motor boats in charge of a Sub-Lieutenant. He told us that he had started over with the other boat but they had both been machine-gunned and the other boat disabled. Commander Clouston who was in it had told him to go on and leave him. Clouston and his boat were not seen again and I had to send the survivor back as it had only one engine and was too badly damaged to be if use.

We got over about 2030 and went in and picked up General Alexander and his staff. I transferred them to a destroyer shortly after, and in her General Mansergh was later killed by a machine-gun bullet from a plane when close to Dover. Tennant and the last of his party left in an M.T.B. as soon as the last of the British troops had gone.

The outer part of the East Pier was not built solid but was of concrete piles through which the West going tide set. This, coupled with a fresh Easterly wind, made it very difficult for ships to get alongside until the tide turned about 2300. We used the M.A.S.B. to push one destroyer in and tried to get other small craft to do likewise. By this time the French had come to life and a large number of their small craft of every sort, size and description filled the narrow harbour. To make matters more complicated the M.A.S.B.'s clutch went wrong and she could not go astern. Turning in that harbour became most dangerous in consequence as boats of all sorts bore down on us from both directions. By 2200, however, in spite of the tide and wind, 4 destroyers had got away and the last of the B.E.F. was clear soon after.

Then there was a long pause. The French should have followed our men on the East Pier but they did not appear. I could see crowds of behelmetted figures at the West quay and there seemed a scarcity of French ships, so I sent two personnel ships in there. One was the *Royal Sovereign* who was handled magnificently, turning and going alongside bows out. Another was the *Rouen*, a French cross-channel steamer. I don't know what happened to her but in getting away she got broadside on to the wind and grounded just to the Westward of the quay; there she lay showing up clearly against an oil fire behind her. The tide was falling and I had visions of her still there in daylight – full of men and

361

a sitting target for bombers. I went outside the harbour and sent in a tug to try and help her but the tug drew too much water and could not get near. I also sent a lifeboat to her to try and get men away. The men, I think, were got away, but she remained there until she floated off with the next tide in daylight and then returned in safety.

June 3

This was a most disheartening night; for some reason the flow of French troops to the East Pier stopped for some hours. One report said they were held up to make a counter attack, but to us there were ships waiting to be filled and no one appearing it was most exasperating. Even when the French did come it was almost impossible to get them to the ships at the end of the pier, they all wanted to get into the first one they came to, and the pier was so narrow that they blocked the way to any ship beyond. One ship lay 3½ hours at the end berth waiting for men. At last they started to trickle down but by then it was obvious that many of the ships waiting outside could not be used and I had to send back empty two personnel ships, three destroyers and several Fleet sweepers.

As it started to get light the French came down faster and as the time of leaving got closer I was hailing them to make them run down the pier. Even then they were quite hopeless. I can remember seeing men, who were on their way to a ship that was alongside the end of the pier, turn and run back down the pier because they saw another ship coming alongside further in.

Again I ordered the ships to leave at 0300, and I waited to see the last go, and to hail the two blockships as they passed up the harbour shortly after, accompanied by M.T.B.s who were to take off the crews.

One of these ships was sunk as arranged across the channel but the other shifted as she was blown up and lay up and down the channel leaving a clear passage. Either this night or the next one block ship was blown up on a magnetic mine just outside the harbour. After seeing the blockships pass up the harbour the M.A.S.B. took us back to Dover where we arrived in time to have a couple of hours rest before breakfast.

This had been a very disappointing night and only 24,000 were embarked. Many more could have been taken but for the long pause when the flow of men to the East Pier ceased for some hours. After the Naval ratings had left at 2300 there was also difficulty in getting ships berthed as the French did nothing to replace our men, although the Port was the headquarters of a French Naval Command and there was always a considerable number of French marines in evidence.

In the Vice Admiral's office I learnt that there was to be another embarkation that night but that this really would be the end. Each night had been thought to be the last and then each day the ships had been asked for one more effort. By this time many of the Commanding Officers and men were at the limit of their endurance and the Vice Admiral did not feel he could order ships to go over. Accordingly a signal was made asking what ships would be ready and able to go, and finally 10 transports, 6 destroyers, 8 minesweepers, 4 paddle sweepers, 2 corvettes, 2 yachts, 1 gunboat, 10 drifters, 5 scoots and 1 tug were collected. Besides these there was a large number of small craft and boats as before.

For this night the time was cut down by an hour to between 2230 and 0230. The small craft were to go right up to the quays and docks of the inner harbour, the transports, destroyers and 4 paddle sweepers were to use the East Pier and the remainder the West Quay. Arrangements were also made to bring off the French Admiral in M.A.S.B. No. 7 as his own M.T.B.s were said to be out of action.

Naval pier and berthing parties for the East Pier under Commander Buchanan were to go over early in H.M.S. *Whitshed*. I went over in M.T.B. 102, the same that had brought me away from the *Keith*. This boat had a cruising engine which was very useful when we were moving about inside in the confined waters of the harbour, which were crowded with small craft. On the way we passed other ships who had started earlier, and in the distance they seemed to be having a hot time from an air attack.

I got over at 2200 to find the harbour swarming with French fishing craft and vessels of all sorts. They were yelling and crowding alongside the East Pier which was already thick with French troops. At one time it looked as if they would get in the way of the Transports and destroyers which were on their way, but I managed to get them to go on up the inner harbour and out of the way in time.

Whitshed arrived at 2220, but owing to a fresh Easterly wind and the West going tide she could not get alongside the pier where there was no one who could be persuaded to assist by taking a line. She was soon followed by *Sabre* and *Kingfisher*. The *Kingfisher* was sent into the West quay but the others were backing and filling in the narrow harbour trying to get alongside and being continually set off. The situation was not made easier by the stream of French craft coming in or leaving the harbour and the seamanship displayed was really magnificent. A small handy tug to push them in would have been invaluable. I could not use the M.T.B. for this as a similar attempt on a previous night had put the M.A.S.B.'s engine out of action.

About 2300 I took some of the berthing party from the *Whitshed* to land them on the pier but had great difficulty in getting alongside even in the M.T.B. Finally, however, they got ashore, and by 2330 three personnel ships, *Whitshed* and *Sabre* were alongside. When it is remembered that there was a wreck alongside the pier itself, a wrecked trawler off the end of the piling on the West side of the up harbour channel and block ships sunk up this channel, the task if these ships manoeuvring to get alongside against the wind and tide could hardly have been more difficult. Luckily the tide was high. In the meantime, Scoots, French T.B.s and Fleet sweepers had been making there way into the West Quay and the embarkation from there was going well.

The hold up at the East Pier had however thrown out the programme of ships entering the harbour and there was great congestion in the entrance. I had to stop ships coming in at times so that other ships could get out in safety, but there seemed never a moment when ships were not on the move in the dark, in waters that were alive with small craft, and the handling of the ships in these congested waters was marvellous. It was hardly to be expected however that there would be no collisions, and *Kingfisher* was hit and badly holed by a French trawler. She transferred her troops to a trawler as her D.G. cable was cut and there were plenty of magnetic mines about. Then she was sent back to Dover.

June 4

At 0100 there came a report of 6 enemy M.T.B.s proceeding South West from off Ostend. This was rather disconcerting news with several transports, destroyers and other craft lying stopped off the entrance to the harbour. There were other troubles as well, for the *Kellett* reported at 0140 that she was aground. The tide was falling and she could be seen right up against the Western breakwater. Luckily a lifeboat managed to tow her stern clear and she got afloat again. It was then too near daylight to risk keeping her.

The West quay was occupied and it would be some time before she could be loaded. By then so slow a ship would be exposed to great danger on her return as she might not be able to get back while our fighter patrols were operating. I therefore sent her back empty. The flow of men on the East Pier was better than on the preceding night but there were bad pauses. The first group of personnel ships and destroyers got away by 0100 and were quickly replaced with others. All the time there were crowds of men at the West Quay and it was obvious that more ships could be used there, so at 0145 I led a large personnel ship, which did not know the way, into this berth. As soon as she was clear, another – the *Royal Sovereign* – went in and stayed there until 0300 – half an hour after the time intended.

At the East Pier the *Malcolm* left with 1,000 men on board at 0245 and the *Express* left at 0300, after I had taken off Cdr. Buchanan and the berthing party who were in her. When she left there were still about 200 men on the East Pier and these were brought off by the *Shikari* who came in later escorting the last two block ships. Of all the ships sent over only one paddler and the *Kellett* were not used. I had some difficulty over the French Admiral. The M.T.B. sent for him had failed to find him and he finally came away in one of his own M.T.B.s.

The light was growing and the harbour was empty but for the two block ships and an attendant M.T.B. as I left it for the last time and set off for Dover. On the passage it was foggy but we found our way. At Dover the first ship to come in out of the fog was the *Sabre* whose compass was wrong and who had gone over to Dunkirk in company with another ship on that account.

I do not know the exact figure but I think that at least 30,000 men were embarked on this night in about 3½ hours, which is a sufficiently remarkable figure. Even so a number of men were left behind and I once heard that there were still 30,000 French there. The total evacuated amounted to 330,000 altogether.

During the forenoon I paid a visit to the office where the Vice Admiral was trying to get out some quick report on the operation and the atmosphere was one of comparative relaxation after the tenseness of the past week. Ships were being sent back to their home ports to give 48 hours leave, and in the meantime they were having the first rest they had had for many days. I made arrangements to return to their proper owners various articles of clothing I had acquired and returned to London with my staff by an afternoon train. The French Admiral and a General also travelled up by this train but kept severely apart from one another. I slept in the train a good part of the way and woke to the thought of returning to my office desk in London – it was rather like waking up from a dream. Curiously enough I slept that night for no longer than my normal hours and never felt any lack of sleep in the least; I found, however, that I had lost 7 lbs. in weight.

SENIOR NAVAL OFFICER DUNKIRK
Captain William Tennant RN

Captain William Tennant's account is dated 7 June 1940:

I have the honour to forward herewith my Report of Proceedings in the Dunkirk area between the 27th May, 1940, and the 2nd June, 1940. The

Report has been made up in the form of a Daily Log with the more important signals included …

By good fortune the mission entrusted to me in the first place by the Admiralty and ultimately by you was completed by 2300 on 2nd June, and I would like to record herewith that the chief factors responsible for this successful conclusion were: a) The ready help we always received from Dover whenever asked for. b) The fearlessness and splendid seamanship of destroyers and minesweepers and nearly all the personnel ships coming to the pier. c) The help of Rear-Admiral Wake-Walker in distributing ships between the pier and the beaches. d) The magnificent work of the Officers and men, and particularly of the pier party who worked with little rest for 7 days. Of these, no one is more deserving of praise than Commander Clouston.

SUNDAY, 26th MAY, 1940

P.M. I was given details of arrangements being made for the provision of shipping for the evacuation of the B.E.F. from Dunkirk and the beaches to the Eastward thereof, by Captain Jeffery, and at 6 p.m. I was ordered by V.C.N.S. to proceed to Dunkirk to take control of the naval shore embarkation parties. The officers and men of my party for the pier and beaches proceeded direct to Dover.

I left London 8.35 p.m. for the Nore, and explained the Admiralty plan for embarkation to the Commander-in-Chief. I continued my journey to Dover early next morning where I received my final instructions from V.A. Dover. After going through the plan for embarkation with him I left Dover in H.M.S *Wolfhound* at 1345 with a naval party consisting of 12 officers and 160 ratings, plus signal staff. The weather was fine and clear.

We proceeded North of the minefield – a voyage of some 90 miles – and about half way over the first dive bombing attack took place. These attacks continued at about half hour or 40-minute intervals until we reached Dunkirk at about 1800. There were several very near misses but only minor damage was done to the ship. This was an unpleasant introduction to the war zone, and dive bombing was certainly more alarming afloat than ashore, as we were soon to discover. On reaching Dunkirk we turned and proceeded alongside in the middle of a very heavy bombing attack.

I disembarked my party, divided them up into sections and told the officers in charge of each section to scatter them round the port to make them less vulnerable to bombing attacks, while I proceeded to the Bastion Naval Headquarters to investigate the local situation.

The town was heavily on fire, the streets being littered with wreckage of all kinds, and every window was smashed. Great palls of smoke from the oil depots and refineries enveloped the docks and town itself. On our way up to the Bastion we had to take shelter from two more raids by enemy bombers, the bombs from the last of which fell unpleasantly close. There were a number of British troops in the town and we passed a good few dead and wounded in the streets – evidently the victims of these air raids.

I held a meeting with Brigadier Parminter, Colonel Whitfield, Area Commandant, and Commander Henderson, B.N.L.O. After this meeting the pier and beach parties were at once organised, told off and dispersed.

At 1900 I took over as S.N.O. Dunkirk.

2005. The following signal made to V.A. Dover: "Port continuously bombed all day and on fire. Embarkation possible only from beaches east of harbour. Send all ships there. Am ordering *Wolfhound* to load there and sail." V.A. Dover had intended to keep a destroyer in Dunkirk as W/T link, but I decided on arrival that this was not possible so ordered *Wolfhound* to sail.

NIGHT OF 27th MAY

Signal 1958/27 to V.A. Dover: "Please send every available craft to beaches East of Dunkirk immediately. Evacuation tomorrow night is problematical."

The naval party were spread out along the beach to act as police.

Troops in the district were directed to the beach and ordered to disperse along the sands so as to afford smallest possible targets for enemy planes.

It was originally decided to embark a small proportion from the East Pier and the rest from the beaches by lighters or barges. The pier method, however, proved so effective as regards speed and order that it was used exclusively, parties of 50 men coming along the beaches to the pier and embarking.

Due to adequate air protection there was comparatively little enemy attack on the area. During the night there were probably 6000 men embarked and cleared.

DAY OF TUESDAY, 28th MAY

Commenced embarkation of B.E.F. from end of Eastern Mole. The Germans were contenting themselves with bombing the town and port.

Situation Report 0935/28: "There are 2000 men on Dunkirk beach and 7000 men in sand dunes for whom I have had no ships. They are now in need of water and Army cannot supply. Unlimited numbers are falling back on this area and situation will shortly be desperate."

The embarkation was continued throughout the day but few ships arrived except destroyers. The enemy air action was again slight due to adequate air protection and also due to the fact that a heavy pall of smoke from the burning town covered the operation most of the day – the only attacks that occurred were those when our aircraft were some distance off at the further points of their patrol. During the morning three shells fired from an enemy battery Southwest of Dunkirk landed near the embarkation point, but did no damage.

Signal 0840 to V.A. Dover: "Evacuation practicable. Vessels urgently required."

In the meantime some destroyers and small craft, including some Dutch Skoots, had arrived off Bray beaches, and I sent an M.T.B. down there to supervise the embarkation arrangements. I ordered the Dutch Skoots to anchor as close to the shore as possible and the destroyers to send all their boats to ferry the troops between the shore and the Skoots. As soon as the scoots were full they went alongside the destroyers to discharge their troops and then returned to their position near the beach. In this way we were able to get some 4000 men away during the afternoon and evening. This operation was continued through the night and it was estimated that a further 3000 men were embarked. On her return the M.T.B. was sent home as she was running short of fuel.

At 1420 heavy bombing on Bray took place and I ordered more troops to march to Dunkirk. During daylight hours probably 12000 troops were embarked from the Eastern Mole.

At 1725 the following signal was made to Admiralty: "Suggest magnetic minesweeping of channel being used from Dunkirk is advisable and preferably at night."

[At] 1835 signal made. Signal sent pressing for all possible shipping whatever their "breed" be sent for troops during dark hours.

NIGHT OF 28th MAY
Evacuation from the Eastern Arm proceeded steadily, embarkation being at average rate of 2000 an hour. Enemy air action was slight due to our air protection but there was some shelling from the same point as during the day. There were a good number of ships throughout the night and at times they exceeded the inflow of troops.

The port was now undergoing bombardment and a situation report was sent at 2245/28 as follows:

"French General appreciation is that situation in port tomorrow will continue as for today. Provided aircraft fighters adequate, embarkation can proceed full speed. French General assures me no German guns at Gravelines Beacon and that area is clear of Germans. Possibly you will consider further test of the West Channel. French have taken over Belgian line in the vicinity of Nieuport. German guns to Southeast are now shelling Dunkirk but so far of little matter. Fighter protection has been invaluable and bombing only sporadic. Please inform me for C. in C. B.E.F. total number of men now evacuated. Rear personnel, 3 corps, now reaching the beach. Please pass to War Office."

DAY OF WEDNESDAY, 29th MAY

0630. Transport *Mona's Queen* mined and sunk two miles East of Dunkirk pier. Very heavy explosion.

Situation Report 0709/29 from S.N.O. Dunkirk: "No enemy interference at present. Embarkation going at 2000 an hour. This can be kept up provided supply transport is maintained. Swell prevents use of beach. All ships to Dunkirk. Enemy air attack would be disastrous. Maximum fighter protection essential. Passenger transport mined and sunk about 2 miles East of Dunkirk Pier Light."

At 1001 made Situation Report as follows: "Embarkation is going on well. Enemy is leaving us alone. The situation ashore is obscure and ominous. I have sent Captain Bush by M.T.B. with an appreciation. There is little food or water in Dunkirk. These should be sent as soon as possible, also a staid force for control of traffic. Armies are unable to help or organise anything. Keep on sending any ships. Cannot West Channel be used? A good Medical Officer with Staff should be despatched. Army unable to provide."

Embarkation proceeded at rate of 3 to 4,000 an hour. Troops were now consisting mainly of the Fighting Corps, all the non-combatant troops in the area having been evacuated. The display of this Corps Troops was noticeably superior – previous detachments had reached the embarkation point in a straggling manner with scarcely any semblance of order. The Corps Troops marched in formation along the beaches, quickly scattering during an air raid, and reforming and continuing afterwards. It was this order which enabled such a high rate of embarkation to be maintained.

At 1200 I proceeded with Brigadier Parminter by Motor Boat to La Panne to G.H.Q. to report on the difficult situation vis-à-vis the French over evacuation. When on board *Express* I made a signal to the Admiralty and to V.A. Dover giving an appreciation of the situation as follows: "Bombing of beaches and Dunkirk pier has now commenced without opposition from fighters. If they hit Dunkirk pier embarkation will become very jammed. Beach at La Panne covered with troops congregating in large numbers. Very slow embarkation taking place from Eastern Beach. The French Staff at Dunkirk feel strongly that they are defending Dunkirk for us to evacuate, which is largely true. To continue evacuation my appreciation is as follows – "The perimeter must be strongly held, food and stores immediately provided, and bombing of Dunkirk pier must be prevented.' There is no other alternative evacuation to take off more than a tithe of men now on each beach before they are bombed continuously."

In Dunkirk itself we were left in comparative peace by enemy aircraft until the evening. V.A. Dover's 1906/29 received, reading: "Evacuation of British troops to continue at maximum speed during the night. If adequate supply of personnel vessels cannot be maintained to Dunkirk East Pier destroyers will be sent there as well. All other craft except Hospital Carriers to embark from beach which is extended from one mile East of Dunkirk to one mile east of La Panne. Part 2 follows."

Part 2 received as follows: "Whole length is divided into 3 equal ports referred to as La Panne, Bray, Malo, from East to West with a mile gap between each port. La Panne and Bray have troop concentration points each end and in middle; Malo at each end. These points should be tended by inshore craft. Pass this message by V/S to ships not equipped W/T, as opportunity offers. Destroyer at Dunkirk pass to S.N.O. Dunkirk."

This was exactly what was required.

In the evening a series of fierce air attacks were made on the Eastern Arm. These resulted in H.M.S *Grenade* being bombed while embarking troops. It looked for the moment as though she might sink and block the entrance to the harbour but a trawler and drifter were sent to assist her and managed to guide her into a pocket to the Westward of the main channel. She burned fiercely for some hours and eventually blew up with a loud explosion.

A trawler was also bombed and sank in the channel about 50 yards from the East Pier about two cables in from the Eastern Lighthouse.

The transport *Fenella* was sunk while loading at the outside extremity of the Eastern Arm. She was practically fully loaded but the troops were transferred to another ship with very little loss.

A troop transport, *Crested Eagle*, was bombed and rendered unusable. She drifted down both towards Bray where she ran aground, A "J" Class destroyer was bombed off the beaches but was taken in tow by another destroyer.

NIGHT OF MAY 29th
Enemy activity was reduced during the night, only two bombing attacks being made. It was intended to recommence embarkation

from Eastern Arm under cover of darkness but apparently due to some misunderstanding the only ships that arrived were 4 trawlers and a yacht. Consequently a great opportunity was missed. Probably 15000 troops could have been embarked had the ships been forthcoming.

As a result of the bombing of the Mole referred to above, the pier itself was hit by a dive-bomber and severely damaged, but a brow was put in place which permitted the passage of troops.

In reply to V.A. Dover's 2057/29, asking whether the harbour was blocked, I replied at 2150: "No. Hope to get a good move on tonight but it is doubtful if much more can be done during daylight hours."

Apparently incorrect information as to the blocking of Dunkirk Harbour had been telephoned by Commander Dove from La Panne. This unfortunate incident reduced the shipping entering during the night to a minimum.

Passenger transport *King Orry* had been damaged by a near miss p.m. 29th May, still alongside the Pier at midnight. I saw the Captain and told him he must go and gave him the alternative of beaching himself on the Eastern beach if his ship was not seaworthy, or of proceeding to England without troops with the escort of a trawler. At 0230 he was observed endeavouring to clear the harbour. It was subsequently found out that he sunk about 4 cables outside the entrance.

At 0039/30 made the following signal to Dover: "There is a shortage of ships and boats. I have no destroyers."

There were no air attacks in the early morning and all was quiet. Later when ships began to arrive, in view of the heavy target presented by a number of ships being alongside the Mole at one time, destroyers were ordered alongside the Pier one at a time. Arrival of the first destroyer was a signal for an attack by one bomber. Subsequently, however, the bright sunshine of yesterday gave way to mist and it was possible to speed up embarkation without undue risk.

0755 following signal was made: "Great opportunity missed during night when only three drifters arrived. No water or food yet provided on Dunkirk beach for large number of troops. Sporadic bombing."

At about 0800 store ship arrived with provisions but no water. This caused so much congestion on the Pier that in view of the urgent need to send off every possible man, unloading was, after about half the food had been unloaded, abandoned and the store ship filled with troops. A certain amount of water was obtained from destroyers.

One personnel ship arrived about 0920, the first one since the previous day. Other ships (three drifters) filled shortly after. Embarkation proceeded thereafter at a good steady rate.

Following signal was made at 0930 to V.A. Dover: "Troops are concentrated in unlimited numbers just east of Dunkirk Beach, on Bray beaches and at La Panne. Please do your best to distribute. I am getting along splendidly here. Send two hospital ships now. If mist persists I will bring them in on arrival."

At 0943 the following Situation Report was made: "Concur are 1700 k/cs. I have no M.T.B. and can only communicate with U.K. by French wireless station, or when destroyers are in sight. If conditions remain as at present a destroyer alongside continuously for embarkation would be a magnificent help. The moment bombing starts all must shove off."

At 0950 I made following signal: "If this weather persists I want a ship every half an hour".

The whole morning was misty and ideal for embarkation but few ships arrived and a great opportunity was again lost. Hospital ships also did not arrive until afternoon and there were over one thousand wounded waiting for transportation.

At 1600 two destroyers arrived.

At 1700 a car was sent for me to go to G.H.Q. and I turned over duties of S.N.O. to Commander Maund.

Friday at 1836 following signal was made: "Am leaving for G.H.Q. for about two days and I have turned over the job of N.S.O. to Commander Maund who fully understands the situation and has everything well in hand."

At 1846 following signal was made: "Embarkation proceeding steadily despite intermittent bombing attacks and bombardments. Conditions appear favourable for good progress tonight. Request all available craft may be made available both for Dunkirk and beaches. Number embarked to date only with destroyers 18,000."

At 2025 a Situation Report was made as follows: "Despite intense bombardment and air attack four thousand troops have been embarked during last hour. Every possible effort will be made. I consider Dunkirk will be untenable by Friday morning. Embarkation will be continued until last moment but depend upon large ships and destroyers at Pier tonight."

As ships had now arrived in good numbers it was necessary that the rate of embarkation must in some way be speeded up. The troops coming down the Pier were, therefore, urged to quicken their pace and eventually the thousands of troops, tired and without food and water for days, broke into double and kept it up the whole length of the Eastern Arm for more than two hours. During that period it is estimated that more than 15,000 troops were embarked.

NIGHT 30th – 31st MAY
Shelling was heavy during the afternoon and night and operations were greatly hampered. However, ships arrived in some numbers and with the cessation in the shelling between 3 and 4 a.m. about ten thousand troops were embarked. This relieved the congestion on the beaches which had been very great in the evening. In the early morning the beaches were very nearly clear of troops.

I remained at G.H.Q. for the night and telephoned the naval situation to the Admiralty. I was present with the C. in C. at several meetings, my main object being to explain to the Military that if the evacuation of the B.E.F. was to be largely accomplished, it could only be done by means of Dunkirk. Even given good weather embarkation from the beaches must be very slow. A destroyer going full out with her boats to the beaches could only embark 600 men in 12 hours, whereas this could be done in 20 minutes at the Pier.

Some of the G.H.Q. staff expressed disappointment that more could not be done to push on with the embarkation off the beaches in a surf. I was satisfied that when the weather permitted everything possible was being done by the officers I had placed there, but I continually stressed that troops should be moved to Dunkirk and maximum numbers should also be available.

Political pressure was now being brought to bear on the C. in C. that the evacuation must be on a fifty-fifty basis with the French. My only stipulation was that at all costs we should be allowed free use of the Eastern arm while the French used the port, outer harbour and beaches.

I made a signal to Commander Maund at Dunkirk to provide personnel ships for General Laurencie's troops (some 5,000 in number) at C. in C's. request. I also asked Admiral Wake-Walker to keep Dunkirk going at 100%.

Little progress could be made off the beaches owing to the surf.

G.H.Q. informed me that a plan was being worked out for naval co-operation to bombard advancing German tanks in the later stages. This however, was never necessary, as far as I am aware.

FRIDAY 31st MAY
The following signals were made:
0320 "Request more ships to load Dunkirk."
0445 "Every available ship will be required at Dunkirk during the next two hours to evacuate rest of army."
0605 "Embarkation proceeding satisfactorily in spite of bombardment. I would again stress the need for more ships and constant fighter protection.

0633 "Am now receiving a number of Frenchmen. I have raised no objection to their embarking in British ships and am allowing them to do so.

0940 "Request you will inform me whether troops are now being ordered to march to Dunkirk from the beaches.

0945 "Sun is now coming through and I have a big target of ships in harbour. Request special air protection for next two hours.

0957 "Lord Gort has agreed that 5,000 French troops should be embarked here this evening after dark in British vessels. Request necessary ships may be sent to arrive at dusk.

1044 "We have been continually heavily bombarded and they are gradually finding the range of our loading berth. I would rather only enter ships as necessary for the flow of troops.

Continuous and heavy shelling all the morning, but the evacuation proceeded fairly speedily. At last ships were arriving in large numbers and strong air protection kept bombing attack away. The only thing necessary was to stop the shelling.

At 1200 a signal was received from the Air Liaison Officer at Dover asking for position of enemy battery. This was not known with any certainty as the battery was probably mobile, but it was in the district of Loon Plage Brouge Kerk Soch. A reply was made to this effect.

The bombardment, nevertheless, become [sic] more intense and a great deal more accurate. Very heavy attacks were delivered during the evening but were concentrated chiefly upon derelict ships in the roads. Dive bombing attacks were carried out on the ships loading but without success. The embarkation proceeded smoothly.

At 1800 approximately Lord Gort embarked at La Panne for the U.K.

At 1937 the following signal was made: "As it is vital to carry on the evacuation of troops throughout every available moment day and night it is intended to place two white lights at eastern and western pier head as a guide to ships in the hours of darkness. It is requested that all H.M. ships and other vessels who are likely to enter port to-night be warned accordingly."

At 1945 a further signal was made: "Slow British progress in the port due to shelling, bombing, and wounded and French troops using quay. Weather fine and clear, sea moderate, good prospects for night embarkation from beaches."

I returned Dunkirk with General Alexander and discovered that totally different instructions had been given to General Alexander by Lord Gort and by Lord Gort in writing to Admiral Abrial and General Fagalde.

Lord Gort had told the French authorities that General Alexander would assist in holding the "perimeter" for the French to embark and that he was to place himself and his divisions under General Fagalde's orders. General Alexander, however, was told by Lord Gort in my hearing that he was to do nothing to imperil his army and was ultimately responsible for their safety and evacuation.

I suggested to General Alexander that he should at once return to La Panne before the telephone was cut off to telephone to the Secretary of State for War, and to get the matter cleared up. This he did. The Secretary of State instructed General Alexander to act on his own discretion and to proceed with the evacuation.

Admiral Abrial asked me to take charge of the British and French embarkation, which I did. I also asked for French officers to assist, and they were provided.

The following signals were despatched [at] 2028: "I have felt it necessary for the operation to disregard your verbal instructions to return home, and hope you will approve. With the approval of Lord Gort I have returned here as S.N.O Dunkirk and to assist the British Commander."

At 2353 the following signal was made: "In view of the decision request maximum number of transports and air protection to-morrow Saturday, and particularly air and sea protection for the following day, when enemy will have no other occupation. Unfortunately some hours are passing to-night without a single ship entering Dunkirk for French or ourselves."

Shelling took place all night during embarkation causing some casualties on the beach.

La Panne was evacuated and troops fell back on Bray.

A situation report was made as follows: "No ships entered between 2230 and 0400. Unsuccessful dive bombing attack has just taken place. British fighters arrive. Smoke covers pier. Embarkation re-commenced. Reported heavy shelling of beaches and an improvised pier smashed. Please despatch by M.T.B. morphine and field dressings."

SATURDAY 1st JUNE

0715. "Attended meeting of French Staff at Malo Barns. Witnessed very heavy dive bombing on ships off shore. Discussed evacuation and arranged that more ships should be given to the French.

At 0910 a further signal was made reading: "Ships are urgently required."

Much bombing had taken place for rest of day. H.M.S. *Keith* and *Ivanhoe* were bombed and H.M.S *Mosquito* on her way to entering the port was bombed and sunk. H.M.S. *Worcester* sailed and received such heavy bombing that I gave orders that no more ships were to sail in daylight and requested that henceforth none should arrive before dark.

At 1841 the following signal was received from C.I.G.S. for Senior Officer: "We do not order any fixed moment for evacuation. You are to hold on as long as possible in order that the maximum number of French and British may be evacuated. Impossible from here to judge local situation. In close co-operation with Admiral Abrial you must act in this matter on your own judgement.

At 2315 I made the following signal: "Withdrawal now proceeding according to plan. Shall have certain reserves here to-morrow to assist French. Intend to complete evacuation to-morrow by midnight."

A motor boat was sent to the mouth of the harbour at dusk and allocated berths to the ships as they entered, the requisite number of the personnel vessels being sent to the embarkation pier in the Western harbour to embark French troops. A good number of ships entered harbour and embarked troops, and the seamanship displayed by destroyers, sloops and transports was most praiseworthy under exceedingly difficult conditions.

I gave orders to evacuate a large proportion of naval personnel during the night.

All those that did remain until the final withdrawal had performed their duties magnificently.

SUNDAY 2nd JUNE
0400/2 – from S.N.O. Dunkirk: "Request again maximum number of transports for British and French. At 2130 June 2nd it is intended that all British shall be evacuated by midnight. Request M.A.S.B. at 2300.

At 0405 – from S.N.O. Dunkirk: "Admiral du Nord requests that block ships will arrive at 0300 to-morrow night. He will signal if their placing is to be postponed.

At 0730 – from S.N.O. Dunkirk: "Wounded situation acute. Hospital ships should enter during the day. Geneva Convention will be honourably observed. It is felt that the enemy will refrain from attack. (This signal was made *en clair*).

At 0830 – from S.N.O. Dunkirk: "About 5000 British remain. Bofors ammunition short. Sporting chance of embarking to-night. Maximum number of fast motor boats as 2130 at inner end of Long Pier would assist. Early this morning the drifter *Lord Cavan* our depot ship, was sunk by shell fire. As it had been decided to cease evacuating troops in daylight, there remained little to do except to prepare the maximum staff to-night."

The following signal was made at 1435/2: "Please direct proportion of shipping to the French. Arrangements of embarkation in the Novul D'Avant Port."

1536/2. From S.N.O. Dunkirk: "Situation of wounded desperate. Shortage of medical stores and accommodation. Demand two hospital ships forthwith."

At 1538/2 the following situation report was made: "French still maintain front line except for area east of Bergues where the Germans have penetrated two miles on a two-mile front. Counter attack being made at 1500. In port no movement. Present situation hopeful."

At dark vessels of all kinds arrived and were berthed alongside the eastern arm on the French jettys and further up the harbour. Berthing was carried out by an officer with a loud speaker at the pier head.

At 2230 the last of the B.E.F. started down the quay and were safely embarked by 2250 at which time I made a signal as follows: "Operation completed. Returning to Dover." I then embarked in a M.T.B. and left for Dover.

After my return from G.H.Q. on 31st May I was closely associated with General Alexander who remained in command of British Troops. He was a tower of strength and delightful to work with at a very difficult time when it did not seem probable that we should succeed in getting away the last of the British Expeditionary Force. Although my report does not make it clear, all signals from S.N.O. Dunkirk referring to military matters were made with his concurrence and approval.

He finally left Dunkirk with Admiral Wake-Walker in a M.T.B. at 2130 on 2nd June.

Appendix I
ACTIVITY OF ENEMY AIRCRAFT

As the enemy aircraft seemed to work in distinct phases, I think it will be as well to devote an Appendix to their operations.

On our arrival, they were chiefly occupied in wrecking Dunkirk and the port. It was quite out of the question to use the harbour at all, and my first reaction was that evacuation would have to be done from the beaches. It soon became obvious, however, that they were not including the pier in their attentions. At times they were held off by a fine morning mist which sometimes persisted until afternoon. At times, when the wind was favourable, a heavy pall of smoke from burning oil tanks, to the westward, largely obscured the pier.

377

During the morning they made attempts to machine gun the beaches, but were held off by anti-aircraft fire. The beaches were also bombed but only for a brief period. Had they persisted, they would have inflicted terrible losses on us, for there were seldom less than 10,000 troops on the beaches. They later attacked the pier, with dive bombers, sunk three ships and damaged the pier. Had they persisted in these successful attacks on the pier and ships alongside, the evacuation could never have been achieved. They soon, however, turned their attention to ships lying off the beaches, and on one day (31st), no less than 100 bombing attacks were made on ships within two miles of the pier. Happily, at least 24 bombs were dropped on one large wreck and many bombs on other wrecks.

By this time also, Bofors guns were being collected and this seemed to make them more shy of attacking the pier. The heavy attacks on ships at sea compelled me to stop all sailings and arrivals during daylight.

On the last day, they appeared once more to return to the bombing of Dunkirk and its port and bastion.

Enemy fighters were occasionally in evidence escorting their bombers. At times our own fighters gave us a great measure of relief, but the sky is a big place and it was often difficult to know if our aircraft were present or not. When our aircraft did arrive the French, and less frequently the British, opened fire on them.

Appendix II
OFFICERS WHO PERFORMED VALAUBLE SERVICES

Captain Howson
Commander Maund*
Commander Lewis (late P.S.T.O. who joined my party and did very good work.)
Commander Ellwood
Commander Henderson
Commander Richardson
Commander Surtees*
Commander Gotto*
Commander Clouston*
Lieut. Commander Junor
Paym. Lieutenant Brockett, R.N.R.
Lieutenant Balfour
Commander Conway
Commander Otway-Ruthven

Lieutenant Commander Cubison of the Drifter *Lord Cavan*
Commander Kerr
> * Name already given to V.A. Dover for special recognition in the first despatch but all the remainder are worthy of mention but particularly those I have underlined.

SENIOR NAVAL OFFICER, BRAY BEACH
Commander Hector Richardson

The following report, entitled 'Situation on the Beaches', was attached to the account provided by Captain Tennant:

At about 1930 on Monday 27th I met the Captain of the *Wolfhound* ashore and he told me that our instructions from the Senior Naval Officer were to proceed to the beaches.

2. I proceeded in close company with Lieutenant Commander Dowling and his platoon. En route we met the head of the Army who were proceeding in the same direction.

3. We arrived on the beaches after about ½ hour's march. During this march there was continuous bombing.

4. On arrival at Bray beach at about 2100/27 it was apparent that the first flight of the Army were showing signs of lack of discipline and for about 20 minutes we had a difficult time to restore order.

5. I ordered the soldiers in my vicinity to sit down and at the same time placed my platoon across the road to prevent any more men coming on the beaches. I then called for Army Officers to assist me and about 7 or 8 approached me.

6. I divided the soldiers up into parties of 30 and placed them under the care of an Army Officer or an Able Seaman and dispersed them at intervals along the beaches in the direction of Dunkirk.

7. As each party arrived on the road leading on to the beach they were met by [a] seaman who marshalled them into parties of 50 and then led them on to the beaches.

8. Quiet was then maintained and the embarking in boats commenced.

9. At about 2100 Commander Clouston sent a message to say that large parties could be taken off at Dunkirk … [page missing]

16. At about 1200 Commander Ken and I motored into Dunkirk to report progress as embarkation on our beach was then impossible. On our return our lorry was heavily machine gunned and hit. At this period a heavy bombing attack took place on the Fleet and beaches.

17. On return to our headquarters (a lorry) we decided to make contact

with General H.Q. but unfortunately our car broke down and we had to walk back 5 miles.

18. During the night another naval embarkation party arrived on the beach to the eastward which reduced the limits of our beach.

19. Early on Thursday morning 30th I proceeded to Brigade H.Q. and offered the suggestion that piers be built by running lorries out to sea. This was quickly done and was successful.

20. I then drove Colonel Whitten and Colonel Mackenzie into Dunkirk to see Captain Tennant and then drove them back to Brigade H.Q.

21. During the afternoon and dogwatches the French poured into our beaches but no boats arrived within 1½ miles of our H.Q.

22. During the last dog the Germans directed most accurate artillery fire on our beach. This fire continued throughout the night and our lorry was hit. The beach was completely evacuated by allied soldiers.

23. We had however taken up quarters in a watch-boat that was ashore at low water. No boats had now been in for 16 hours on our beach.

24. During the night the weather became bad once more – and a heavy surf was running. At about 0300 31st May it was impossible to carry out embarkation on the beaches.

25. Our men were showing signs of extreme exhaustion and as it was impossible to communicate with the Senior Naval Officer we decided to take over a whaler that we had salved and to go to the nearest destroyer to report to the Senior Naval Officer.

26. We waited for high water and at about 0730 put to sea. There was a very heavy surf running and we had only an uneven set of oars, rope crutches and only an oar to steer by.

27. We approached two destroyers but they both got underway. Two other destroyers passed us at about 7 cables but paid no attention to us.

28. After about an hour as if from nowhere appeared the Margate lifeboat. We asked the Coxswain to take us to the nearest destroyer but all were underway at this time. He was returning to Margate and so we came back with him.

29. The men in my party were completely exhausted and were asleep within five minutes of being onboard the lifeboat.

30. On arrival at Margate I phoned the Chief of Staff at Dover and reported our return.

31. I was ordered to return to Chatham with my party.

The points that I would like to bring home in the way of general criticism are:

(1) When being bombed in daylight and at night it is apparently the Army training for the men to lie over on their faces in a huddled heap and to await the completion of the air raid. I consider that if one lies over on one's face during an air raid, one gets the impression that the bombs when falling with very horrid shrieking noises are each and all coming to land right in the small of one's back. There is little doubt that the Army were considerably cowed by the bombing and I do feel that this form of inactivity during a raid is psychologically bad. I would have thought it better that the men be trained to stand up and take cover and loose off their rifles and anyhow look at the bomber, especially by day. It appeared to us obvious which aircraft was going to be anywhere near us and which was going to be miles away, while to watch the Army lying down with their faces to the ground with the bombs shrieking, one could see that they were going through a tricky time by being in such a position. I saw no sign, except in one very isolated case, of any of the Naval ratings being at all genuinely upset by the bombing. Machine-gunning, though, was quite embarrassing.

(2) I thought the pom pom fire of the Fleet and 4" barrage fire to be most effective and consistent. The absence of fighters was a source of great discussion and in many cases bitter words. Although the reason for the absence of fighters has been explained by the Prime Minister, I do feel that it is psychologically right to have a few bombers directly over the men taking part in such an operation. There is no doubt that when fighters were present bombers did not come, but as soon as the fighters left, they seemed to know the exact moment in which to approach.

(3) Lack of satisfactory communication arrangements was most noticeable. There were no portable wireless sets ashore with the beach parties nor were any field telephones supplied by the naval parties. The only method of communicating messages to ships embarking from the beaches was by a written message sent off in a boat.

BEACH OFFICER, BRAY
Lieutenant J.G. Wells

I have the honour to forward a report of the operations carried out by the Naval Beach Staff at Bray during the embarkation of the British Expeditionary Force on Thursday and Friday, 30th and 31st May, 1940.

2. On arrival in Dover with the other Lieutenants selected for service at Dunkirk, the situation was briefly explained by Commander M.G. Goodenough. He gave us the necessary orders for policing the beaches

and expediting the embarkation as much as possible. A definite stipulation was that Naval personnel were not to be exposed to danger and that we were to evacuate the beaches as soon as enemy action made the risk serious.

3. At 2000/29 we embarked in H.M.S. *Esk* with about 60 ratings. Each of the twelve officers in charge of embarkation were to have a party of one Petty Officer, one Leading Seaman, two Able Seaman and a Signalman. The ship sailed for Dunkirk at 2045 and, en route, Rear Admiral Wake-Walker and the Commodores attached to the beaches explained our duties in greater detail.

4. At 0125, I was landed at Bray with three other officers and the parties of ratings. Commodore Hallett, who was in charge of the beach as a whole, remained afloat. We never saw him at all as I believe his boat broke down and he had to be towed clear of the danger area. It was obvious that naval personnel were needed for the embarkation of the large number of troops then waiting on the beach. They were all very tired and eager to get off the beach at any cost. Some had been waiting for 48 hours and all had witnessed the bombing that day by German aircraft.

The system that produced the best results was to organize them into a long queue at each of the three embarkation points at Bray beach. The queues were three deep and were spaced out in groups of ten, this number being most suitable for the types of boat available. The following group could be used for shoving off a loaded boat, which took a good deal of moving at half tide owing to a bar running parallel to the sea.

The Army pontoon boats proved most suitable owing to their draught, double ended construction and general handiness. Fortunately the weather was favourable for the operations, the sea remaining calm all day and a gentle Northerly breeze assisting in the recovery of drifting craft. An overcast sky and the presence of our fighter patrols seems to have deterred the enemy aircraft from bombing.

5. The main difficulty lay in the insufficiency of naval ratings to take charge of the outgoing boats and bring them back to the embarkation points. As a rule the soldiers detailed to return them did not carry out orders and it was necessary to swim or wade out for drifting boats, causing a delay that was perpetually slowing up the operation. One can hardly blame them as it was clearly our responsibility. I asked for more ratings and a signal was made to this effect from outlying warships. However, none arrived.

6. Another handicap was the bad communication between ships and shore. A motor cycle headlamp is a poor substitute for an Aldis Lamp. Semaphore was not easy and we failed to find the W/T sets that had been promised at Dover.

It was necessary at one at one period early in the forenoon of Thursday to get more ships to lie off Bray as they seemed to be concentrating on La Panne and Dunkirk. The signal asking for more support did not reach the right authority afloat for over an hour as the signalman had to bicycle for three miles along the beach and eventually send the message by boat.

At no time during Thursday were there more than three warships off Bray until 2200, when the situation became much easier. Between 1300 and 1700 only 120 men were sent off, which was disappointing as we had plenty of small boats available.

7. The Royal Engineers constructed a pier from lorries to the level of low tide. This facilitated embarkation at nearly all stages of the tide, particularly at night. I endeavoured to get another one built and one was started on Friday morning. Derelict lorries, which had been abandoned below the high tide mark proved a serious danger to boats. I saw no less than three come to grief on these submerged wrecks and one boat was damaged irreparably.

8. The conduct of the troops on the beach was splendid and their discipline and morale of the highest order. At times the sporadic embarkation was most disappointing but I never heard any complaints. Their behaviour under shell fire later in the day was a fine example to the sailors, who soon picked up the idea of lying flat on the stomach and singing: "Roll out the barrel", to pass away the time.

Enemy 4-inch Howitzer shelled the beach at 2230 and thereafter at hourly intervals. Initially there was a number of casualties on the dunes, but as soon as the troops were organized on the beach, few received any injury. The effect on morale was more dangerous as it made one realise the proximity of the enemy, who was then about 5 miles distant.

9. At 0100/31 I was informed that naval personnel would have to evacuate at dawn if the present shelling continued. Some officers, not in our original party had already left, and at 0300, I swam out to fetch a boat for the Brigadier in command of the 42nd Division. Unfortunately I lost all my equipment in doing so but we managed to take him off at about 0330.

The shelling of the beach then looked fairly effective and the order was passed from Headquarters that as the embarkation would probably be over at dawn the following day, all naval personnel were to embark forthwith. Accordingly I remained on board H.M.S. *Halcyon*, where we had taken the Brigadier.

Halcyon arrived at Dover at 0845 on Friday, 31st May, and the officers that had then returned were later told that they were no longer required. I returned to H.M.S. *Excellent* at 2300 that day.

383

BEACH OFFICER, BRAY
Lieutenant G.W. Vavasour

Lieutenant G.W. Vavasour's report was submitted to Vice-Admiral Dover on 7 June 1940 by Captain E.J.P. Bund, the latter being the commanding officer of HMS Excellent *at Portsmouth. In his covering comments, Bund wrote that 'Lieut Vavasour had a very difficult situation with which to deal, no one seeming to know anything when he asked for information & the Commander in Para 8 completely misled him about the state of Dunkirk – though that may not have affected the situation. [He spent] 25½ hours on the beach.'*

DISPOSITION OF OFFICERS
We were split up into three groups of four lieutenants
ABCD sections were the La Panne end of the beach.
EFGH were in the middle of the beach (Bray)
IJKL sections were the Dunkirk end of the beach.
Commodore Stephenson was S.N.O. LMNO sections.
Commodore Hallett was S.N.O. EFGH sections.
On landing – as far as I know – no Commodore was responsible for IJKL sections.

I was in G Section under Commodore Hallett. Other officers under Commodore Hallett were Lieutenants Wells, Tibbbits, Cameron.
    Before landing Rear-Admiral Wake-Walker told us of our dispositions. He said that the information available was extremely small and that we should have to meet situations as they arose. We were told that on no account were our parties to be captured and that we were to leave when we thought fit.
    Rear Admiral Wake-Walker explained that he would stay afloat and that whatever ship he was in would hoist the Red Ensign at the main as a distinguishing signal, and that the 'Blue Peter' would be the signal for the Naval Party to leave in an emergency.

ACCOUNT OF 'G' SECTION
Commodore Hallett explained the following organisation to his officers before leaving. He was to be afloat approximately in front of his section of the beach. Signals were decided as to how he would call us up and how we could communicate with him.
1. He informed us that we were to be the sole judges of when to evacuate the naval party and that if one party had to leave to communicate along the whole beach so that all would have the warning.

2. The section Lieutenants decided that as their sections were so very small, that all four sections should remain close together in case there should be trouble with the soldiers over boats or seizing the food and water bottles of the sailors.

3. 29/5. We landed at approximately 2330 May 30th [sic] in two whalers. The Admiral and the Commodore decided to remain until daylight in the destroyer from which we disembarked. On landing we took up our positions – the four sections each covering a frontage of approximately four hundred yards.

4. When we landed there were no signs of any boats ashore or of any soldiers. Within two minutes of landing, approximately 5,000 soldiers left their cover in the sand dunes and approached the boats.

5. 30/5. The soldiers were on the whole easy to control. We had been prepared to find a very bad situation with French and English fighting among themselves. There was nothing like that at all. Any organisation for forming groups for the next boat was constantly ruined by streams of stragglers coming down to the waters edge. At that time only junior army officers were present. They had little or no control over the men. Our orders and the orders given by the naval ratings about boats were obeyed implicitly; orders about forming groups and queues for the boats were very much more difficult to enforce – chiefly due I think – that stragglers were continually arriving and forming batches out of their turn.

6. The morale of the soldiers was very good. They had experienced bitter disappointment in that some of them had been waiting as long as two days to be evacuated, and there had been only a few boat loads at very long intervals. Considerable discontent was felt against the French – not only as to their fighting ability which the British soldiers described most fluently – but as they were mingling with our soldiers waiting for evacuation. A few wholesome lies to the French soldiers as to the position of their own ships soon cleared the area. They formed to the eastward of our sections but between ABCD sections and ourselves. We discovered that a headquarters was established in one of the houses along the front, but we decided not to contact with them until daylight. There was no acute distress for food and the soldiers although extremely weary were not exhausted. The general feeling was one of depression for evacuating in daylight hours as on the previous day and Wednesday morning the German aircraft had made the beach almost [illegible].

7. From 2330, when we landed, until daylight at 0500 evacuation was practically non-existent. In Commodore Hallett's sections it is doubtful if we got off 80 men. A few boats appeared but when the soldiers

reached their ships they all abandoned it and left it drifting as there were no boat keepers.

8. 30/5. At dawn we contacted headquarters. We saw one Captain RN and two Commanders R.N. There were no sailors anywhere except for our own little party. No suggestions or orders were issued from headquarters. The Commander R.N. informed us that they had come from Dunkirk which was now out of action with the moles in ruins.

9. The boat situation was now acute. There was one destroyer and one sloop opposite our area, and at dawn we must have had 15,000 soldiers on our section of the beach.

10. 30/5. Shortly after dawn some of the more senior army officers started to arrive and we managed to move this large body of men, which were considerably strung out, away from the water's edge, and to settle down in the sands. We managed by 0600 to collect a considerable number of collapsible boats from the R.E.s.

11. By 0700 approximately we had sent off these collapsible boats averaging parties of ten in each boat but in spite of all efforts in the vast majority of cases all the soldiers left their boats when they arrived at their ships, and left their boats floating with no one to bring them back to the beach. To make matters worse, these boats were drifting to the East and coming ashore abreast the French who were using them to go off to British ships. At this time there were no power boats at all and whaler trips were extremely infrequent. The rate of evacuation was appallingly slow. I informed one of the Commanders RN – The Captain RN had departed to La Panne and I did not see him again – that I proposed to act with my section as boatkeepers and to leave the beach.

12. By 0730 more ships had arrived. Evacuation was going quicker as we had formed boatkeepers but was still far from satisfactory. The soldiers were extremely clumsy in getting into the boats in the surf and we had to wade out shoulder deep to keep the boats stern on to the beach. I decided that we should go onboard H.M.S. *Anthony* to get a change of clothing. While onboard HMS *Anthony* we managed to procure a motor boat from the *Daisy Bell*? which was alongside with only one man in her with little idea of action. My 2 P.O's, signalman and myself remained in that boat until she broke down twelve hours later.

13. The first object was to recover the majority of boats which were now being used by the French, and to bring them back to our area. This was successfully done and we proceeded to start a ferry service.

14. 30/5. At 0900 we made contact with Commodore Hallett who was then in a drifter. I informed him of what I was doing. He approved. He informed me that he was very short of coal at 0930 approximately, the

Commodore steamed away to seaward. I did not see the Commodore again.

15. At 0930 – there was only one other motor boat working within five miles either side of us. It was a destroyer's motor boat which had been left behind, when the destroyer sailed, due to being aground.

16. During the forenoon, evacuation proceeded satisfactorily. There were boats of all descriptions – cutters, whalers, collapsible boats – available.

17. By noon all ships that I could see had departed fully laden. There was a full half hour or more with no ships left to pick up our evacuation boats.

18. 30/5. At this time (1230) the general opinion of the more senior Army officers that we met was that the infantry could not hold out for more than 24 hours.

19. After this appreciable interval with no ships present a destroyer arrived and anchored slightly to the eastward of Bray. We towed as many boats as we could to her. It looked certain at this time that the Navy had abandoned the evacuation. Lieutenant M.A. Hemans closed this destroyer in a boat. We found onboard two officers – Lieutenants Stubbs and Fletcher from A and B sections – who had been told to leave by their Commodore. Rear Admiral Wake-Walker was onboard and he told Lieutenant Henmans and myself to carry on with boats. We took them in again but still there was a long interval with no ship to which to tow the boats.

20. That was the last time that I saw Rear Admiral Wake-Walker.

21. At about 1300 a considerable number – about ten – ships started to arrive – trawlers, drifters, sloops, paddle minesweepers.

22. Evacuation then continued as fast as possible but the whole day we saw only two other motor boats operating. We asked each destroyer and ship for sailors to act as boatkeepers but not one ship could let us have them.

23. 30/5. At 2000 it appeared again that the Navy had abandoned the evacuation. All ships except one – the *Royal Eagle* – had departed fully laden and no more ships were arriving for more soldiers. At this time air operations started and our section of the beach from which we were now operating (to the westward of the stranded *Crested Eagle*) was bombed twice successfully.

24. Firing from the shore was also appreciably closer and occasional bursts of shells started to come over.

25. The *Royal Eagle* signalled me to come onboard. Her Captain – a Commander RN – informed me that his ship was almost full, that it appeared that the evacuation was over and that I was to tow some of the

closest boats of soldiers to his ship and then bring my sailors onboard for evacuation.

26. I ordered my Petty Officer to do this, while the Captain of the *Royal Eagle* continued to question me about the general situation. While the motor boat was away it broke down and started to drift to the eastward.

27. About 2100 – just after dark – many destroyers and sloops started to arrive. My sailors in the motor boat were picked up by a destroyer that anchored close to us. I signalled the Captain of this ship to ask him to send the sailors and motor boat back as evacuation was still possible now that more ships had arrived. He replied that he had received orders to proceed to La Panne and he could not get them back to me. He weighed immediately and departed; that was the last time I saw my own group of sailors.

28. For half an hour I was stranded in the *Royal Eagle* with no means of getting off. Before she sailed a Commodore RN in a flat bottom power driven boat arrived alongside. I went onboard and returned to the shore with him. The *Royal Eagle* sailed almost immediately.

29. 30th/31st. Unfortunately, at midnight we grounded on the ebb tide and filled our circulation with sand. Low water was not until 0100.

30. 31/5. The Commander remained with the boat for the tide to turn and I left to try and get another boat. I found a pulling boat aground with twenty soldiers sitting in her trying to get her off by pushing with three paddles. I do not think they realised that they were aground!!

31. We got her off after about half an hour by carrying the boat bodily out to sea. We were pushed back continually to ground by the surf as the soldiers were loathed to wade out chest deep before getting into her. This was one of many examples where naval boatkeepers were so urgently required.

32. 31/5. After a very long interval and immense labour we succeeded in reaching the eastern most ship of the line with our three paddles. It was approximately 0100.

33. The ship that we boarded was a paddle minesweeper.

34. I was now stranded on board without boatkeepers or power boat. The shelling on the beach was now more intense. I decided that there was nothing more that I could do at present. The paddle minesweeper sailed shortly afterwards and arrived 1215 at Harwich.

35. On arrival at Harwich, I reported by telephone to Commander Goodenough in Vice Admiral Dover's office.

36. On arrival at H.M.S. *Excellent* I found that the remainder of Commodore Hallett's Lieutenants were back. They had been told to abandon the evacuation at midnight approximately by the S.N.O. of the beach – a Commander.

I beg to submit the following suggestions:
1. The rate of evacuation could have been carried out at a really great speed if there had been sufficient sailors as boatkeepers and sufficient motor boats for towing.
2. I felt most limited in my activities by the very definite orders that I had received that on no account was the naval party to be left behind. No accurate information was available.
3. Although it may have been unavoidable, a definite and fixed headquarters afloat would have helped immensely, where fatigue from wading in the surf and rowing of boats could have been alleviated. The other Lieutenants of EFGH sections fully concur about this, and in all our cases, a change into dry clothing and an hours rest and we were fit again for duty.
4. I was unable to obtain any information at all from any single one of the large number of ships to which I towed boats during the day and night.

BEACH OFFICER, BRAY
Captain John Howson

I reported to Vice Admiral Dover, about 0530 on Wednesday, 29th May. As a result of a report of an Army Officer recently evacuated, it was decided that a party of Naval Officers was required on the beaches between La Panne and Dunkirk. Accordingly, I together with Commanders Gorton and Otway-Ruthven, Lt. Commander Cockburn, R.N., Lt. Commander [illegible] and Lts. Whalley, Nettles and Jones, embarked in *Sabre* about 1400, eventually sailing for Dunkirk about 1600.

Captain Bush, who had also arrived from Dunkirk in the morning, took passage with my party. On arrival at Dunkirk about 1820, the Western side of the town was in flames and vast volumes of smoke were drifting to the Southward. *Grenade* was seen to be heavily on fire and sinking in the inner harbour. A trawler was sinking alongside the Eastern pier and a transport sinking at the outer side of the Eastern pier.

We disembarked at once, and proceeded to the inner end of the pier where we met Captain Tennant's (S.N.O. Dunkirk) staff. Captain Tennant had proceeded to G.H.Q in the morning and was expected back at any time. Our arrival coincided with periods of heavy bombardment which went on almost continuously until dusk. *Sabre* had to clear the harbour as soon as possible owing to the bombing, and it was therefore impracticable to transfer the W/T sets she had brought prior to her leaving for the beaches. Captain Tennant returned about 1200(?) and proceeded to a conference before I had time to seek his instructions as to my party's disposal. Before leaving Dover, my function had been mainly to act either as a double-back for Captain Tennant or alternatively to work on the beaches according to S.N.O's decision.

During the above shelling and bombing, 3 or 4 transports were sunk or disabled. *King Orry* manoeuvring in the entrance to the harbour was ordered to proceed clear, but before doing so was damaged by a near miss and subsequently rammed the Eastern pier making a large hole, and remaining there until towed alongside by a drifter. The pier was holed by a bomb making the outer part useless.

A hospital ship about to enter was ordered to proceed clear and return alongside after dark. As darkness fell, a considerable number of stretcher cases which had accumulated were despatched in the only three ambulances available to the quay the other side of the harbour in readiness for the hospital ship's return. Large number of walking cases were transferred across the harbour by drifter to the same quay.

Captain Bush in the meanwhile proceeded in an M.T.B. to embark in *Hebe* as S.N.O. afloat of the beaches, the M.T.B. being directed to return to transport me to the beaches later if necessary.

About 2330(?) S.N.O. returned and said he wished my party to proceed along the beaches. On passage across the Channel, I had tentatively divided my officers into two parties, one to work from La Panne to Bray and one from Bray to Dunkirk. Commander Gorton proceeded along the beach with his party to work East of Bray and later I with Commander Otway-Ruthven and two other officers also proceeded along the beach to Bray. There were vast number of troops on the beaches round Malo Le Baine. Enemy aircraft were heard overhead and they and the guns west of Dunkirk were bombing and shelling Malo and Dunkirk Fort. The night was very dark, the tide was low and as we proceeded to Bray we met many large bodies of troops making their way westward including a certain number of French, who asked if they could be sent off.

I informed these that French ships might be expected in due course.

Half way to Bray were sighted some ships at anchor off the beach but we heard nothing in reply to our hail. Later we passed the *Crested Eagle* high and dry and still burning. A little further another ship was sighted to seaward and a boat also observed. On hailing her, she proved to be from *Medway Queen* lying off. Later a second boat and a power boat also came in. We sent off 700 to 750 troops in these boats to *Medway Queen*. As we approached Bray in the lightening dawn, a number of destroyers, sloops and scoots were seen to be lying off and embarkation was proceeding in such boats as were available. Several boats were aground, others were holed, and some had no oars.

At about 0500(?) I reached Bray and made contact with Headquarters. By about 0600 all destroyers, sloops, etc., had cleared for England and there were no further ships available. At Bray I also met some Naval Officers who had apparently been working on the beaches for some time and later some Naval Lieutenants and Naval Ratings who had apparently arrived from *Excellent* and *Vernon*. The latter were few in number and had a certain amount of signal lamps. Before leaving Dover I had understood that there would be 24 Signal Ratings along the beaches adequately supplied with Aldis lamps, but these I never saw, and their need was certainly felt. In any case, communication along so many miles was very difficult if not impossible with so many troops on the shore, and I also sorely felt the need of better communication with passing ship or ships anchored off beaches. Similarly there was no communication until Thursday afternoon between La Panne and Bray and never between Bray and Dunkirk.

About 0800 I proceeded on a motor bicycle to La Panne where I met Commander Dove who I felt was in a very fatigued and ineffective condition. He took me to see Q.M.G. with whom I discussed the position. There were very many French troops between Bray and La Panne and some of these had been allowed to embark on British ships, but before I took steps to stop this, the French had been ordered to move westward to Malo.

Off La Panne there were two or three destroyers and sloops, and embarkation appeared to be proceeding satisfactorily. Not many British troops were in evidence on the beaches, but possibly they were inshore among the dunes. On the return to Bray an hour later the sky was then overcast and a Scotch mist prevailed which was a Godsend, for throughout the forenoon vast masses of French troops quite apart from British troops were proceeding along the beaches, and had aircraft attacked, the carnage would have been dreadful.

No further ships arrived during the forenoon off Bray or La Panne and a great opportunity was missed for embarking troops undisturbed. During the forenoon the Sappers in conjunction with the First Division, built a long pier of lorries off Bray into the sea, with plank decking. This was an excellent piece of work and proved invaluable later as a pedestrian pier, but it was insufficiently stable for such craft as paddle steamers to go alongside. Nor was it desirable for smaller pier craft to go alongside in safety especially in a lop. It was, nevertheless, later invaluable for embarking troops into small boats.

During the forenoon I proceeded to Dunkirk and met S.N.O. He informed me that embarkation had proceeded very satisfactorily during the night and estimated that 12,000 to 13,000 troops had been embarked. I told him that I estimated 6,000 to 7,000 had embarked during the night from the beaches, and I stressed the urgency for more ships to arrive and more and more boats, but few if any ships arrived during the forenoon.

On my way to Dunkirk, I found the water lighter *Claude* high and dry, but with ample supplies of water, and on my return to Bray arranged with the Military Authorities for lorries and men to collect and distribute this sorely needed requirement.

Acting on S.N.O's instructions, I sent officers on board the *Crested Eagle* to destroy any secret equipment still in her, but fire had already done all that was necessary. In the afternoon (Thursday) one or two scoots and 2 or 3 motor yachts and paddlers arrived and anchored to the westward of Bray, where no doubt they first observed large bodies of troops waiting embarkation. None, unfortunately, preceded East of the Bray Pier where the First Division had waited many hours patiently and most orderly. Eventually some of the First Division proceeded to Dunkirk where they hoped embarkation facilities were better. One or two destroyers or sloops passed en route from the westward to La Panne, and I tried without success with a very ineffective improvised lamp to tell them to anchor off the pier.

Eventually I managed to get a signal to Rear-Admiral Wake-Walker in a passing ship asking him to arrange for this. I sent an officer with a representative of the First Division staff to Dunkirk to represent the urgent need for destroyers to anchor off Bray. (Not until two days later did I learn that all the destroyers, etc., had been given specific instructions as to which beaches they were to anchor off). Later a certain number of destroyers, sloops and scoots had anchored off Bray and the embarkation proceeded satisfactorily. Unfortunately however, owing to a lack of Naval Ratings, time after time did one see the procession of boats going off loaded with troops, only to be cast adrift empty floating seaward.

About 1700(?) I paid a further visit to G.H.Q. to clear up a point about the allocation of troops to the several beaches, and returned to Bray.

About 2000 I decided that I must go and interview Admiral Wake-Walker who I believed to be embarked in a ship off Bray. Before leaving I gave instructions that in the falling tide, arrangements were to be made to ensure that all craft should be kept afloat in not less than one foot of water pending ships being available to embark troops. I also discussed with the Brigadier, the need for ensuring that troops would be properly fallen in when the final evacuation took place to prevent so far as possible an almost inevitable ugly rush, but nothing definite could be fixed up in this matter pending the promulgation of the final plan not then received.

I learnt that the final evacuation was expected to take place on Friday, 31/5 completing on Friday night, in view of the closing in of the enemy and as I had specific instructions that my beach parties were not to be taken prisoner and in order, for psychological reasons, to avoid the undesirability of the Naval personnel embarking to the possible exclusion of Military personnel (even if they could do so), I left instructions that half of the personnel were to embark between midnight and the early hours of Friday.

At about 2000 I again set of for La Penne intending to return that night as soon as I had seen the Rear-Admiral. There were many men embarking in the few boats available going off to about 2 or 3 destroyers and sloops lying off La Panne and I had considerable difficulty in getting a passage off. I eventually found the Rear-Admiral was using *Worcester* as his Flagship, but he himself was ashore. I decided to wait for his return which did not occur until 2230. Meanwhile, enemy aircraft were active in the vicinity and destroyers were filling up with troops. I stressed to the Rear-Admiral the urgent need for ships and boats already obvious, and mentioned to him the question of covering fire during the evacuation, but my main object was to get his concurrence which he gave me, to my embarking the following day in a motor boat off the beaches to rectify the projected recurrence of emptied boats being cast adrift.

It was too late to return to Bray that night by land, and after the Rear-Admiral had transferred to *Express* she sailed for Bray in the early hours, disembarking me onto the trawler *Olvina* at about 0400(?). At this time there were a very considerable number of destroyers, paddlers, trawlers, scoots, etc., off Bray and embarkation was proceeding satisfactorily but a lop had already started. From Bray I transferred to *Scimitar*'s motor boat and later to *Ankh*, one of about ten motor yachts which arrived from England. These craft drew 6 to 7 feet and were unable to get close to any of the beaches.

I used *Ankh* as my headquarters during the day, and instructed half the yachts to proceed to La Panne and the other half to work off Bray. During the forenoon considerable [illegible] of empty craft towards the beach was carried out and only about two boats were allowed to get adrift and ultimately aground. With the falling tide, however, quite a number of boats were seen to ground and remained ashore till the tide rose in the afternoon. These included the ALC fast motor boat and a lifeboat. Other power boats broke down. Nevertheless the embarkation much hindered by the lop proceeded satisfactorily.

As destroyers and sloops arrived, I instructed them to lower their motor boats and whalers where this had not already been done. These boats, especially destroyers' motor boats were quite invaluable.

During the morning, a certain amount of interference was felt from enemy aircraft and also from a gun shelling from inland which embarrassed embarkation. La Panne was clearly being bombed and shelled and the few destroyers and sloops lying off had to clear to the westward. About noon, the lop began to subside, and with the rising tide, conditions for embarkation very greatly improved. More boats were sent in and more boats floated off and things were proceeding very well, when the gun at La Panne started to shell the beaches and off shore with great accuracy. *Mosquito* which had anchored close in off the pier had many near misses. A certain number of light craft were sunk. The ALC broke down and was towed away by a steamer. *Mosquito*, destroyers and sloops proceeded westward clear of the firing.

About this time the Rear-Admiral who had been cruising between Dunkirk and La Panne arrived off Bray and I reported the position to him. He directed me to tell the destroyers not to go too far to the Westward, which I did.

At this time a motor yacht arrived from England with 6 smaller power boats. These I ordered into the beach about a mile west of Bray where I was proceeding myself, when the bombardment again started and ships once more had to proceed to the Westward. Shortly after this, some 30 enemy bombers escorted by many fighters appeared overhead. Most proceeded to Dunkirk which they bombed heavily, but others dropped many bombs in our vicinity.

One of these was a very near miss to my yacht which started leaking at the stern and forward. Moreover there was a unhealthy metallic sound under the stern as if the A bracket was shaking. My electric pump was out of action and I considered that the craft was not capable of further rough treatment and accordingly when some two or three miles to seaward decided to return to Dover keeping the yacht *Amulree* as escort. The yachts *Isla II* and *Caryandra* closed me. One reported she was short of fuel and as the drifters *Lord Keith* and *Lord Collingwood* which had been promised had not turned up, I told her to return to Dover to refuel. The other I told to close destroyers inshore unless she had insufficient fuel. Further, she was short of lubricating oil, and her astern gear was stripped. I tried without success to report these facts to the Rear-Admiral.

This reduction of 4 craft was indeed regrettable, and looking back on it I recognised that it would have been better for me to have made my way back unescorted especially as it was later found possible to keep the water down by bailing, and it was particularly unfortunate, since the *Amulree* was later cut down and sank off the Gull by *Vimy* in the early hours the following Sunday morning. On my arrival at Dover I reported to the Vice Admiral's Office and requested to return to the beaches, but I was admittedly in an extremely exhausted condition and had completely lost my voice.

Within the Admiralty files are two reports by Captain Howson. Dated 3 June 1940, the second is as follows:

I have the honour to submit the following report on events after I left Dover in *Sabre* about 1600 on Wednesday 29th May 1940:-

2. On arrival at Dunkerque about 1820, the western and inner part of the town were heavily on fire with vast volumes of smoke drifting to the southward. *Grenade* recently bombed was heavily on fire and sinking – a trawler was sinking at the inner side and a transport had been hit at the outer side of the eastern breakwater. *Sabre* berthed inshore of the trawler and Captain Bush and my party of officers at once proceeded to the inner end of the breakwater to report to Captain Tennant, S.N.O. Dunkerque for orders.

3. On leaving Dover the intention had been that Captain Bush should transfer to *Hebe* as S.N.O. afloat, that my Officers should work on the beaches in two batches either side of Bray and that I should either double-bank the S.N.O. or alternatively work on the beaches with H.Q. at or near Bray, the whole being subject to S.N.O.'s wishes on our arrival. S.N.O. was found to have proceeded to La Panne in the morning to see Lord Gort, his staff remaining at Dunkerque – I decided to await his return, expected at any moment.

4. Our arrival coincided with a renewal of air bombardment and for 2 hours or more until dusk we were subjected to continuous heavy air and gun bombardment.

5. *Sabre* left the harbour as soon as possible to go to the beaches and there was no time, in the circumstances, to disembark the wireless sets which she had brought.

6. During the shelling and bombing some 3 or 4 transports in the vicinity of and to the east of the harbour entrance were sunk or damaged. *King Orry* manoeuvring in the entrance was told to clear out, but before being able to do so had her steering gear disabled by a near miss and rammed the breakwater. A hospital ship entering was ordered out and to return after dark. The eastern pier was hit, the outer end being out of action.

7. S.N.O. returned after dark but before I could obtain his instructions he left again for a conference, not returning until about 2300.

8. Captain Bush subsequently embarked in a M.T.B. to join *Hebe* off the beaches, the M.T.B. being told to return to Dunkerque later to transfer me and my party as requisite.

9. In the gathering darkness a number of army stretcher cases were collected and sent round to the hospital ship quay in such few ambulances as would run, a lengthy process, and in addition a very considerable number of walking cases were transferred by drifter to the same quay. Later I sent Comdr. Gorton and 3 officers to walk up the beach to the eastern side of Bray.

10. When S.N.O. eventually returned he decided that he did not want to be double-banked: accordingly my party of 3 officers and myself set off along the shore about 2330. Aircraft were overhead and enemy guns west of Dunkerque kept Malo and Dunkerque under fire.

The night was very dark and the tide low, and though some ships could be seen off the beach, no replies could be got to our hailing.

Very large numbers of British troops were gathered at Malo and we continuously met many large bodies making their way towards Dunkerque: these included some French troops who were told that some French ships might be expected for them, a pious hope.

11. About 0100 a boat was hailed and proven to be from *Medway Queen* anchored off. A second pulling boat and later a power boat also appeared: troops in the vicinity were hailed and some 700 – 750 were eventually sent off by early morning. Later we passed *Crested Eagle* high and dry and still burning after being bombed.

On approaching Bray in the lightening dawn 4 or 5 sloops and destroyers, and some scoots were found off the shore and men were embarking in the few boats of various descriptions that were available. Several boats were ashore, holed, or without oars.

All destroyers, sloops etc. proceeded to sea about 0600? on 30th May.

12. At about 0600? I made contact with Corps H.Q. in a house in Bray and also met Comdr. Gorton of my party, and some naval officers who had apparently been working on the beaches for some time before our arrival. Later I proceeded on a motor bicycle along the beach to make contact with G.H.Q. at La Panne. Two sloops or destroyers were off La Panne and embarkation appeared to be proceeding slowly but satisfactorily. There were many French troops – but not being embarked except for small numbers: there were not great numbers of British troops in evidence.

After discussing the situation with Q.M.G. (I had also met Comdr. J.S. Dove, R.N. who gave me the impression of being a tired and ineffective person), I returned to Bray making contact en route with Naval Lieutenants and their parties who had apparently come from *Excellent* and *Vernon*. I also learnt of Rear Admiral Wake-Walker's presence in a ship lying off and signalled to him re the urgent need for naval boat-keepers.

13. Before leaving Dover, I had understood that we should find some 24 signal ratings and an adequate supply of Aldis lamps on the beaches: this may have been a misunderstanding on my part, but they were not seen and throughout the operation their need was sorely felt both for intercommunication along the immense length of beach and for communication with passing ships. In any case, communication would have been difficult with so many thousands of men on the beaches and dunes; further motor boats were too precious and too few in their urgent employment as embarkation craft, to spare them for despatch work. Telephone communication between La Panne, Bray and Dunkerque was urgently needed but only on Thursday evening was a line run by the Army between La Panne and Bray. W/T communication was also badly needed, but it had not been possible to establish this. An improvised V/S lamp was established at Bray H.Q. on Thursday evening, but it was too weak to be very effective.

14. On Thursday the French troops were ordered to concentrate at Malo and throughout the day <u>vast</u> bodies of them covered the beaches and dunes on their route westward. It was indeed a heaven sent condition that a Scotch mist prevailed during the morning, or the havoc that would have resulted from enemy air action is dreadful to contemplate.

15. Thursday morning was quiescent and more and more British troops continued to arrive, but there were practically no ships for them to embark in and only a few boats and pontoon craft and perhaps a couple of power boats. An A.L.C. operating off La Panne appeared to be invaluable.

I had hoped from what I was told at Dover that *Locust* and *Mosquito* and some 30 small craft from Ramsgate would have arrived off the beaches but they were not seen that day.

16. Soon after my return to Bray, I left by motor cycle for Dunkerque to meet S.N.O. and ascertain progress there. En route I found the water carrier *Claude* high and dry 3 miles west of Bray. Water was a most urgent need for the troops, and on my return to Bray later, I informed the military authorities with a view to carriers and cans being sent to collect and distribute the water.

S.N.O. informed me Dunkerque had evacuated some 12-13,000 the previous night and morning and I estimated the beaches had embarked 6-7,000. But SHIPS and BOATS were <u>urgently</u> wanted and especially small power boats.

There were at this time vast numbers of British troops at and just east of Dunkerque and <u>many</u> French troops at and near Malo.

17. On my return to Bray I arranged in accordance with instructions from S.N.O. for *Crested Eagle* to be visited and any sound equipment to be destroyed. The fire had, in fact, done all that was necessary.

18. During the day the R.E.'s assisted by 1st Division had constructed a long pier of lorries and planks off Bray – this should have given about 10 ft. of walk at high water and was invaluable later as a pedestrian pier and for small craft to lay alongside, but it was insufficiently stable for large ships to secure to and liable to damage small craft by holing themselves, especially in a lop.

19. Apart from a Scoot or two, no ships arrived off the beaches during the forenoon, but some paddlers and a yacht or two arrived from the westward during the afternoon and anchored <u>west</u> of Bray where no doubt they first observed bodies of waiting troops.

Later two or three destroyers and sloops passed eastward to La Panne and I tried without success to signal them to anchor to the east of the pier where the 1st Division had been waiting in vain for ships and boats. (I did not learn till some days later that all ships from Dover had been given specific instructions as to their destination.) Later in the evening I passed a message to Admiral Wake-Walker asking him to detail a ship to anchor east of the pier and also sent an officer to Dunkerque for this purpose. Meanwhile many of the 1st Division troops set off for Dunkerque where it was hoped transport was available.

20. In the late afternoon I paid a second visit to G.H.Q to clear up a point re the allocation of troops to beaches and returned to Bray in the evening.

21. Whilst watching the embarkation at Bray it was noted how time after time, boats laden with troops on reaching the ships were cast adrift without boat keepers – a tragic and most serious position. In the absence of naval boatkeepers, it was very evident that there was an urgent need for power boats to collect and tow them back under direction and I accordingly decided to go to La Panne that night and propose to Rear Admiral Wake-Walker that, although I was a Naval Officer-in-Charge of beaches, I should best be employed afloat working inshore and directing this traffic the following day.

22. During the evening I learnt that the enemy were closing in and that it might be expected that the final evacuation would take place during the following day (Friday) or Friday night at latest. If this were so, it seemed inevitable that <u>very</u> many troops would be left ashore. My orders being that beach parties were not to be taken prisoner and since it was anticipated that the final embarkation would be hectic, it would

have been morally undesirable for all naval personnel to embark in the final rush – even if that were possible. Accordingly, before proceeding to La Panne I arranged that half the naval personnel should embark during the early hours on Friday (31st) and although I intended returning myself to Bray that evening I left instructions to ensure that during the falling tide, arrangements would be made for all boats to be kept in not less than 1 ft. of water whilst awaiting the arrival of shipping off the beach.

23. I also spoke to the Brigadier at Bray H.Q. re the need for ensuring troops falling in to avoid an "ugly rush", though without knowledge of the final plan – not yet promulgated – this could but be anticipatory.

24. I left for La Panne about 2000 and eventually embarked in Admiral Wake-Walker's "flagship", *Worcester* about 2100. The Admiral came off from the shore later and we all transferred to *Express*. Meantime the ships at La Panne were continuing to embark troops – it was too late to return to Bray that evening and the Admiral having approved my proposal as to my going afloat the following day told me he would disembark me off Bray on his way down the coast during the early hours.

25. On arrival off Bray about 0300 Friday 31st/5, I transferred to H.M. Trawler *Olvina* [*Olivina*] and later to *Scimitar*'s motor boat which was engaged in bringing off laden boats to various destroyers, sloops, scoots etc. anchored off Bray.

26. Later when some 10 or 12 motor yachts arrived from England I transferred to *Ankh* and used her as my H.Q. for the remainder of the day. Half of these I ordered to La Panne, the remainder to work off Bray. These craft mostly drew 6-7 ft. and therefore could not work close inshore to the beaches. In addition there were two lifeboats, and certain other power boats and the valuable A.L.C.

Some of the small yachts had motor boats and when weather conditions permitted, lowered these, but in the lop their small freeboard precluded their being much value.

27. During the early hours and forenoon there were ample ships for embarkation but the wind had freshened causing a lop which added seriously to difficulties and delays in getting heavy laden boats off.

28. With the falling tide a considerable number of boats grounded and remained ashore till the afternoon, including the A.L.C. and a lifeboat and a speed boat. Thanks to towing boatkeepers boats inshore after unloading, few boats were left to drift.

As destroyers arrived I instructed them to lower their motor boats and whalers where they had not already done so. The boats from destroyers did <u>invaluable</u> service and <u>especially</u> their shallow draught motor boats. Conditions at Bray therefore were a great improvement on the previous day in the matter of available transport. At La Panne, however, there appears to have been a great shortage of boats and suitable power boats.

29. The lop subsided about noon on Friday and conditions for embarkation improved. A number of enemy aircraft appeared periodically and bombed the dunes, beaches and off shore, and enemy guns inland opened fire on ships seaward, which delayed embarkation and sank various small craft. No. 9 motor yacht reported she was making water and I told her to beach herself if necessary.

30. The Rear Admiral proceeding in *Keith* between La Panne and Dunkerque arrived off Bray and I closed him as necessary.

31. With the rising tide after low water conditions much improved, more boats were floated or sent in, and *Mosquito* arrived and anchored close into Bray pier. Embarkation was accelerating rapidly, when an enemy gun beyond La Panne opened an accurate fire on *Mosquito* and other ships and craft inshore, necessitating their withdrawal to the westward – a most disappointing situation at this moment. I closed the flagship, then arriving from Dunkerque, and informed him of the position and by his instructions was closing destroyers to tell them not to proceed too far west when the gunfire again opened up: meanwhile the flagship with a sloop proceeded towards La Panne, presumably to draw fire. About this time a yacht towing 6 small power boats arrived and I told them to proceed inshore to bring off troops a mile or so to the west of Bray where I was also proceeding. I learnt that at this moment that the A.L.C. was out of action but in tow of a steamer.

32. As we closed the beaches, some 30 enemy bombers escorted by many fighters appeared overhead. Most went on to bomb Dunkerque heavily, others bombed *Mosquito,* destroyers, sloops and small craft. Many bombs fell in the vicinity, one being a very near miss to my yacht.

33. She started making water forward and also through the stern glands and I noted an unhealthy metallic sound as from the A brackets. In the circumstances and observing that the electric pump was reported defective, I was of the opinion she would be unlikely to stand up to further "rough treatment" and after due consideration regretfully decided to return to Dover, ordering the yacht *Amulree* to keep company. We were then some 2-3 miles to seaward in the falling light and I was unable to pass a message to the flagship. *Isla II* and *Caryandra* – yachts – in my vicinity closed in. The one reported she was short of fuel and as the fuel drifter had not arrived I told her to return to Dover and I instructed her to tell the others to close destroyers inshore if she

had fuel. She was short of lubricating oil, had a leak and had stripped her astern gear, and consequently they returned in company to Dover. These four were a regrettable reduction in available small craft.

34. Looking back on it, I recognise that I should have been better advised to have returned unescorted and to have let *Amulree* proceed inshore. In the circumstances at the time I decided it was a wise precaution.

35. As it turned out, the passage was made without incident, the water being kept down by baling and it is all the more to be regretted since on reaching the vicinity of the Gull in the dark *Amulree* was run down by *Vimy* fortunately without loss of life.

36. On arrival at Dover, I reported to the Vice Admiral's office and requested to return to the beaches. I was, however, admittedly in an extremely fatigued condition and had completely lost my voice. I was accordingly directed to rest and hold myself in readiness for further duty.

SENIOR NAVAL OFFICER, LA PANNE
Lieutenant Commander J.W. McClelland RN

Lieutenant Commander McClelland's account, predominantly presented in a chronological manner, was written at the Royal Naval Hospital Chatham on 2 June 1940:

I have the honour to forward the following report on the final evacuation of "A", "B" and "C" beaches, La Panne, during the period 1600/31 to 0300/1 at which time, I was the senior naval officer there.

2. I regret that this report is written from memory as, during a period of shelling at about 0130/1, I saw fit to bury my notes and signal log, as they contained information which might have proved of value to the enemy.

3. The rapid changes of Headquarters, to which I was attached at La Panne in the period covered by the report – four in six hours – has also made it impossible for me to remember the names or titles of some of the various army officers with whom I was associated.

4. I also beg to report that all communication personnel with me, seven signalmen and two telegraphists, carried out their duty with courage, cheerfulness and efficiency.

FRIDAY 31st MAY, P.M.
On Friday afternoon, on my return from a visit to Bray Dunes, I was instructed by Captain Tennant, R.N., to arrange for the evacuation of

the Army Commander-in-Chief and staff, and to take over his duties as S.N.O., La Panne, and to join General Montgomery, IInd Corps.

At that time, an enemy 18 or 25 pounder battery near Nieuport had been ranged by kite balloons on the beach and embarking ships, which had withdrawn. I accordingly arranged with the remaining unwounded beach officer, Lieutenant Greatwood, R.N., and the 12th Lancers, to complete the building of a second pier of motor transport, on "A" beach, and for the repair of the eight pulling boats and pontoons still serviceable.

Parties were also organised to provide all the buckets and to collect all the oars and boats that could be found. Damaged boats were made watertight as far as possible with discarded clothing. I also ordered one of the naval Lieutenants, who had been wounded in the hand, to embark in a small motor cruiser to run a ferry service off to ships.

The intention at this time was to recommence the embarkation of troops at 2030 with two ships, when it was hoped that the fire from the enemy's battery would be less effective. Further quantities of the essential boats and power boats had been promised and the local situation appeared promising even if difficult. To make it easier, certain army units which had arrived at La Panne were ordered on to Bray, to reduce the numbers waiting to be embarked.

1630/31 At about 1630, arrangements were made direct with Vice Admiral, Dover for the evacuation of the Army Commander-in-Chief, from a point 2 miles westward of La Panne at about 1800, which I considered would be out of gun range of the enemy battery near Nieuport.

1800/31 At 1800, the Commander-in-Chief, who had been delayed by a change in the military situation, left with his staff in cars, and I joined General Montgomery, IInd Corps.

1830/31 Very soon after a staff officer returned to say that the Commander-in-Chief had not arrived at the rendezvous, nor could they attract the attention of the ships there. I therefore went with him to the rendezvous and asked for boats by signal, but, before these could be sent, *Keith*, flying the flag of R.A. Dover, arrived, and, on being informed of the situation, sent boats inshore. At the same time another staff officer joined the party with the information that the Commander-in-Chief, had embarked nearer to La Panne. The other of the wounded naval Lieutenants also embarked under my orders in this boat.

During the embarkation, a few bombs were dropped near the boats, and a large number of bomber squadrons attacked La Panne. The enemy battery also opened fire on the two piers of motor transport, and some damage was done, which was, however repaired.

The two remaining signalmen of my party who had accompanied me to ensure the embarkation of the Commander-in-Chief, I employed to help in handling the boats on shore, and then sent on to Bray Dunes to assist there.

1930/31 On my return to La Panne, I gave orders for the destruction of all equipment and confidential gear which was not in actual use.

2030/31 At 2030, two ships arrived and the boats, which had already been filled, put off. As, however, no additional boats had arrived, the rate of evacuation was only about 300 an hour and, as darkness set in this fell to about 150 an hour. With between 5 and 7 thousand men awaiting embarkation before 0400, at which time the beach would become exposed to the fire of, if not actually in the hands of, the enemy, a rate of at least 1,000 an hour was requisite.

Accordingly, urgent representations were made to V.A. Dover, M.L.O. Bray Dunes, and ships in the vicinity for more boats, but these never arrived.

During the period of darkness, low flying enemy aircraft patrolled continually overhead and all lights shown were promptly bombed. This made communication with the ships difficult but not impossible, although further interruptions were caused from time to time by a few, "spy hunting" disorganised troops, who suspected the flashing.

2200/31 By 2200, the situation had become serious, as only about 600 troops had been embarked and the few boats available had dwindled to three, principally owing, I believe, to mismanagement in the darkness by the inexperienced army personnel, who were doing the naval duties of rowing and turning the boats. At this time as the telephone to Dover was still working, I destroyed the wireless set, and despatched the two operators to Bray.

2300/31 At about 2300, the situation became critical, as troops, for whom there were no boats, commenced to pile up on the beach and the withdrawal, which would leave La Panne in no-man's-land by 0400 the following morning, was in full swing.

To make matters more awkward, the enemy battery near Nieuport opened a slow fire on the beach, which caused casualties with almost every shell and must have been very nerve racking to the waiting men.

0000/1 Finally, after a conversation with General Johnston, commanding IVth Division, to whom I had now attached myself, and after he had conferred with the Duty Captain at Dover, it was decided to march the 6,000 odd men, who remained to embark at La Panne, on Dunkirk, by way of Bray Dunes. This decision was reached after I had made a personal reconnaissance up and down the seaport, above and below the beaches, without finding any more ships or boats, and had informed the G.O.C. in reply to a direct question that I thought that they would not arrive. I therefore informed Dover about 0500 that I was closing down the telephone line as the headquarters were now being abandoned.

0100/1 Whilst this decision was being taken, further enemy batteries had come into action on the town, and the rate of fire on the beach was increased.

As it was desired to leave a few men behind to embark at la Panne, and as I had already lost touch with General Montgomery, commanding IInd Corps, who had left earlier, I apologised to General Johnston for the non-arrival of the boats, and informed him that I would go down to the piers and assist in the embarkation of those who were not to march.

0130/1 It being dead low water, it was now about half a mile to the end of the piers, which were now high and dry, and whilst walking there, I was twice knocked down by H.E. bursts, one splinter smashing the box signalling lantern I was carrying and another slightly injuring my left ankle. Several houses on the front were now blazing fiercely.

When I reached the embarkation point, I was informed that there had been no boats in for over half an hour, and the naval beach party had apparently left. This was probably in accordance with my orders that they were to go off in the last boat.

There being neither ships nor boats now at the beaches, I ordered a general retirement westward of all the groups on the beach, without waiting for further orders, with the object of getting them inside the defended perimeter outside Bray Dunes, which had been arranged for 0400. Whilst these orders were being carried out, I rounded up all the stragglers I could find and sent them off after the other bodies of men with officers.

0200/1 After this was done, I set out to Bray Dunes, walking along the edge of the water to avoid the shelling, and collected a few other men of all units.

About two or more miles down the beach towards Bray, I made out three ships at anchor and soon after met a small party, who informed me that they had endeavoured to attract attention by firing shots without success. There being further large parties ahead whom I could see by flashes had no boats, and being anxious that the naval authorities should be informed that all troops were being withdrawn from La Panne, I thought it best to swim off, and managed to get close enough to *Gossamer* to be picked up by a lifebelt on a line brought to me by one of the ship's company.

I then informed the captain of the change of plan and the state of the beaches, and asked him to inform R.A. Dover, by cypher, to avoid the possibility of boats being sent where they were not required.

Being very exhausted, and unable to walk because of my left ankle, which had recovered from its numbness, I regret to state that I remained in *Gossamer*, as I felt that I should be more of a hindrance than a help if I returned ashore.

BEACH OFFICER, LA PANNE
Lieutenant Commander T.G.P. Crick RN

As the Senior Officer of H.M. Ships *Abel Tasman*, *Alice* and *Kaapfalga* (Dutch barges), I have the honour to make the following report on operations at La Panne on 28th May.

2. *Abel Tasman* was loaded with ammunition, *Alice* and *Kaapfalga* with provisions. The destination of La Panne was received at Dover at 1900 on 27th May and ships sailed forthwith.

3. On arrival at about 0500 ships were beached shortly after high water. A number of H.M. Ships were in the process of evacuating troops.

I proceeded ashore to make arrangements with the Military for unloading. It was extremely hard to get any information at all or to understand the situation. After 2½ hours search I was able to locate G.H.Q. and reported to General Adam, who was in command of the Adam force. He stated that it was of paramount importance to evacuate

405

as many troops as possible on the beaches between La Panne and Dunkirk. I accordingly made those arrangements.

There was great air activity all day and at about 1400 approximately 6 bombers commenced a wave of attacks with bombs and machine-gun on the three ships and the personnel in general on the beach. The military were about to commence embarking. I had left orders that in the event of attack the crew were to take cover on the beach, or elsewhere than on board, where there was still a quantity of ammunition. Immediately after the second attack I went on board *Abel Tasman* to see that my orders had been carried out. The crew of 9 were extremely young and 6 of them had not been to sea before. I found one rating on board and got him ashore. There was only time to take cover under the ship close up to the keel. I was wounded in the foot by a machine-gun bullet during one of the attacks.

When the attacks were over my wound was dressed on the beach. I was in considerable pain and did not feel that I could adequately perform the duty of getting my ship back to Dover. I therefore turned over to the next Senior C.O. Later on I learned that my 1st Lieutenant had been very badly wounded. I therefore determined to return to Dover. I was feeling much better after receiving proper medical attention. Ships were due to sail at 1700, and I felt that I could carry out the navigation with one of the 1st Lieutenants in charge of the ship and that by stationing the ship with the sole Officer astern in the line that the three ships would return safely to Dover with the troops.

Accordingly I was carried down to the beach at 1630 by the military, only to find that two of the ships had sailed. I could get no answer from the remaining ship by hailing. Apparently it had been decided to sail as soon as possible after the bombing was over and as there were only 4 Officers for the three ships only two of the ships sailed. I consider that this was a proper decision having regard to the circumstances. The inexperience of the crew and the strangeness of the ships and also the locality made a passage an extremely arduous affair.

The close proximity of the German army made it imperative to return to England as soon as possible. Accordingly I was put on board H.M.S. *Calcutta* early to-day en route for Chatham Hospital.

4. During the time ashore at La Panne I was besieged with requests for a passage to England or France from French and Belgian Officers. These Officers all stated that their desire was to re-form and fight again. I informed them all sympathetically that I could not give them a passage without the approval of General Adam. As this was not forthcoming in the majority of cases, about 20 of them got a Diesel engined boat from the beach and requested that they might come across to England in

company with me. I readily acceded to this request and was prepared to tow them if necessary.

5. I understand that the admiralty were informed by the Military that my 1st Lieutenant and myself had become casualties.

EMBARKATION OFFICER, DUNKIRK HARBOUR
Commander H.M. Troup

I left Ramsgate on the night 2nd-3rd June in War Ministry fast motor boat *Haig* with three other fast W.M.M.B's. I took with me the French Naval Attaché Captain de Revoir who came over to see how the embarkation was going on on the pier. I gave instructions to the Officers in charge of boats to act independently and ferry troops to ships taking a final boat load back to Ramsgate.

I entered Dunkirk harbour and proceeded alongside the centre pier and with great difficulty persuaded 40 French soldiers to come aboard. These I took to a big ship outside and returned for more. After loading 39 I again proceeded out and just in the entrance was rammed by a French tug on the port beam; as the hole was a good foot above the water line I went on. I had not gone more than 200 yards when another French tug altered course and rammed me in the forecastle, cutting halfway through the upper deck and right up to the keel.

I managed to get clear quickly and took the boat alongside the *Westward Ho* and got the soldiers out, one of whom got his shoulder smashed in the collision. A destroyer coming across the bow of the *Westward Ho* caused her to go astern and the wash from her paddle filled the boat up with water and washed her away from the ship. As soon as the ship stopped I again got alongside and as it was now three o'clock and the Captain had been ordered to clear out everyone else having gone, I decided to abandon the boat and get on board the ship with my crew and return to Margate. On the way over Captain de Revoir told me there was some difficulty on the pier and suggested he should go there the following night and help. I therefore arranged to take him.

On night of 3rd-4th I left Ramsgate in the W.M.M.B. *Swallow* at 2000, but I left without Captain de Revoir who missed the boat, arriving at Dunkirk at 2230 going straight alongside the centre pier where I landed and sent the boat off ferrying, with orders to come back at 0330 for me.

I found I could be useful as was suggested by Captain de Revoir in making ships fast, finding out the number of men they could take and then getting the French Officers to help me embark the troops quickly.

So I decided to make myself Piermaster and everything else combined. The French soldiers were very loath to be separated from each other, their companies or their Officers but by promising them they would only be separated for two hours and would meet again in England they moved quicker. I embarked at least 10,000 troops. The French Officer Captain le Comte le Chartier de Sedouy on the staff of General Lucas of the 32nd Division was very helpful and I arranged with him to take the general and a staff off with me not later than 0330. I had some qualms about the boat returning for me as her engines were somewhat groggy I instructed the Officer in the boat if he was in any doubt to close one of the other boats and order him to come in by 0300 at the latest. It so happened that he broke down altogether and told no one and it was just by luck that the motor boat which took me off came into harbour about 0305 just at the time I was beginning to wonder.

I would like to put on record the wonderful discipline of the French troops when the last ship left about 0300.

About 1,000 men stood to attention 4 deep about half way along the pier, the General and his staff about 30 feet away and after having faced the troops; whose faces were indiscernible in the dawn light, the flames behind them showing up their steel helmets, the Officers clicked their heels, saluted and then turned about and came down to the boat with me and we left at 0320.

COMMUNICATIONS OFFICER
Commander Michael Ellwood

On arrival at Dover at about 1000, Monday 27th May, I was placed in charge of communications.

D.G. CODE
A private code, known as the K.D.G. Code, consisting of a simple letter transposition was arranged between the Flag Lieutenant to V.A. Dover and myself for communication with Dover should other means fail.

EQUIPMENT
The Flag Lieutenant gave me to understand that one military portable wireless set would go over to Dunkirk in the *Wolfhound* and that two or possibly three Naval Sets and personnel would follow almost immediately. It was unfortunate that none of these sets materialised until Thursday 30th, when one Naval set arrived.

SIGNAL STAFF
One Yeoman of Signals and 24 Signalmen were attached to the landing party. These were told off so that one Yeoman and 8 hands should be available for Headquarters, leaving 2 signalmen for each of the various embarkation parties. They were provided with hand flags but the total equipment other than these consisted of one Aldis Lamp, which was taken over from the British Naval Liaison Officer and made to function with the help of a battery acquired from a French Motor Car.

SIGNAL STATION
A H.Q. Signal Station was established at the shore end of the pier for communication with ships arriving, but for some days no means of communication existed between Headquarters and the various parties, nor between one party and the other, except by Despatch Riders, distances being too great for the effective use of Semaphore.

Beach parties improvised signalling arrangements as best they could with the help of lamps of commandeered motor cars.

W/T MESSAGES
Messages for transmission by W/T were sent either through the French Station at the Bastion in Anglo-French or K.D.G. Code, or, for the sake of greater secrecy as well as of convenience, through destroyers. These were taken by hand down the pier.

All messages were received through the French Station.

ARRIVAL OF MORE EQUIPMENT
On Thursday 30th, Lieut. Balfour arrived with:

2 Telegraphists and 2 Signalmen.

A W/T set. (T.V.5).

A Portable Loud Speaker equipment, which proved invaluable for passing instructions to troops marching down the pier and also later for controlling ship traffic from the pier head. A number of these instruments would have been of great value.

Two Field Telephones, with which it was at last possible to establish effective communication between the Pier Master and the H.Q. Signal Station.

One copy of Syko Code.

Two Aldis Lamps.

Reception on the W/T set was established by 2300 Thursday, 30th, but owing to a defective transmitter full communication was not established with Dover on their set until daylight Friday 31st, when R/T

409

had to be used. Transmission broke down altogether on Saturday evening 1st June, probably due to sand in the generator.

On Saturday 1st June, the Royal Corps of Signals established a W/T Station in a lorry by the Bastion, working on 1700 k/c, and also a much needed telephone communication between the Bastion and the H.Q. Signal Station. Owing to the intense bombing and shelling of Sunday, the line was more than once severed.

DESTRUCTION OF RECORDS
In view of the possibility of the arrival of enemy forces on Sunday 2nd, all signal forms and records were destroyed.

REMARKS
During the week under review, the French wireless Staff had ceased decoding messages in the Code Franco-Brittanique, and had turned this over to Paymaster Lieutenant Brockett, who worked untiringly and with great efficiency, helped only from time to time by the S.N.L.O. or myself.

The K.D.G. Code was used almost entirely for outward messages. This was because the only copy of the Code Franco-Brittanique possessed by the French was the French version. Consequently to transmit a message by this code it was first necessary to translate it into French. This meant that the message when do-coded at Dover by the English version might differ in some detail from the original message. The do-coding of messages in, was fairly straightforward as an English De-Code was kept by the French.

The main objection to the Anglo-French Code was the time taken in decyphering. To give one example, a long message from Dover timed 0900 was received by me at 1300 and the text was finally obtained at 14.30. With events moving at the speed they were, quite often the purport of these messages had been anticipated some hours before.

SIGNAL OFFICER AND SIGNALLING EQUIPMENT
The arrival of Lieut. Balfour was a great relief. Efficient communication in an undertaking of this kind is of such paramount importance that a Signal Officer, fully up-to-date and technically conversant with all the most modem equipment would seem to be a first essential of the organisation.

Adequate means of establishing daylight and night signalling, telephone communication wherever possible, independent W/T communication and loud-speaker communication would greatly have eased the situation and saved much valuable time in getting important messages to their destination.

Lieut. Balfour carried out his work with coolness and precision and was of the highest value.

COMPARISON OF RECORDS

Since all records were destroyed it is not possible to make a complete comparison. Speaking from memory, however, it would seem that all messages in and out duly reached their destination, even though in some cases the delay in transmitting and decoding caused them to be of somewhat doubtful value.

High praise is due to the Signal Staff in general. They were kept constantly on the look out with short spells and undertook a large volume of visual signalling.

In particular I would bring to notice the work of:
Yeoman of Signals Piper
Signalman Waters
Signalman Jones
Signalman Mulheron
Signalman Simmonds

OFFICER IN CHARGE No.3 PARTY, ROYAL MARINES
Lieutenant Commander, R.H. Buthy RN

Lieutenant Commander Buthy's report was written at RN Barracks, Chatham, on 6 June 1940:

I have the honour to report that this party left R.N. Barracks, Chatham at 0415, 29th May 1940 for Dover, where it arrived at 0630.

2. The party consisted of "C" Company of Nore First Battalion and 120 Stoker ratings from the M.T.E.

3. On arrival at Dover I reported to the Commodore, who was the principal S.T.O. of the Division, and was informed that the party would be required in small groups to augment the crews of the merchant ships being used in the transport of troops from Dunkirk, or as armed guards in the event of any disturbances taking place in these ships.

4. I then contacted Lieutenant Commander Eykin, R.N., First Lieutenant of H.M.S. *Lynx*, who afforded me great assistance by arranging accommodation for the party during out stay in Dover. The first night the party was accommodated in the Citadel, but was subsequently

transferred to the Transit Camp near the harbour as this was more convenient for getting emergency parties away quickly. A small party was kept on duty outside the P.S.T.Os offices for emergencies.

5. The parties sent to merchant ships, both Seamen and Stokers were reported to have had a very heartening effect on the crews of these vessels. They helped work the ship and formed the nucleus of boat crews working from Dunkirk beaches.

SPECIAL REPORTS

6. Dutch boat *Ngaroma*. The Captain of this vessel reported that his engineers were unwilling to sail in the ship, and I was asked to provide Engine-room ratings who could work a Diesel-engine. Stoker Petty Officer Jenner and Leading Stoker Linden volunteered for this Duty. I also sent an armed party of six hands and Petty Officer Burge to augment the crew. On their arrival on board the Captain obeyed orders to sail immediately and the crew, heartened by our party, all did their jobs. Owing to the delay in sailing, the ship did not arrive at Dunkirk until daylight and was consequently subjected to constant fire from shore batteries during the time she was there. Lateness of arrival was also caused by two engine failures on the way over. The ship was carrying provisions and water, but the shelling prevented her from getting alongside. Two attempts were made but proved impracticable. It is regretted that casualties incurred were, four killed and three injured. A list of Naval casualties is attached.

7. S.S. *Seiriol*. It was reported that the Captain of this ship had refused duty. As there were no spare crews for Merchant ships in the port, Lieutenant McEwen, R.N.R. was ordered to take command of the ship. Petty Officer Harding and six armed ratings, with one Stoker Petty Officer and six Stokers joined the ship at 1000 on 29th May, 1940. The Captain was put under open arrest and the ship proceeded. The Naval ratings manned the Lewis Guns and Bren Guns in the ship and on arrival at Dunkirk were standing by to take lines ashore had it been possible to get alongside. This was not possible so they manned the only two boats left in the ship. The only ships ratings who assisted were one Officer and a Steward. They embarked survivors from S.S. *Crested Eagle* which was on fire, and H.M.S. *Grenade* which had been sunk alongside. They also embarked soldiers from the beach. About two hundred men were brought on board, half of whom were badly wounded. As there was no medical party on board the ship left before being fully loaded on account of the latter.

8. Hospital Ship *St. Julien*. It was reported that the crew of this ship were very tired and shaken and required assistance in working the ship. A party of twenty-two hands under Sub. Lieutenant Radcliffe, R.N.V.R. was sent for this purpose, half of whom were to assist in the engine-

room. The crew were very willing and the Naval party lent practical and moral support. The ship proceeded to Dunkirk on May 31st, where she arrived at 0850 and went alongside the pier. She remained there until 1015 and was under heavy fire during the whole of this time. All the Naval ratings except the Stokers on watch were ashore bringing off stretcher cases. No casualties were sustained. Sub. Lieutenant Radcliffe was himself ashore carrying stretchers and was the last man on board having seen all his men returned.

FOLKESTONE

9. At 0500 on Sunday 2nd June, 1940, it was reported that three ships – S.S. *Malines*, S.S. *Ben-my-Chree*, S.S. *Tynewald* – were giving trouble. An armed party under Petty Officer Hollingsworth was sent over to take guard duties on these ships. The Petty Officer had instructions that no-one was to leave these ships under any circumstances. Shortly after the arrival of this party the ships were sent out to anchorage. Nothing untoward occurred before 1400 when a relief party under Leading Stoker Booth took over duties.

At 1850 S.S. *Ben-my-Chree* came alongside the jetty. Three sentries – A.B. Clithero, O.Smn. Tomlinson, A. Cook Blackman – were placed on the gangway, the remainder being posted at intervals along the ship. As the ship was being berthed the crew were demonstrating and shouting that they were going to leave the ship, and on the brow being run out they attempted to do so with their kits.

Leading Stoker Booth ordered his men to come on guard and advance up the brow. The crew thereupon returned on board at once, where they remained until the relief crew arrived.

S.S. *Tynewald*, came alongside at 1910. The crew did not attempt to leave the ship, but contented themselves with shouting abuse at the sentries. Relief crews for these two ships arrived at 1950, and the old crews were then allowed to leave. Complete lists of their names and addresses were taken and given to the S.T.O. Folkestone. These ships subsequently sailed as ordered.

S.S. *Malines*, had left the harbour with no instructions at about 1600, and was subsequently found to have proceeded to Southampton.

10. The Chief Gunner's Mate of the Company – Chief Petty Officer Ward rendered the most valuable service in the Transit Camp, not only by regulating our own party and sending out guards and Stoker parties with the utmost despatch, but also by keeping a complete record of all Naval ratings passing through the Camp. These included survivors, Lewis Gun parties, U.P. Parties etc.

11. The following ratings were also outstanding – Petty Officer Harding, Petty Officer Burge, Petty Officer Willock, Leading Stoker Booth – The

whole party remained in good spirits throughout and were always cheerful and eager for any duties, that were to be performed.

12. The party had proceeded to Dover in buses from Maidstone and District 'Bus Company. Two of these were retained in Dover and I would like strongly to commend the Drivers, who were only too willing to turn out at any hour of the day or night to transport our various parties, so saving time, and also turned to themselves in shifting gear and stowing in the buses for transport when necessary

APPENDIX

1. Armed guards had to be placed on the following ships at various times during the operation.
>   S.S. *St. Helier*
>   S.S. *Manxman*
>   S.S. *Seiriol*
>   S.S. *Ben-my-Chree*
>   S.S. *Tynewald*
>   S.S. *Malines*

2. A guard was sent to the Dutch boat *Ngaroma* but she sailed on their arrival.

3. Parties to supplement ships' crews were also lent to the following ships, besides those mentioned above:
>   S.S *Canterbury*
>   S.S. *Lady of Mann*
>   S.S. *Princess Maud*
>   H.S *St. Julien*
>   and various Drifters and Motor-boats

DYNAMO MAINTENANCE OFFICER
Rear Admiral A.H. Taylor

I have the honour to report that on Monday 27th May, after getting final instructions from the Vice Admiral, Dover, I proceeded to Sheerness and commenced duty as *Dynamo* Maintenance Officer; my staff consisted of Commander H.R. Troup, R.N., who accompanied me from Economic Warfare Division, and Lieutenant Commander D.E. Holland-Martin, R.N. We had the invaluable assistance of the Fleet Engineer Officer, Captain T.E. Docksey. Lieutenant Commander Guinner, R.N. in command of the Schuit *Princess Juliana* which had broken down, helped for the first day, he then left to join N.O.I.C.

Ramsgate whose need was greater. Lieutenant Commander Filleul, R.N., from Weymouth Contraband Base, also joined but was sent away in charge of a lighter with petrol cans of water and subsequently joined N.O.I.C. Margate. Lieutenant R.S. Hellby R.N.R. who came from Weymouth Contraband Base, but was not fit enough to go to sea, took his place.

2. Officers, ratings, volunteers and boats commenced to arrive on Tuesday, and the work of preparing boats for service occupied the whole of daylight hours for the remainder of the week.

3. The first group consisting of 20 cutters with half crews sailed for Dover on Tuesday in tow of the *St. Clears* and *Sun V*. The first group of motor boats sailed for Dover on Wednesday. Subsequent groups were sent either to Ramsgate or direct to the beaches, as directed by the Vice Admiral, Dover.

When there were insufficient Officers available, boats were sailed in groups with at least one Officer trained in navigation in each. Lighters were as far as possible given motor boats to attend them.

4. Officers and Coxswains were given broad instructions that failing orders and guidance from Officers on the spot they were to find the places where troops were waiting, ferry them off to ships off shore, and continue the work as long as possible, retaining enough fuel in reserve to get back to Ramsgate. As far as I have been able to judge, good use was made of the wide discretion given.

5. Requests were made from time to time for rafts, ladders, lifebuoys and water. These and all the other demands were met wholeheartedly by the Dockyard and H.M.S. *Wildfire*.

6. Most of the owners and crews who brought boats volunteered to serve in them; more would have been done so had it been possible to tell them before sailing for Sheerness what they were wanted to do. Many volunteers who had commitments went away to clear themselves and came back to join, although their own boats had already sailed. Crews who lost their boats joined others at Dover and Ramsgate, or came back to Sheerness to find another. There were I am glad to be able to say, very few exceptions to the general enthusiasm.

In *X213*, the Master, a man of 60 years who had served at the Dardanelles, did all he could to get away and induce his drivers to take her. They went away to Chatham. S.N.S.O. sent them back. They made a most unfavourable impression on me and I suggest that the Dockyard would be well advised to get rid of them. I feel sure that they could not be relied on in any emergency and would have a bad effect on others. One, I regret to add, is an ex-service man.

Greatly to the Master's disappointment, *X213*'s machinery was not in a good enough condition for her to be used.

7. Owing to a misunderstanding, not here, which I have been unable to trace, the motor boats which should have reached Sheerness from the Thames on Friday 30th did not arrive until 24 hours later. Suspecting that the fifth column was at work I informed your Chief of Staff, D.S.V.P., V.A. Dover, N.O.I.C.s Ramsgate and Margate of the circumstances, and of my intentions to ignore any such messages. No possible harm could have been done by sending boats on, at any rate as far as Ramsgate. Had these boats not been delayed, they would have been available on the last day on which evacuation from the beaches was still going on. Some of them were employed on the last two days in the vicinity of Dunkirk.

8. The type of machinery fitted in many of the boats and its defective state, presented F.E.O. and Sheerness Dockyard with some difficult problems and a great deal of hard work, which was tackled, night and day, with great zeal and energy.

Some of the boats broke down later on, much to the disappointment of their crews, who had done their best. Most of them, I think succeeded in joining other boats and making at least one trip to the French coast.

9. The total number of craft prepared for service and sent out from Sheerness was as follows:

    100 Motor Boats
    10 Lighters
    7 Schuits
    1 Oil tanker
    6 Paddle Steamers

10. On Sunday June 2nd, having got away all the personnel and everything afloat that was sufficiently in good condition to do useful service, I went to Ramsgate with Commander Troup, arriving about 1600, in order to help N.O.I.C. and to endeavour to assist in the cooperation of motor boats with larger vessels.

I went in with a group of Schuits and slow motor boats to the beach at St. Malo Les Bains, where a British Officer who had just got back reported that there were British troops who had been unable to get into Dunkirk. None were found. I have no doubt, however, from later enquiries that they had got into the town. A volunteer whose name I have not yet been able to get [a note in the margins states it was Sidmouth-Willing, a Sea Cadet Lieutenant], landed from one of the Schuits and walked along the beach to make sure there were none left. We brought him off and his boat's crew, and a number of French soldiers who were pulling for England in a small boat.

Commander Troup took the fast Army motor boats into Dunkirk alongside the centre pier and brought off 79 French troops when his boat was rammed by a French tug and had to be abandoned.

11. On Monday night I took a group of slow motor boats up to the Quay Felix Faure, at the top of Dunkirk harbour. I went on ahead in the fast boat *Marlborough* to identify the quay. The motor boats were led in by the *Mermaiden*, Sub Lieut Beale who did very well to find the place in the dark. 300 French Marines were embarked in the motor boats and a French trawler. Their bearing was excellent.

As the quay was now clear, and machine gun fire was getting a little near, I decided not to get the motor boats back on the chance of another load of troops. At this period through no fault of the Officer at the wheel, we had the misfortune to scrape over some masonry that had fallen from the quay, losing our propellers and rudder.

Eventually a motor yacht got us in tow and took us to Dover.

Commander Troup went with the fast motor boats to the outer port. He made himself Piermaster on the western mole and conducted the embarkation of about 10,000 French troops. He also had some anxious moments, as the boat which was to fetch him broke down. Another turned up in which he embarked with a French General Lucas and many Staff Officers and men; and thus had the honour of being the last man to leave Dunkirk.

12. As Officers and Coxswains pass through Sheerness, endeavour is being made to extract full accounts of their adventures. N.O.I.C. Ramsgate is doing the same. These reports are being forwarded to Vice Admiral, Dover, but copies of those obtained here are attached. Even so it will be impossible to do justice to the services of these young Officers, ratings and volunteers, most of whom were acting independently, without anyone to see how they conducted themselves. A list of those who came under my personal observation is attached.

13. Until all reports have been compared and lists of Officers, men, and volunteers going out and returning have been checked, the number of casualties remains uncertain. Many boats have had to be abandoned owing to grounding, collision or fouled propellers, but in most cases the crews transferred to other craft.

One craft is known to have been sunk by bomb, *New Prince of Wales*. Large motor craft. Officer in command, Sub Lieut. P.H.E. Bennett, R.N., now in R.N. Hospital, Chatham. Two ratings are believed to have been killed, but I have not been able to get this confirmed.

Several motor boats sailed direct from Southend for the beaches with volunteer crews who had not signed on. There may be others, of which there will be no record.

417

Considering the heavy bombing, shelling and machine gun fire experienced by many of the boats, the casualties seem to be lighter than might well have been expected.

14. It would be impossible to speak to highly of the spirit which has animated all those who have been concerned in "Dynamo". Everyone tried to do their best for the Armies at Dunkirk, and those whose fortune it was to get across and bring some of them off, will always look back on it with deep satisfaction. Some of the crews got their boats as far as Ramsgate, only to find that owing to the shortcomings of their vessels, they could get no further, but many of them succeeded in finding another boat with room for them.

A young Able Seaman, whose boat sunk after bringing 1,000 men, did much, by his cheerful talk and bearing, to bring about this happy result.

Here at Sheerness the Commodore and his staff, H.M.S. *Wildfire*, and the dockyard did all that man could do to hasten the preparation and sailing of the varied fleet of craft which arrived here, some of them needing much attention. With the exception of the Thames steamers which could not run in salt water, though they had a good try at it, very few craft failed to achieve at least one trip to the French coast. Many men from the *Wildfire* offered their services, though only a few could be allowed to go, and more would have done so had it been possible to spare their services.

Of the Officers, ratings and volunteers who formed the crews I need say little. The services they have done and the narratives which have, with no little difficulty, been extracted from them, speak for themselves. No one can say again that the young men of this country, or the older ones amongst them, lack initiative, common sense, and resourcefulness. One young Acting Sub Lieutenant who took his lighters in to the beaches, where they were exposed to bombing, shell and machine-gun fire, after praising the steadiness of the civilian volunteers, adds "The Naval members of the crew acted as expected". An echo it is good to hear.

MALO LES BAINS
June 2nd – 3rd

1. I reached Ramsgate with Commander Troup about 4 p.m. on the 2nd. The operations were to be for fast craft only, but hearing from a Colonel, who had just come ashore, that he thought there were some British troops and others near St. Malo who had not been able to get to Dunkirk, I got permission from V.A. Dover to go there with a group of Schuits, motor boats and life boats. Commander Troup was to take the fast boats into the Avant Port and Commandant Anduse-Faru arranged for the

French motor fishing boats to go to St. Malo and ferry troops to a French ship and a paddle steamer. The larger ships, however did not sail, and the fishing boats went to Avant Port instead of St. Malo. 3 Schuits and 12 motor boats were available. They sailed between 1800 and 1900. I was expecting a M.A/.S.B. from Harwich and waited as long as I could for her, as I thought her armament might be useful during our withdrawal. As she did not come I went in the 12 knot motor boat *White Wings*, Sub Lieut. Mullins. We left about 2045 and owing to a head sea and some trouble with the starboard engine, did not overtake the slow convoy.

2. I found the three Schuits in the appointed place between E.12 buoy and the shore and went in to close the motor boats. They had already been in and found the beach deserted. After giving one boat which had broken down to a Schuit to tow, I ordered them all to return to Ramsgate and went back to the beach to make sure no one was left behind.

3. The battery of four 6 inch guns near Nieuport, which had been shelling a point somewhere near La Panne, where I supposed some Allied troops to be holding out, and had been dropping an occasional shell in our neighbourhood, now started to register on the eastern mole. They got the range with about four rounds, and then landed a salvo on the mole itself, all direct hits & one just short of it. Though evidently fired at extreme range, the salve fell well together. Another round struck and sunk a transport which was entering. It was now time to leave, but as it got lighter we made out a ship's lifeboat pulling off with very tired men in her. This was a party from the Schuit *Hilda*, in charge of a volunteer from one of the yachting associations. I hope it will be possible to get his name [Sea Cadet Lieutenant H. Sidmouth-Willing]. He had been ashore and along the beach to make sure there was no one there.

4. There were hundreds of troops lined up on the Mole, but it was clearly impossible for us to do anything but report. We also discovered a motor boat ashore (the *Singapore*) at the foot of the mole. The lifeboat went ashore and our volunteer waded along the beach to help her off. The boat's crew decided to wait till the tide lifted them, keeping under cover so that aircraft should think the boat deserted. As my boat drew too much to get anywhere near her, I decided to withdraw. The *Singapore* got away and returned to Ramsgate in company with the motor boat *Kitcat*, which had been into Dunkirk.

5. Off Dunkirk we picked up 6 French soldiers who were pulling for England in a small fishing boat. I saw in the distance another of my boats towing a life boat full of troops, but I do not know her name. 8 German bombers flew out of the smoke cloud, but turned off to the westward, ignoring us. Many British aircraft were seen on the return voyage.

QUAI FELIX FAURE
June 3rd – 4th
1. For the final evacuation, 12 of the best slow motor boats were to proceed on tow to Dunkirk and thence to the Quai Felix Faure some way up the main harbour. I started in the leading motor boat but transferred to the Army fast boat *Marlborough*, in order that I might if possible get into contact with the French Naval Authorities and make sure we had got the right places, and also to give us a boat to get away in, leaving the motor boats free for ferrying.

2. Our quay was not easy to identify, even in the light that remained, and I was very glad that I had gone ahead of the tow. The quay was deserted, but after a time some troops passed along the road in rear, on their way to Avant Port. Sub Lieutenant Karminsky who came ashore with me as interpreter, tried to find someone to tell me whether we had got to the right place but received the reply "sorry I'm a stranger".

Eventually we found we were correct. About 2300, 300 French Marines arrived and explained that they were all we had to take off. Then followed a bad half hour of waiting for the motor boats, which had been delayed on passage. I sent the *Marlborough* to look for them, and soon after 1300 was relieved to see them coming. The leading boat *Mermaiden* Sub Lieutenant Beale had done very well to find the place in the dark. Some of the boats had missed their way and no doubt went into the Avant Port where I expect they did good work.

My anxieties were entirely relieved by the arrival of a large French trawler, who took all that the motor boats could not and had room for more. Sub Lieut. Karminsky tried to induce the Officer of some troops returning along the road to embark, but they said they had their orders and could not vary them.

3. By about 0200 the quay was clear and as machine-gun fire was getting a little near I decided not to get the motor boats alongside this part of the harbour on the chance of another load and so re-embarked in the *Marlborough* and started to move down harbour. In avoiding two French vessels, we had the misfortune to strike a heap of fallen masonry which removed our propellers and rudder. After some adventures fully described in the attached narrative by Sub Lieut. Edge-Partington, we got a tow and returned to Dover.

4. The three Officers in the boat with me were Sub Lieuts. Don, Edge-Partington, and Pool. All did well, and showed coolness and resource in the somewhat interesting situation in which we found ourselves.

5. The report from *Mermaiden* has not yet been received. The Sub Lieut. In command did well, and his name also deserves mention.

Index

Numbers listed in bold indicate a main report.

421